Economic Development
of a Small Planet

Economic Development of a Small Planet

BENJAMIN HIGGINS

University of Ottawa

AND

JEAN DOWNING HIGGINS

W · W · NORTON & COMPANY

New York · London

COPYRIGHT © 1979 BY W. W. NORTON & COMPANY, INC.
All rights reserved. Published simultaneously in Canada by George J. McLeod Limited, Toronto.
Printed in the United States of America.

Library of Congress Cataloging in Publication Data

Higgins, Benjamin Howard, 1912–
    Economic development of a small planet.

    Includes index.
    1. Underdeveloped areas.   2. Economic development.
I. Higgins, Jean, joint author.   II. Title.
HC59.7.H45   330.9'172'4   79–13316
ISBN 0–393–05697–X
ISBN 0–393–09084–1 pbk.

2 3 4 5 6 7 8 9 0

Contents

Preface

This book was originally intended to be no more than a short, simplified version of the senior author's textbook, *Economic Development: Problems, Principles and Policies*. However, the character of the present volume has changed substantially in the course of preparation.

The metamorphosis began as we adjusted the text to a less specialized audience than that of the earlier book. Deciding to deal more with concrete policy and less with the niceties of economic theory, we found ourselves drawn into a global approach. We could not propose viable development programs and policies without consideration of the interactions among events and trends in advanced and underdeveloped countries, and without analysis of much needed changes in the economies of advanced countries. In order to provide a more balanced picture we have also included some coverage of socialist experience.

Warnings of an impending environmental crisis began to swing the book's focus around from a somewhat simplistic acceptance of growth as a vehicle for development to contemplation of the startling idea that continued growth at the global level might be both impossible and undesirable. The increasing attention paid to the "quality of life" and to the physical environment added new dimensions to the preparation of development programs. Taken together, environmental and physical limitations gave new credence to suggestions emanating from the Third World that Western style industrialization might not be a good thing for traditional societies living harmoniously and independently within the limitations of their own physical environments. Even in countries where incomes are unacceptably low there has been a search for a better "style" of development.

Meanwhile, as we rewrote, the emerging failure of Third World development efforts was forcing economists to put content into a new concept of development (embodied in the "basic needs" and "unified" approaches) within which poverty is attacked directly.

The energy and food crises gave the book—and its potential readers—a final strong push towards recognition of the global nature of the development problem. The 1973–76 recession revealed the inefficiencies of the economies of advanced and Third World economies alike, and their vulnerability to each other's economic fluctuations. Thus, world events and our own ideas converged, enabling us to offer the book in its present form.

Economic Development
of a Small Planet

1

A system of mutual vulnerability

For some years now, a massive wave of doubt has been building concerning the whole philosophy of "development"—the goals of industrial societies (both socialist and private enterprise), their socio-economic systems and received economic doctrines. The shocks of the 70s brought our misgivings into sharp focus, magnified a number of economic problems to the point of comprehension, and at the same time set in motion a new and powerful process of change.

An early and deceptively simple interpretation of this change was put forward by the Third World Forum in 1975 at its inaugural meeting in Karachi. The Forum concluded that the then current world economic crisis was neither a "normal" recession nor merely the result of the oil problem. It marked the crumbling of an old order in which a group of rich nations had continuously expanded their economies by the use of energy and raw materials provided at cheap prices by the poor nations. Subsequent massive changes in the world's economic power structure have substantiated the Forum's point. The overwhelming question which now confronts us is what the new international economic order will be.

Although primarily concerned with the effects of the power changes on its own objectives, the Forum had pinpointed and linked two major issues at the core of the continuing international debate concerning reorganization of the world economy: first, the implications of the 1973–76 world recession and subsequent economic instability; secondly, the changes which the enormous pressures of a shrinking world are already making on the old order, particularly the pulverizing effect of the Third World's confrontation with the advanced world. These issues, taken together reflect the striking increase in international interdependence, thereby raising a key question: Is "one world" really desirable?

While the system of dependence, which began nearly five centuries ago when Columbus and Vasco da Gama opened the way for global trade and subsequently for colonialism, is now crumbling, it has not resulted—as we

1

might have hoped—in a world of truly independent countries. On the contrary, we find ourselves—advanced and developing countries alike—caught in the uneasy embrace of a highly interdependent global economic system. On the one hand, Third World countries have gained enormous new bargaining power in world affairs through increasing global dependence on their oil and other raw materials. On the other hand, old economic links remain, and new ones have been forged; Third World countries continue to be dependent on the advanced world for capital investment, technology and markets, and, increasingly, for food. This "mutual vulnerability" emerges not only from resource interdependence, but from the extraordinary extent of integration in the world economy as well.

Perhaps the most important point the Third World Forum made was that the then current economic crisis was not a "normal recession." The "slumpflation" of 1973–76 differed from earlier recessions in two major ways: for the first time—as the freshly coined term suggests—the "slumpflation" in capitalist countries was not accompanied by falling prices as in the past but by accelerated inflation and increasing unemployment. Politicians and economists were caught short, with no ready-made formulas to deal with the phenomenon. Also for the first time, economic fluctuations became synchronized on a world–wide scale; the sharp differences among countries in the timing and amplitude of cycles characteristic of previous recessions had all but disappeared. Reportedly, even the communist countries were affected simultaneously by the 1973–76 slump, thus rendering all countries highly responsive to economic fluctuations in other countries.

All in all, the upheavals of the seventies have thrust a number of smouldering problems to the surface. Advanced and developing countries are querying orthodox doctrine concerning national economic systems. The Third World is challenging the advanced world's whole organization of the global economy, not only in terms of social justice, but also in terms of sheer efficiency. Meanwhile, advanced countries have extended their inquiry into Third World development from a largely humanitarian or intellectual exercise towards a hard-headed, self-oriented assessment of what is taking place in this increasingly influential sector of the global economy. Evidence of the extreme vulnerability of all nations resulting from this economic and environmental interdependence is raising questions as to the costs, benefits, and possibilities for particular countries—rich or poor—should they decide to uncouple from the international economic system. Is it advisable to remain within an inefficient world economy consisting of a number of malfunctioning national economies? In designing better economies and a better international economic order should the objective be efficient development within a well-integrated world economy or should autarchy be the goal? Above all, what went wrong with the brave new world designed with such high hopes at the end of the World War II?

ECONOMIC INTERDEPENDENCE

At the close of World War II the design for a better international economic system was based on the idea of One World—a more integrated global economy which would bring a world-wide spread of individual welfare and increased prosperity in the wake of the fast vanishing colonial era. This idea was based on a long-held view of orthodox economics that a more highly integrated world economy would also be a more efficient one. The 1973–76 recession exploded this piece of conventional wisdom. Far from reflecting a smoothly working world economy, the recession crowned with resounding failure the postwar international development effort, thus calling into question its whole approach. Was the approach essentially wrong? Was it right but badly executed? Would it have eventually worked had the energy crisis not crippled development efforts? Does the energy crisis, presaging world-wide shortages, call for a new kind of economics?

Postwar development strategies for a more integrated world economy had raised high hopes, based as they had been on a strategy of freer trade and growing capital movements in contrast to the "beggar-thy-neighbor" forms of economic warfare which had characterized the inter-war period. At first it seemed to work. Massive capital infusions funnelled into Western Europe under the Marshall Plan had laid the foundation for subsequent "miracles" of national economic growth. The same "pump priming" with capital aid and expertise was expected to effect similar economic miracles in the Third World.

When President Harry S. Truman announced his Point Four Program in 1949 much was expected from a simple transfer of know-how from technologically advanced to technologically retarded countries. An underdeveloped country was broadly distinguished at the time as one with a per capita income of $600 or less a year and with most of its labor in low productivity agriculture using centuries old technology. The idea was by means of judicious infusions of capital and expertise to set in motion the development process which had been so successful in the past: to industrialize, to "get rid of farmers" by transferring a large proportion of agricultural labor into industry and services (trade, banking, insurance, transport, education, etc.). This *structural change* had, in the past experience of both socialist and nonsocialist countries generated burgeoning national incomes, and ultimately improved levels of welfare.

As rich countries (both socialist and nonsocialist) joined in this new experiment in international cooperation, capital and technical assistance began to flow to the Third World, directed mainly towards building up infrastructures (especially transport, power, and irrigation) and modern industry. Meanwhile, prospering advanced countries were pulling the developing world along by offering them bigger markets, while advanced technology was also being diffused by private investment in modern industry and in resource exploitation in the Third World. To the surprise of many, as the cold war thawed, "Free World" enterprise even began moving into the socialist bloc.

Global corporations were already viewing the world as one economic unit, IBM's Jacques G. Maisonrouge declared, planning, organizing and managing on a global scale, "making possible the use of the world resources, with a maximum of efficiency and a minimum of waste."[1]

In the fifties, advanced world economies prospered and national incomes in the Third World, as a group, rose rapidly. But by the time President John Kennedy called for a "development decade" in 1960, Third World populations were exploding, unemployment was growing, and the gap in per capita incomes between economically advanced countries as a group and underdeveloped countries as a group was growing rapidly. These problems were dismissed by some as mere growing pains, and were expected to disappear during the First Development Decade (DDI).

THE DEVELOPMENT DECADE 1960–70 (DDI)

Certainly during DDI growth rates generally continued high. Developing countries as a group slightly exceeded the target of 5% average annual growth. But unemployment also continued to grow at alarmingly high rates.[2] The average annual increase in prices was 5%, but rates of inflation ranged upwards to 40% for Brazil and Uruguay to nearly 800% for Indonesia. As for welfare levels, Robert McNamara, president of the World Bank, declared bluntly that "the state of the developing world today is unacceptable". Despite the progress in terms of growth of national income, the world remains one "in which hundreds of millions of people are not only poor in statistical terms but are faced with day to day privations that degrade human dignity to levels which no statistics can adequately describe. Children under five years of age account for 20% of the population of the world but 60% of the deaths. Two-thirds of the children who live on will have their physical and mental growth stunted by malnutrition. There are 100 million more adult illiterates than there were twenty years ago. Education and employment are scarce, squalor and stagnation common." All in all, "we can no longer take much satisfaction in the simple statistical achievement of the overall GNP growth goal of 5% by the close of the First Development Decade."[3]

The question immediately arises, of course, as to how such high rates of growth of income could bring such disappointing results. In the first place, these overall high growth rates in developing countries were very deceptive since richer Third World countries were growing much faster than the poorest ones. Major oil exporting countries, with less than 4% of the population of the developing world, enjoyed a growth of GNP of 8.4%.[4] Countries with per

[1] Jacques G. Maisonrouge, *"How International Business Can Further World Understanding"* (Speech delivered Sept. 16, 1971). Quoted in Richard J. Barnet and Ronald Muller, Global Reach (New York: Simon and Schuster, 1974), p. 14.

[2] OECD 1970 Review Paris December 1970 p. 16.

[3] Robert McNamara, Address to the United Nations Conference on Trade and Development, Santiago, Chile, April 14, 1972 (published by the International Bank of Reconstruction and Development, Washington, D.C.), pp. 2–3.

[4] The United Nations had classed oil rich countries as underdeveloped because large numbers of their population still seek a livelihood in traditional agriculture.

capita GNP above $500 (comprising 9% of Third World population) grew at 6.2%. Countries with a per capita GNP of between $200 and $500 (comprising 67% of Third World population) had a growth rate of only 3.9%. When growth of *per capita income* is considered rather than *national income* as a whole, the picture is even worse for the simple reason that rates of population growth tended to be higher in poor countries than in rich ones. For the poorest countries (comprising 67% of the Third World) the rate of growth of per capita income was only 1.5%. For countries in the $200–$500 category the rate was 2.4%, and for those in the over $500 group 4.2%. For the oil countries the rate was 5.2%. Thus, the maldistribution of income among nations was seriously aggravated rather than improved during DDI.

Income distribution within countries followed the same increasingly unequal trend. Thus, in Brazil, with a respectable growth of real per capita income of 2.5% during the decade, the share of national income of the poorest 40% of the population fell during the decade from 10% to 8%, while the share of the richest 5% rose from 29% to 38%. In Mexico, the overall growth rate of per capita real income was even higher—3% per year—for the fifties and sixties combined. In these twenty years, the share of the bottom 20% dropped from 6% to 4%. A study of forty countries shows that at the beginning of the First Development Decade the richest 20% of the total population received 56% of the income, and the poorest 60% only 26%. Preliminary estimates indicated that the situation was worse at the beginning of the Second Development Decade.

Some observers still adhered to the idea that these problems were growing pains not so different from those felt by the now advanced countries during their transition to industrial states, and that eventually prosperity would be more evenly distributed. In Brazil and Indonesia for example, in spite of increasing inequalities, there is evidence of absolute improvement in real income in lower income groups. However, during the seventies, rather than Third World conditions drawing closer to the advanced countries, problems were emerging in advanced countries curiously similar to those of the Third World.

DD–II.

The oil crisis exposed long submerged problems in the advanced world economies, and smashed development efforts in many countries in the Third World.

After a promising start in the first three years of DDII, growth bogged down. Higher oil prices and the consequent drain on foreign exchange threatened many development plans; the increased flow of aid from OPEC countries could hardly compensate for the $100 billion increase in annual energy costs for the developing world. Both the food crisis and the energy crisis (which are related because petroleum prices affect the price of fertilizers and pesticides) hit the poorest countries hardest. The commodity boom brought short lived gains to some countries, but these proved less durable than the effects of inflation and the dislocation of economies in advanced countries.

The economic woes of advanced nations had unfavorable repercussions on the terms and balance of trade of developing countries; not only did declining production in advanced countries diminish demand for exports from developing nations, but accelerated inflation increased the cost of imports from the advanced countries. Thus, developing countries found themselves caught up in a global depression which they saw as not of their own making, but instead a highly undesirable export from the advanced countries, creating a particularly disastrous kind of recession. In nearly every developing country, growth rates tapered off after 1973. Malnutrition became famine in West Africa and South Asia. Meanwhile, advanced countries, in spite of international difficulties, had enjoyed per capita incomes over the 1965–75 decade that rose in absolute amounts more than in any comparable period in history. Deep seated problems, however, were rising to the surface.

By the middle seventies, the world economy had become a highly interdependent system, functioning so badly that the trend towards integration seemed to be doing more harm than good. The large gaps between the incomes of advanced and developing countries continued to widen; at the same time accelerating inflation, mounting unemployment, and falling output were suffered by rich and poor countries alike. Advanced nations found themselves sharing other Third World problems as well: shortages of resources, increasingly unequal income distribution, urban blight and congestion, social unrest, and political instability. An observer from Latin America, Yale Professor Carlos F. Diaz Alejandro, remarked that the United States was enduring "inflationary recession, campus disorders, frequent power shortages, creaky and bankrupt railroads, erratic mails," all problems familiar to the Third World.[5] Even the food crisis did not leave the advanced world untouched.

The food crisis of the early and middle seventies not only revealed the failures of the Development Decades, but also the extent of global interdependence. The death by starvation of hundreds of thousands of people in West Africa, South Asia and elsewhere, led to emergency food being sent to the stricken areas by the United States, Canada, and Australia. These gifts, coupled with sales of food to Russia and China when their crops failed, resulted, in rising domestic food prices in the United States and Canada. Their citizens in turn became alarmed by the soaring coasts of bread and meat. Together with the energy crisis, the food situation pointed up the narrow environmental margins on which the world was operating, and raised controversy afresh concerning the true dimensions of the environmental crisis and the possiblities of continued world development.

ENVIRONMENTAL INTERDEPENDENCE

When the Club of Rome published its first major study, *The Limits to Growth* in 1972, its predictions of imminent exhaustion of world resources

---

[5] Carlos F. Diaz-Alejandro, "Latin America: Towards 2000 A.D.," in Jagdish Bhagwati, *Economics and the World Order: From the 1970's to the 1980's*. (London: Macmillan, 1972) p. 249.

was deemed alarmist by many in the economics establishment.[6] Yet by the time the Club of Rome's calculations were proven faulty (among other things, they slipped a decimal point in one of the strategic variables) and it appeared that Doomsday might be postponed, the errors no longer seemed important. By the mid 1970s it had become clear that we were already in a state of critical shortages. The worldwide energy crisis along with the shortages and spiraling prices of other raw materials and foodstuffs indicated that the Club of Rome's warnings had some basis. This element of surprise (after unheeded warnings) permeates predictions concerning world collapse, human extinction by pollution or by wars fought over resources.

THE POPULATION EXPLOSION

The major warning which recurs throughout predictions of world collapse is the swiftness of its approach and unexpectedness of its arrival, because of the exponential growth of the variables involved. Exponential growth is illustrated with an old French riddle about a water lily growing in a pond. The lily plant doubles in size each day; it will completely cover the pond in 30 days, choking out all other forms of life in the water. Nobody worries about it until it covers half the pond. On what day will that be? On the twenty-ninth day of course. There is one day left to save the pond.

The growth of world population over the last three hundred years bears a chilling resemblance to the growth of the lily plant. It took hundreds of thousands of years for the world population to reach three billion (2,982 million in 1960) but if the current rates of growth continue, the second 3 billion will be added in less than thirty years (6,494 billion is predicted by 200 A.D.)[7] Taking the world as a whole throughout human history, the curve of population shows a sharp break around 1750 and accelerated growth ever since. Whereas it may have taken as much as 1650 years for world population to double after the year 1, it took only 200 years (1650–1850) to double a second time, only 80 years to double a third time (1850–1930), it took only 45 years to double a fourth time (1930–75) and a further doubling is likely to occur within some 30 years (1975–2010). While it appears that population growth rates are tapering off, the Second Development Decade has seen the largest growth of human numbers in the history of mankind.

Based on this enormous population growth and accompanying exponential industrialization, pessimists' predictions have included: human extinction through overheating of the earth by increasing dissipation of energy in the form of heat; growth of physico-chemical pollution which could reduce the length of life of the biosphere as an inhabitable region for organisms to a matter of decades rather than millions of years; world economic collapse through exhaustion of resources and pollution. The Club of Rome derived from its first World Model the conclusion that if exhaustion of industrial resources

[6] Donella H. Meadows, Dennis L. Meadows, Jurgen Randers, William W. Behrens III *The Limits to Growth* (London: Potomac Associates, Earth Island, 1972).
[7] United Nations, *The World Population Situation in 1970* (New York: 1971).

does not bring economic growth to an end, then pollution will; if resources are diverted to preventing or offsetting pollution, food supplies and health services will fall off, resulting in world collapse.

UNLIMITED RESOURCE POTENTIAL?

These predictions have been attacked mainly on the basis that technological progress itself will be an exponentially increasing variable leading to an extraordinary acceleration of world economic growth due to man's rapid increase in control over matter.[8] Optimistic futurologists predict that metal supplies will be maintained by new discoveries and through better mining methods (picking up nodules from the ocean floor). They argue that since total natural occurrence of most metals in the top mile of the earth's crust is about a million times as great as present known reserves, we have enough to last about a hundred million years, and we shall have plenty of time to discover how to mine to the depth of a mile. We shall find alternative materials where necessary; microminiaturization with integrated circuits will lead to a fantastic reduction in the physical volume of machinery and thus of the metals required. Technological advance could bring a glut of food; since only 3% of the globe's surface is now farmed and in most poor countries a serious "green revolution" leading to the best possible methods and crops has not yet taken place. Moreover sensible management could increase available resources: 70% of crops in some poor parts of the world are eaten by easily destroyable pests; the world's cows eat more grain than do all the world's people; in future, food will be "reared" by conversion of cellulose by enzymes and of petroleum wastes into single-cell high-protein organisms.[9]

All in all, world GWP (gross world product) could grow much more quickly in future. Norman Macrae argues that since real GWP has been increasing between 1950–73 at an annual average of 5% (doubling about every 14 years), the world has the potential to grow in future considerably more quickly than that. But even if gross world product (GWP) continued to grow at the rate of only 5% per annum, then by 2059 it would have passed $350 trillion. Guessing that world population might be around 15 billion at this time, Macrae concludes that most people—with per capita incomes standing at about $23,000,—would not be interested in becoming much richer.[10]

[8] For example, Lord Zuckerman, recent Chief Scientific Adviser to the British Government, maintains that "the growth of human knowledge" is exponential, cf. "Science Technology and Environmental Management" in Maurice Strong, ed., *Who Speaks for Earth?* (New York: W. W. Norton, 1973), pp. 138–139, see also H. S. D. Cole et al., *Thinking About the Future: A Critique of the Limits to Growth,* (London: Chatto & Windos for Sussex University Press, 1973), especially Chapter 9, "An Evaluation of the World Models."

[9] For a more detailed version of the optimists' outlook, see Herman Kahn, *The Next 200 Years* (New York: Hudson Institute, 1976).

[10] Norman Macrae, "America's Third Century," *Economist,* Oct. 25, 1975, p. 17–25.

LIMITED GROWTH BY CHOICE?

These mind-blowing possibilities of technological advance, suggest a future world of peace and plenty in which considerable self-sufficiency might eventually be achieved by most countries. The Club of Rome itself, in its Third Report, turns away from supposed insurmountable physical limits to growth and asks rather how growth can be maximized within existing economic and environmental restraints.

That the day may come when no one wants to be any richer is also an acceptable notion in light of the changes in thinking and behavior that have already taken place in affluent countries—shifts in taste from further accumulation of "things" towards consumption of high-level sophisticated services—high education, the arts, recreation; less interest in moneymaking, lagging rates of productivity, antibusiness attitudes and disappearance of the "work ethic." The environmental crisis evoked explicit opposition to "growthism" (the idea of growth for growth's sake). When the Club of Rome suggested zero growth of capital goods and population as a solution to the environmental crisis, many conservationists adopted the idea as a philosophical goal—an end in itself rather than a mere economic expedient. According to economist E. J. Mishan:

> If it is acknowledged that, once subsistence levels are passed, the sources of men's more enduring satisfactions are to be found in mutual trust and affection, and . . . the unfolding of nature . . . great art . . . it is just not possible to believe that sustained attempts to harness the greater part of man's energies and ingenuity to the task of amassing ever larger amounts of material possessions—fashion goods, gimmickry, motorized implements, novelties, and tasteless inanities—can add much to people's happiness. On the other hand, it is entirely plausible to believe that the competitive pressures of the technological society, the stifling specialization that makes material progress possible . . . will come to grind ever harder against the grain of men's intuitive needs.[11]

THE 29TH DAY?

However, reaching a stage when *no one* will want to be any richer will require a great deal more development—and a much better distribution of the world's wealth. World Models which followed the Club of Rome's First Report have increasingly concerned themselves with these two objectives.[12] The Club of Rome's Second Report warns that ever widening gaps between

---

[11] E. J. Mishan, "Ills, Bads, and Disamenities: the Wages of Growth," *Daedalus,* Fall 1973, page 85. This volume is reprinted as Mancur Olson and Hans H. Landsberg, *The No-Growth Society.* (New York: W. W. Norton, 1973).

[12] See for example Mihajlo Mesarovic and Eduard Pestel, *Mankind at the Turning Point: The Second Report to the Club of Rome* (New York: E. P. Dutton, 1974). Jan Tinbergen and others, *Reshaping the International Order: Catastrophe or New Society* (New York: E. P. Dutton 1976). United Nations, *The Future of the World Economy: A Study of the Impact of Prospective Economic Issues and Policies on the International Development Strategy,* (New York, 1976). Fundacion Bariloche, *Catastrophe or New Society? A Latin American World Model* (Ottawa: International Development Research Center, 1976).

rich and poor countries are intolerable and inconsistent with a stable, viable world. The outcome could be "wars of redistribution", nuclear terrorism or final collapse of the world economy with widespread famine and pestilence. "The relevant question" declares Brazilian economist Diogo Adolpho Nunes de Gaspar "is whether there will be violent discontinuity, or whether it will be possible to make a quick response . . . which will satisfy human needs? This question is likely to be answered by sheer population pressure if nothing else".[13] In the year 2,000 the Third World will constitute some three-quarters of the world's population. It is in this context that the lily plant riddle makes most sense.

The major share of the world's exponential population growth is at present taking place in the Third World. Advanced countries' population, growing presently at the rate of only 1 percent is predicted to increase from 1,080 million in 1970 to 1,454 million by the end of the century—an increase of less than 500 million. Developing countries, with current explosive population growth rates running close to 2.4 percent, will increase by over 3 billion, making a total Third World population probably exceeding 5 billion. In the poorest countries, pessimistic predictions are already a fact. People have been starving to death, quickly and with publicity during the famines, slowly and silently the rest of the time, through deteriorating nutrition. At the same time, sheer weight of numbers is already exerting increasing pressure on world resources, not only in terms of consumption but in terms of destruction of resources by misuse and pollution.

Irresponsible waste and pollution are mostly associated today with the advanced countries, with throwing cars and other durable consumer goods on trash heaps rather than repairing or recycling them, with manufacture of highly advertised inanities for the sake of "creating demand," with principles placing "progress" first at the expense of disfigurement and pollution of the environment. The Third World is moving into the position to do—or not do—the same kind of thing. In poor countries irresponsible waste is less flagrant. It exists in the form of luxury consumption by the rich but at the same time some of the oldest cars in the world still take to the roads where enormous human ingenuity keeps them running; in the poorest countries, even an empty bottle or tin can is treasured. Nevertheless developing countries have wasted and are still wasting natural resources by overexploitation and mismanagement, such as soil degradation, ecologically destructive agricultural and grazing practices, water pollution, depletion of sea resources. Moreover, as industrialization proceeds pollution problems are growing; and Third World attitudes do not always favor controls. Some leaders were enraged by suggestions for expensive curbs to pollution put forward at the environmental conferences of 1971–72. In their eyes, the Third World's relatively unpolluted environments had become resources in themselves. "We have plenty to pollute" roared a Latin American delegate at one of the conferences "and we're going to go right on polluting!"

[13] Diogo Adolpho Nunes de Gaspar, "Beyond Conference Ritual," *Development Forum*, July–August 1976, p. 2.

THE EXTENT OF MUTUAL VULNERABILITY

In sum, while no economist can presume to predict whether or not the human race is headed for extinction, there is every reason to believe that ingenuity and good management can overcome environmental restraints, conserving resources and discovering new ones, while curbing pollution and population growth—*if men make up their minds to do so, take the right decisions, and act soon enough*. Environmental exigencies introduce new forms of international interdependence and vulnerability, forcing difficult choices between international advantage and short-range national advantage, and among conflicting environmental and economic goals. Will, for example, some Third World countries forgo curbing pollution (which observes no national boundaries) in order to provide their people with desperately needed food and other necessities? What research will the advanced countries (who have the greatest capacity in research resources and expertise) choose to undertake—research which will make them independent of the Third World, or research based on international needs which could be quite different? Moreover, many of the predicted cure-all technological advances are still far from achievement. "In general the distant future . . . is glowing with promise," comments Lincoln Gordon, economist of Resources for the Future in Washington D.C. "while the near-term future is full of hazards and uncertainties."[14]

Great hazards lie in the increasing income gaps and uncertainties concerning their solution. A major conclusion to which newer world models come is that growth alone will not solve inequalities. The Club of Rome's second and third Reports stress the need for increased transfers from rich to poor countries. The United Nations World Model, with nearly 3000 equations, describing 15 regions of the world in terms of 45 sectors of economic activity, and designed to analyse interactions between economic and environmental policies, shows that the targets for developing countries during DD II are unattainable by growth alone. The world model assembled by the Fundacion Bariloche of Argentina (which asks what would be needed to assure a decent standard of living to the bottom 20 percent of the world income scale by the year 2000), leads to the conclusion that the target cannot be achieved by any possible rate of growth but requires redistribution within and among countries. Here, once again—according to Robert MacNamara—the limits are not environmental but human:

> The external assistance needed by the poorest nations over the past few years to achieve reasonable rates of economic growth, and to move towards meeting the basic human needs of their people, *has been within the ability of the wealthy world to supply*.[15] And it would have been made available had the developed nations met the target, agreed on in the United Nations in 1970, of contributing 0.7% of their GNP to Official Development Assistance (DA)—and had 0.2% out of this been earmarked for programs benefiting primarily the absolute poor.[16]

[14] Lincoln Gordon, "Limits to the Growth Debate," *Resources* No. 52, Summer 1976, p. 4.
[15] Italics added.
[16] Robert MacNamara, Address to the Board of Governors of the World Bank Group, Manila, Philippines, October 4, 1976.

But the target has not been met, MacNamara winds up dryly, "Nor is there any present indication that it will ever be met." Economists are asking whether there is another way out through new directions of development.

THE DEVELOPMENT CRISIS

Today's world models are changing focus from purely environmental considerations to the much broader issue of world development. Questions are being raised concerning conservation of resources, redistribution, and new directions for development. A popular nostrum being put forward at international conferences is that the richer countries should decrease consumption and change their life styles to permit greater transfers of resources to poor countries and that in return poor countries should curtail population growth. This prescription has been described as simplistic; but it might be better interpreted as "giving history a push." Not only can incentives be devised to accelerate the present shift into services and other forms of qualitative growth; history can also be given a push in the developing world by measures to speed up the decline in fertility rates. China and India, along with a number of smaller countries, have engaged in vigorous propaganda and educational campaigns in family planning; however history suggests that so far the greatest push towards smaller families has come from development itself. But what is the new development to be?

Although development problems are basically the same, approaches will necessarily differ between advanced and developing countries because development in advanced countries is virtually a *fait accompli* in need of modification of style, improved income distribution, and better management (discussed later). In developing countries, by definition, the process is not complete. Some countries believe they can choose a different more relevant development path, and are even contemplating "uncoupling" from the world economy, apparently willing to forgo the advantages of geographic specialization and of borrowing capital and technology in order to free themselves from the international economy's vagaries, inefficiencies, and increasing maldistribution of income in order to design their own development.

Recognition that the international economic policies pursued during the 1950s, 1960s, and 70s have not worked satisfactorily for any group of countries, but that they have worked better for rich countries than for poor countries—and better for rich people than for poor people in poor countries—has for years been the basis for economic analysis in the Third World.

In considering what has gone wrong within countries, many Third World economists put the blame on misguided efforts to apply Western development formulas where they do not belong. The basic formula for development taken over from the West—which was such a success in socialist and nonsocialist countries alike—was "getting rid of farmers": transferring agricultural labor into industry and services (trade, banking, insurance, transport, education, etc.) As noted above, this process of structural change, together with capital accumulation and technological progress in both industrial and agricultural sectors, generated economic growth in the past, burgeoning national incomes, and ultimately improved levels of welfare. Development however has taken a distorted form in the Third World.

The main divergences from the advanced countries' pattern of development in the Third World seem paradoxical: extraordinarily high growth rates have outdistanced those of the now advanced countries during their period of industrialization, yet rapidly rising national incomes are not guaranteeing "development" in the sense of widespread, deeply implanted and continuing improvements in welfare. Nor has the Third World gotten rid of its farmers. On the contrary, the rate of occupational structural change has been slow. The great majority of the populations remain in peasant agriculture, yet almost no developing country is self-sufficient in foodstuffs. Apart from the lack of structural change, differences in the development process appear most strikingly in population growth patterns, technological and sociocultural dualism (i.e., the development of a small modern economy and society alongside the traditional economy and society) and in related social problems of overurbanization and unemployment. All these characteristics are evident in all three major regions of the Third World. However, since population problems are greatest in Asia, dualism is particularly striking in Africa; and Latin America—most advanced—demonstrates directions in which social problems are headed, these differences will be examined in a broad scanning of these three major regions.

POPULATION PRESSURE: ASIA

Successful development largely hinges on the outcome of the race between the growth of population and gross national product. A major reason for failure to increase welfare in the Third World is the high rate of population growth, which has absorbed the lion's share of increases in output. In the 1950s the population of the developing countries grew at about 2 percent per year. By the early sixties the rate had increased to 2.5 percent and in the late sixties to 2.6 percent, *much higher and more prolonged than population growth ever was in the advanced countries*. Particularly in Asia, where the world's population problem is concentrated (with over 800 million in China, 700 million in India, over 125 million in Indonesia, 75 million and 60 million in Bangladesh and Pakistan respectively) population explosions have inundated spectacular economic achievements.

Independence gained by Asian countries after World War II released extremely rapid rates of industrialization and of technological progress (measured in terms of output per man-year in manufacturing), considerably higher than in the world as a whole. In small states such as Singapore, Hong Kong and South Korea, average rates of industrial expansion ran at 19 percent, 14.3 percent, and 14 percent respectively. Since they also experienced substantial decreases in birthrates, they achieved high per capita income growth rates as well (5.2%, 8.4%, 6.8%). In the vast, very poor, heavily populated Asian countries where high rates of industrialization were also achieved, but where birthrates fell more slowly, per capita income grew much more slowly. India's growth performance is a case in point.

India's main achievement since World War II has been the building up of a diversified industrial structure, largely through indigenous effort. Between 1950 and 1971 output of capital goods industries rose 10–11 percent annually, while the output of basic goods industries rose at the rate of 8–9 percent. These indicators reflect growth in the iron and steel, mining and power generation sectors, and the achievement of virtual self-sufficiency in supplying equipment for rail and road transport communications. India is also manufacturing machinery to equip a number of traditional industries (such as textile, sugar, and cement) while technology for processing raw materials has been developed to produce fertilizers and rayon and to dissolve pulp. Competent consultancy services can now provide design and engineering skills to erect power plants, to design and commission steel mills, while know-how is also available in fields such as heavy inorganic chemicals, sugar, cement, paper, aluminum, and coal mining. The extent of this expertise has allowed skills to be exported to other countries, not only in Asia and Africa, but also to Western Europe and South America.

At first glance, achievements in agriculture are less impressive; output rose at an annual rate of 3.2 percent, yet if one takes into account that methods were mainly traditional, the increase is an achievement. The ratio of savings to income nearly doubled from 5.7 percent to 10.0 percent, while the ratio of investment to income also doubled from 5.6 percent to 11.1 percent during the 1960s—large percentages in a country where per capita income was in the neighborhood of $70 in the early fifties, rising to $110 a year by the end of the sixties. Statistics of improvement in education and health services are also impressive. Primary school, secondary school, and university enrollment grew at an annual rate of 5.9 percent, 9.6 percent and 19 percent respectively. The admission capacity for higher technical education rose at an annual rate of 9–11 percent. The number of doctors and beds in hospitals rose 3.5 percent and 4.3 percent, respectively, each year, while primary health centers have increased at a rate of 14 percent annually. The literacy rate jumped from 16.6 percent to 29.4, while life expectancy at time of birth has shot up from 32.5 years to 52 years—*thus population growth rates also shot up*. While family planning programs have spread the awareness of the problem as well as the availablity of various methods of contraception to the remotest parts of the country, and the birthrate declined from 41 per 1000 to 39 per 1000 by 1965, and is declining slowly still, *this reduction fails to balance the highly successful reduction in death rates; population growth accelerated from 1.95 percent during 1951–61 to 2.25 per cent per annum during 1961–71.*

As a result, all these achievements have had disappointing overall results in improvement of welfare and employment creation, because the precentage gains, starting from a low base and swamped by population growth and the vast poverty of India, have all but disappeared. The high percentage rates of increase in industrial production melted into an average growth rate of national income of 3.6 percent. This rate was further negated by the population growth so that per capita income grew at only 1.4 percent per annum. The increase in food-grain production of some 1.4 percent per annum was therefore literally swallowed up by population growth; yet it is estimated that over 40 percent of the population do not have enough food to eat in terms of required caloric intake. To be sure the common man can now buy steel and aluminum utensils, plastic-ware, synthetic fibers, bicycles, radios, and watches—if he is gainfully employed—but population growth also undercuts the efforts at employment creation. Employment in the organized sector grew at about 5 percent per annum, but even if employment grew at 10 percent per year, the modern sector could not absorb as much as half the annual addition to the labor force. In fact, the rest of the labor force is absorbed by occupations mostly just adequate for basic subsistence.

In general, the population explosions in Asia have not only dissipated increase in output, imposing severe burdens on infrastructure (schools, hospitals, transport) and diverting national income from investment to consumption, but have also imposed a drag on structural change by flooding the labor market. The bulk of the population still remains in low-productivity agriculture and in relatively poor regions. Yet even thinly populated countries are having difficulties "getting rid of farmers."

TECHNOLOGICAL AND REGIONAL DUALISM: AFRICA

Africa is very thinly populated for the most part; why, then, does one find (even more than in Asia) the vast majority of the population trapped in low-productivity, low-income traditional agriculture?

The black continent remains least developed largely because it has had least to work with in the past. While there are a few relatively advanced countries, such as Algeria, some rich ones such as Libya, and others beginning to industrialize and urbanize rapidly, such as Nigeria, a number of "least developed countries" (to use the United Nations classification) have harsh, resource-poor environments, where most of the inhabitants must seek out a meager living in a traditional agriculture, virtually untouched by the modern world. Though thinly populated, they might still be described as overpopulated in relation to their *known* resources.

When a new resource is discovered, a mine opened, or a new crop introduced, one might expect a chain reaction creating jobs in other sectors of the economy, as occurred in now advanced countries. Instead, Third World countries often experience "high-growth without development". There is simply no relationship between the consequent high rate of growth, confined to the small modern sector, and the lives of the great majority of the people in the traditional sector where per capita income remains close to subsistence level and the traditional cultures remains essentially undisturbed.

One might expect that this technological and cultural dualism would diminish as the modern sectors grow and attract people from traditional sectors. Since their populations are relatively small, one might expect that such African countries would thus absorb their farmers into the modern sector in due course. However, it must be kept in mind that nations where population is growing relatively slowly (such as the Middle African countries) often have high population growth potential because the revolution in public health has not yet taken place. If the death rates are cut in half, as they may well be when public health campaigns are launched, rates of population growth could double, thus causing future unemployment problems. Latin America countries, for example, which are much more advanced in development than Africa, and where population is also relatively thin, have only partially succeeded in absorbing their farmers.

SOCIAL PROBLEMS: LATIN AMERICA

While more advanced in terms of structural change, education, and incomes, Latin America can more rightly be called an "underdeveloped" continent in terms of resources than the other regions of the Third World. Argentina, Brazil, Chile, Colombia, and Venezuela in many ways resemble the United States a century ago: all still have frontiers, with usable agricultural land and the promise of new mineral discoveries, awaiting settlement and development. In spite of rapid population growth, overall population densities are still low. Because of this favorable constellation of conditions, Latin American incomes are, on balance, the highest in the Third World. Venezuela and Argentina, with per capita incomes in the neighborhood of $2000, should probably not be classified as "less" developed at all. Uruguay, Mexico, and Brazil have all passed the $1000 mark and Chile should soon do so. Most other Latin American countries are in the $200 to $500 category: No Latin American country except Haiti, has a per capita income below $200. Most Latin American countries also have high rates of growth of national income, although growth of per capita income, is somewhat less impressive due to high population growth. In Uruguay, Haiti, and Cuba per capita income actually fell during the sixties. However, Latin America as a whole now falls into the "transitional" classification in terms of population growth. Death rates are already low; fertility rates are tapering off, and many demographers would expect fertility rates to drop further, following the pattern set in the past by Europe, North America, Australasia, and Japan. With so many parallels to North American conditions, development might be expected to follow advanced countries' patterns more closely, yet Latin America still fails to assimilate the entire population into the modern economy.

While Latin America has been successful in "getting rid of farmers" in that less than half the working force remains in agriculture, there has been only partial success in reemploying them: droves of unskilled, rural laborers are flocking into the burgeoning cities, creating enormous urban problems. This "urban drift" characterizes other parts of the Third World but is most advanced in Latin America. Asia has huge urban conglomerations where misery and squalor abound, and Africa now has the highest rate of urbanization, but the great bulk of Asians and Africans still live in the countryside (75%). By contrast, over half the population of Latin America is urbanized; Mexico City,

Sao Paolo, Rio de Janeiro and Buenos Aires are among the world's fifteen largest cities and still growing.

Similar migrations characterized the development process of advanced countries in the past, but gainful employment awaited the migrants, and really large cities did not appear until per capita incomes were already fairly high. Unfortunately urbanization in the Third World today is outrunning industrialization. Only a fraction of these rural-urban migrants are being absorbed by the industrial sector; the rest remain unemployed or enter the swollen services sector. On the other hand, good jobs are sometimes left unfilled because people with the right skills are not available. Ill-adapted education has been blamed.

Developing countries have been expanding their educational systems rapidly, in the firm belief that education is the keystone for equalized opportunity as well as development, as it was in the advanced countries. But of all the advanced countries' recipes for a better life, education has been one of the bitterest disappointments. There are a number of reasons for failure. Elitist education systems, inherited from colonial days have often been inadequately adapted to development needs. Population explosions have swamped the schools; moreover, improved education brought higher levels of production in the advanced countries because it was accompanied by capital accumulation and resource discovery that provided the jobs and the opportunity to use the education. Here one of the stalemates of underdevelopment emerges: legions of educated unemployed swell, because employment opportunities do not match the graduating students in volume owing to insufficient economic development.

NEW DEVELOPMENT PATTERNS?

Leaders and development planners of the developing countries have been trying to interprete these trends, and to create new patterns of development that, as Soejatmoko of Indonesia declares, "are not simply a repetition of the phases and directions that the industrial nations have gone through in the past."[17]

SHOULD TRADITIONAL CULTURE BE PRESERVED?

Planners are reexamining Western development formulas for their appropriateness to Third World conditions and trying out some modifications of their own. They are turning from unquestioning introduction of Western technologies to a search for "intermediate" technologies which, whenever possible, use local materials and techniques, employ more people, and are thus more suitable to the local scene. The choice of technology is one aspect of a much

[17] Soedjatmoko, "Technology, Development and Culture," unpublished paper 1972, prepared for a colloquium organized by the Institute for Religion and Social Change, Honolulu, held at Santa Barbara, California April 10 through 12, 1972. Soedjatmoko is responsible for sociocultural aspects in the Ministry of Planning.

broader and more fundamental choice: how much should traditional societies be changed, if at all? Objections are raised against traditional institutions being swept away without being adequately replaced. The built-in social security systems of village society, for example, where the aged and the sick are taken care of within the extended family circle, the village, or the tribe, and where (since unemployment is not acceptable) income is shared by sharing work, should not be lightly cast aside.

A long standing controversy as to whether some very stagnant traditional societies highly resistent to change can or should modernize has developed into a discussion as to whether they should modernize in the light of the environmental crisis. Some discussants insist that sociocultural barriers to economic development reflect contentment with things as they are, and believe that some societies would be better off if they sidestepped pollution, an environment defaced by industrialization, a society filled with tensions, and instead took advantage of the many virtues of traditional life.

When confronted with setting a course of cumulative change in a tranquil civilization such as Bali, the planner may pause with good reason. With an average income of about $100 a year, with 90 percent of the people in agriculture, the island of Bali is certainly an economically underdeveloped region. Yet volcanically renewed soil and a bountiful rainfall enable the Balinese to feed, clothe, and shelter themselves with a few hours of work a day; with the rest of the time devoted to refined use of leisure—to pursuit of painting, sculpture, architecture, ballet and music, the study of philosophy. Some kind of change must come about in Bali to offset population pressure, but does it have to be Western-style modernization of either socialist or nonsocialist brands?

Few countries are as fortunate as Bali; in the case of the abject poverty of India and Bangladesh, or famine-stricken West Africa, for example, it is clear that much has to change. In general, leaders of the poor countries are determined to achieve higher standards of living and initiate a process of development that will offer their people opportunities for a richer and more varied life. However, they also want this richer life to retain indigenous social and cultural heritages. But is it possible to retain traditional modes along with modern development? The militant neo-Marxists insist that development cannot proceed without a sweeping revolution and declare that what appears to others as backward traditional societies is really the result of deliberate exploitation. The leaders of the many right-wing military revolutions also see the need for radical change, although their preferred style of revolution was very different. Is it indeed necessary to have a revolution, Cuban or Maoist or Brazilian style, establishing totalitarian or near-totalitarian regimes, or are there other internal solutions? Or should the Third World "uncouple" from the advanced world?

INDEPENDENCE OR INTERDEPENDENCE?

While all the distortions of development listed above contribute to continuing poverty, Third World leaders have also come to the conclusion that a great deal of the problem lies in the fact that the countries are so poor to begin with. It is a matter of simple arithmetic that when per capita income starts to grow from a low base of $70 per year, as India's did in the early 50s and increases to $110 within two decades, the overall increase is impressive, but the country still remains very poor. Moreover, the poorer the country, the harder it is to save and achieve high growth rates. As already noted the "richest" poor countries enjoyed much higher rates of growth than the poorest ones.

A group of economists sometimes labelled the "radical political economists" have taken this idea much further, presenting a "dependency theory" which explains the widening gaps between rich and poor countries, and between rich and poor in poor countries in terms of consciously planned collaboration between the powerful capitalists of the advanced countries and the less powerful and subservient capitalists of the developing countries. It is the aim of this international capitalist conspiracy to keep peasant incomes and wages low in order to keep profits high. Governments of developing countries (indeed of all nonsocialist countries) are mere creatures of the dominant capitalist class and do its bidding.

Even among more moderate leaders the view is held that the Third World has never been accorded the full advantages of trade expansion and technological advance. They have been dissatisfied with the conditions of technology "sharing" (particularly when introduced by foreign investors), with their mounting national debts (since aid is increasingly taking the form of loans), with trade restrictions against their products on the part of advanced countries, and above all with their deteriorating terms of trade—that is, the tendency for prices of their exports to fall relative to prices of imports from advanced countries. Advanced countries have maintained that this tendency results naturally from the working of the market mechanism, but a widely held view in the Third World is that the phenomenon is due to malpractice on the part of the advanced countries, or at the very least, advanced countries have been guilty of a monumental lack of comprehension of the problems involved.

This lack of comprehension was suggested in the opening address by Mahbub ul Haq at the Karachi meeting of the Third World Forum where he explained the devastating effects of deteriorating terms of trade by means of the advanced countries' own experience in 1973 at the hands of OPEC. Ul Haq (Director of Policy Research at the World Bank) began by recapitulating the terms of trade controversy:

> When we protested against deteriorating terms of trade for our countries, we were quietly informed that this was merely the workings of a free international market mechanism and we were left to puzzle for ourselves why, by some curious coincidence, the market mechanism always worked to the detriment of the poor nations.[18]

When the shoe was on the other foot, Ul Haq went on to observe, the same "grand sounding principles" changed with amazing suddenness:

[18] The Third World Forum: Intellectual Self Reliance, *Development* Vol. XVII Number 1, 1975, p. 9.

When the OPEC nations demanded a higher price for their oil exports, it was dubbed as "exploitation" and "blackmail" rather than the working of the international market mechanism. When terms of trade turned for once against the industrialized countries last year, it was characterized as the beginning of a world depression and an unmanageable adjustment problem, even though it meant a transfer of merely 2% of the GNP of the developed world. But the industrialized countries conveniently forgot that the developing countries have often lost 10–15% of their GNP through the deterioration in their terms of trade in the 1960's and were forced to make a far more painful adjustment in the consumption levels at a much lower level of income.[19]

He also used this 2% transfer of the advanced countries' GNP to explain how Third World countries viewed the volume of foreign aid:

When the rich nations were obliged to transfer a mere 2% of their GNP—and that too in financial rather than in real terms—they suddenly became so 'poor' as to protest that they could not carry on the burden of aid to the developing countries. They quietly ignored the fact that their average per capita income was still about seven to eight times that of OPEC. (He might have added "and for some rich countries as much as 40 times the incomes of the poorest countries").[20]

Finally, Mahbub ul Haq explained Third World countries' reticence concerning acceptances of foreign investment by the same device.

When some of the surplus funds were used by the OPEC nations to acquire a partial control over some Western corporations, there were screams of protest from the very people who had lectured us on the virtues of foreign investment, and criticized us for too much national sensitivity over issues of foreign control.[21]

Belief in the theory of dependence leads naturally to demands for independence or autonomy. The theory has a particularly marked vogue in Latin America; and in Latin America in particular it leads to demands for independence from advanced countries for capital, markets, entrepreneurship, and technology. It is better, the argument goes, to be content with the level and rate of development made possible with the countries' own resources, than to put up with the growing inequalities and the partial loss of sovereignty implicit in being dependent on advanced countries. Even foreign aid is seen as a device for building up the modern sectors of developing countries in order to enhance profits. Some Latin American economists go so far as to maintain that their countries would be better off if they limited their production to commodities which require only resources, equipment, and technology of a kind available within Latin America (assuming some sort of economic integration within the region) rather than being dependent for any of these things on advanced countries.

Such a solution may be acceptable for transitional countries with relatively good resource endowments, such as Argentina, Brazil, Chile, Mexico, Venezuela, and Malaysia. Over the next few years, with their new bargaining power, along with their own achievements, such developing countries as a

[19] Ibid., p. 9.
[20] Ibid., p. 9.
[21] Ibid., p. 9.

group can hope to reduce their dependency on the advanced countries for capital, technology, and scientific and managerial skills. Since the sixties the Third World has been financing 85% of its own development; centers like Sao Paulo, Hong Kong, Singapore, Seoul, Taipeh, Calcutta, Bombay are advanced enough in their technologies not only to look after themselves but to export technology. However, for countries such as Haiti, Cambodia, Niger, or Mauretania it would seem to be truly a council of despair; it is hard to see how such countries can escape the vicious circle of poverty on the basis of their own resources and technological capacities alone.

Independence of this type or to this degree, however, is not what the Third World's negotiating bloc—the Group of 77—have in mind. The Group of 77, which pushed the Declaration and Program for a New International Economic Order through the United Nations, and which inaugurated the Third World Forum, is composed of countries with a wide range of wealth and resource endowment, from very rich to very poor. A deliberate choice has been made by the members of the group to operate as a unified bloc within the world system, with the strong helping the weak, particularly in bargaining with the advanced world. OPEC, for example has given strong support at international bargaining tables to the ''77,'' (who had previously enjoyed little clout as a negotiating bloc for the Third World). Above all, OPEC had, in the early days of the oil crisis, shown what can be done by a group of developing countries acting in unison to achieve certain aims. Thus, in spite of rivalries within the Group of 77, (which has now expanded to about 130) their delegates have arrived at subsequent world conferences with documentation well prepared, and have displayed remarkable unity of purpose in marked contrast to the disunity and general disarray of the advanced countries.

Rather than independence, then, bargaining with advanced countries remained, in the mid-1970s, within the framework of a New International Economic Order, including all countries of the world, rich and poor, socialist and nonsocialist, within one articulated global economic system. If dependence is rejected, so for the moment is isolationism. At the same time, the demands could be interpreted as paving the way towards freedom from interference by foreign governments or foreign corporations in the determination of their economic policies, their own social and political system, and their own ideologies and cultures.

The recently enhanced bargaining power of the Group of 77 does not really bring them any closer, as yet, to solution of their fundamental development problems; ''instant development'' cannot be negotiated. All that can be *negotiated* is enlarged net transfers of resources, to increase the *means* for development at the disposal of the Third World, and new institutions. As we have seen, the mere existence of an ''integrated'' world economy is no guarantee of its smooth performance, let alone of international peace and harmony. An interdependent global system must be carefully *designed* to assure harmony and efficiency. Moreover, even with the best imagineable set of international institutions, the global economy cannot function better than the national economies of which it is composed. Above all, there remains the central task of making the best use of scarce resources, in other words, of sound economics. The viability and justification for any program for national development, as well as any proposed new international order, should be judged in terms of solid economic analysis. But does today's economic science provide a solid basis?

CONCLUSIONS: THE CRISIS OF ECONOMICS

Some of the keenest minds in the whole field of economics contributed to the Third World Forum inaugural meeting. When they spoke of the old order "crumbling" one thing in the delegates' minds was certainly the crumbling of confidence in long-defended economic principles and economic systems. The crises of the seventies gave rise to a massive wave of new doubts concerning the goals of industrial societies (both socialist and nonsocialist), existing socioeconomic systems and received economic doctrine.

Above all, the energy crisis and 1973–76 recession spotlit the inefficiencies of the market economies,[22] and the shortcomings of standard economics when it comes to dealing with shortages, with simultaneous inflation and unemployment, mass poverty, pollution and waste, and social injustice within and among nations. In the early seventies a complacent economics establishment declared that the market would ration scarce materials through higher prices, and encourage research for alternatives. But as shortages emerged, it became clear that the market did not have sufficient foresight, that the price system cannot create resources where they do not exist and that the market rations badly; while expensive oil continued to fuel big industry, smaller enterprises dropped out of production, and petroleum-based fertilizers and pesticides moved beyond the reach of the poorest peasants in poorest countries.

It is not only a question as to whether the private enterprise system's keystones—the free market and the price system—will indeed ration resources efficiently, but also a question as to whether or not "free world" institutions work well from any point of view. Until the seventies the expansion of the world economy and growing affluence had masked and allayed the full effect of their inefficiencies, at least in the richer countries. Nothing illustrated more strikingly their profound shortcomings than the repercussions of the oil price hike in the form of acceleration of world inflation and aggravation of world unemployment. Yet the relationship between price increases by monopolistic groups of employers and workers and inflation and unemployment is only the visible tip of an iceberg of inefficiency. In particular, standard economics, in its search for "rigor" and "freedom from value judgments," has always ducked the issue of inequalities of income distribution. Yet today questions of equity and social justice are paramount, and the private enterprise system seems to have less satisfactory answers to these questions than the socialist

[22] "Market economy" is the United Nations term for nonsocialist countries, with little or no centralized planning, where free markets play a major role in resource allocation.

system, especially in its Maoist version. It is clear that economists and others who prefer to find solutions to economic and social problems within a non-socialist system must be prepared to tackle problems of income distribution—within and between nations.

Not only are economists confronted with new sets of economic, social, and environmental problems, added to old ones, but changing attitudes have eroded a number of basic assumptions concerning man's economic behavior and aims. Increasing numbers of people in both rich and poor countries refuse to accept the equation of expanding consumption of material goods with improved quality of life. This attitude has crystallized in attacks on the concept of economic growth itself.

From the birth of economics as a separate discipline, (often linked to the publication of Adam Smith's *Wealth of Nations* in 1776) economists have taken it for granted that economic growth is a good thing. While they have been ready to admit inefficiencies in the operation of the world economic system, they have greeted attacks on "growthism" as a mortal challenge, particularly the equating of "growthism" with materialism. "You would think," declared economist Robert Solow "that you favor growth if you are the sort of person whose idea of heaven is to drive at ninety miles an hour down a six-lane highway reading billboards, in order to pollute the air over some crowded lake with the exhaust from twin 100 horsepower outboards, and whose idea of food is Cocoa Krispies. On the other hand, to be against economic growth is to be a granola-eating, back packing, transcendental-meditating canoe freak." [23] Implicit in Solow's argument is the point that growth is neutral in terms of style of development. We might do better to "contemplate great art" rather than to buy electric toothbrushes; and indeed some countries may not need further growth; although other countries will. As the famous British economist and parson, the Reverend Phillip T. Wicksteed once remarked, "It is difficult to be a philosopher, a poet, or a lover unless one has fairly recently had something to eat."

Meaningful discussion must start with a clear distinction between economic growth and development, and between "productivity" and "production." Economic growth in this study means growth of national income and accumulation of industrial capital. Development means increased productivity, i.e. increased capacity to provide *whatever* people want, whether it be food, leisure, temples, unpolluted sylvan scenes, ballet, heated houses, or national independence. To offer all these things to all people in the future will involve a great deal of economic ingenuity, political skill, and last, but not least, technological advancement. *Higher productivity* does *not* necessarily mean *higher production of material goods*. Technological progress achieves goals with *less* use of capital, raw materials, and human effort. Any economic, environmental, or social problem can be more easily solved with technological advancement than with stable or falling man-hour productivity. For example,

[23] Robert M. Solow, "Is the End of the World at Hand?" *Challenge*, March/April 1973, p. 40.

if the present experiments with microbial pesticides succeed in replacing petroleum based pesticides, *productivity* will have improved, because microbial pesticides are much less harsh on the environment. Moreover, such a switch would save an increasingly costly, increasingly scarce resource. Productivity, unfortunately, has been rising too slowly, evoking a major reassessment of economic management and economic systems, the role of political and socio-cultural factors in development, patterns of foreign trade and investment, and the international economy as a whole. This study essays such an assessment. It therefore begins with a review of the leading economic-political systems and of long accepted economic doctrines and principles.

2

Panaceas
for progress

The world today is confronted with two major *systems* for development. One is presented by the *market economies*—the predominantly private enterprise economies, with varying degrees of government regulation and ownership, formerly known as "capitalist" countries. On the other side are the *centrally planned,* socialist countries.

It is not easy for people to choose their system by looking at the record. A glance at Table 2.1 shows that the rich countries are nearly all market economies; in terms of the speed of recent growth, however, the advanced centrally planned countries have done better than the advanced market economies. The performances of the developing countries are mixed. Except for Libya with its recently found petroleum reserves, the most impressive performance in terms of growth has been registered by private-enterprise Japan, and the worst by socialist Cuba. Each group of countries can dismiss its failures as special cases; they make their appeal mainly on ideological grounds.

Behind the two rival economic systems are two rival systems of thought, both of long standing. The market economies' rationale rests on the liberal or classical economics of the late eighteenth and early nineteenth centuries, as modified in the twentieth. The centrally planned economies base their faith in their system on Marxist economics, also a nineteenth century product, although since the Russian Revolution interest has shifted in socialist countries from theorizing about the process of capitalist expansion and collapse to hardheaded planning for further socialist development. Some of the most powerful minds ever concerned with questions of economics belong to the classical and Marxist schools. Does either system of thought, even in its most modern version, provide a real panacea for economic ills? To answer this question, let us look at the key features of both systems of thought.

TABLE 2.1   GNP PER CAPITA 1970 AND GROWTH RATES 1960–70

	GNP	Growth Rates: 1960–70
Market Economies		
U.S.	$4,760	3.2
Sweden	4,040	3.8
Canada	3,700	3.6
Switzerland	3,320	2.5
Denmark	3,190	3.7
France	3,100	4.6
Germany West	2,930	3.5
Norway	2,860	4.1
Australia	2,820	3.1
Israel	1,960	4.7
Japan	1,920	9.6
Libya	1,770	20.4
Centrally Planned (Advanced)		
East Germany	2,490	4.2
Czechoslovakia	2,230	3.8
USSR	1,790	5.8
Hungary	1,600	5.4
Poland	1,400	5.2
Bulgaria	760	7.4
Centrally Planned (Developing)		
Romania	930	7.7
Albania	600	4.8
Cuba	530	−0.6
Mongolia	460	0.0
Korea North	330	5.1
China	160	2.1
Mixed (Developing)		
Hong Kong	970	8.4
Singapore	920	5.2
Mexico	670	1.6
Brazil	420	2.4
Taiwan	390	7.1
Korea South	250	6.8
Sri Lanka	110	1.5
India	110	1.2
Burma	80	0.6
Indonesia	80	1.0
Mali	70	4.4

Source: World Bank Atlas

THE CLASSICAL THEORY OF CAPITALIST DEVELOPMENT: GROWTH AND STAGNATION

The term classical school refers to a group of economists, primarily English, writing in the late eighteenth and early nineteenth centuries—the period of the Industrial Revolution in Europe. Best known are Adam Smith, David Ricardo, Thomas Malthus, and John Stuart Mill. French contemporaries were Cantillon, Dupuit, and Cournot. Living through a period of accelerated economic growth, these men were very much concerned with the conditions for economic progress; they analyzed the process of growth that was taking place; seeking to explain differences in growth rates among nations and to isolate the requirements for continued development.

The classical school provided the economic philosophy of the intellectual liberalism prevalent in the eighteenth century. Like other adherents to the liberal ideology, the classical school believed in the essential harmony of the universe. They considered the free market to be the instrument of harmony in the economic sphere, and an explanation of the surge of development they were then witnessing. Because it advocates a free market, created by free trade, free competition, and in general a policy of laissez-faire, classical economic thought is often regarded today as the antithesis of socialist economic thought, which calls for centralized decision making and planning. Rather than opposing such centralization (a proposal which had not yet presented itself), the classical economists were reacting against the remnants of feudalism which were impeding growth. They were opposed to the "ill-gotten gains" of the landlords, considered to be unearned, and endorsed the struggle of the craftsmen and merchants to free themselves from the rules of the guilds, the restraints on foreign trade, and the municipal regulations concerning domestic trade. Marx himself drew heavily on classical thought, and today socialist and nonsocialist economists alike still apply principles and propositions first stated by the classical school.

Classical thought also throws considerable light on the poverty of the underdeveloped countries; the epoch of the classical school coincided with the spread of colonialism. During the seventeenth, eighteenth and nineteenth centuries, international trade between the colonies and the imperialist powers burgeoned, and the seeds of the present problems were sown.

In sum, the classical economists have much to offer today's developmentalists: they not only contribute basic economic principles, they have an essentially modern approach to their treatment of the economy as a *system,* and their forecast of exhaustion of resources and stagnation is remarkably similar to the predictions of "zero growth" by the Club of Rome.

THE ECONOMIC MECHANISM

The classical school made its major contribution to economics in its analysis of the workings of the economic system as a whole. These economists conceived the operating economy as a working mechanism; they interested themselves in the whole system of causal relationships which direct the economy's course, examining the factors governing the flow of capital, natural resources, and labor into production and distribution of goods for consumption. They were particularly interested in the natural forces of the competitive market. They believed that the economic mechanism would function automatically and at its best if the market were left free to allocate the means of production to the best advantage; free, that is, from either government or private interference.

PROFITS

The classical economists regarded profits as the mainspring of growth in creating surpluses available for further investment and stimulating further expansion. There is a good deal of misunderstanding about this concept. Many educated people in developing countries—and even in advanced countries—regard the interpretation of profits as the mainspring of growth as an apology for ruthless exploitation within a capitalistic system, for unhampered entrepreneurial activity, which they associate with colonialism, and as a crass, materialistic, devil-take-the-hindmost form of robber baronry. But to understand fully the role of profits in the classical system it is necessary to remember two basic points. First, the classical economists were resolutely opposed to *monopoly* profits; they justified only profits that were wrung out of success in keenly competitive markets. Second, and in a way more important, the classical school was very severe with landlords. They regarded rents as an unjustified and unnecessary form of exploitation which ought to be eliminated. Now with rents excluded, profits in the national economy are simply the surplus over wages and salaries paid out.[1] In countries not yet arrived at affluence, wages and salaries tend to be spent almost entirely for consumption. Thus profits are necessary in order to have a surplus available for investment, without which growth is impossible even in a socialist country. Marx himself fully understood the need for profits, or "surplus-value," for economic growth to take place.

Therefore, while the expectation of profits motivated industrialists, farmers, and merchants to invest their capital, this concern with gain was not deemed antisocial, because profits are a prerequisite to increases in national income. The classicists expected these capitalists to reinvest the bulk of their profits rather than to dissipate them on extravagant living; profits thus activated the flow of capital, natural resources, and labor into productive activity.

THE PRODUCTION FUNCTION

The desire for profits not only impelled capitalists to invest, but also encouraged investors and entrepreneurs to use available resources to their best advantage. Again the classical economists expected this motivation to serve the common weal, since individual efforts to maximize income would tend to maximize productivity of the economy as a whole, and thereby maximize

---

[1] Profits in this context means total returns to capital and entrepreneurship. At the level of the individual firm it is the common sense concept of profits, as total receipts minus total costs, or total value of product sales less total costs of product: wages and salaries, rents, interest on loans, payments for raw materials and equipment. When resolved into shares of national income, all interest payments become part of profits, and payments for new materials and equipment become wages, salaries and rents paid by producers of new materials and equipment plus the profits of those producers. Thus at the level of the national economy, Profits = (Total value of production or sales) − (wages and salaries plus rents).

total output. Here we come to the central problem of economics: finding the best use of available resources in order to maximize total output.

Smith, Ricardo, Malthus, and Mill all had it quite clearly in mind that total output depends on three main elements:

1. The factor endowment—the size of the labor force, the stock of capital, the amount of land available (meaning the supply of known and economically useful natural resources)
2. The proportions in which these factors of production are combined
3. The level of technology

All these conditions are referred to collectively as the production function. For every factor endowment there is an optimal combination of the factors of production and an optimal product mix, an optimal choice of products to be manufactured.

Factors of production would be combined according to their relative abundance or scarcity. If abundant labor were available for agriculture, a farmer could engage in labor-intensive agriculture, such as vegetable cultivation or poultry farming, combining relatively large amounts of labor with small amounts of land. If labor became scarce, a farmer would combine smaller amounts of labor with larger amounts of land, raising sheep, as the farmers did after the Black Death (discussed below). Similar optimal combinations of resources would be made—if wood were plentiful and cheap and metal were less plentiful and more costly, wood would be used in preference to metal— where practicable—in the manufacture of a good.

THE INVISIBLE HAND

Within the classical system, the allocation of the factors of production would be ultimately determined by what Adam Smith referred to as the "invisible hand"—the natural forces of the competitive market. Resource allocation would be resolved in the marketplace: "demand" would reflect what people wanted to buy while "supply" would reflect the costs involved in producing the goods.

By revealing what goods people wanted to buy and how much they cost, the market "decided" what would be produced in such a way as to bring about an optimal allocation of the factors of production among industries, regions, and nations. The market also decided just rewards to these factors; in a competitive market, rewards to the factors of production would be highest where their productivity was highest, and factors would tend to flow into their best use. The market also acted as a warning device, signaling bountiful supplies of factors of production and indicating scarcities: higher interest rates would signal growing scarcity of capital; rising wages rates would provide the same information for particular types of labor skills and likewise rents for land. Price movements would automatically encourage the use of bountiful factors and curb the use of scarce ones.

EQUALIZING EFFECTS

At the same time the market was thought to have an equalizing, spread-the-wealth effect. Some countries or regions might be better endowed with capital or natural resources; however, differences in productivity and incomes would tend to disappear through one or another of the more or less automatic mechanisms triggering the movement of men, capital, and goods. Migration moves labor from low-wage to high-wage regions, tending in the long run to equalize wages. Capital would tend to flow automatically to sectors or regions where it was scarce, because returns to new investment would be higher there. The inflow of capital would raise productivity of labor, and so labor's income in the area. Pure competition was also supposed to assure the limitation of profits to the "normal" level, just high enough to retain the interest of investors and entrepreneurs. In other words, they again saw the market as the best allocator of capital and determinant of its rewards.

COMPARATIVE ADVANTAGE

Even without movements of men or capital, movements of goods through international trade would lead each region and country to specialize in those goods and services for which it had a "comparative advantage".

Comparative advantage was a subtle concept. It was not simply a matter of every country doing what they were best at. A country might have *absolute* advantage in everything, but it would still pay the country to specialize in the field where its *comparative* advantage was greatest. For example, England produced corn and wool efficiently, but in the following situation, it might be better in the long run to concentrate on wool. Suppose that for a given cost,

England can produce:	*France can produce:*
3 tons of corn	2 tons of corn
or	or
2 tons of wool	1 ton of wool

thus in England, 1 ton of corn costs ⅔ tons of wool and in France, 1 ton of corn costs ½ ton of wool.

It is obvious that it pays France to export corn and import wool. It is less obvious that it also pays England to specialize in wool despite her absolute advantage in growing corn. At any price for corn below two-thirds the price of wool, it pays England to get her corn by importing it in exchange for wool. As we shall see later, the distinction between comparative and absolute advantage is at the root of current controversies between advanced and developing countries with respect to trade between them.

GOVERNMENT ACTION

With their faith based on the free market as the optimal allocator of resources, the classicists had little to say concerning government policy in the belief that so long as a country installed a sociopolitical economic system based on the principles of *laissez-faire* free trade, free competition, and minimum government interference, economic growth would take care of itself.

They were implacably opposed both to government interference in the market and to monopoly profits.[2] Monopolies, the classical school believed, would lead to unfair profits, distorted factor values, and a consequent misallocation of resources. Government interference could have similar bad effects. The classicists, for example, advocated the repeal of the Corn Laws which restricted importation of grains into England. Their repeal was deemed to have accelerated the nation's industrialization, allowing England to turn to her true comparative advantage, which was at that time mainly sheep raising and manufacture of woollen goods. The classicists' recommendations for government policy were, in general, limited to similar efforts to free the market.

However, alongside these efforts to free the market from ill-founded interference by the national government, and the petty regulations of local governments and guilds, Adam Smith approved limited intervention where the free market did not bring social justice in accordance with his own value judgments. He approved of minimum wage legislation, legal limitations on profits, progressive income tax, price ceilings on necessities, curtailment of exploitation by landlords, and extension of public enterprise to fields of social importance which are not, or should not be, allowed to become profitable for private enterprise.

Apart from this "patching" of the market to effect social justice, the classicists believed that given a free market, economic progress would be a natural state of affairs (as it was at that time in England). Absence of growth was held due to human folly, sloth, or indulgence.

THE SUCCESSES OF LAISSEZ-FAIRE

The records of the countries developing at the time substantiate the classical view. The "invisible hand" did a respectable job in the nineteenth century in moving men, capital, and goods to advantage in industrial Europe and subsequently in the United States, Canada, and Australasia. The fact that men, capital, and goods have failed to move to the best advantage in the underdeveloped countries is a basic cause for the problems of those nations today, and opens up for us important lines of inquiry.

The capitalists of the epoch also behaved as the classicists expected. They invested most of their profits rather than squandering them on extravagant living; instances of profits being dissipated merely confirmed the classicists' opinion that sloth and greed could bring about economic stagnation. It is with the threat of stagnation that the classical model is ultimately concerned.

---

[2] In this context *monopoly* means any departure from "pure competition," where there are so many firms that none of them can influence price. It means that there are only one or a few sellers of a particular good or service. *Monopoly,* therefore, covers the cases of "oligopoly" (few sellers) and "monopolistic competition" (several competing sellers).

THE CLASSICAL SYSTEM

The classical economists recognized that a healthy, well managed, growing economy may eventually stagnate through limits to growth imposed by excess population and by exhaustion of resources. They saw the process of development as a race between population growth on the one hand and capital accumulation, technological progress, and expansion of markets on the other. Technological progress and capital accumulation were regarded as closely linked; capital accumulation permitted a finer division of labor, the introduction of new techniques, and more tools and equipment per man. Expanding markets also permitted a finer division of labor through geographic specialization. Investment evoked by these opportunities reaped profits, leading to a feedback of these profits into further investment and expansion of the market, a circular movement of success breeding success. However, this favorable progression was constantly threatened by steady population growth and the accompanying specter of "diminishing returns" which would eventually lead to stagnation.

THE LAW OF DIMINISHING RETURNS

The classicists believed that additions to total agricultural output, as the labor force grew, would increase for a while, then as the total area of land became utilized, the addition to output with higher employment on the land would decrease, and ultimately fall to zero. This was their famous "law of diminishing returns." If the stock of capital utilized were increased, or the technique improved, labor productivity would rise temporarily; but with continuing population growth, diminishing returns to agriculture would soon set in again. The labor force, employment, and the population were generally conceived to vary together. Of course, the classical economists could ignore neither the existence of unemployment nor variations in the amount of unemployment, especially in the decades of depression following the Napoleonic Wars. But on the whole they regarded unemployment as an aberration, at least in a growing economy, and felt that population growth and employment must move together. This belief provided the basis for their "iron law of wages."

THE IRON LAW OF WAGES

The classicists' pessimism rested not only on their expectation of eventual exhaustion of resources (diminishing returns) but also on their conviction of the inevitability of population growth if investment increased, thereby raising the "wages fund"—the amount of accumulated capital available for employing labor.

Few of the basic propositions of the classical school have been so vehemently attacked as the "iron law of wages." The general idea is that the rate of population growth depends on how much money (working capital) is available to pay wages. If the total wages fund is increased and real average rates rise above the subsistence level, larger numbers of working-class children can survive to become members of the labor force. There are no checks on the size of working-class families except the amount of wages available to them and the number of children that can subsist on those wages. Thus there is a constant tendency for real wage rates to return to the subsistence level. An increase in wages paid may bring a temporary improvement in living standards, but this improvement will soon be swamped by an increased rate of population growth.

This argument often seems farfetched to people living in advanced countries today, but it probably gave a fairly accurate description of what happened in Europe in the late eighteenth and early nineteenth centuries. It also seems to be true of peasant societies in Asian, African, and some Latin American countries today.

In Europe in the eighteenth century, as in Asia, Africa, and Latin America in recent decades, health and nutrition were improving, while most people could not visualize a significantly higher standard of living to be achieved by acceptable and available means of limiting family size. Thus they were probably rather indifferent to family planning. When wage rates rose, more children could be brought to maturity without impinging on the customary living standards of the working class, and consequently population growth could increase. There was no strong incentive for limiting family size, and no cheap and convenient ways of family planning were available. Under these conditions, the classical theory of population makes good sense.

Thus population growth eventually brought a decline in incomes due to "diminishing returns," *unless* offset by technological progress. Historically increasing returns, especially in industry, offset this tendency through improvements in technique. Which force is more powerful is a question of fact, not of pure theory, and varies from country to country and from time to time in the same country. Most classicals felt that technological progress was for the time being winning in their own country (England) but that it could not win for very much longer.

Sooner or later in an advanced or "mature" economy, diminishing returns to land and the consequent rise in labor costs will outrun effective technological progress. Surpluses available for investment (profits) will fall and eventually disappear. Net investment drops eventually to zero, technological progress is brought to a halt, the wages fund ceases to grow, and so population also ceases to grow. In the classical model, the end result of capitalist development is stagnation. Of course, levels of income in early nineteenth century Europe were rising and already high in comparison with many poor countries today; Europeans could hope to attain reasonable standards of living before the stagnation set in. Thus the classical concept of the "stationary" state was essentially a concept of a mature economy. There might still be a rising standard of living due to improvements in the art of living and increased leisure through technological progress, but national income would cease to grow.

The classical school did not regard the stationary state as something de-

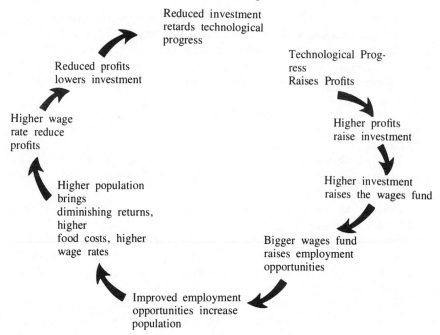

Reduced investment
retards technological
progress

Technological Prog-
ress
Raises Profits

Reduced profits
lowers investment

Higher profits
raise investment

Higher wage
rate reduce
profits

Higher investment
raises the wages fund

Higher population
brings
diminishing returns,
higher
food costs, higher
wage rates

Bigger wages fund
raises employment
opportunities

Improved employment
opportunities increase
population

FIGURE 2.1

voutly to be wished. Apart from the cessation of general improvements in welfare associated with the stationary state, Adam Smith believed that the stationary state would be "dull" and the declining state "melancholy," in contrast to the "cheerful" progressive state. But the inexorable logic of the classical system led to the conclusion that the ultimate end of capitalist development is stagnation, like it or not.

THE CLASSICAL MODEL

In sum, the classical school envisioned a circular causation in the economic system; Figure 2.1 illustrates this "feedback system," with its interacting causal factors forming feedbacks which could either spiral towards prosperity or turn into a vicious circle leading to stagnation.

To get the system going, any innovation—or better—a set of innovations, such as those which triggered the Industrial Revolution of the eighteenth and early nineteenth centuries—is enough. Since in those days, wages lagged far behind any increase in productivity, technological innovation brought increases in profits. These in turn raised investment, swelling the wages fund and raising industrial employment, especially industrial employment. Improved employment opportunities encourage population growth. But population growth brings diminishing returns to labor on the land, raising costs of subsistence and thus raising wages and reducing profits. Reduced profits reduce investment, retarding technological progress, shrinking the wages fund, reducing employment opportunities (especially in industry), and discouraging population growth.

It is apparent that the approach to the stationary state rests on an empirical judgment regarding the pace of technological advance on the one hand (especially in industry) and the rate of diminishing returns in agriculture on the other. The classical school thought technological advance would win for a while, but not for long. Mill put the advent of the stationary state in Europe before the end of the nineteenth century. He was a bit premature in his gloomy predictions. Technological progress was able to keep the lead longer than that.

THE MALTHUS VERSION

We cannot leave our discussion of the classical theory of development without drawing attention to its refinements in the Malthus version. Thomas Malthus was a nineteenth century English parson who took a direct interest in the underdeveloped countries of his time, and was particularly interested in the factors *limiting* growth. Book II of his *Principles of Political Economy* was concerned with "The Progress of Wealth":

> There is scarcely any inquiry more curious, or, from its importance, more worthy of our attention, than that which traces the causes which practically check the progress of wealth in different countries, and stop it, or make it proceed very slowly, while the power of production remains comparatively undiminished, or at least would furnish the means of a great and abundant increase of produce and population.[3]

He defines the problem of development as explaining any difference between potential gross national product ("power of producing riches") and actual gross national product ("actual riches").

There is nothing automatic about economic growth, Malthus warns. To say that population growth by itself is enough to bring economic advance is absurd. In the first place, population growth—despite the strength of the psychological and physiological forces tending to bring it about—is an end product of the whole economic process; "an increase of population cannot take place without a proportionate or nearly proportionate increase of wealth." As evidence that neither population or income may grow he cites such "underdeveloped" countries as Spain, Portugal, Hungary, Turkey, "together with nearly the whole of Asia and Africa, and the greatest part of America."[4]

Population growth encourages development only if it brings an increase in *effective command.* "A man whose only possession is his labor has, or has not, an effective demand for produce according as he is, or is not, in demand by those who have the disposal of produce."[5] Thus a country need neither be overpopulated nor landhungry to stagnate if a certain minimum level of effective demand is absent. Speaking of Latin American countries Malthus writes:

---

[3] The first edition of Malthus' *Principles* appeared in 1820, the second in 1836. (Page references are to the Augustus Kelly reprint of the 2nd ed.; New York, 1–51).

[4] Ibid., p. 314.

[5] Ibid., pp. 311–12.

> Except in the neighborhood of the mines and near the great towns, the effective demand for produce is not such as to induce the great proprietors to bring their immense tracts of land properly into cultivation: and the population, which, as we have seen, presses hard at times against the limits of subsistence, evidently exceeds in general the demand for labor, or the number of persons which the country can employ with regularity and constancy in the actual state of its agriculture and manufactures.[6]

While large landowners have no incentive for more intensive cultivation with the present limitations of the market, the peasants lack the capital that would be needed for efficient cultivation, which alone would permit them enough to induce the landlords to rent some of their land:

> In the midst of an abundance of fertile land, it appears that the natives are often very scantily supplied with it. They would gladly cultivate portions of the extensive districts held by the great proprietor and could not fail of thus deriving an ample subsistence for themselves and their families; but in the actual state of the demand for produce in many parts of the country, and in the actual states of the ignorance and indolence of the natives, such tenants might not be able to pay a rent equal to what the land would yield in its uncultivated state and in this case they would seldom be allowed to intrude upon domains. . . .[7]

Thus lands capable of supporting thousands of people instead support a few hundred cattle. And, Malthus emphasizes, if the agricultural sector of a country does not expand, the industrial sector remains limited in total size. Malthus points out that each sector constitutes the market for the output of the other sector (in the absence of international trade). Thus failure of either sector to expand acts as a drag on the growth of the other. In underdeveloped countries the development of the industrial sector is limited by the poverty of the agricultural sector. A certain minimum level of effective demand is needed before cumulative growth can set in.

Finally, Malthus links these limitations to growth to the "indolence of the natives." Denying that the indolence characterizing underdeveloped countries is due to the tropical climate, Malthus links this "backward sloping supply curve of effort"[8] (as it would be called today) to the absence of incentives.

How then, can one initiate economic growth? Malthus suggested land reform as one means of creating incentives and expanding output, and that broadening international trade could provide incentives for additional expenditure of effort. Thus the economy could get "over the hump" to the point where its own production was sufficiently varied to provide all the incentive needed for further growth.

However, when cumulative growth sets in, Malthus (like the other classicists) envisaged a process of increasing population pressure on the land but he went further by expressing the problem in quantitative terms. Once all the fertile land is occupied, he argued, further increases in food production de-

[6] Ibid., p. 341.
[7] Ibid., p. 341.
[8] The preference for leisure to more income.

pend on agricultural improvement, but the natural tendency is for the fertility of the soil to decrease, not increase, whereas population, given an adequate food supply, would continue to expand indefinitely.

Taking the whole earth, supposing the present population equaled a thousand million, the human species would increase as the numbers 1, 2, 4, 8, 16, 32, 64, 128, 256, and subsistence as 1, 2, 3, 4, 5, 6, 7, 8, 9. Here we have the "law" most frequently associated with Malthus: the geometric growth of population and the arithmetic growth of means of subsistence.

If the industrial sector does not expand enough to absorb a large share of the increase in population, population pressure on the land continues to increase, and per capita productivity and income in the traditional rural sector fall.

In sum, as will be seen below, virtually all the modern ideas regarding technological dualism and the population explosion and exponential growth have been anticipated by Malthus.

APPRAISAL OF THE CLASSICAL SYSTEM

Indeed, even though the classicists underestimated the potential of technological progress, their prediction of stagnation, while premature for the advanced countries, describes in many respects what happened to the underdeveloped countries. In most cases population won the race against technology; and their economies stagnated at low levels of living. The description of population growth in relation to workers' wages fits very well the process of population growth at subsistence level as it has occurred in the underdeveloped countries. The idea of circularity, that success breeds success, and failure breeds failure goes a long way toward explaining the problems of the underdeveloped countries today. This idea is implicit in Gunnar Myrdal's "backwash theory" (reviewed in Chapter 4) and in the "feedbacks" of systems analysis. Their warning concerning the dangers of monopolies are well illustrated by present day experience. Finally the market is proving a powerful automatic signaling system of approaching shortages; today, steadily spiraling prices presage the problems which the Club of Rome and the classicists forecast.

It is unfortunate that the association of the classical economists with *laissez-faire,* which is rejected by most planners, has diverted attention from home truths these economists introduced. Planners or politicians (in other socialist or nonsocialist countries) who ignore them do so at their peril. If they "repeal" the law of supply and demand, they may find their shops filled with goods no one wants to buy, and shortages emerging of goods people do want. Bottlenecks may appear in industry, if capital goods industries overproduce or underproduce, creating excess capacity in certain sectors and undercapacity in others. If they do not pay close attention to factor combinations, they may have open unemployment, and/or "disguised unemployment." Any country—whether private enterprise or socialist—which fails to make profits (to maintain a spread between wages and salaries paid out and the total value of production) will have nothing left over for investment and will end up with a stagnant economy. In sum, once the need for profits in this sense is admitted, the feedback system outlined in Figure 2.1 (P. 34) could apply to any socioeconomic system.

THE MARXIST MODEL: GROWTH AND COLLAPSE

Karl Marx is one of those influential thinkers about whom much more has been written than he himself ever wrote. As the prophet of doom for capitalism and chief saint in the communist hierarchy, he is revered by hundreds of millions of people, and also reviled by hundreds of millions. Because of the continuing importance of his ideas in shaping policies in Russia, China, and other communist countries, and in determining the programs of communist parties the world over, some knowledge of Marxist thought is essential to the understanding of these systems.

Here, however, our purpose is quite different; we shall make no attempt to evaluate the Marxist system as a whole, but will isolate the basic elements of the Marxist theory of capitalist development and breakdown, and present only the essential ideas as they apply to today's development problem.

HISTORIAL EVOLUTION OF THE SYSTEM

In contrast to the classical idea of an innate harmony in human society being achieved through the market, where rational human beings expressed their wants, Marx conceived of social and economic change brought about by a process of conflict. He believed that the pursuit of wealth and power by some and the effort of others to survive resulted in a struggle amongst social groups. With this idea, Marx introduced a powerful new stream of thought, based on the essential notion that technological, economic, sociocultural and political change interact as they move together through time. This basic concept has been picked up and elaborated by economists and other social scientists ever since, including many who would reject the Marxist label.

Marx considered technological change rather than profits as the prime mover of the whole system. The technology of each stage in a country's development determines not only the economic situation but also the style of the whole society. The hand mill created the feudal lord, he declared, and the steam mill the capitalist. Each stage of social evolution, with its characteristic technology and "style," breeds its particular kind of class struggle, which leads to its breakdown and the emergence of the next, higher form of social organization. For Marx, capitalism is merely one of a series of stages in the evolution of society towards the communist state, which is the inevitable final form of economic, social and political organization. Marx took the philosopher Hegel's concept of "the dialectic" as a process whereby scientific progress is made, and translated it into a theory of class struggle; hence the expression "dialectical materialism" associated with Marxist thought.

For Hegel the prevailing ideology at any point of time is the "thesis"; this ideology generates an opposing ideology, the "antithesis"; and the clash of these two ideologies produces a new set of received doctrine, the "synthesis." The synthesis then becomes the new "thesis," creating its own antithesis, and thus breeding a new "synthesis." The theory of evolution is sometimes presented as a form of the dialectic; each species is analogous to a "thesis," the environment is the "antithesis," leading to the appearance of mutations or new species, analogous to the "synthesis"; and so on.

According to Marx, in the process of social evolution the equivalent of the "thesis" is the ruling class of each period. Opposed to this class is another, as "antithesis," which gradually gains enough power to bring fundamental social change, and the emergence of a new ruling class, analogous to the synthesis. This class in turn generates new opposition from an oppressed class, leading to new social revolution, a new "synthesis," and a new ruling class. Note that in contrast to the classical system, this is not really a feedback system; it is a one-way street. (There are of course, feedbacks or "loops" *within* the system). Thus the European feudal system (which arose out of primitive communism) was dominated by feudal lords. Capitalism brought a very high stage of technological advance, and gradually the power of the commercial capitalists grew, until they were able eventually to take power in their own hands (Cromwell in England) and replace the monarchy with a system of parliamentary democracy (with limited franchise). Governments are "creatures" of the ruling class at every phase of history, with no function but to serve the interest of the ruling class. Commercial capitalism was succeeded by industrial capitalism, and then by "monopoly finance capitalism," the higher stage of capitalism.

In this phase the "antithesis" is the working class, or proletariat. Exploitation of this class becomes increasingly severe with the capitalists' desperate effort to maintain their profits, and the workers become "increasingly miserable." Eventually they rise up in arms, overthrow the capitalist system, and establish the "dictatorship of the proletariat," and the socialist system. In this system poverty will disappear; moreover there is no class conflict and thus no need for government; the state "withers away." The end of the line (equivalent to the "climactic state" of biology) is full-fledged communism, which would also be anarchy, since government would have disappeared, having no function in a classless frictionless society. It would be an affluent society, based on a philosophy of "to each according to his need, from each according to his capacity."

THE CAPITALIST STAGE

Marx never underestimated the capacity of the capitalist system for economic expansion. He expected that this growth would fluctuate in the form of a series of booms and depressions, and that the entrepreneur would be the key figure in initiating this expansion. True, he expected capitalism to break down, but only after a very high degree of development, and for sociological reasons, not because of stagnation.

In essence, Marx believed that labor-saving technologies would cause technological unemployment, leading to an ultimate reduction of profits and a final collapse of the system. With wages steady at the subsistence level, an increase in man-year productivity (by introducing labor-saving device) would permit an initial increase in profits. But Marx regarded technological progress as being labor saving *and* capital absorbing. In his day, with technological change dominated by capital-intensive innovations such as canals, railroads, steamships, steel, and heavy chemicals, he was probably right. Thus, according to Marx, there was a tendency for capital per worker to rise. As time went by, not only the amount of capital per worker but also the amount of capital per unit of output would rise. The implication of these tendencies is apparent: the increase in capital per worker must result in a fall in the *rate* of profit (unless increasing technological progress takes place). By this process, Marx explained the tendency of profits to fall rather than through diminishing returns to labor on the land caused by population growth.

Marx did not believe that the working class tended naturally to reproduce on such a scale as forever to bring wages back down to subsistence level; he regarded this Malthusian doctrine as ''a libel on the human race.'' Mass poverty is to be explained only by capitalist exploitation. It cannot continue in a communist society, whatever the level and rate of growth of the population.

Since he regarded innovation as essentially labor-saving, Marx also put a good deal of emphasis on technological unemployment. An investment boom would tend to increase employment while it lasted, but each addition to the stock of capital would tend to swell the ''reserve army'' of technologically displaced workers. Marx therefore incorporated the analysis of unemployment into his system. Population and employment in the Marxist system cannot be treated as varying together as they do in the classical system.

Technological unemployment would, in turn, reduce the workers' purchasing power. Marx attached great importance to workers' consumption. He argued that investment cannot be profitable unless consumption increases enough to absorb the increased output of final products, and that however luxuriously capitalists may live, it is the workers who provide most of the market for consumers' goods.

What then determines the level of profits? Marx believed that, unfortunately for the capitalists, a contradiction exists at this point: maintaining profits requires reducing the wages bill relative to gross national product; but a successful reduction of the wages bill and its consequent reduction of workers' purchasing power would in turn mean that part of the output would go unsold, and profits would be reduced after all.

THE SYSTEM IN OPERATION

We can see the pincers in which the capitalists are caught. In order to survive the competitive race, they must be continually introducing improved techniques, which means accumulating capital, using more capital-intensive and less labor-intensive techniques. But technological progress is a treadmill for capitalists; they must run ever faster just to stand still, for technological progress must always keep one step ahead of the rate of capital accumulation. However, labor saving innovations help in another way; they displace workers, adding to the "industrial reserve army" of unemployed. Chronic technological unemployment weakens the bargaining power of workers, who are always competing for jobs against their unemployed brethren, thus making it easier for the capitalists to keep wages down to the subsistence level. Third, hours can be increased or work speeded up without raising wages. Fourth, monopoly positions can be strengthened, to raise prices without raising wages.

Everything the capitalists do to maintain profits helps pave the way for revolution: not only does "the misery of the working class" increase; as well, the middle class begins to disappear. In the late stages of "high capitalism", capitalists become desperate indeed. Encountering increasing resistance at home, they turn to colonies for more ready exploitation of labor. Colonies also provide sources of cheap raw materials, new outlets for investment, and new markets in which to establish monopoly positions for the sale of final products. So valuable are these colonies in staving off the collapse of capitalism that the advanced capitalist countries fight imperialist wars for their possession.

All in vain. At best these desperate measures of desperate men can bring only temporary respite. The rate of profits continues to decline, and capitalists cannot resist turning the screws on workers a bit more in the effort to save their way of life. Eventually the workers can stand it no longer; by sheer strength of numbers, they overthrow the system through revolution.

APPRAISAL OF THE MARXIST MODEL

As indicated above, any appraisal of Marx is likely to displease more people than it pleases; it will have too little villification for some and too little veneration for others. But let us try, nonetheless, remembering that we are reviewing the earlier literature for the light it may throw on the development problems of today.

Obviously, Marx was a bad prophet. He was right, of course, in predicting the spread of communism, but both the establishment of communist societies and their subsequent evolution have taken forms very different from those envisaged by Marx. In particular, the countries that have become communist have not been those in which capitalist development has been most advanced but those in which it has lagged. For in the advanced capitalist countries workers have become increasingly prosperous rather than more miserable, and the middle class, far from disappearing, has grown until it now dominates society. And in the communist countries, poverty has been slow in disappearing and there are no signs of the state's "withering away."

We cannot attempt here to explain all the reasons for Marx's failure as a prophet; we are concerned only with his analytical framework as a means of explaining economic growth. One obvious mistake was in not foreseeing the rise of powerful trade unions; but it may be questioned whether trade unions would have become so strong if the competitive position of unorganized labor had not become increasingly favorable in the first place. Let us note only two fundamental analytical errors. First, Marx did not see that innovations can be capital saving as well as labor saving. If the ratios of capital to output fall through improved techniques, as they frequently do (electronics, synthetics), the rate of profit can rise even though wages rise too. Second, Marx was trapped by the labor theory of value which he took over from the classical school. By measuring everything in terms of man-hours, he attached a quite wrong significance to a fall in the rate of profits in terms of man-hours. He did not see that a rise in man-hour productivity and in real wage rates can be accompanied by a rise in money profits (and real profits), even though profits in terms of man-hours fall as man-hours become more valuable. And what really counts for capitalists is their actual income, not the number of man-hours' worth of labor a given amount of profit will buy. In other words, Marx did not foresee a process of economic development in which technological progress brings such increases in productivity and total output that both wages and profits can rise together.

On the other hand, Marx introduced certain ideas into the theory of economic development that have remained ever since. Virtually every writer on the subject since Marx has incorporated in his system the basic idea that technological progress is the mainspring of economic growth, and that innovation is the main function of the entrepreneur. By the same token, investment decisions and capital accumulation are the core of most modern theories of growth, and in all theories these decisions are related somehow to the rate of return on capital. Another fundamental idea is that economic development under capitalism tends to take the form of fluctuations; economic growth is a destabilizing phenomenon. While Marx had little to say about how to manage a socialist economy once created, his ideal of an egalitarian society in which the means of production were owned in common has formed the keystone of the economic systems of socialist states today.

So far as its pure economics is concerned, Marx's system is less directly applicable to problems of underdeveloped countries than that of the classical school. Marx did not really think of underdevelopment as an enduring state; underdeveloped countries were simply precapitalist ones, which, unfortunately, would have to go through the capitalist phase before they could attain the Elysian Fields of communism. His exclusion of the possibility of population pressure is a severe handicap in trying to apply his system to most underdeveloped countries.

The Marxist sociological and political theory, however, provides some clues to the economic history of underdeveloped countries. It suggests that part of the explanation of underdevelopment in the former colonies might be traced to colonial policies. As we shall see in more detail below, in some underdeveloped countries conditions occurred rather like those Marx predicted for advanced ones: labor was indeed exploited; wages were indeed kept close to subsistence levels; a "reserve army" of chronic unemployment did in fact exist; the class structure was sharply defined and a middle class virtually nonexistent; in some cases there is even evidence of "increasing misery." That such conditions could result in revolution of one sort or another few people would deny.

We must be wary of the pitfalls in the Marxist system, but for all its errors the Marxist theory of economic development has much to contribute to an understanding of development or the lack of it.

THE NEOCLASSICAL SCHOOL

Around 1870, Stanley Jevons and Alfred Marshall in England, Carl Menger in Vienna, and Léon Walras in Lausanne, apparently independently and almost simultaneously, discovered the principle of "marginal utility." The neoclassical school was founded and economics was never to be the same again. Marshall took longer than the others to get his ideas into print, but two generations of students were brought up on the successive editions of his great *Principles of Economics*.[9]

With the introduction of "marginalism" the neoclassical school constructed a much more refined and sophisticated apology for the free private enterprise system than the classical school had done. "Utility" is the satisfaction derived from consumption of a good or service. "Marginal" utility is the additional satisfaction obtained by consuming one more unit. Marginal utility was said to decline as the amount of any commodity consumed increased. This idea led easily to the concept of consumption of any commodity increasing as it price falls, because at a lower price the satisfaction foregone by buying one good rather than another is reduced.

The neoclassicists went further, however, and turned even costs into psychological considerations. Where the classical school regarded costs as labor effort expended in production, the neoclassical school talked of "opportunity cost," the satisfaction that is foregone by producing and consuming one commodity instead of all the others that might have been produced with the same bundle of resources. However, for the neoclassical economists this "opportunity cost" would be accurately measured by money costs in a freely competitive market. In such a market each factor of production (land, labor, or capital) would be rewarded according to the value of its "marginal product," the increase in total output through adding one more unit of that factor. If any entrepreneur tried to pay less, the factor would be bid away from him; and no one would pay more. Thus "marginal cost"—the cost of producing one more unit of output—becomes a measure of "opportunity cost" to society of producing that unit; that is, the value of all the other things that could have been

---

[9] W. Stanley Jevons, *The Theory of Political Economy,* (London, 1871); Carl Menger, *Grundsätze der Volkswirtschaftlehre.* (Vienna, 1871); Léon Walras, *Eléments d'Economie Politique Pure,* (Paris, 1874); Alfred Marshall, *Principles of Economics* (London: MacMillan, 1st ed. 1890, 8th edition 1920).

produced instead. When these propositions are put together we arrive at a startling conclusion: under "pure competition," when no buyer and no seller controls enough of the market to influence prices (including prices of factors of production), "equilibrium" (position from which there is no tendency to change) will be established with marginal cost equal to price. And since price measures the marginal utility of the commodity to all people buying it, and marginal cost the marginal utility of all the goods and services sacrificed to produce that commodity instead, "welfare is maximized." It was this identification of market prices with relative marginal utilities which enabled the neoclassical economists to claim scientific objectivity (freedom from value judgments) for their analysis of welfare.

Another essential feature of the neoclassical system is that economic change is seen as a series of very small and essentially continuous increases or decreases in the basic variables. This view opened the door to the use of differential calculus to express economic relationships, leading to the conversion of economics, from that time onwards, into a mathematical science.

Apart from J. B. Clark and Joseph Schumpeter, who will be discussed below, the neoclassical school had relatively little to say about economic development. When they wrote, there was little evidence that the dire predictions of Marx and the classical school were correct. Technological progress continued to outstrip population growth, and standards of living continued to rise, although slowly by present day standards. The world economy was expanding and the neoclassicists were confident that attractive investment opportunities would continue to appear and that capitalist economies would thus continue to expand. With their deep faith in the efficacy of a free market apparently confirmed, and having divested themselves of the responsibility of making value judgments, the neoclassicists were more social astronomers than social engineers. They were essentially nonoperational in their analysis, more interested in exploring the economic system and its functioning than in trying to change it.

If sometimes things seemed to go wrong, as during inflations or depressions, or when large pockets of poverty seemed to resist all efforts to remove them they looked for "interference" with the system and sought to eliminate it. Thus they supported legislation for elimination or control of monopolies, and statutes to regulate the banking system, which they thought to be at the root of "business cycles." If misbehavior of the credit system could not be simply "outlawed" by banking legislation, then it must be regulated by the policies governing interest rates and credit expansion administered through the central bank such as the Bank of England, or the Federal Reserve system in the United States, which are the ultimate source of reserves for the whole banking system. Their formula was, in essence, "tight money to correct inflation" (high interest rates); easy money (low interest rates) to combat depression."

If the neoclassical economists paid little attention to the problems of poor countries, it was in large measure because they expected these problems to be solved through international trade. In their hands, the theory of international trade became an extremely elaborate structure, which proved—to their own satisfaction—that with free movement of factors of production, or even with free trade plus pure competition and complete mobility of factors of production in each country, there would be a tendency towards "equalization of factor prices." In other words, under the stipulated conditions trade between England and India should equalize wages in the two countries. They accordingly regarded international trade as a powerful "engine of growth." How they reconciled this theory with the ever widening gaps between advanced and underdeveloped countries is not easy to understand. The basic idea, of course, was that so long as factor prices in any field of production were low the country would have a "comparative advantage" in that field, and exports of the commodity would expand. Prices of factors of production would be bid up to attract them into that industry, until the cost differential disappeared and factor prices were equalized. Most of their analysis was conducted within a "static" framework, without population growth or labor-saving inventions. Indeed much of the effort was directed towards analysis of the "stationary state," without capital accumulation either.

It is thus not surprising that the elaborate structure of theory built by the neoclassicists over a period of seventy-five years has proved of little use in prescribing policy, not only for development, but even for stabilization. In the Great Depression of the 1930s neoclassical theory proved worse than useless, leading to policies, such as wage cuts, that only made matters worse by further reducing incomes, demand, and prices. The idea that depressions could be cured by lowering interest rates was also proven tragically wrong. It is now recognized that savings depend much more on levels of income than on levels of interest, while investment depends on a good many things, including the intensity of the desire to keep capital in safe and liquid form.

One neoclassical concept is still accorded considerable importance in development theory today: external economies and diseconomies. Costs of one enterprise may be reduced (or revenues increased) by something taking place completely outside the enterprise itself. Thus completion of a railroad or a power plant may lead to expansion of several enterprises whose costs are thereby reduced, creating an external economy. Conversely, they may lead to pollution of air and water, generating external diseconomies. The concept leads to consideration of interactions in the economy as a whole, which can lead to quite different policy conclusions from those reached by looking at only one enterprise at a time.

In general, however, since they believed fundamentally that a free market guaranteed "maximum welfare," the neoclassicists had little to offer beyond "patching the market" whenever holes in its fabric appeared. As Joan Robinson tersely sums up the neoclassical contribution:

> Apart from the advocacy of Free Trade there was not much to say on practical questions. The policy recommended was *laissez-faire,* and there was no need to describe in any detail how to do nothing.[10]

[10] Joan Robinson, *Economic Philosophy* (New York: Doubleday, 1964) pp. 63, 73, 74. For a more exhaustive analysis of the limitations of neoclassical economics by an economist brought up on it, see I. M. D. Little, *A Critique of Welfare Economics* (Oxford: Oxford University Press, 1950).

Yet among the neoclassicists was a group of mavericks, who, far from bogging down in "contemplation of the ultimate stationary state," were interested in dynamic theories of growth. In accord with the Marxist concept of technological, economic, and social change moving together through time, these economists studied "the seamless web" of human behavior, wherein economic behavior was an integral part. In doing so, these mavericks participated in a highly modern trend of inquiry.

The Seamless Web

In the late nineteenth and early twentieth centuries, a major line of inquiry into economic development was taking place which stood somewhat apart from both the Marxist and neoclassical camps. In some respects it was the forerunner of the contemporary approach to development theory. Its participants insisted on looking at the facts, and in doing so in an interdisciplinary manner. In Germany, the "historical school," led by Werner Sombart expressed their disdain for the abstract theoretical models of the neoclassicsts. They insisted on looking at the facts over a wide sweep of time and space. At the same time, German sociologist Max von Weber and English economic historian Richard Tawney theorized about economic and social change on the basis of historical observation. (These ideas will be briefly reviewed in the following historical chapter). In the field of economics, mavericks of the neoclassical school attempted to construct dynamic theories of growth, with attention to changes in human behavior within the development context. J. B. Clark and Joseph Schumpeter worked on theories of development, taking into account the institutional setting and attitudes required for encouraging lively entrepreneurship. A group of economists in the United States, led by Thorstein Veblen, falling heir both to the European interdisciplinary approach with emphasis on empirical research, and also to J. B. Clark's ideas concerning the institutional setting for growth, attempted to build a sociodynamic theory which came to be known as the "institutional" theory of growth.

JOHN BATES CLARK'S THEORY OF ECONOMIC PROGRESS

J. B. Clark, the leading American representative of the first generation of neoclassical economists, was a "marginalist" like the others, yet he also tried hard to develop an economic dynamics, and presented a theory of economic growth. Moreover, whereas most of the neoclassical literature discusses economic behavior in terms of "laws" that are presumed to be true always and everywhere, like the laws of physics, Clark explicitly recognized the existence of two groups of countries, one advanced and one underdeveloped, and stressed differences in economic behavior between them:

> We must draw a boundary line about the area of active movement, of lively interchanges, and of general sensitiveness to economic influences, thus separating it

from the broader zone of sluggish movement of capital and population, of slow response to economic stimuli, and of generally backward economic conditions.[11]

The lively economic center included Western Europe, most of North America, Japan, and parts of Australia; the sluggish outer zone virtually comprised today's underdeveloped world. However, Clark believed that the boundaries were not fixed; eventually, through international trade, labor and capital flows, and the exchange of techniques the outer zone would be assimilated into the dynamic centers.

For Clark, growth was the essential feature of a satisfactory economic system, because only economic growth could assure the ultimate achievement of an acceptable standard of living for the working class. Clark therefore (very astutely) measured economic growth by the effects on the real wage rate of five dynamic variables: population growth; growth of capital; changing consumer wants; improvement in methods of production; and changes in industrial and business organization. He concluded that these dynamic forces could result in continuous and cumulative economic growth.

Clark opposed the Malthusian theory that *population growth* would soon vitiate an increase in the wage rate, calling attention to the upward trend of the wage rate during the nineteenth century and the declining rate of population growth. He explained this inverse correlation by the determined resistance of the people to a fall in their standard of living and status in society. Moreover, he believed that *consumer wants* were insatiable, expanding qualitatively as well as quantitatively, as a result of intellectual and moral growth.

Clark regarded *technological progress* as the most important variable. He believed that the proper institutional setting was necessary for a rapid rate of invention; an effective patent system would encourage not only individual invention but also internal research by the firm. Yet he attached great importance to the maintenance of a competitive economic system; monopoly must be handled by vigorous government action. Not only would monopoly have a stagnating effect on innovation, but, as well, the separation of ownership from control in monopolistic corporations lessens the guidance of profit for decision-making managers. By the same token competition was required to stimulate the entrepreneur to seek *improvements in organization.*

By hinting at the idea that economic advance needs the proper institutional setting, Clark laid the groundwork for others. Joseph Schumpeter was to explore the right "climate" for entrepreneurship. The "institutionalists" (although they attacked Clark's theories) were to expand the idea even further.

JOSEPH SCHUMPETER'S THEORY OF ECONOMIC DEVELOPMENT

Joseph Schumpeter ranks among the all-time greats in the history of economic thought. He has special interest for this volume because virtually alone

---

[11] J. B. Clark *The Essentials of Price Theory* (New York: MacMillan, 1907), p. 9. The present writer did not fully appreciate the significance of Clark's contribution to growth theory until it was presented in a term paper (since published) by John Pisciotta, then a graduate student at the University of Texas.

in his generation his main interest was in economic development. The German edition of his *Theory of Economic Development*[12] was published in 1911, and throughout his career, he continued to elaborate and refine his theory. His eclectic and synthesizing approach was no doubt partly due to his wide range of experience.

Schumpeter's range of experience was unusually wide for his generation; born and reared in Vienna, his career included the post of Minister of Finance in the Austrian government, Professor of Economics in Tokyo and Bonn, and Professor at Harvard from 1927 to his death in 1959. He was of course nurtured on neoclassical economics, especially in its Vienna version. He leaned heavily on Marx, sharing his conviction that economic fluctuations and growth are inseparably intertwined. He also acknowledged his debt to J. B. Clark; Schumpeter's own theory was largely concerned with entrepreneurship, innovations, and their institutional setting, and his ideas on these elements of development have become stock in trade for all development economists.

Like Clark, Schumpeter maintained that the most important part of private investment is determined by such long range considerations as technological change. He stressed innovation as the mainspring of this type of investment. Any "doing things differently," that increases the productivity of the bundle of factors of production available is innovation. The entrepreneur is not the inventor; he is the man who sees the opportunity for introducing an innovation—a new technique or a new commodity, an improved organization, or the development of newly discovered resources. The entrepreneur raises the money to launch the new enterprise, assembles the factors of production, chooses top managers and sets the organization going. Schumpeter believed that growth is associated with booms and recessions because successful innovations tend to bring "clusters of followers," with investment financed largely through new credit, resulting in a boom; then, when the new plants are in place, debts are repaid just as output increases, prices fall, and the recession sets in. However, Schumpeter did not feel that deep depressions like that of the 1930s were necessary; like other neoclassicists he believed depressions represented mismanagement of the monetary system.

In Schumpeter's system the supply of entrepreneurship is the ultimate determining factor of the rate of economic growth. This supply in turn depends on the "social climate," a complex phenomenon reflecting the whole social, political, and sociopsychological atmosphere within which entrepreneurs must operate. It would include the social values of a particular country at a particular time, the class structure, the educational system, the attitude of society toward business success, and the nature and extent of the prestige and other social rewards, apart from profits, which accompany business success in the society. A particularly important factor in "climate" is the entrepreneur's understanding of the "rules of the game," the conditions under which he must operate. Sudden changes in the rules of the game are particularly dele-

[12] Joseph Schumpeter, The *Theory of Economic Development* (Cambridge: Harvard University Press, 1934).

terious to an increasing flow of enterprise. In general, the climate is appropriate when entrepreneurial success is amply rewarded, and where there are good —but not too good—chances of success.

In contrast to Marx, who thought of "capitalists" as a "class" almost in the sense of caste, a group to which workers could not aspire, an essential aspect of Schumpeter's vigorous capitalist development is rapid circulation of the elite. If entrepreneurs are social deviants, the society may oppose them in some degree, accepting them only after they have proven successful. The Schumpeterian entrepreneur is untraditional and ambitious; success in the innovational process must lead to the top of the social ladder—if not for oneself, then at least for one's son or grandson—as it did in nineteenth-century Europe.

Capitalism, however, produces, by its mere working, a social atmosphere that is hostile to it, and this atmosphere, in turn, produces policies which do not allow it to function. Thus Schumpeter explained the depth and duration of the Great Depression of the 1930s in terms of the labor legislation, social security, public works spending, progressive tax structure, public utilities regulation, and other New Deal policies introduced in the middle and late 1930s. These constituted a change in the "rules of the game" so drastic as to discourage enterprise and thus retard investment.

Schumpeter was an extremely independent thinker, and something of an enigma. He has sometimes been taken for an apologist for private enterprise, but that is not quite true. Schumpeter admired and enjoyed the kind of society produced in capitalist countries, especially the European ones at the turn of the century. Yet he was Minister of Finance in a socialist regime in Austria, and in his *Socialism, Capitalism, and Democracy* [13] he stated explicitly that the socialist formula is superior to the capitalist one. Late in his career he advocated the corporative state (maintaining its basic Catholic philosophy and eliminating its fascist trappings) as a middle way likely to work better than either. However, his development theory was neutral. The crucial role of entrepreneurship and innovation in economic development is not tied to the capitalist system. Socialist countries have need of new techniques, new products, new resources, and new organizational systems; and the men who see and seize the opportunity to introduce these new "ways of doing things differently," bring together the factors of production and organize them into effective enterprises, play a significant role in economic progress in any society and tend to be rewarded for this role one way or another.

THORSTEIN VEBLEN AND THE INSTITUTIONALISTS

Thorstein Veblen, a student of J. B. Clark, wrote at the time of the American "robber barons," when American capitalism was at its most vigorous, most lusty, most brutal, most uninhibited, and irresponsible. At the same time, the economist-theologians who did most of the teaching of economics in

---

[13] Joseph Schumpeter, *Socialism, Capitalism, and Democracy* (New York: Harper and Row, 1947).

the United States were carrying *laissez-faire* principles to extremes, echoing eighteenth century liberal philosophy. They saw men as both rational and spiritual beings, and treated the free enterprise system as almost literally divine. Veblen found the combination hard to swallow.

Veblen began by attacking the very fundamentals of neoclassical theory. In his famous first book *The Theory of the Leisure Class* published in 1889,[14] he challenged the hypothesis that economic behavior is rational. Rather than regarding them as rational spiritual beings Veblen considered men as not yet far removed from the jungle, remnants of superstitious fears, tribal myths, tabus, ceremonial rites, and magic. Where the neoclassicists saw essential harmony in society, Veblen (like Marx) saw conflict and coercion. The entrepreneur, declared Veblen, is not so much concerned with improving resource allocation as in copying his neighbor, emulating those still richer than he, coercing those who are weaker, and conspiring to increase his power. He is concerned, not with producing, but with "making money," which is an entirely different thing. "Man's behavior in respect of using and handling and 'making' money is varied, irrational, complicated, and often confused," as a contemporary "institutionalist," John Gambs, puts it.[15] It is the engineers and their machines who produce goods, Veblen argued, while entrepreneurs produce profits, by controlling, restricting and manipulating production, and speculating on the results; thus businessmen become saboteurs, rather than the motivating force of the economic system.

To confirm this point, Veblen used a cross-disciplinary approach, which has remained an essential feature of "institutionalism." He looked at primitive societies such as the American Indians, the Ainus of Japan, and the Australian aborigines, and found no "leisure class." Then he looked at the Polynesians, the ancient Icelanders, and the shoguns of Japan, and found well-defined leisure classes. True, these leisure classes were not always "idle"; they were busy seizing wealth from others. In time these leisure classes became rich and powerful enough to become respectable, and so their means of acquiring wealth became respectable too. Veblen thought that the financiers and industrialists who comprised the European and American leisure class of his day were much the same.

For one whose blast against the establishment was so powerful, Veblen's own proposals for revolution seem rather tame. What Veblen wanted was a technocratic society. His admiration for machines spilled over into an admiration for the men who make them, the scientists and engineers. Machines impose a discipline on men, strengthen their productive propensities, and make possible an industrial republic run by engineers.

Veblen, therefore, saw the rate of economic progress as the outcome of

---

[14] Thorstein Veblen, The *Theory of the Leisure Class* (New York: Macmillan, 1899). Reprinted in the Vanguard Modern Library Series.

[15] John S. Gambs, *Beyond Supply and Demand* (New York: Columbia University Press, 1946), p. 18. The standard work on Veblen is Joseph Dorfman, *Thorstein Veblen and His America* (New York: Viking Press, 1934). A lively shorter treatment can be found in Robert L. Heilbroner, *The Worldly Philosophers* (New York: Simon and Schuster, 1972).

a conflict between technological progress and irrational, magical, and ceremonial resistence to technological change—sociocultural obstacles, if one chooses. Here Veblen identifies one of today's major development problems: science and technology are the forces of progress; cultural lags, superstitious fears, ceremonial patterns, and ingrown conservatism of thought and action are the opponents of progress.

This concept of the growth process was enlarged and refined by a disciple of Veblen, Clarence Ayres of the University of Texas. Like Veblen, Ayres saw development as a race between technological progress and the inhibiting role of ceremonial patterns and tradition, particularly as embodied in religious institutions. Ayres added the idea that the inhibiting role of tradition may be weakened in a frontier society. Thus Western Europe's headstart in industrialization is explained by the withdrawal of the Romans, which left Western Europe essentially a frontier society, with a technology inherited from older civilizations, but without the social arteriosclerosis associated with deeply imbedded traditional institutional power. "Almost certainly it was this composite character which made the civilization of medieval Europe the parent of industrial revolution,"[16] Ayres points out: by the same token, the ever-moving frontier played an important role in the later development of the United States. By definition a "frontier" is a region into which people come from an older center of civilization, bringing with them the tools and materials of this civilization, and while they also bring their traditional values and folkways, these are weakened by a frontier environment. On the basis of Ayres theory, one might draw a parallel between the retreat of the Romans and that of the colonial powers, and expect a new, postindependence dynamism in the developing countries; and this expectation would be well founded.

The institutionalist approach had two major facets: the insistence on a stern empirical approach, on what Veblen called "the opaque fact," in contrast to the delicately woven but transparent cobwebs of abstract theory of the neoclassical school; and the insistence on a cross-disciplinary or multi-disciplinary analysis. Since, in their view, social behavior is a *Gestalt* or pattern, a seamless web, it is futile to try to separate out something called "economic behavior" to the exclusion of all other aspects of a particular culture which determine how people behave, in the marketplace or anywhere else.

In these regards the institutionalists were undoubtedly right. All economists today admit the importance of quantitative analysis, and all those who have seriously tackled the problems of developing countries admit the need for knowledge outside the scope of standard economics in order to understand the development process.

The classicists, Marxists, neoclassicists, and institutionalists all had one thing in common: they were all more concerned with socioeconomic organizations and *systems* than they were with day-to-day, or even year-to-year, policy measures. It is this characteristic, more than any other, which differen-

---

[16] Clarence E. Ayres, *The Theory of Economic Progress*, (Durham: University of North Carolina Press, 1954) p. 137.

tiates the economics of the nineteenth and early twentieth centuries from contemporary economics, which is highly operational.

Economics Becomes Operational: Socialist Planning and Keynesian Management

The era of unbridled private enterprise and armchair theorizing on communism came to an end with the Russian Revolution of 1917 and the onslaught of the Great Depression of the late twenties and thirties. The leaders of the new Russian socialist society found that the decades of debate about Marxist theory had provided little guidance in how to run a socialist economy once you had it. Similarly, in the capitalist countries, the onslaught of the Great Depression of the 1930s showed both neoclassical and institutionalist economics to be of little use in dealing with such a catastrophe. These cataclysms ushered in a change in economic thinking, from accepting economic growth as a natural state of affairs—once you had the right system—to believing that for an economy to work smoothly it requires constant, appropriate intervention.

THE RUSSIAN EXPERIMENT: THE PLANNED ECONOMY

The introduction of the planned economy was the great Russian contribution to development theory and practice. Not that planning was a new idea; the Jesuits, for example, planned for Paraguay in the sixteenth and seventeenth centuries, and in 1884 the Japanese completed their great thirty volume "Kogyo Iken" (advice for the encouragement of industry) which was a comprehensive plan for development. Moreover, the Russians first took planning ideas from the German methods of organizing their war economy during World War I; but in the hands of the Russians, planning became a much more comprehensive and sophisticated affair.

Diametrically opposed to the private enterprise system, the Russians believed in public ownership of the means of production. They believed in the dynamism of the economic mechanism, but deemed the private enterprise system to be uncontrolled, unbalanced, and full of "contradictions." They wished to leave nothing to be determined by the market. They believed that planning could greatly improve the functioning of the economy, accelerating growth and improving distribution.

Behind their planning approach is a theory of maximum economic growth, relating to necessary structural change, and in practice giving high priority to the rapid expansion of heavy industry. "Target planning" involved the selection of "key sectors" for special development efforts and the establishment of production targets (iron and steel, power, chemicals) is fundamental to this approach. Everything else both "upstream" and "downstream" from these sectors is derived, in terms of "balances" of inputs or use of outputs, from the targets for the key sectors. This technique of balancing inputs and outputs is the essence of "balance planning" which will be discussed in more detail in Chapter 8. Technical "norms" (quantitative standards partly derived from past experience and partly based on ideas of what ought to be) to some extent took the place of the market as an indicator.

In the early days, the Soviet planners shied away from projections of demand and reliance on the market for guidance as to how much of what should be produced. They were also reluctant to include interest on capital as a cost. They felt obliged to follow what they regarded as Marxist principles even if it was often a nuisance to do so. Marx had taken over from the classical school the idea that value is determined by labor cost and that rents are a form of exploitation, and added the idea that returns to capital are exploitation too. To the Soviet planners before World War II, therefore, to take account of differing costs in terms of land or capital would be to succumb to "bourgeois thinking." It was argued that the law of value was *replaced* by the planning process. Planning accordingly was restricted almost entirely to technological and engineering relationships, graced with the term "teleologic principle" and comparisons of costs and benefits of alternative investment were scarcely made.

This general switch from microeconomics to macroeconomics was later parallelled in the capitalist world when those countries switched to managed economies after the Great Crash in 1929.

THE KEYNESIAN REVOLUTION AND THE MANAGED ECONOMY

The era of unbridled private enterprise came to an end the year of the Great Crash. The collapse of the New York Stock Exchange in October 1929 ushered in an international financial crisis, followed by ten years of deep depression. In the United States, national income dropped by one-third, and the total value of output did not regain its 1929 level until 1941. In 1933, when the depression was at its worst, unemployment in the United States exceeded 25 percent of the labor force, and was even worse in some European countries. The neoclassicists applied their formulas of "easy money" and wage cuts to no avail. The protectionism of the 1920s (which had replaced free trade policies) intensified into "beggar thy neighbor" policies in the 1930s. These negative measures weakened the world economy and deepened the depression. It began to look as though earlier predictions of the collapse of capitalism might come true.

KEYNES "GENERAL THEORY"

Two affluent men on opposite sides of the Atlantic, however, decided that the collapse need not and must not occur: John Maynard (later Lord) Keynes, and Franklin Delano Roosevelt. The first had radically new ideas about how to raise levels of income and employment, the second was prepared to put them into practice. Keynes' basic idea was simple enough: income is created by spending, since one person's income is derived from someone else's spending; and income and employment move together, since one has to sell something in order to employ people. If private spending is inadequate to create full employment levels of national income, and once everything possible has been done to raise private spending by cutting taxes and lowering interest rates, the only solution is to increase public spending, which Roosevelt did. In order to persuade his professional colleagues of the truth of this simple prescription, however, Keynes had to present a brand new framework of economic analysis, in what seemed at the time an extremely complicated form. This he did in his famous *General Theory of Employment, Interest and Money,* published in 1936.[17] It was this book that launched the "Keynesian Revolution."

The chief reason why the book seemed so revolutionary was that it destroyed once and for all any remaining illusions about a *natural* tendency towards equilibrium of the economy as a whole with stable prices and full employment, which would be automatically achieved if only imperfections in the market mechanism were removed. Keynes did not dispense with the notion of equilibrium, as a situation which might prevail for some time once established; but he showed that such an equilibrium might be established almost anywhere, depending on conditions, including a position with deep unemployment. It could also be established with steady or even cumulative price increases, at least for short periods (and in the long run we are all dead, as Keynes reminded his critics). But there was also in the Keynesian system the conclusion that in order for capitalist systems to function well they must be continuously and expertly managed. This concept of a permanently "mixed economy" involving continuous intervention by government rocked neoclassicists and Marxists alike, the former because their belief in *laissez-faire* died hard, the latter because of the implication that *if* capitalist systems were well managed they could last forever.

From the standpoint of methodology, the essential feature of Keynes' General Theory was that it shifted the focus from the behavior of the individual firm, entrepreneur, consumer, or worker (microeconomics) to the operation of the economy as a whole (macroeconomics). The Keynesian system consists of large aggregates: total consumer spending ("C"), total private investment ("I"), aggregate government spending ("G") and national income as a whole ("Y"). The basic proposition is: $Y = C + I + G$.

If total spending, or national income which is the same thing is not enough to assure full employment, a government may seek to encourage consumer spending by cutting taxes or providing consumer credit at low interest rates and easy terms; or it may try to promote private investment by reducing interest rates and easing credit, or cutting business taxes; but if these devices fail, the only solution is to raise government expenditures. The higher government outlays must not be offset by higher taxes, since these discourage consumer

---

[17] John Maynard Keynes, *The General Theory of Employment, Interest and Money,* (London: MacMillan, 1936).

spending and private investment. Unemployment, therefore, calls for easy money and budget deficits. Conversely, inflation requires cutting government expenditure without offsetting reductions in taxes, or raising taxes to reduce consumption and investment, and higher interest rates with tighter provisions for lending. In short, inflation calls for tight money and budget surpluses. This "gospel" is now accepted by the governments of virtually all advanced countries and is at the root of most decisions regarding monetary and fiscal policy. This statement holds even for socialist countries, since (as will be seen below) what the socialists call the "financial balance" is really the same thing as the Keynesian equilibrium.

But whereas in Russia and Eastern Europe much of production is planned directly, the Keynesian approach of the "mixed and managed" economy relies mainly on monetary and fiscal policies, designed to generate the appropriate stream of total spending, so as to assure steady growth with full employment and no inflation. However, during World War II, allied economies became noticeably more similar to the Soviet model. Not long after the publication of the *General Theory,* Keynes found himself in the British Cabinet Offices, not fighting unemployment but trying to fight a major war without inflation. That was done with great success, not only in the United Kingdom but in Canada, Australia, and the United States as well, by applying essentially Keynesian policies, designed in wartime to limit spending rather than increase it.

Managing the War Economy: Keynes and the Econometricians • Success in wartime planning was due in large measure to a happy marriage between Keynesian economics and econometrics, or "quantitative economics." The Keynesian system led to the rapid development of national accounts, so that statistics were available for the strategic variables within the system. Dutch, Scandinavian, and American economists led the way in econometrics; and to their work was added a major contribution by American expertise in Operations Research and Systems Analysis, notably in the Office of Naval Research, the Rand Corporation, and the Office of Strategic Services. Wartime pressures to determine "the appropriate stream of total spending" and its optimal allocation, applying the Keynesian analytical system and the analysis of intersectoral flows, led to a rather sudden conversion of economics from a somewhat rarefied academic exercise into a quantified and operational science, much closer to the natural sciences in its basic methodology. The Keynesian system was cast in terms of easily measured variables, leading directly to econometric models in which the strategic relationships determining the behavior of an economy were not only set forth but quantified as well. Sophisticated analytical tools and mathematical techniques, linear programming, input-output matrices, and econometric models were developed or refined by the neo-Keynesians, while giant strides in statistical theory, vast improvements in the supply of data and the development of high-speed computers, all occurring at about the same time, put economics on an operational basis. It provided tools for both socialist and nonsocialist planners, and paved the way for the managed economy in the Western world with a major war as its first test. Thus the management of the World War II war economies of the United States, Britain, Canada, and Australia became a virtuoso performance of Keynesian economics and econometrics. The "war economy approach" involved a massive expansion of government spending and credit to private enterprise, achieved without inflation. Keynesian tools and techniques were used in conjunction with a battery of controls, within a planning framework which bore a strong family resemblance to Russian "balance planning."

Great strides were also made in systems analysis during this period. This analysis was developed to deal with a limited supply of resources, a system of "either/or"; is it better to use steel for guns, for ships, for tanks, for plant and machinery to produce war material, or more steel in relation to everything else going on in the war economy? Indeed, the basis of systems analysis is the recognition that the *structure* of any system, the many circular, interlocking, feedback relationships among the components, are often as important in determining its behavior as are the individual components themselves; systems analysis seeks to chart and predict these changes, as, for example, in the M.I.T.-Club of Rome model of the world economy. Systems analysis is being used increasingly by socialist and nonsocialist planners alike for solving all manner of economic problems today, from those of individual enterprises to those of the national economy.

Towards a Workable International Economic Order • There is one more contribution which Lord Keynes may yet make to economic history. Keynes did not confine his interests to the management of individual economies; he was also greatly concerned with the establishment of a workable international economic order, expecially in its monetary aspects. He severaly criticized the international gold standard, which finally collapsed because it required deflationary monetary policies in countries with international balance of payments problems (when the value of the imports exceeded the value of their exports). This requirement involved higher interest rates to attract funds from abroad; discouragment of borrowing at home, thereby reducing investment; and forcing down domestic prices to a point where imports became unattractive and exports easy. Keynes attributed the peculiar depth and length of the Great Depression of the 1930s partly to misguided application of these rigorous "rules."

At the international monetary conference at Bretton Woods in 1944, which set up the new international monetary machine comprising the International Bank for Reconstruction and Development (the World Bank) and the International Monetary Fund, Keynes and the United Kingdom delegation made a bold proposal: to establish a true world central bank with powers to regulate the flow of a new international currency called "bancor." But this proposal seemed too bold for the United States delegation, headed by Harry White of the U.S. Treasury, who had his own plan, with the U.S. dollar as the international monetary unit and with less transfer of sovereignty to any international institution.

The final outcome of the debate was closer to the Canadian proposal than to any other, mainly because the Canadian "plan" was a compromise between British and American views to begin with. The new postwar system was certainly a great improvement over the rigid gold standard of the 1920s. But it was still far from perfect, and recent discussion has tended toward the original "Keynes plan" as we shall see in Chapter 10.

In sum, by the end of World War II, Keynesian economics had not only proved able to alleviate the Great Depression and to operate a war economy successfully without inflation, but had, together with quantitative economics perfected a set of tools for both managed and planned economies, and had suggested a new, more workable international monetary system. The question then arises as to why, after this brilliant start, Keynesian economics now seems to have failed. Why is the free world today confronted with inflation, unemployment, and balance of payments problems all at once?

PROBLEMS OF POST-WORLD WAR II ECONOMICS

Economists on both sides of the socialism versus capitalism debate emerged from World War II full of confidence, bordering on euphoria and arrogance. In the capitalist countries, it seemed that Keynes had been proven correct; if government spending were high enough, full employment was assured, and need not entail inflation either. The sharp declines in prices, output, and employment that had followed earlier major wars did not appear; it looked as though managed economies, Keynesian style, had licked the prewar business cycle, with its alternations of inflation and unemployment. The socialist countries, and particularly the USSR had demonstrated an enormous productive capacity and considerable flexibility in patterns of production, and socialist economists felt sure of the effectiveness of socialist institutions and planning. The more orthodox among them, along with the political leadership, were also confident enough of their Marxist theory to believe that this time, capitalism was going to disappear altogether in a gigantic postwar depression. Some of the socialist economists suspected that the Keynesian medicine might just possibly work, although it was dangerous to say so (witness the case of the Russian economist Vargas, who was stripped of his several high posts for predicting that capitalism *would* survive one more great depression). Meanwhile, in the warm glow of the postwar international economic cooperation, when the new international aid agencies were starting and no one questioned the importance of foreign aid or liberalized trade, it was possible to look at the world economy and see signs of improvement. Everyone was destined to receive rude shocks, which led to major changes in economic policy and inquiry.

SOCIALIST DISAPPOINTMENTS

For the socialists, it became apparent as the fifties drew to a close that capitalism was not likely to disappear in the foreseeable future, and the the two sets of countries would have to learn to get along together. Disappointments arose also from the appearance of severe shortcomings of centralized planning, which diluted incentives and reduced efficiency.

Even before World War II, Soviet economists began to realize that centralized planning had disadvantages as well as advantages. Such catastrophic failures as the collapse of the Donbas mining industry in 1939—when the miners went unpaid for months—led some Soviet leaders to feel that "teleological planning" was not good enough, and that something was missing from the Soviet planning calculus. They met the problem by a degree of decentralization of decision making, placing a heavier emphasis on regional planning; they also placed more reliance on the price system.

Central planning reduces some of the risks entrepreneurs face in a private enterprise economy; on the other hand, it lacks the danger signals of a system of cost-price comparisons: absence of rents for scarce natural resources can lead to waste of mineral wealth and uneconomic use of land. Implementation of ill-calculated investment decisions may continue too long before being corrected where capital cost-accounting is imperfect. The lack of a pricing system which reflects relative scarcities may lead to waste of resources, as in the case of overdevelopment of Russian hydroelectric power. Stalin himself eventually encouraged new thinking about Soviet economics, and referred cautiously to the "operation of the law of value in an altered form" in the socialist economy.

It was not until 1954, however, that any real progress was made towards a more rational basis for Soviet planning. In that year, a meaningful debate took place on light versus heavy industries and in the following year discussion began on the importance of capital depreciation and obsolescence, opening the door to a consideration of capital costs. Since that time, while the stress remains on key sectors, and on balances and norms in areas where the market cannot be relied upon to produce desired results, there has been a steady increase in the importance attached to the price system by Soviet planners.

The inflexibility of resource allocation in responding to consumer tastes also resulted in unsold stocks of some commodities and lengthening queues for others, leading to Soviet planners relying increasingly on the market for guidance with respect to production of consumers' goods. Projection of demand elasticity has now become a standard part of planning practice in socialist countries. This "revisionism" however, was to lead to bitter attacks from more orthodox Marxists, particularly Mao Tse Tung's attack on "economism" during the Chinese Cultural Revolution.

"Economism" was a term applied to tendencies in Soviet Bloc countries, which some Chinese leaders favored, giving a larger role to price-cost relationships in planning, making more use of income incentives for getting things done, and establishing a chain of command in the economic sphere. Mao regarded such ideas as rightist and bourgeois, an infiltration of capitalist ideology. To keep the Revolution intact and stay on the true road to socialism, he considered it essential to rely on a spirit of selfless service to the people for basic motivation. This Maoist strategy resembles other contemporary approaches to economic development in one fundamental respect: it is based on social engineering rather than on a distinctive system of pure economic analysis as we shall see below.

Meanwhile, curiously enough, capitalist countries were running into trouble, partly because of unwillingness of trade unions, employers, farmers, and governments to accept the "classical medicine" imposed by a free market.

THE NEO-KEYNESIANS

After the wartime successes, most economists thought postwar stabilization was going to be easy. With wartime pressures on limited resources relieved, controls were lifted and private enterprise was once again given its head. The gigantic postwar depression confidently expected by the Russians and feared by not a few Americans, did not take place in the "free world." Instead, the Marshall Plan, along with neo-Keynesian economic policies shored up free world economies, and a period of what seemed at first to be steady growth ensued.

The Quest for Steady Growth • Meanwhile, the Keynesian school did not rest on its laurels. They had posed themselves the task to prevent booms and depression altogether. The American economists, Alvin Hansen, in his stagnation thesis, had already diagnosed the causes of the peculiar length and depth of the Great Depression as being: the fall in rate of population growth, disappearance of frontiers, capital-saving innovations, and lack of "great new industries," all of which diminished investment while savings tended to increase. Thus total spending was too low to generate full employment. Hansen came to the same conclusion as Keynes: if private spending cannot be raised sufficiently, increase public spending. That was in fact done. Attention then turned to *maintaining* steady growth. The basic questions behind the new spate of "growth theories" of the 1950s were: "How can we assure steady growth with full employment and stable prices?" and "What is needed to maximize the rate of growth?"

The Harrod Model • Roy Harrod of Oxford was one of the first to show that achieving steady growth was no simple affair. The Harrod model demonstrated that, far from there being an inherent tendency toward equilibrium in a free market, if equilibrium is disturbed, there will tend to be a cumulative movement away from it. If the actual growth of national income is more than sufficient to satisfy investors, they will increase their investment, accelerating growth further; if actual growth is disappointing, investment will be cut, eventually bringing growth to a halt. Therefore to achieve steady growth not only must the income and the output generated by the same investment process fit each other, but the rate of growth must be just enough to satisfy entrepreneurs and thus persuade them to repeat their investment decisions period after period.

The Domar Model • Whereas Harrod's theory was cast in terms of behaviour of individual entrepreneurs, Evsey Domar of M.I.T. was concerned with the mechanics of the economic system as a whole. Since in the Keynesian system the rate of growth of output depends on the *level* of investment, and the rate of growth of income (or spending) depends on the *rate of increase* in investment, how can we be sure that the two growth rates will be the same, so as to permit both unemployment and inflation to be avoided? The answer was: we cannot be sure at all. To have steady growth with full employment and stable prices there must be full employment and stable prices to begin with. Even then, it is unlikely that this happy state will continue without astute management of the economy by government. For steady growth, the percentage rate of growth of investment must equal the percentage rate of growth of income. Moreover, this rate must be at a certain level, and at that level only: namely, the rate equal to the ratio of output to the stock of capital, multiplied by the ratio of increases in savings to increases in income. There is just no way the operation of a free market can guarantee all these equalities.

These two theories (sometimes lumped together as the "Harrod-Domar thesis"), by showing the need to match growth of output with growth of effective demand so as to avoid both unemployment and inflation, underscored the need for management of the private enterprise or market economy. In the postwar years, the application of neo-Keynesian economics did in fact modify booms into relatively smooth expansion and turned "depressions" into mild "recessions". The Domar model also provided one basis of development planning in the developing countries. That is, targets were set for growth of national income, and calculations made of the rate of investment needed to achieve steady growth at the target rate. However, the ultimate results have been far from satisfactory, in advanced and underdeveloped countries alike.

Limits of Keynesian Economics • The shortcomings of Keynesian economics became evident soon after World War II when Western-trained economists first attempted to deal with the problems of the Third World. Then, for the first time, economists encountered the peculiar phenomenon of serious inflation and widespread unemployment occurring simultaneously. It became clear that the Achilles heel of Keynesian economics is the underlying assumption that inflation and unemployment would alternate, as had been the past experience in the advanced world. The prewar business cycle had consisted of alternating booms and depression, of full employment with rising prices giving way to unemployment with falling prices. Obviously the Keynesian formulas of easy money and budget deficits in depressions and tight money with budget surpluses in times of inflation made good sense under these conditions; but they become inoperable when unemployment and inflation exist side by side. At first Keynesians explained this phenomenon in terms of the peculiar dualistic structure of underdeveloped economies. It was therefore an even greater shock when during the 1950s the same phenomenon emerged in advanced countries as well. How had this awkward situation come about?

In the case of the Third World, mismanagment arose largely from inexperience. In the case of the advanced world, it is now common knowledge that effectiveness of simple Keynesian policies have been frustrated by monopoly power, combined with ill-advised government action which have been building up inflationary conditions ever since World War II, In affluent, advanced societies, and even in the more rapidly industrializing less developed countries, the process has been begun by trade unions bargaining for wage increases (even in the presence of increasing unemployment); employers then grant wage increases and offset them by raising prices; and governments respond by increasing the money supply so as to make sure that the higher wage-price structure can be sustained without reducing sales, output or employment. This pattern negates the efficient management of the money supply that the Keynesian formulas were supposed to furnish. Since costs and prices are rising together, profits need not be much affected, and thus the process of inflation need not lead to any increase in real investment or any reduction of unemployment. With a growing labour force plus innovation of a labor-saving type, the coexistence of unemployment and inflation is all the more likely under these conditions.

While these monopolies were mainly exercised by corporations and unions, monopolies gained by government protective measures also prevent the market from eliminating inefficient enterprises. The essence of the classical system was mobility of capital and labor. As the classicists warned, monopolies prevent resources from flowing as they should from one sector to another, and from one region to another. The process of raising wages everywhere, irrespective of productivity, then requiring support from the government through protection against imports, subsidies and monetary expansion to support higher prices, ties up capital and labor which could be more productive elsewhere—in another sector, or another region. Through the distorted use of the Keynesian formulas, the cyclical reductions in private investment that brought depressions in the old, prewar framework, are now translated into a declining rate of increase in employment (with a growing labor force, increased unemployment) and sometimes accelerated inflation as well. In sum, various interest groups have eluded the discipline of the market, and the managers of market economies have not had the courage or understanding to tackle the real problems.

In such a situation governments try to select the best "trade-off" between reducing unemployment at the expense of more inflation and vice versa. This set of options confronting a government is known as the "trade-off curve."[18] Once the trade-off curve becomes a reality, there is no simple, aggregative, central government monetary or fiscal policy uniformly applied throughout a country which will reduce the rate of price increase, accelerate growth, and

---

[18] The "trade-off curve," relating unemployment to *price* increases, is related to, but not identical with, the "Phillips curve" which relates unemployment to *wage* increases. The term "Phillips curve" came into the language of economics as the result of a seminal article by A. W. Phillips of the London School of Economics. A. W. Phillips, "The Relation Between Unemployment and the Rate of Change of Money Wage Rates in the U.K. 1861–1957," *Economica* 25 (Nov. 1958).

reduce unemployment all at once. The existence of a trade-off curve is a symptom of deep seated structural weaknesses and inefficiencies which must be attacked directly.

At this point, the basic limitation of the Keynesian system emerges: it is concerned with money flows, not production. The Keynesian world is essentially one of superabundance of resources, and the basic economic problem is to create enough effective demand to use them. There is even a suggestion that it does not much matter how the effective demand is created. Keynes himself proposed burying jars of banknotes in city dumps and letting out contracts to dig them up. When *The General Theory* was published, Keynes's emphasis on effective demand made sense. There existed in the advanced countries not only massive unemployment, but also excess plant capacity, and unutilized entrepreneurial, managerial, scientific and technical skills as well. All that was missing was adequate *effective demand* to absorb the output these resources were capable of producing. In such a situation, it was reasonable to think that if *effective demand* could be generated, output, income, and employment would all rise together, as indeed they did. "Postwar planning" of the 1940s was also very largely a matter of guessing how large the deflationary gap would be, the *shortfall* of consumption and investment which would have to be offset by government spending. But *inefficiency* in using scarce resources rather than lack of effective demand has emerged as the major problem.

The basic problem has shifted back to assuring adequate *supply,* rather than assuring adequate *demand.* Growth models have, however, continued to be concerned with money flows, rather than with raising productivity. Consequently, they have become increasingly remote from reality. Keynesian economics is an economics of abundance, and thus of limited use in a world of scarcities. Economists working in developing countries had been aware of this defect in Keynesian economics for some time. The energy crisis brought the point home in the advanced world. Lord Keynes had inadvertently diverted economics away from its main purpose: to determine the way in which *scarce* resources can best be used to improve the welfare of mankind.

Clearly, there is no use in making growth models ever more elaborate and more refined if they run in terms of savings, investment, consumption, capital: output ratios and national income, while the strategic variables in raising productivity are such things as technological change, entrepreneurship, training and education, organization and managerial capacity, receptivity to technical and social change, health and nutrition, and interactions among sectors and regions. This shortcoming becomes particularly noticeable in terms of the problems of developing countries. There is nothing in the Keynesian system to tell us how to raise output where capital, entrepreneurship, and managerial, scientific and technical skills are all scarce.

The Keynesian theory is not a theory of development nor is it a theory of optimal allocation of resources. Full employment without inflation is not the only social goal to be sought through a managed economy, and control of the money flow is not the only instrument needed to achieve it. Indeed, to explain simultaneous inflation and unemployment, economists are being driven back to microeconomics.

While macroeconomics are still used to determine the main financial balances, economists are turning to studying and working with microcosms of the economy—sectors, industries, firms, cities and regions. They study the behavior of the decision makers—consumers, investors, managers, entrepreneurs, and workers. This new interest in these "actors in the economic process" has stimulated an interest in "noneconomic" aspects of economic development—sociocultural, political, historical, technological, and environmental considerations.

This switch reflects the larger change from "rigor" to "relevance". As will be seen below, this change-over involves reassuming responsibility for making value judgments, and an expanding of the scope of economics to permit an interdisciplinary approach. This trend had already been started years earlier by development economists, an approach reminiscent of the institutionalists.

CONTEMPORARY DEVELOPMENT ECONOMICS

Development economists came to realize early in the postwar epoch that no aspect of human knowledge is completely irrelevant to the process of development. Eugene R. Black, after his fourteen years as president of the International Bank for Reconstruction and Development, said in 1960 that to deal with the problem would "require a philosopher, widely schooled in academic economics, with a good command of history, who held a degree in civil engineering, with geography and anthropology as minor subjects, and who had taken a postgraduate course in modern social psychology."[19] This awareness arose both from the fact that western formulas and strategies were not working successfully in the developing world, and from the fact that Third World leaders themselves were insisting that development should take new directions in the developing world. Each nation must "develop its own vision of the future out of the materials of its own history, its own problems, its own national makeup and geographical location."[20]

Certainly the development problem required something beyond the narrow approach of "pure economics." What, for example, did an economist do when people responded to innovation, but *not* in a manner conducive to further dynamic development? Take the case of some very poor fishermen in Kakinada, Andra Pradesh, who were provided by the Indian government with nylon fishing nets which were stronger and held more fish than their own primitive nets. Some men caught more fish with each cast of the new nets, but stopped fishing when they had caught their usual number. Others fished

[19] Eugene Black *The Diplomacy of Economic Development and Other Papers* (New York: Atheneum, 1963) p. 3. (Originally published by Harvard University Press.)
[20] Soedjatmoko "Technology, Development, and Culture," unpublished paper, 1972.

longer, but used the extra income to buy more liquor. Thus economists now found themselves obliged to take account of differences in individual behavior in varying sociocultural settings. How, for example, can modern irrigated agriculture be introduced in the Senegal River Valley? The people cooperate in their traditional agriculture on a tribal basis; modern irrigation projects operate on a bigger scale, requiring the cooperation of several tribes. Would intertribal cooperation be a reasonable possibility? Or should one start afresh with modern institutions? And what to do about traditional societies strongly resistant to change?

In recent years, the importance of sociocultural and political influences has brought about a significant synthesis of thought and action among the social sciences, as well as an ever growing exchange of ideas and techniques. Not only are economists paying attentions to these new areas of inquiry, but sociologists and anthropologists are bringing their own techniques to bear on development problems and, for good measure, borrowing the quantitative techniques of economists. Concern with directly improving welfare is leading to closer collaboration among economic, physical, environmental educational, and health planners.

A further global confluence of interests results from the similarity of economic problems currently emerging in developing and advanced countries alike, from shared problems, such as globally synchronized economic fluctuations, and from environmental limitations. A synthesis is also taking place between socialist and nonsocialist approaches, particularly at the planning level, where strategies are virtually the same and techniques are almost indistinguishable. In Eastern Europe, a story was told in the 1960s about an East European and a West European planner who met at a United Nations Conference. "We have so many problems at home," said the Westerner, "but we have found a solution, We call it planning." The Easterner replies, "We too have our problems. But we too have found a solution. We call it the Market." This borrowing of approaches is not limited to planners. A Senate Finance Committee report on U.S. global firms states:[21]

> The coordination of MNC (multinational corporations) operations requires planning and systemization of control of a high order. In the largest and most sophisticated MNC's, planning and subsequent monitoring of plan fulfillment have reached a scope and a level of detail that, ironically, resemble more than superficially the national planning procedures of Communist countries.

CONCLUSIONS

This borrowing brings us back to our original question: does either the private enterprise or the Marxist system of thought provide a panacea—a uni-

---

[21] Senate Finance Committee on the planning capabilities of multinational corporations in *Implications of the Multinational Firm for World Trade and Investment and for U.S. Trade and Labor*. Report to the Committee on Finance of the United States Senate and its Subcommittee on International Trade, Investigation No. 332-69, (Washington, D.C.: 1973) Government Printing Office, p. 159.

versal remedy for development? From the purely economic point of view the answer is clearly "no." In the development field, neither socialists nor non-socialists have a monopoly of knowledge or wisdom. Rather, in spite of differences in conviction, economists have built on each other's findings in the common search for the well-being of man. Marx borrowed from Adam Smith and Malthus, Schumpeter borrowed from Marx, Keynes borrowed from Schumpeter, and everyone borrows from Keynes. The current synthesis continues this long tradition. The difference, of course, emerges at the political level. The NeoMarxists or—as some of them prefer—"the radical political economists" insist that the present less developed countries cannot really hope to develop without first having revolutions of a Russian, Chinese, or Cuban type.

Anyone is entitled to the view that one social system *ought* to be replaced by another, moreover, revolutions do occur from time to time. However most Third World governments have decided that revolution of the communist variety need not be a prerequisite of development for all countries. "Class hatred, fueled by deliberate class struggle and welded into an instrument of power, may be the trigger," Soedjatmoko declares "but so also can the simple desire for freedom and justice and the yearning for a better life."[22]

Some developing countries have—with much justice—cried, "A plague on both your houses," and have flatly refused to accept the idea that the choice is limited to either socialism or capitalism and have set out to construct their own social and economic systems, attempting to select what is best from both systems and to build on their own institutions to create an indigenous democracy. Such an ambitious undertaking is extremely difficult, creating problems of its own; development may take longer with the trial and error approach which it often involves, but it is a solution with strong appeal.

In any case, selecting the system is but the beginning. Once the revolution is won—or even if it does not take place—the leaders, old or new, in advanced and Third World countries alike, must get down to the job of making their system work so as to improve the lot of the people. From the standpoint of *economics*—the *design* of a system is less important than its construction, maintenance, and operation. Any system must apply knowledge and skill continuously, if it is to work well. It is towards the problems of management of economies of different political and social construction that the efforts of economists are properly directed. The real significance of Table 2–1 is not so much that it shows that success can be achieved by either system; the wide range of performance of countries—whatever the political system—reflects an enormous range of environmental, historical, sociological, as well as economic conditions influencing performance, problems which must be faced and solved by socialist and nonsocialist economists alike.

We will continue this inquiry by asking what is relevant to today's development problems in the process of development of the now advanced countries?

---

[22] Soedjatmoko, "Technology, Development, and Culture."

3

Development of advanced countries: capitalism and socialism

Economic difficulties experienced by developing countries today are being increasingly blamed on the ill-advised application of Western formulas (both socialist and nonsocialist) which worked well for the now successful advanced countries but proved imperfect for developing countries. Development economists have become uncomfortably aware that, after all, they derived much of development theory from the patterns of economic growth of Europe, Japan, and Russia, and that it was presumptuous to apply unquestioningly what had worked in the now advanced countries to Third World problems.

Yet while today's countries will follow different paths, the experience of these now-advanced countries may offer certain guidelines for successful development. Moreover, the now-advanced countries of Western Europe, Russia, and Japan once had many conditions in common with the Third World. They were once poor, agricultural, and tradition-bound by feudalism. They were also stagnant. Questions arise as to: How did they break free from poverty and stagnation and progress ultimately to become affluent societies? To what extent is development influenced by historical happenstance so that formulas which work in one situation may not work in another? What *are* the essential requirements for successful development? The basic formula for development is based on industrialization:

1. The successful transfer of an agricultural surplus (along with the farmers) to the industrial sector.
2. The generation of mutually stimulating interactions between the sectors.
3. As these activities proceed, it is expected that suitable banking institutions and other services (insurance, commerce, transportation) will emerge in response to need.

4. As the economy expands, labor becomes scarce, wages rise, consumption increases and welfare spreads.

This process is clearly evident in European economic history whence the formula was mainly derived.

THE RISE OF CAPITALISM

The striking feature of the growth of the European countries is that their structural change was a "natural state of affairs." Some chance historical events combined with favorable economic and cultural conditions, starting and sustaining a process of change to which the Europeans responded with vigor, but for a long time with little comprehension of the process of growth in which they were participating. Actually feudalism in Europe was being gradually replaced by constitutional democracies and industrialized, urban economies in the course of the three-and-a-half centuries between 1500 and 1850.

COMMERCIAL CAPITALISM

Modern theories of development usually specify the need for a "challenge" or "outside shock" to start the development process. Those who would associate the rise of capitalism with the development of medieval commerce would stress the role of the Crusades in providing this initial stimulus. These basically religious movements had as their chief results the colonization of unsettled districts and the economic development of the Italian cities; they opened up new Mediterranean markets and ports; the subsequent growth of European trade with the Near East led to the introduction of new commodities and new techniques into Europe; navigation improved; capital and foreign exchange markets were better organized; the new commercial capitalists began to absorb the old feudal aristocracy. By stimulating international trade, the introduction of new or improved technologies, better organized financial institutions and social change, the Crusades had set a vast feedback process in motion.

In the period following the Crusades, a highly organized international trade developed in Europe centered around what we would today call the "growth poles" of the trading cities. Although Italian cities took the lead in the Mediterranean trade, Spanish cities such as Barcelona and French cities like Marseilles were not far behind. They traded with North Africa and the Near East, largely in luxury goods. Almost contemporaneously the north-to-south trade was developing through the organization of fairs such as those of Champagne, Antwerp, Lyon, Avignon, Bruges, and Brussels. The traders were true capitalists earning large profits and often becoming nobles on the proceeds of their financial success.

Financial institutions emerged to handle the accumulation and transferring of capital. Capital was provided mainly through a variety of partnership arrangements and often obtained through issuing shares. Ships were sometimes state-owned. Not only the traders, but also church finance called for financial institutions because the heavy taxes imposed by the Popes necessitated transfer mechanisms and credit. Financing the state also offered a way for commercial capitalists to increase their wealth by lending to the royal houses at usurious rates—witness the Medici and other great trading families. Out of the commercial capitalism of the Middle Ages, the capital accumulation it made possible, and the financial organization it required, grew the industrial capitalism of later periods.

CAPITALISTIC AGRICULTURE

Meanwhile, the growth of the towns and cities, by offering a market for exports from the nearby manors, triggered the beginnings of the Agricultural Revolution. Here we see the hallmarks of structural change: the transferring of the surplus agricultural product and surplus agricultural labor to the industrial and services sectors, of mutually stimulating interactions between the sectors, a "ratchet effect" by which progress in one sector provided a firm base for further progress in the other sector.

The landlords began around 1400 to enclose open fields and common land previously cultivated by peasants in order to grow vegetables and run poultry and livestock on it, for sale to the towns. From the thirteenth century onward, a gradual transition took place from farming for consumption to more specialized and more efficient farming for the market. The enclosure movement was accelerated by the Black Death, a plague which swept Europe in a series of waves. This crisis precipitated the next phase of development, "getting rid of farmers." The resulting depopulation made it desirable to replace labor-intensive industries with land-intensive activities such as sheep farming, providing a further encouragement for enlarging land-holdings which paved the way to further agricultural improvement.

Enclosures concentrated ownership into fewer hands; scattered strips were amalgamated into more workable plots, arable land was converted into pasture and the commons were appropriate for production. Sheep farming became the most important agricultural industry, and yielded large profits. This production of wool in turn stimulated the textile industry.

URBANIZATION

The growth of activity in the towns also effected the crucial transfer of the agricultural population into industry and services in the towns. The demand for labor in the towns led to the freeing of some serfs; others, attracted by higher wages, simply ran away. The enclosures accelerated this transfer. At the same time, cottage industry was transplanted from the manor to the town. By the sixteenth century, large workshops had come into being, particularly in the textile industry; their sheer size contributed to the accumulation of capital. However, we must distinguish between a mere collection of workers under one roof and an increased use of machinery and division of labor. Technical specialization, the chief characteistic of industrial capitalism, was still rare in the sixteenth century.

THE DISCOVERIES AND THE COMMERCIAL REVOLUTION

The industrial specialization of the seventeenth century was made possible by the expansion of markets and trade trigggered by the great geographical discoveries of the fifteenth and sixteenth centuries. The North American continent was discovered in 1492, the Cape Route to the Orient in 1498, Brazil in 1500, and Magellan circumnavigated the globe in 1522. These events precipitated the Commercial Revolution. Navigation vastly improved; European commerce (domestic and international) expanded enormously. Important population movements (the slave trade and emigration) provided new raw materials and markets for finished products.

This commercial expansion, in opening up new markets and creating new demands, facilitated the division of labor and led to technological improvements. The Commercial Revolution completed the overturn of the medieval economic organization of guilds, manors, and town control of foreign trade. Guild organizations, unable to set up plants involving investments greater than individual craftsmen of guilds could provide, crumbled and gave way to the capitalistic employers.

THE PRICE REVOLUTION

The discoveries not only expanded commerce, but also provided the "easy money" which staked the beginnings of the Industrial Revolution. The vast influx of gold and silver in the sixteenth century came first to Spain and Portugal and was distributed throughout Europe in payment for import surpluses. Prices quadrupled and wages and rents lagged, giving an incentive to speculation, capital building, and promotion of new industries. The important aspect of the gold inflow was its effects on liquidity and bank reserves. In a monetary system where the volume of bank credit depends on the size of the nation's reserves of precious metals, the influx of these metals results in low interest rates and "easy money." The volume of investment and the consequent rate of economic growth is accordingly maintained on a relatively high level.

The flow of precious metals also broadened the area of trade; tremendous profits were made from goods from the Orient without need to sell an equal value of European goods. Without the influx of gold and silver the "unfavorable" trade with the Orient could not have been continued. Much of the metal coming from the Americas travelled finally to the Orient. Were the obverse effects of this flow of treasure into Asia the beginning of the East-West economic gap? It should be pointed out that the mere possession of precious metals cannot itself provide an incentive to economic development. The countries richest in "treasure" have not always been the most economically advanced. Spain and Portugal, which received gold and silver from their colonies had no need to develop new industrial exports to pay for imports. Northern European countries with no access to precious metals had to do so; they exchanged new industrial products for luxury goods from the Orient, ending up with handsome profits to reinvest. Spain and Portugal bought goods with gold and silver, and did not participate in the Industrial Revolution. The oriental countries ended up with gold and silver paid for with traditional goods. Trade brought to them neither genuine enrichment nor industrial change. In the long run the countries which developed industries were much better off than those who relied on treasure from the New World, which is a reason why Spain and Portugal were numbered among the underdeveloped countries in the post–World War II years.

THE AGRICULTURAL REVOLUTION

The Agricultural Revolution of the eighteenth century was, in turn, accelerated by the expansion of trade and commerce following the discoveries. Growing markets and rising prices encouraged farmers and landlords to put land to the most profitable use.

The eighteenth century was marked by the belief in the "principle of change," by technical experiments, and by a brisk interchange of ideas and techniques among countries. Virtually every ruler imported merino sheep from Spain; "spirited farmers" and "improving landlords," particularly in England, introduced new crops, tools, and methods from France and Holland. Jethro Tull, Arthur Young, Robert Bakewell, and "Turnip" Townshend pioneered new methods in England, breeding improved types of cattle and sheep, and experimenting with crop rotation. Dutch engineers were sought wherever a drainage problem had to be solved. Innovating Danish landlords developed highly efficient dairy farms, while the smaller farmers developed cooperative methods at every point.

The Industrial Revolution later contributed to agricultural advance by mechanization. The Agricultural Revolution in turn provided the basis for the Industrial Revolution by moving people from farm to factory without undue strain on the supply of foodstuffs.

THE INDUSTRIAL REVOLUTION

The discoveries, the consequent expansion of markets and commerce better nourished workers, and the "easy money" made possible industrial specialization with increased used of machinery and division of labor. This transformation of the European economy was completed between 1600 and 1850.

Economic historians point out that the Industrial Revolution was more than industrial and less than revolution. Labor-saving inventions such as the spinning jenny had revolutionary effects, but technological progress was gradual, more continuous than erratic, a continuous advance in the ability to exploit natural resources. New know-how changed the way work was done, reduced the cost and increased the volume of output. New cheap ways were found to extract and use metals; new kinds of power, especially steam, were developed; coal and later oil were used as fuels; better tools were designed and the invention of machines continued apace. Railroads, steamships, and motor transport reduced barriers of space and time. Agriculture, industry, commerce, transportation became more capital intensive while large investments were made in post office, highway, military, and public health facilities.

At each stage of this development process, men emerged to accept the great risks that accompanied the new opportunities. One of the most frequently cited reasons for lack of development is entrepreneurship. Developmentalists today are therefore taking a keen interest in how the free wheeling, daring "capitalist spirit" emerged from the tradition bound societies of the Middle Ages.

THE CAPITALISTIC SPIRIT: EXPLOITATION

Karl Marx was one of the first to interest himself in capitalists as well as capitalism. He had a comparatively simple conception of the capitalistic spirit. All that was needed to assure capital accumulation was the power and the opportunity to make profits by exploiting workers and peasants. In the early stages of industrial development, this conception had some basis. Not only did capitalists have the opportunity to make profits by considerable exploitation of workers, but also the fiscal systems of most Western countries as well as the economic systems were such as to redistribute income from poor to rich. Taxes consisted almost entirely of customs and excise duties, which fell relatively heavily on the poor, who spent most of their income for consumer's goods. Income and inheritance taxes were unknown. Government expenditures on the other hand benefited mainly the upper-income groups; interest on government bonds, subsidies to private enterprise, transport facilities all added to the flow of savings and investment.

To be sure this mobilization and concentration of capital into entrepreneurial hands accelerated development, which eventually led to a better life for workers than Marx would have expected. However, while the statistics are none too good, it seems possible that the material standard of living of European wage earners *declined* in the first stages of the Industrial Revolution.

THE CAPITALIST SPIRIT: THE PROTESTANT ETHIC

Other students of capitalism, such as Max Weber and R. H. Tawney, felt there was more to the spirit of entrepreneurship than simple greed and a will to exploit. They felt that an appropriate religious and ideological climate was necessary to nurture the "delicate plant of entrepreneurial endeavor."

According to Weber,[1] impulse to acquisition is common to all times and all places, but Roman Catholicism held in check the pursuit of profit and the ac-

[1] Max Weber, *The Protestant Ethic and the Spirit of Capitalism* (New York: Scribner, 1930).

cumulation of wealth which characterize capitalism. In the Middle Ages the acquisition of wealth was considered the lowest kind of avarice; after the Reformation, this conduct became highly respectable. At the beginning of modern times, it was not the existing entrepreneurs who represented the capitalistic spirit, for they were bound by traditionalism: fixed profits, limited interest rates, just wages, and just prices. It was in the lower middle class that the spirit was strongest. This spirit, and not new streams of money, stimulated the rise of capitalism.

The chief reward for making money was the feeling of having done the job well. This concept is to be found in Luther's doctrines under the name of the "calling," the idea that each individual is "called" to do a certain job and to do it as well as possible. The net result was to justify the pursuit of wealth, provided that happened to be one's "calling." Poverty was not required, but the pursuit of riches must not lead one to reckless enjoyment. Profits are as holy as wages, and interest is not wrong unless wrung from the poor. The cardinal sin is idleness. Thus the Reformation gave to the entrepreneur and to the capitalist a clear conscience to pursue profits to the best of their ability. In condemning expenditure, it provided the basis for capital accumulation. The profits of this era were not absorbed into luxurious living of a new nobility but were reinvested.

R. H. Tawney[2] emphasized the influence of John Calvin on entrepreneurial attitudes. Luther, he says was opposed to the accumulation of wealth, usury, monopoly, high prices, speculation, and the luxury trade with the East. But Calvin saw economic life with the eyes of a peasant, and recognized frankly the need for capital, credit and banking, and large-scale commerce and finance. Thrift, diligence, sobriety, and frugality are the Christian virtues, and profits and interest are not necessarily evil gains.

While acquisitiveness is not a characteristic exclusive to Protestants, it is fairly generally agreed today that the Protestant ethic was one element in the acceleration of capitalistic development. The relationship between predominant religion and per capita income is too close for religion to be dismissed out of hand as a factor in economic history. Moreover, in parts of the world other than Europe, quite different religions have produced the spirit of enterprise; the parsees of India; the Indians in Burma, Africa, and Malaysia; the Chinese in South East Asia; and the Jews and Lebanese all over the world have all proven themselves astute capitalists. Here the common denominator is not religion but the fact that they are all subdominant élites, sometimes persecuted, who have been denied the conventional routes to prestige and power and have sought safety and power in wealth. Other examples are the persecuted Protestants who immigrated into England, West Germany, and Holland, bringing with them technical skills, scientific knowledge, and managerial talents. Later religious persecution contributed to the development of the New World.

It should be added that the Reformation itself had economic effects more

[2] R. H. Tawney, *Religion and the Rise of Capitalism* (Gloucester, Mass.: P. Smith, 1954).

direct than those entailed in the change in ideology it introduced. The dissolution of the abbeys and the confiscation and sale of church properties transferred capital from less enterprising to more enterprising owners. Thus the Reformation contributed capital as well as an ideological impact to the extraordinarily favorable constellation of historical, economic, and sociological conditions which led to "the rise of capitalism".

STAGES OF ECONOMIC GROWTH

Within this mosaic of chance events and human response, economic historian Walt W. Rostow[3] discerned a pattern of development, which he translated into a "stages" theory according to which the history of each national economy (or region) may be broken down into phases. He discerned five stages: The traditional society; establishing the preconditions for takeoff; the takeoff; the drive to maturity; the age of high mass consumption.

Rostow defines the social structure of *traditional society* as hierarchical with little scope for vertical mobility. Because productivity is limited, the people are obliged to devote a high proportion of their resources to agriculture. *The preconditions for takeoff* are likely to be established somewhere in the primary sector, usually an increase in food production, although wool, cotton or silk, timber, rubber or oil may also play the role of leading sector. An essential increase in agricultural productivity and production provides necessary inputs into the leading sector. At the same time, other "clusters" of leading sectors impart net spread effects to the rest of the economy, while transportation and other forms of social overhead capital are improved. Here Rostow comes close to Colin Clark's recipe for economic development, which consists of first raising agricultural productivity and then improving transport facilities, after which industrialization is supposed to take place more or less automatically. Like most economic historians, Rostow makes a bow to the entrepreneur. He hints that there must also be an interest in modernization on the part of the "effective political coalition."

The main feature of the take off is an increase in the ratio of savings and investment to national income from about 5% to 10% or more. Usually, the beginning of the take off can be traced to some particular sharp stimulus, although what is essential is not the form of stimulus but the fact that the prior development of the society and its economy result in a self-reinforcing response to it. Then one or more substantial manufacturing sectors develop with a high rate of growth, and the political, social, and institutional framework (which either already, exists or quickly emerges) exploits these impulses to expansion in the modern sector.

The take off period is pinned down to an interval of about twenty years followed by the *drive to maturity*—a long interval of sustained if fluctuating

[3] W. W. Rostow, *The Stages of Economic Growth: A Non-Communist Manifesto* (Cambridge: Cambridge University Press, 1961) p. 1.

progress with 10% to 20% of the national income steadily invested "permitting output regularly to outstrip the increase in population." Maturity is generally attained some sixty years after take off, with new leading sectors gathering momentum to supplant the older leading sectors. Thus, the drive to maturity seems to be a sort of "striptease stage" during which the economy just goes on taking off and taking off. With the achievement of maturity the economy continues to grow until the final stage of *high mass consumption* is reached.

There is a certain circularity in Rostow's reasoning. For a society to absorb new production functions in ways which generate the spread effects on which the takeoff depends, he says, requires massive prior change away from the pattern of traditional society. There must be changes in the economy's infrastructure, working force, agricultural and foreign-exchange earnings or borrowing capacity. There must also be "changes in rules of behavior," particularly the emergence of a minimal initial group of entrepreneurs. Rostow seems to be saying that for a takeoff to occur in response to some "sharp stimulus" the conditions for takeoff must be present. But how does the developmentalist initiate these massive sociological changes? As one graduate student asked, "Well, what do we do? Launch a Crusade or find a subdominant elite and persecute it?"

Since the growth of Europe was "a natural state of affairs" which cannot be reproduced, its history offers limited guidance. It points to agricultural and industrial development in a series of stages but only the luckiest countries today can emulate the pattern.

Experiments with Promoted Growth

More pertinent to the problems of the developing countries than the European and New World experiences is that of Russia and Japan. In these two countries, growth did not just happen as it did in Europe; in both cases the countries' leaders vigorously promoted industrial growth in response to the "sharp stimulus" of fear of foreign domination. Their basic formula was the same: hard work, a heavy emphasis on education, large-scale investment made possible by "abstinence" (sacrifice of present consumption for future output), and imported technology. This formula was applied, however, in very different ways, and under very different circumstances.

THE RUSSIAN EXPERIMENT

Soviet Russia's approach to development was based on nationalization of resources, centralized planning, and strong centralized control of the economy. When they came to power, the Soviets first expropriated rural properties of landowners and the church, without compensation, and nationalized the banks. Workers took control of industrial enterprises and a process of nationalization began. The main sectors of the national economy were transferred to public ownership and state bodies were created to administer them. The Supreme Economic Council, established to administer the nationalized enterprises, was charged with making the first plan.

Conforming to Marxist theory (and also fearing invasion by the Western powers), the Russian planners emphasized the role of heavy industry. Lenin outlined a plan that increased the production of fuel and iron, developed the machine building and chemical industries, and raised the technological level of the economy. Divided into sections and departments for fuel, metals, finance, etc., with a central coordinating office, the council evaluated plants and factories, and fixed production targets for the various enterprises. A rough estimate of requirements was made for essential machinery and consumer goods; the extent to which these requirements could be met by domestic production was determined and the prospects explored for importing the balance. The council prepared an economic plan on the basis of this data, but its implementation was prevented by civil war and the disorganization attending profound social change.

Soviet Russia's first ten years of experiment were chaotic; the economy was in a state of deterioration after World War I; civil war raged, and the new socialist administration was inexperienced. The Soviets printed money to cover governmental expenditures, creating a wild inflation. Food supplies were requisitioned from the pesants and distributed by rationing, but these measures provided only half the food supply of the cities; a black market emerged to supply the rest. There were problems in industry, since the managers and technicians were often hostile or had defected. By the time the civil war had ended in 1921, the economic strain had led to the introduction of the New Economic Policy.

This interim policy involved partial restoration of the market economy. The system of rationing and compulsory deliveries was ended, and trade was restored to market channels. Some small state enterprises were leased to individuals or cooperative groups, and there was a general effort to cooperate with the bourgeois technicians. This system lasted until 1928, at which time industrial output was only one-third higher than in 1913, while agricultural output was only up by one-quarter, a performance substantially inferior to that of the capitalist countries.

In the meantime, however, the Russians had improved their planning techniques. In 1920 a more ambitious, long-range plan was begun, what we would today call a "perspective plan." Heavy emphasis was to be placed on the "main links of the chain" giving precedence to main objectives, but also aiming to provide a unified set of directives rather than a collection of disparate schemes. Lenin emphasized that the plan should not be a narrowly technical document, but rather a program for the transformation of the entire economy. The basic transformation was to be the electrification of Russian industry, and the making of the plan was entrusted to the newly established State Commission for the Electrification of Russia.

The Commission took an inventory of the country's resources and made projections of its economic development over the following ten to twenty years. These projections were translated into concrete production targets, estimates were made for every sector of the economy, and the balances of the various sectoral plans coordinated into a unified economic plan. The first of the famous Five Year Plans followed (a five-year span because it took roughly that long to put in a major electrical power installation).

The launching of the first Five Year Plan in 1928 initiated a new phase in the Soviet experiment. The plan introduced ambitious goals for both growth and socialization of the economy. The range of state control was greatly extended; firms were organized into state trusts, and agriculture was collectivized. The period from 1928 to 1937 proved to be one of high achievement; gross national product increased at the rate of some 9% per year; the nonagricultural sector rose from 29% to 46% of employment, and nonagricultural output rose from 52% to 69% of total output. This rapid structural change was attained through high investment ranging from 12.5% to 26% of GNP, but at a high cost to the people. Consumption was sacrificed to the extent that the workers' already low standard of living fell during the period. Agricultural output spoilt the record with a low growth rate of 0.9%.

World War II interrupted the general progress, but recovery was rapid; by the time Stalin died in 1953, the output of the economy had trebled, the state had achieved ownership and control of all means of production, and the development process had spread to a considerable extent throughout the country. Industrial performance has continued to be impressive; industrial productivity today is higher than in several Western countries and about half that of the United States.

Major reasons for Russia's industrial success are:

1. High investment: a willingness to sacrifice present consumption for future gains.

2. Technical training and wage incentives for technical jobs. The Russians have made great strides in science and technology, the result of a very deliberate concentration of education in scientific and technological fields, and the planning of education in relation to development.

3. Technical assistance. Particularly during the Depression years, when Western technicians were more available, the Russians imported Western technology in the form of hiring people (in the early years few Western countries would sell them machinery).

4. Large-scale operations. Russia's huge internal market offers opportunities to save capital in terms of scale; large-scale standardization reduces costs, although gains in quantity are often at the expense of quality and variety for the consumer. Russia also saves capital by using capital stock very intensively as in the case of transport facilities. While these genuine economies of scale can be gained through large-scale enterprise, they are popular with Russian planners because they are also easier to administer from the center.

Enjoying direct control, the government can decide on income distribution without having to heed trades unions or employers; to a large extent it can determine the level of overall demand. However, centralization can create a high administrative burden in a country of Russia's size. Efficiency can be very high in key sectors, at the expense of lower priority sectors. The Russian emphasis on key sectors was translated in practice into selection of one industrial sector after another for a "big push": electricity, iron and steel, chemicals all had their turn. This strategy can be a good one when the supply of resources and expertise are limited, but it has led in Russia's case to imbalance in the form of shortages of some items and oversupply in others.

The Russians have made significant decentralizing modifications in organization to offset drawbacks of central planning. Gosplan (State Planning Commission) established in 1921 was for years the chief organ of centralized planning; sectoral planning was largely the responsibility of the sectoral Ministries for Ferrous Metallurgy, Petroleum, Textiles, Light Industry, etc. In 1957, the sectoral ministries were replaced by regional planning. The country was divided into 103 territories, each with a regional economic council, and nearly three-quarters of state industrial production was put under their control.

A warning lies in Russia's failure in her agricultural sector. Virtually every observer of the Soviet economy (including the late Chairman Khrushchev) had commented on the failure to raise agricultural productivity in Russia, and the consequent drag on rapid industrialization. Productivity of both labor and land rose more slowly in the Soviet Union than in other European countries because Russian agriculture suffered from special disadvantages of soil and climate, from high population densities in good agricultural areas, and from the backward technologies of the peasants. Also, however, Russian agriculture seems never to have received sufficient attention.

In the early 1920s there were strong arguments made in favor of starting development with a "big push" in the agricultural sector, to create a demand for industrial products and to permit a transfer of resources to industry. The proponents of this view, however, lost out in the debate to the advocates of all-out industrialization. Moreover, Alex Nove warns that the measures that were taken to solve the peasant problem should not be a model for anyone. "The Soviet type of industrializing ideology in fact tends to strengthen these elements which have a contempt for peasant agriculture and are all too ready to neglect agriculture." [4] Certainly the first Five Year Plan which featured the collectivization of agriculture had mixed results. Angus Maddison lists the major problems which were thus created:

1. The process of change from peasant ownership to collectives was costly and did lasting damage. The peasants resisted the change which was eventually achieved with brutality and suffering.

2. The management units were inefficient; collectives were excessively large, private plots were dwarf-sized, and machine tractor stations separated control of equipment from the farm enterprise.

3. The use of centralized directives and the absence of efficient market prices were particulary inappropriate in agriculture.

[4] Alec Nove, *The Soviet Economy* (New York: Praeger, 1961) p. 305.

4. Agricultural research was inefficient; experiments were undertaken without adequate preparation in soil studies, production of appropriate seeds, etc.

5. The peasantry was an exploited class. Heavy taxation became a major disincentive to production; the peasants' efforts to increase income by working private plots were hindered by severe controls, and did not benefit from extensions services or agricultural credit. Nor were farm workers entitled to social security benefits; other social and educational facilities were poor; shops, merchandise, transport and entertainment were worse in the countryside than in the cities.[5]

At the close of the Stalin regime, farm income per head was only half of the average for the economy as a whole.

After 1953, agricultural investment increased until it absorbed about one-fifth of total capital formation, and incomes of peasants improved. However, in 1958 Khrushchev himself commented that agricultural productivity was still several times as high in the United States as in the USSR and argued to the effect that the Russian system of collective farms was a form of "disguised unemployment" designed to hold people on the farms and to provide them with a livelihood, rather than permitting them to emigrate to cities where they might be openly unemployed.

While Russian agricultural output has grown considerably since then, it is important to note that Western Europe enjoyed an Agricultural Revolution *before* the Industrial Revolution really began; if we compare the Russian story with that of Western Europe, it is precisely in this "agricultural lag" that the major difference lies.

While the Russian experience offers valuable guidelines for development, it must be borne in mind that Soviet development was attended by circumstances which apply to few developing countries. Russia was already the fastest growing country economically in Europe at the time of the Soviet take-over. Russia had shared in the effects of the Industrial Revolution in Europe (although somewhat belatedly) and was busy catching up at the time. Russia already had a basic railway network, a capital goods sector and a steel industry; moreover, Russia had a wide range of natural resources and the rate of population growth was quite low compared with many developing countries today. Yet it was a big country with a population big enough to offer a substantial domestic market, permitting large-scale production.

The Japanese situation was somewhat closer to that of the developing countries today. To be sure, Japan also had a low population growth over the long term, partly due to the fact that her expansion took place when medical technology was less advanced. Japan also had an internal market big enough to permit large-scale production in many industries. However, unlike Russia, Japan had almost no margin of unexploited natural resources; Japan was also

---

[5] Angus Maddison, *Economic Growth in Japan and the U.S.S.R.* (New York: W. W. Norton, 1969), pp. 112–13.

more backward and more isolated than Russia when she resolved to industrialize. With a large population in relation to her resources, her situation parallels that of many poor lands today.

THE JAPANESE EXPERIMENT

Cited today as a prime example of the successful private enterprise economy, nevertheless Japan was launched into economic growth by vigorous government action. Her leaders' driving motivation in emulating the West was intended to make Japan secure from Western imperial ambitions. In the seventeenth century they had secured themselves by closing their doors to foreign trade and foreign contact; when Commodore M. C. Perry arrived in Edo Bay in 1853 at the head of an American flotilla, and conveyed American demands for free access to Japanese markets, Japanese policy was forced to change. The Japanese leaders then decided that they could keep their country's freedom only if they adopted Western industry and technology. The Meiji government's policy of Shokusan Kogya (more production through industrial enterprise) was initiated in 1868 and lasted until the early 1880s.

The Japanese began by taking advantage of foreign technology. A group of Japanese toured Europe and the United States for nearly two years, studying factories, communications, schools, parliamentary procedures, elections. Western experts were subsequently hired to initiate the new technologies in Japan.

The capital needed to effect modernization of the economy was provided mainly by the Japanese themselves, since they did not want to risk borrowing from foreigners. Land taxes were the mainstay of government finances, enabling the government to take the lead in making investments in new industries. Important industrial concerns were nationalized; all facilities for manufacturing arms and ships were taken over and managed by the central government, as well as all engineering and mining facilities. Telegraph lines, iron foundries, and factories for producing cement, paper, and glass all came in for government investment. Railroad building and commercial shipping were helped with subsidies.

The government also made a number of institutional changes: feudal restrictions (such as the local monopolies on specific products and techniques) were abolished, limitations on interregional trade were relaxed, prohibitions on change of occupation and interregional movement of the people was repealed. These measures were designed to stimulate the participation of the people and in fact led to the rise of private enterprise.

During the first years of the Meiji reforms, the government had serious financial difficulties; tax revenues were inadequate for its massive commitments. This lack of capital resulted in large budget deficits along with great national debt and inflation. Foreign trade was chaotic, leading to violent price fluctuations. Many of the governmental activities concentrated in heavy industries were not financially successful. At the same time, the mushrooming private enterprise sector experienced a great many business failures—more than fifty-two-thousand in the first five years.[6]

The Japanese were inexperienced and lacked appropriate skills; "because of their lack of knowledge about machines, Japanese cannot even open a lock if it is a little complicated," commented a contemporary review.[7] They also lacked commercial skills, and were unfamiliar with advanced commercial organizations, while the legal system was inadequate for a commercial society. All in all, industrialization proceeded slowly; as late as 1900, factory production in the private sector had not attained 8% of National Domestic Product and one-third of the net value came from foods, beverages, and tobacco.[8]

These failures evoked the Kogyo Iken, a long-range plan completed in 1884, which included a review of the Japanese economy, a program of economic development, targets for a ten-year time span, and a set of recommended policies. The planning function of the government was stressed, and the need to establish clear objectives. An environment was to be created conducive to a smooth-functioning market economy; domestic and overseas markets were to be stabilized or expanded; emphasis was to shift from industry to agriculture (agricultural performance had been disappointing and attempts to borrow British and American extensive cultivation techniques had been only partially successful). The most remarkable feature of the plan was its stress on the improvement of techniques in the traditional sector, making this "quasi-agricultural" sector the strategic leading component in the transformation of the structure of the Japanese economy.[9]

A group of strategic products was selected for encouragement (such as raw silk, tea, rice, tobacco, wax, lacquerware, metal products, weaving), according to practicality, suitability to local conditions, and the *possibility of gradually shifting from labor-intensive to capital-intensive techniques*. While the eventual establishment of large-scale factory production was kept in mind, these local industries, carried out mostly in small rural workshops by family labor, were judged to have the potential vitality to serve as the leading sector of the economy if they were given adequate guidance and technical assistance:

> It is necessary in the present situation to direct the people to avoid promotion of new enterprises unsuitable to their capital, and to begin with things with which they are quite familiar. For example, farmers must be directed to improve the use of fertilizer and methods of cultivation, and to select the kinds of plants suitable to their land. Manufacturers are to be directed to postpone the establishment of a factory with big machines, and at present to pay more attention to the improvement of machines which they now use. . . .[10]

The program was predominantly self-help. While some foreign technical assistance in agriculture was sought in Germany and Holland, the Japanese

[6] Ichirou Inukai and Arlon R. Tussing, "Japan's Ten Year Plan, 1884," *Economic Development and Cultural Change*, Vol. 16 No. 1, University of Chicago, 1967.
[7] "Kogyo Iken," reprinted in *Meiji Zenki Zaisei Keizai Shiryo Shusei* (Tokyo: Meiji Bunken Shiryo Kankokai, 1964) p. 70
[8] Inukai and Tussing, "Japan's Ten Year Plan," pp. 53, 63.
[9] Inukai and Tussing, "Japan's Ten Year Plan," p. 63.
[10] "Kogyo Iken," p. 436.

government concentrated on diffusing the practical techniques of traditional agriculture through extension work, and promoted meetings to discuss new techniques and exchange seeds. Practical, concrete prescriptions were furnished for improving indigenous production. Significantly, this policy of seeking out traditional industries with transitional potential is being followed in some developing countries today, notably India and China; these experiments are discussed later.

The stress on transitional industries proved well advised; in the subsequent process of industrialization, these small industries expanded alongside the modern sector, and gradually became part of a clear-cut manufacturing sector. As the economy strengthened, the government began to withdraw from direct production by selling its interests to private enterprises, and after 1895 until World War I, a large amount of foreign investment was allowed into the country.

Japan's subsequent imperialism built up the economy further, making available large supplies of raw materials; yet since World War II Japan's economic performance has continued to be brilliant, not only without the vast empire of the past, but also without the near totalitarian conditions to which Japan's earlier success have been attributed. In recent years, Japan's rate of growth has been one of the fastest in the world. Until 1973 growth did not fall below 7% and has sometimes risen to 9% and 10%. Wages have risen, and the new wealth is spread more evenly through the population. With a population of 100 million, Japan's per capita annual income, now well over $2,000 (1978) could exceed Western Europe's in the 1980s if recent growth trends could be maintained.

What is Japan's secret? It seems to be a matter of doing everything right: a high ratio of savings and investment of national income, a careful adaptation of product-mix and technology to factor endowment, large expenditures on research and application of its results to technological improvement, discerning use of technical assistance and foreign private investment; vigorous promotion of foreign trade. These policies were possible because development-minded governments were willing to plan economic development with the help of highly qualified technicians and at the same time encourage initiative at the grassroots level. They carried out the necessary institutional reforms; they enforced harsh levels of taxation; they were ready to act—where necessary—as entrepreneurs, and at the same time to cooperate with and encourage private entrepreneurship.

Can the developing countries follow this same path? Probably not, because their historical circumstances are different. Japan used her opportunities well, but she was also lucky. The semiannual pilgrimages of the Daimyo (feudal lords) to Kyoto (on their compulsory visit to the King) preconditioned Japan for development in much the same way that the Crusades preconditioned Western Europe. Japan was able to build up her tea and silk exports in a period when international demand for primary commodities was still expanding fast, and when the huge markets of India and China were virtually free of tariff protection. Her silk industry gained when a silkworm disease crippled the European silk industry in the 1860s. Domestic conditions were also favorable. The Japanese administrative machine was efficient and centralized; its bureaucratic, authoritarian, sell-educated Samurai elite could draw on strong national unity and a tradition of obedience. Compared with China or India, the country was small, compact, and easy to administer. Few developing countries today have comparable conditions to support development.

CONCLUSIONS

The economic growth of today's advanced countries was stimulated by an extremely favorable constellation of circumstances. They were underpopulated through most of their rapid-growth period; moreover at the beginning their per capita income was in the neighbourhood of $300. Today many of the poor countries are overpopulated, creating less favorable resourse ratios, and have income per capita closer to $100 a year. One significant parallel pattern of experience is the fact that both Russia and Japan had an initial period of attempting drastic change, of trial and error; then a period of reassessment followed by policies more carefully adapted to their particular situation. In general the economic histories of the advanced countries provide important guidelines rather than complete formulae for the developing countries today.

However, they open up further important lines of inquiry. While it is impossible and in some cases undesirable to duplicate the various events which stimulated the growth of these countries, it is important to note that one of the greatest stimuli—the expansion of foreign trade following the discoveries of the New World and the Cape route to Asia—was shared by the presently developing countries; and at a time when their populations were more comparable with the European countries. Why did the growth of international trade work so much better for the European participants than for the Asian, African, and Latin American? Why did Europe respond to the challenge while her trading partners stagnated?

Colonialism is the obvious answer but an incomplete explanation. Spain, which received rich treasure from the New World, was nevertheless for generations afterward poorer than some of her colonies. The colonists of Australia, the United States, and Canada opened up their countries with natural resources comparable to those of Brazil, Mexico, and some of the other Latin American nations, and fared much better. What constellation of circumstances precipitated these differences?

4

Economic stagnation: colonialism and foreign trade

When the Europeans found their way around the Cape of Good Hope in 1498, there was no clear difference in the level of development between Europe and Asia. Indeed, the refined civilizations of Southeast Asia and China may have been the more advanced. India, Indonesia, and China had firearms, navigation instruments, modes of land and water transport, techniques of manufacture and agriculture, and education systems that compared favorably with Europe's best. Indonesians in particular were heavily engaged in the expanding international trade of the fifteenth and sixteenth centuries. The Javanese dominated the trade of the whole archipelago and even of the Malay peninsula and the Philippines. The bustling port of Malacca controlled the East-West trade through the straits.

Moreover, it cannot be demonstrated that in 1500 the standard of living of either rich or poor was significantly higher in Europe than in Indonesia. Peasants and unskilled workers lived near subsistence level in both places, but princes and merchants engaged in domestic and international economic activities lived well and many lived in considerable luxury. There is evidence that in 1600, Javanese literacy was higher than in 1900; while in 1800, Burma probably had the highest level of literacy in the world. Yet four hundred years after the arrival of European ships in Asian waters, per capita incomes in Europe had become several times as high as those in Asia and the technological gap was enormous.

It is even harder to understand the development lag in Latin American countries. Here the Spanish and Portuguese transplanted European cultures and European peoples to the New World. Brazil, for example, nearly as big as the United States, still with vast, empty spaces, untapped frontiers, and rich in natural resources, failed to raise its per capita income above three hundred dollars in the course of four centuries. What happened?

THE ROLE OF INTERNATIONAL TRADE

Classical and neoclassical economists, except for Malthus, had great faith in the role of international trade as an "engine of growth" in international development. According to them, international trade permitted all countries to specialize in the fields of economic activity for which they were best suited. By exploiting to the full the opportunities provided by "comparative advantage" in one field or another, all countries could benefit greatly from trading with each other. Foreign trade provided a "vent for surplus." The "vent for surplus" was John Stuart Mill's term for an idea at least as old as Adam Smith that expansion of foreign trade, by widening the market and permitting more division of labor, accelerates economic growth. The theory assumes that a previously isolated country about to enter into international trade possesses a surplus productive capacity. Exports can be raised without reducing domestic production by using labor locked inside the closed economy.

Meanwhile the "invisible hand" of the market would allocate resources in an optimal fashion among enterprises, industries, sectors, regions, and nations. Both European and American experience seemed to confirm the theory. Resources did move from low-productivity agriculture to industry and services, and from poor to rich regions. The same forces were expected to operate for the well-being of the underdeveloped countries in Asia and the New World. The relative scarcity of capital in less developed countries would result in high returns to investment there and thus in a flow of capital from rich to poor countries until returns to investments were equalized. Technology and skills would tend to flow from technologically advanced countries to technologically retarded countries to take advantage of the profits at least temporarily associated with such transfers. Goods would also move through expanding world trade. In sum, the classical economists believed that international trade would prevent diminishing returns and stagnation in Europe, while bringing enlightenment and splendid markets to the backward countries.

Marx agreed with the classical economists that world trade prevented diminishing returns in Europe, but he also talked of exploitation. He regarded any European country and its overseas possessions as one economic system. He thought of England and her colonies, or France and hers, as two sectors of a single economy, administered from the metropolitan country in the interests of the capitalists of that country. He claimed that the form trade was taking between advanced and backward countries meant that the advanced countries retained the profits.

Yet during the heyday of nineteenth century trading, the possibilities seemed very bright. *Laissez-faire* held sway: officially free trade and free competition released the "invisible hand." The classical and neoclassical theories seemed proven correct as the rubber plantations of Malaya flourished, the coffee plantations of Brazil prospered, Australia's sheep flocks and Argentina's cattle herds increased, the Dutch developed Indonesian oil reserves, the French sank artesian wells in the Sahara, and English capital opened up mines and plantations and built railroads in America, Canada, Australia, and the rest of the colonies. As these countries were opened up, they in turn provided expanding markets for Europe's industrial goods. Until 1913, many of the developing countries enjoyed rapid economic growth.

Although as we shall see, practice deviated significantly from pure *laissez-faire* theory, the successes of nineteenth century free trade, freedom of immigration, and freedom of capital movements seemed to bear out neoclassical economic theory. During this period, the nations of Western Europe, North America, and Australasia essentially completed their industrial revolutions and emerged as "advanced" countries. Significantly, the stagnation from 1913 to 1939 of the Third World's economies was largely due to the throttling of international trade by trade restrictions including the "beggar thy neighbor policies" of the thirties and the interrelated depression and world wars.

The Great Depression caused stagnation or worse in Europe also, but there was a difference—most of the countries stagnated at a high level of income. In the course of the four-and-a-half centuries of international trade following the discoveries of the new trade routes, an income gap had emerged. The leading European countries, along with the United States, Canada, and Australasia were rich; the rest of the world was poor. Marx's predictions had been closer to the truth. The underdeveloped countries had arrived at a state of chronic disequilibrium and poverty. Much of the blame must be pinned on *laissez-faire* as interpreted in colonial policy, and on the retention of profits in Europe.

Assigning guilt to colonialism, however, does not provide answers to the present development problems. The key to prosperity did not prove to be just a matter of achieving independence, nor just a matter of retaining profits (expectations that explain some of the super optimism of the first years of the international development effort) or the newly independent countries would have done better than they have. Nor can imperialism be blamed for everything. If we compare the incomes of neighboring Southeast Asian countries, it is an ex-colonial country, Malaysia, that is the most prosperous: Thailand, which has never been a colony has a per capita income still below $400 a year; Malaysia next door became independent only in 1957 and has a per capita income of over $700 a year, largely owing to the introduction (by the British) of the rubber tree and the mechanization (by the British) of the tin mines. Senegal owes its relative prosperity among African countries to the introduction and development by the French colonial administration of the large-scale cultivation of peanuts.

Moreover, "economic imperialism" cannot be substituted for colonialism as the sole scapegoat. Malaysia, with its relatively high per capita income, still retains heavy foreign investments within the country. Burma next door gained independence a decade earlier and freed itself from "colonial exploitation" in the form of foreign investment; yet its per capita income has scarcely

risen above $70 since independence. Indonesia expelled the Dutch and expro-
priated their enterprises and in the 1950s and 1960s was one of the few developing countries with falling per capita income. A distinction must be made
between the effects of colonialism and other sources of poverty. Let us first
examine the "opening up" process of an underdeveloped country to economic relations with the outside world under colonial regimes.

THE "OPENING UP" PROCESS: THE EMERGENCE OF DUALISM [1]

On the eve of their colonial era, countries such as Indonesia, Burma and
Malaysia were generally fairly sparsely populated in relation to their potential
natural resources. Foreign enterprise, assisted by colonial government policy,
developed a few primary products for export; measures for economic development consisted mainly in attempts to persuade or force traditional people into
new ways of life represented by the money economy, for example, by stimulating their demand for imports and by taxing them so that they were obliged
to turn to cash crops or work in the newly opened mines and plantations.

The growth of foreign trade failed to bring overall economic development
in Asian and African countries, although these countries did experience economic growth. During the nineteenth and twentieth centuries, their export
sectors expanded very rapidly. The value of Indonesian exports grew over
tenfold between 1880 and 1920; Malayan exports increased nearly fourteen-
fold between 1906 and 1950. Other countries show similarly dramatic growth
of exports; in Burma, exports grew by 5% per year between 1870 and 1900,
and Thailand enjoyed a comparable rate of expansion. Why did the growth in
value of exports not have favorable effects in the rest of the economy?

It is too often assumed that the effects of industrialization and investment
generally will spread quickly to the rest of the economy, determining as Marx
put it the whole "superstructure" of culture, attitudes, and institutions. In reality, it is sometimes the reverse. Since the "spread effects" from industrialization depend a great deal on the availability of education, on prevailing
attitudes and institutions, the spread effects in underdeveloped countries are
often slow and incomplete. In the nineteenth century several factors worked
against spread effects: workers' willingness to accept very low wages (which
were not considered low relative to efficiency) and the abundance of the labor
supply. Some entrepreneurs also believed that it was difficult to recruit an adequate labor force in the light of what they conceived to be the general
indolence of the people, their disinterest in increasng their incomes, and the
lack of accuracy and finish in their work. The reluctance of European entrepreneurs to make heavy investments requiring a large supply of skilled workers, and their preference for simple labor-intensive techniques, left labor productivity low and afforded few training facilities. The same factors also
provided an incentive to choose wholly capital-intensive techniques, requiring

---

[1] This section draws heavily on Hla Myint, *The Economics of the Developing Countries* (New
York: Frederick Preager, 1964), especially chapters 2, 3, and 4.

relatively few skilled workers, where such methods were technically possible. The intermediate kind of technique requiring fairly large numbers of workers in skilled occupations were shunned by entrepreneurs, and it is these intermediate techniques that provide the best means of training large numbers of workers. Some opportunities occurred on the plantations and in the mines, but these were diluted by the high labor turnover; traditional peoples keep one foot in their tribal and village economies and look upon wage labor as a temporary expedient.

Meanwhile foreigners held the managerial positions, and very often even the middlemen between the big European concerns and the indigenous population were foreigners. Indians and Chinese in Southeast Asia, Indians in East Africa, Syrians and "Coast Africans" in West Africa contacted, and in some areas still contact, local consumers and act as money lenders. They operate as a buffer between the indigenous population and the advanced Western society, thus depriving the former of the educating and stimulating effect of direct contact. Here, once again, colonial administrators claimed that the indigenous people were culturally disinclined to engage in these activities.

The most damaging colonial policy however was the failure to promote the spread effects in the secondary and tertiary sectors of the colonial economy. In most Asian and African countries, colonial policy was directed toward promoting those sectors in the "mother country," not in the colony. According to the principle of comparative advantage, the imperial powers regarded themselves as the best producers of manufactured goods and the Asians and Africans as ideally endowed to produce rubber, coconut, other foodstuffs, and raw materials. Most financing, transporting, storing, insuring, and processing of industrial raw materials occurred *outside* the colonial country.

In sum, the contributions of Western enterprise to colonial development were mainly improvements in local transport and communications, discoveries of new mineral resources, and acting as middlemen between the peasant and the world market. Even after many decades of rapid economic development, the majority of the population of many colonial countries still remained as poor, as ignorant, and as remote from modern economic life as they were before.

The question remains as to why increasing capital investment and swelling export earnings did not in themselves bring steadily rising incomes in the colonies. In spite of their inferior bargaining position there is evidence that as peasant producers found new markets for their crops, and as capital flowed into the plantations, mines, oil fields, and refineries, per capita incomes of the native peoples did rise initially. However, resulting improvement in living standards began the population explosion. This impact was augmented by public health measures. As the colonial powers shifted from trading to settlement, the colonists took an interest in public health; by taking measures to eradicate smallpox, malaria, typhoid, plague, and other diseases, they greatly reduced the incidence of these diseases among the native peoples. Maintenance of law and order also reduced death rates by hampering local warfare, while improved transport lessened the impact of famine.

Here we see a further significant divergence in the economic history of the advanced and underdeveloped countries. To be sure, in the advanced countries of the West, also, an initial increase in population growth seems to have followed the first wave of rapid industrialization. The rise in *per capita income* continued long enough, however, and the subsequent drops in fertility rates came soon enough to permit continued economic growth. In many underdeveloped countries, the initial favorable impact of investment was swamped by population growth because of the *longer lag* between the drop in mortality rates in the early stages of industrialization and the subsequent drop in fertility rates. No one knows for certain why this crucial longer lag appeared. Some evidence suggests that the drop in fertility rates in Europe and in the New World was concomitant with urbanization. Development in Asia and Africa, centered as it was on plantations, mines, oil fields, and exports of raw materials initially brought more industrialization than urbanization. Industrialization confined to the production of raw materials can proceed very far without seriously disrupting the pattern of village life led by most of the people. Hence the checks on family size enforced by the urban industrialization of Europe and the New World operated less effectively in the underdeveloped countries.

Had the factories for processing the raw materials been established in the colonies, along with the accompanying services in the tertiary sector, the colonial people might also have urbanized, and their population patterns might have more closely resembled those of the European countries. Instead the fruits of development were swamped by the population explosion.

This difference in the population patterns led to a further crucial difference. Production techniques coming in from the West were designed, almost without exception, to replace labor with machinery. The industrial sector was characterized by relatively fixed technical coefficients (fixed proportions in which factors of production must be combined) or was assumed by entrepreneurs to be so (some production processes, such as petroleum refining actually come very close to having fixed factor proportions). Employment opportunities in the small industrial sector, therefore, did not expand at the same rate as population growth. Thus the population increase had to seek a livelihood in the rural sector, where adaptation does indeed take place, since a wide range of techniques or combinations of labor and capital will give the same output.

The rest of the story follows closely the predictions of the classical economists concerning diminishing returns. In Indonesia, for example, the initial response to population growth was to bring additional land under cultivation. Eventually good land became scarce; and as population continued to grow, techniques became increasingly labor-intensive; irrigated rice culture was substituted for shifting dry rice culture. Finally the point was reached when all the land was already cultivated highly labor-intensive techniques. With continuing population growth, disguised unemployment began to appear. In Indonesia at the time of the transfer of sovereignty in 1949, only 7% of the labor force had been drawn into the modern sector, and on the island of Java, where the peasant-agriculture sector is concentrated, population density had reached fifteen hundred per square mile. In Malaysia, on the other hand, 50% of the labor force had been drawn into the modern sector (mainly into the rubber and oil plantations) by Independence Day; this structural change is why that country fared so much better than its neighbors.

Colonial development left the largest share of the labor force of most under-developed countries in the most inefficient sector of the economy. Peasant agriculture such as that in Southeast Asia was "efficient" in the sense that, through extremely labor-intensive techniques, the peasant contrived to feed his family on a very small holding. But in terms of man-year productivity or ability to compete in world markets, it was highly inefficient. So long as the bulk of the population was employed in the traditional sector, the countries would be poor.

HOLLOW FRONTIERS: "BOOM AND BUST" PATTERNS OF GROWTH

Population pressure is hardly the key problem in the larger Latin American countries, yet there, too, foreign trade failed to bring widespread prosperity. Most Latin American countries have enjoyed periods of rapid growth of exports; Brazil provides a good example. Each era of Brazilian development has had its own special growing point: sugar, livestock, minerals, rubber, coffee, and manufacturing. At one time or another, Brazil has been the world's major exporter of sugar, gold, rubber, and coffee. However, until recently each of these sources of growth has produced the well known "boom and bust" pattern of development: a relatively brief period of expanding activity, followed by stagnation or decline, with only limited impact on the rest of the country. The sugar industry in the northeast, the first focal point of growth in Brazil, became a problem industry, hardly able to hold its own in competition with sugar produced in other regions of Brazil and elsewhere in the world. The mineral boom has passed, leaving ghost towns in its wake. The most spectacular of all boom-and-bust periods was the brief rubber "bubble" which has left behind a small, high-cost industry, unable to meet even domestic requirements, along with empty opera houses and other evidences of short-lived prosperity.[2] Coffee today remains the major export, but it too has become a problem commodity (price instability, crop hazards) rather than a generator of growth for the economy as a whole.[3] The current industrial boom is much more promising. The new wave of industrial development has lasted now for a generation, and since 1964 has brought to Brazil very high rates of growth; there is now good reason to believe that Brazil is at long last on a path of sustained development. The question still remains as to why this take off was so long delayed.

In comparison with other large countries of recent settlement (Canada, the United States, Australia), what is striking about Brazil is this failure of successive waves of development, each based on a new export, to generate

---

[2] When rubber cones were transported to Malaya and Indonesia, Brazil's natural rubber could not compete because of transport costs.

[3] Coffee suffers from fluctuations of world coffee prices.

"spread effects" to the rest of the economy and to populate unsettled areas. The "ratchet effect," so essential to the widespread diffusion of high rates of growth among all sectors and regions of a country, has only recently occurred in Brazil. Except for a modest contribution of capital and entrepreneurship from the coffee sector to the recent industrial development, each new wave of growth has been almost entirely discrete. There has been very little transfer of profits and skills of the "leading sector" and "propulsive region" of one era to the "leading sector" and "propulsive region" of the next, unlike the progressive movements into the interior of the United States and Canada. Since development opportunities were often geographically far apart, sheer distance helped to prevent spread effects, creating "hollow frontiers": large empty spaces were left between developing areas. The frontier towns of Campo Grande and Corumba, for example are separated from the large east-coast urban centers by hundreds of miles of unsettled territory, creating problems of transportation and communications.

Profit transfers also reduced spread effects. In the case of Brazil, most of the profits and much of the expertise generated by the successive waves of development were transferred abroad, particularly in the early phase of development. Later the profits went into luxury consumption rather than investments in other sectors.

In the Brazilian experience we also see the detrimental effects of the trade in precious metals, discussed in the previous chapter. In many ways, the gold discoveries did more harm than good to Brazil. They made it possible for her economy to survive on the basis of gold exports to Europe (mainly to the United Kingdom) without developing her own manufacturing industry. There was no possibility of transfer of technology from Portugal, because Portugal's budding manufacturing industry had been destroyed by the Methuen Treaty of 1703 between Portugal and England which gave Portuguese wines a privileged position in the English market, and English manufactured goods a favored place in the Portuguese market. By comparison, capital and skilled labor were flowing together to Canada, the United States, and later to Australia, where emigrants provided the management and the labor skills for the new undertakings. This movement of capital, accompanied by the needed transfer of skills and technical knowledge facilitated a high rate of technological progress, and goes a long way toward explaining the better economic performance of these countries.

Meanwhile in a decree of 1785, the Portuguese themselves had even prohibited manufacturing activities in Brazil. No one seemed to care very much at the time, because of the greater attractions of the mining activities. But as in the case of the sugar boom, while per capita incomes generated were so high, much of the earnings from gold production were spent on imports, and much of the balance was transferred abroad. The same kind of thing can happen today with oil production. Even Venezuela with her vast reserves of oil until recently experienced difficulty in "sowing the petroleum"—utilizing petroleum earnings to finance more general development. In sum, a "boom and bust" story can usually be explained by transfer of profits abroad, lack of expertise, lack of genuine commitment by domestic government. Limited supplies of other resources—or isolated resources—are also often part of the explanation.

THE ONE-CROP ECONOMY

This latter restraint—a narrow resource base—poses a major problem in many African countries. The "one mineral" economies and "one-crop" economies have difficulty in spreading growth in the form of a variety of economic activity, because of lack of other resources. It is easier for countries as rich as Libya to "sow the petroleum" in spite of its narrow resource base, but for a "one-crop economy," such as Senegal, "sowing the peanut oil" can prove very difficult. In contrast to Southeast Asia and Brazil, Senegal has very little to work with. Situated in the tropics, Senegal soils are for the most part poor and its mineral resources insignificant, and much of the country is arid for most of the year.

However, the soil and the climate that were so forbidding for other forms of agriculture proved to be excellent for peanuts. The peanut plant was imported from Brazil by the Portuguese in the sixteenth century, but for three centuries it served only as a supplementary source of nutrition for the peasants. What made the difference was the discovery in the mid-nineteenth century that an excellent oil could be made from peanuts. Peanuts quickly became the major product of the country; production rose from 180,000 tons in 1913 to 450,000 in 1945 and to nearly 1,000,000 tons in recent years. The whole economy was built around peanuts—the transport system, the financial institutions, the tax system. Processing peanuts became the principal industrial activity. But, unfortunately, there were no other resources to permit significant spread effects from the growth of the export sector, limited as it was to a single agricultural product and its by-products, and limited also by a small population. Annual per capita income rose in the 1950s to about $230 a year, which is fairly high by West African standards, but there it has stuck, although in recent years, efforts have been made to branch out into light industry and tourism.

Thus far we have been speaking of colonialism, and we have found its impact on economic and social development of the colonies to have been mixed at best. But what of countries that were already politically independent in the nineteenth century, but still dependent on foreign investment?

FOREIGN INVESTMENT IN INDEPENDENT COUNTRIES

Foreign investment is often put forward as an effective instrument for transferring needed packages of managerial know-how, scientific and technical skills, and capital. But there is high controversy as to whether foreign investment helps or hinders development.

The argument against foreign investment on economic grounds is based on the cost of servicing foreign debt relative to the benefits it brings. Wendell C. Gordon, for example, has shown that even in the United States, the cost of servicing foreign debt exceeded new net capital inflow from about 1830 on.[4] He also points out that foreign investment may also delay the development of domestic cadres of managers, scientists, and technicians. However, we are confronted here with a matter of fact; the relationship of debt service to net capital inflow is not the only element involved in appraising the contribution of foreign enterprise—nor even that plus the impact on long-run supply of skills. The question is whether in the United States, for example, the railways and the canals could have been built at all, at the time they were constructed, without British capital and high-level skills. The debt incurred was repaid out of the much higher level of income the imported capital and skills helped to produce. The question cannot, unfortunately, be answered with precision; no one can say what would have happened to the rate of economic growth in the United States if no foreign investment had taken place.

However, a striking example of both the advantages and disadvantages that foreign investment may bring is provided by the record of United States investment in Cuba, which ran close to a billion dollars in the years preceding the Castro revolution.

MONO TRADE AND MONO INVESTMENT

When Castro's revolution took place in 1959, Cuba's statistics placed her as economically advanced, compared with most Latin American countries. Per capita income was estimated at $500; only 42% of the labor force were still engaged in agriculture, and her infrastructure was highly developed in comparison to other Latin American countries. On closer inspection, however, the Cuban economic and social situations had characteristics of an underdeveloped country: per capita income of peasant families was below $100 a year, the level of health, nutrition, and education was low. About 40% of the total population was illiterate. No more than .5% had completed a full five years of university education, yet unemployment or underemployment was all too common among lawyers, doctors, engineers, and architects. In general unemployment and underemployment were at very high levels, mainly because the economy was stagnant.

The high level of Cuban income in 1959 was mainly due to the past growth of the sugar industry (where U.S. private investment was concentrated); the stagnation of the economy was a result of the stagnation of the sugar industry. The explanation, therefore, of the failures of prerevolutionary Cuba lies largely in answering why the sugar industry dominated the Cuban economy as long as it did. Why did not Cuba, like other sugar producing countries such as Indonesia, the Philippines, and Brazil, follow the obvious course of diversifying production when sugar no longer enjoyed a buoyant market? Cuba had the soil to do it; most of Cuba's land is extremely fertile, adaptable to large-scale mechanical agriculture, and well-watered. And why did Cuba not develop her other resources further than she did? Her resource endowment is not espe-

[4] Wendell C. Gordon, "Foreign Investment," University of Houston *Business Review,* Fall 1962.

cially rich but the country has large deposits of iron and nickel, and useful reserves of chrome, manganese, copper, limestone, marble, and clay. Why did agricultural productivity remain relatively low, mining relatively insignificant, industrialization relatively retarded? And to what extent was Cuba's major investor—the United States responsible? Let us look at the record.

American promotion of the sugar industry made it a leading sector in the economy for some decades. Cuba's revolution against Spain at the end of the eighteenth century was followed by very rapid growth of the sugar industry through sales to the United States market. During the early decades of this century, Cuba's economy developed rapidly, bringing significant rises in *per capita income*. The sugar industry became more capital intensive and American investors provided much of the capital. The expansion of the sugar industry was able to outrun population growth and ultimately absorb close to a quarter of the Cuban labor force into the modern sector of the economy.

Levels of living seem to have stopped rising about the middle of the 1920s. Once sugar ceased to be a solid growing point, most sugar growing countries diversified; Cuba did not. Part of the explanation lies in Cuba's trading relations with the United States. At a time when other countries were beginning to diversify and industrialize behind a protective tariff wall, Cuba under the United States Reciprocal Trade Agreement of 1934 was lowering import duties, limiting quantitative restrictions on imports, reducing taxes on products originating in the United States, and eschewing exchange control. This agreement was signed following the crash in sugar prices during the downswing of the thirties. The United States introduced a quota system for sugar under which Cuba and other exporters to the United States received a price slightly above that of the world market. No doubt at the time this agreement was deemed good fortune, coming as it did in the depths of the Depression. But the social cost proved very high; Cuba was left in the vise of "bitter sugar," with her chances of industrialization drastically reduced.

By 1958, Cuban foreign trade was overwhelming dependent on the United States for both exports and imports. About two-thirds of Cuban exports went to the United States and about three-quarters of imports came from the United States. From a strictly economic point of view, there is no great disadvantage in such dependence on a single market for exports and imports, provided that the market itself enjoys stable growth without sharp shifts in taste or innovations of a kind that would displace major exports. However, the United States' demand for its main import from Cuba—sugar—became stagnant if not declining.

This excessive dependence on the United States market was aggravated by the predominant position of United States investments in capital movements as well. By 1934, Americans had increased their investments in Cuba to the extent of 1.1 billion dollars; 600 million dollars were in the sugar industry and 235 million dollars in utilities and railways. The intermeshing of the foreign investors with the Cuban elite advanced so far that by 1945 about half the shares of the big Cuban sugar properties came to rest in the elite residential districts of Havana. A similar proportion remained in the United States. There was little overall increase in the United States investment in Cuba between 1929 and 1958, with the result that in the latter years there was a net capital outflow from Cuba to the United States.

Not only was there a net outflow of capital, but investment within the country was not maximizing efficiency in terms of the Cuban economy as a whole. In agriculture, Cuban cane yields were among the lowest in the world. There was little investment in improving cane varieties, in irrigation, or in fertilizers. Instead, large tracts of land were held fallow. This policy is obviously good business from the standpoint of the firm when land is plentiful, and cheap. In 1959 the major sugar concerns controlled nearly one-fifth of Cuban land, yet only about half of it was kept under sugar cane at any one time. The other half was held as a reserve, or put to lower-yield uses such as pasture for cattle grazing. The Annual Report of the Year 1957 of the United Fruit Company states that of the 147,770 acres owned by the company in Cuba, 50,000 acres were held in reserve—that is, fallow. The obvious alternative would have been to introduce subsidiary crops to alternate with the sugar. A pressing reason for doing so was the high seasonality of sugar production, and consequent high seasonal unemployment. Planting, harvesting, and grinding together provide employment for only a few months in the year, but during these seasons, the requirement for labor is heavy; during the "dead season," employment in the sugar enterprises drops to a skeleton staff for maintenance only, together with a small amount of replanting. With secondary reductions in employment in transportation and shipping, it is estimated that at least one-fifth of the total labor force was completely unemployed between August and October, while more than half the gainfully occupied agricultural population was employed for no more than four months in the year. The effect of the dead season was such that for most of the year the rural population had to give up meat, rice, beans, and coffee for plantains, roots, and cane juice.

Solving this problem with diversification of agriculture seems to have been blocked by a lack of dynamic interplay between government and enterprise, a collaboration essential (in either a socialist or nonsocialist country) for launching development. The incentive to introduce subsidiary crops was destroyed, Andrés Bianchi has suggested, because welfare legislation required the sugar factories to pay the same minimum wage in the dead season as during the sugar harvest. "Because of the vast area and financial resources controlled by the cattle and sugar industries, diversification on a significant scale was not possible without their cooperation. Artificially high labor costs, great concentration of land ownership and the pull of routine and tradition made such cooperation unlikely or negligible."[5]

The cattle ranches were operated on much the same principle of extensive land use rather than large expenditures on fertilizers or on storage facilities. Enormous herds grazed on thousands of acres of land. In the wet season, a great deal of grass was wasted for want of silos for storing fodder; in the dry

[5] Andrés Bianchi "Agriculture—Prerevolution" in Dudley Seers, ed., *Cuba: The Economic and Social Revolution* (Chapel Hill: University of North Carolina Press, 1964) p. 90.

season when the grass became sparse, the cattle weight and milk yields dropped sharply.

Industrialization also seemed unnecessarily retarded: production was expanding less rapidly than national income as a whole. According to Edward Boorstein, who worked as an economist in Cuba from 1960 to 1963 for various Cuban government agencies, Cuba's industry was suffocated by the large flow of imports mostly from the United States. In his review of the effects of United States investment in Cuba,[6] he declared that Cuba's internal market was dominated by every conceivable kind of imported good, from cornflakes and tomato paste, to nails, tractors, and passenger cars, from thread to all types of clothing.

The corporations did not deliberately plot to strangle Cuba, Boorstein says; they simply acted in accordance with business principles; their job was to sell Cadillacs or whiskeys, not to decide whether the importing country could put its foreign exchange to better use than providing luxuries to a privileged minority. In sum, what was "good for General Motors" did not prove to be good for Cuba.

From the turn of the century up to the middle-twenties, United States investment provided an effective instrument for transferring needed packages of managerial know-how, scientific and technical skills, and capital; however, once development ceased to be a "natural state of affairs," the interplay between government and investor proved inadequate. A wiser, stronger Cuban government (or even an efficient colonial administration) might have steered private capital investment towards more useful enterprises. Rather than passing welfare legislation insisting on year-round maintenance of wage levels, for example, the government might have done better to pass laws encouraging diversification, and allow a lower wage to be paid in the off season, as has been done in Castro's Cuba. As it was, the Cuban economy fell between the two stools.

To be fair, it must be pointed out that diversification does not always prove to be a panacea, as Castro was to discover in the first years after his takeover. Moreover, even without the Reciprocal Agreements, Cuba would have faced the problems of a small country trying to industrialize, with a small internal market to which the present sluggish state of the Cuban economy bears witness.

THE "BACKWASH EFFECTS" OF INTERNATIONAL TRADE

Myrdal carries the inquiry into causes of underdevelopment far beyond capital transfers, population growth, and narrow resource bases. He contends that the relative lack of development "was not primarily forced upon the underdeveloped countries by devious policy designs by the colonial powers."[7] It was mainly the natural outcome of the market forces. Trade between underde-

[6] Edward Boorstein, *The Economic Transformation of Cuba,* Monthly Review Press, New York, 1968.

[7] Gunnar Myrdal *The Challenge of World Poverty* (New York: Random House, 1970), p. 60.

veloped and advanced countries, far from tending toward equality of productivity and incomes as the classical economists claimed, results in a tendency
away from equilibrium, a vicious spiral bringing increasing discrepancies between productivity of advanced and underdeveloped countries. This unfavorable impact on the development of the backward countries Myrdal calls
"backwash effects."

> In the normal case there is no . . . tendency towards economic self-stabilization in
> the social system. The system is not by itself moving towards any sort of balance
> between forces, but is constantly on the move away from such a situation. In the
> normal case a change does not call forth countervailing changes, but instead, sup-
> porting changes, which move the system in the same direction as the first change
> but much further. Because of such circular causation a social disequilibrium tends
> to become cumulative and often to gather speed at an accelerating rate.[8]

Myrdal begins his analysis with the tendency toward regional inequalities
in a single country. The growing communities exert a strong agglomerative
pull, accelerating their rate of growth and bringing increasing stagnation or
decline in other parts of the country. No offsetting forces arise to prevent the
acceleration of this shift of economic activity from decadent to progressive
regions. Any accident or shock giving a momentary advantage to one region
can start this chain of disparate growth movements.

Myrdal cites the expansion of the north and the retrogression of the south of
Italy following political unification in 1860 as a dramatic example of growing
regional disparities following the "shock" of the liberation of trade. Before
unification, Italy was divided into seven national states, each constituting
more or less a closed economic system, extremely diverse in size and political
and economic institutions. While there was no marked difference in employment structure at the time of unification, the seeds of disproportionate growth
were already there: the north was much better endowed with social overhead
capital (such as education and roads), especially transport facilities. The fu-
sion of these closed economic systems into a unified economy has had continuing effects on regional development. The consequent freeing and widening of the markets conferred such competitive advantages on the industries in
already established centers of expansion that even the handicrafts in the more
backward regions were thwarted. At the same time, regions not touched by
the expansionary momentum could not afford to keep up good road systems
and other public utilities at a level comparable to the expanding centers.

Myrdal also reports two striking correlations discovered in the studies of
the Economic Commission for Europe; first regional disparities are greater in
poor countries than in rich ones, and, second, the disparities are increasing in
poor countries and decreasing in rich ones. A large part of the explanation for
these two broad correlations, he says, may be found in the important fact that
the higher the level of economic development that a country has already attained, the stronger the spread effects will usually be. Generally speaking (as

---

[8] Idem, *Economic Theory and Under-Developed Regions.* (London: Duckworth, 1957), pp.
13, 28, 29.

noted above) at a low level of economic development spread effects are relatively weak.

REGIONAL INTEGRATION IN THE UNITED STATES

Myrdal's explanation fits the American story. Historically the United States has been more successful in achieving regional integration of its economy than any other country comparable in size and geographic diversity. From 1840 to 1880 the overall tendency was centrifugal, that is, the gaps in per capita income of regions tended to increase, resembling the characteristic trend in underdeveloped countries. From 1880 to 1920, however, there was a strong centripetal tendency in regional per capita incomes. While the new movement was interrupted from 1920 to 1930 by a mild centrifugal tendency, after 1930 an extraordinary, almost perfect, inverse correlation developed between the *levels* of per capita income and *rates of growth*. The southeast was the poorest region in 1930 but enjoyed the most rapid growth in the following twenty years. The southwest was second lowest and had the second highest rate of growth from 1930 to 1950. The regions richest in 1930, on the other hand, had relatively slow rates of growth in the following two decades.

The whole history of interregional relations in the United States resembles a colossal game of "follow the leader" in which one region after another takes a turn at being the leader. Lagging regions somehow managed eventually to become leading regions again. It is almost as though Adam Smith's "invisible hand" were operating in the American economy in a fashion never envisioned by Adam Smith himself. A consequence of this tendency for centripetal movements to appear and reappear is that the United States has eliminated the vast regional differences in per capita income that still plague other large regionalized countries of recent settlement.

No other country has enjoyed quite this pattern of interregional relations. The Industrial Revolution of Europe was not accompanied by such mass movements of population and frontier development. By the time the Industrial Revolution came along, most of the centers of European population had already been established, and while there were differences in rates of growth, urbanization took place simultaneously throughout most of Europe. However, something like this "follow the leader" pattern took place in Europe in the post World War II years, but with an accelerated pace. Partly under the impetus of the Common Market, one country after another "took off" into fresh development, with the success of Germany and France sparking fresh development in Spain, Portugal, and Greece. Europe in general seemed "over the hump" into a stage where centripetal tendencies were taking hold.

BACKWASH EFFECTS ON UNDERDEVELOPED COUNTRIES

Myrdal's thesis provides a convincing explanation for the continuing and increasing disparities between rich and poor countries and for the acute regional disparities within underdeveloped countries. The course of the international backwash was probably set when the Portuguese found their way around the Cape of Good Hope. Subsequently the European traders acted as a buffer rather than a link between Asia and the more rapidly progressing parts of the world. The fifteenth century had been one of relative stagnation in Europe and Asia alike; the sixteenth century brought the first stirrings of the subsequent Industrial Revolution to Europe; the transition from feudalism to commercial capitalism was well advanced, and the Agricultural Revolution was on its way. Had Asians carried trade to Europe rather than the other way around some of the "preconditions for takeoff" might have rubbed off on Asians as well. And had the Asians had a suitable education system when the Westerners launched the first large-scale modern enterprises, local staff might have been engaged. Instead Asia continued to stagnate technologically. A basically similar situation developed in Africa, and to a lesser extent in Latin America.

The pervasiveness of the continuing backwash effects appears even in the Green Revolution. Here, one would think, was an opportunity for the poor nations to begin to pull abreast of the advanced nations. Yet new grains and new techniques tend to help the relatively more advanced countries, and to help the richer, more educated farmer, because their introduction requires both capital and new skills. The new cereal strains are successful only when precisely adapted to soils, rainfall, and temperature, when combined with exactly the right fertilizers and pesticides; and when sophisticated modern irrigation systems permit precise waterflow. Higher yields also require increased investment in storage, transport, and marketing facilities.

Marxists are inclined to brand these discrepancies as yet further capitalist failures. However, wealthy farmers, whatever their political complexion, are often rich because their land is rich. In China, wide differences in per capita income among the rural communes are related to such factors as differences in soil fertility, availability of water, climate, and distance to urban markets. A 1965 survey of thirteen communes found that income per worker in the richest commune was 3.4 times as high as in the poorest. In other words, backwash effects must be fought in virtually all aspects of development.

REGIONAL GAPS AND TRADE-OFF CURVE THEORY

Carrying the backwash theory further, we can make an important link between regional gaps and the current phenomenon of unemployment and inflation appearing side by side.

The relationship of trade-off curves to regional gaps became apparent when the senior author was investigating two weaknesses of the Canadian economy: first, among advanced countries, Canada has to explain the acute and *persisting* regional gaps in Canada (for an advanced country Canada's regional gaps are unusually large and intractable); and second, Canada has a particularly unfavourable combination of inflation and unemployment. The two phenomena appear to have a common cause. It was the author's strong hunch, since supported by empirical studies, that inflation is generated in the leading regions; and it was abundantly clear that unemployment runs rampant in the lagging regions. Thus in Canada, inflation is generated in booming Ontario and Alberta and to a lesser degree in British Columbia, and unemployment is concentrated in Quebec and the lagging Atlantic provinces. In Brazil, inflation is generated in the thriving São Paulo–Rio de Janeiro region, and to a lesser degree in the south, while unemployment and underemployment are concentrated in the lagging northeast and the north. In Indonesia, inflation is generated in the rich frontier islands of Sumatra, Kalimantan, and Sulawesi, with an assist from the expanding city of Djakarta, while unemployment and underemployment are concentrated in the rest of Java.

If we apply the classical or neoclassical theory regarding movements of goods, men and capital, it is obvious that large regional gaps persisting within the same national economy indicate some degree of immobility of factors of production. In the case of Canada, distances are vast—as in Brazil—discouraging migration and even capital transfers. Capital does not flow from the rich to the poor region in sufficient quantities to reduce inflation in the rich region and provide jobs in the poor region; nor does labor move to the rich region, to find there higher-income employment, in sufficient numbers to make the gap disappear. Regional gaps, in fact, are a measure of the lack of integration in the economy.

When this analysis is extended to the gap between rich and poor countries, it goes a long way to explaining the disappointing performance of a number of developing countries since independence, and the success of others.

INTERNATIONAL "REGIONAL" GAPS

In the post-World War II period, capital movements and migrations in Europe were major features of development. The United States poured over 25 billion dollars into Europe through the Marshall Plan. As the economies began to pick up, migrant workers from Italy, Greece, and Spain streamed into the northern European countries, notably France and Germany, and in general, European countries experienced a period of vigorous economic development.

By comparison, movements of men, goods, and capital among and within other continents have been much less dynamic during the same period. Migration has been restricted by immigration laws, by the prevalence of unemployment in some of the most advanced countries, and by sheer distance. Trade also has been restricted, while capital has flowed sluggishly to the backward regions of the world, with the result that a widening gap has emerged almost everywhere in the underdeveloped world between import needs and foreign exchange earnings. This gap largely explains the disappointing performance of the postwar years.

All in all, differences today in levels and patterns of development in the Third World can be explained in large measure by ill advised or exploitative colonial policies and their unexpected side effects, along with limitations of the environment and resource endowments. Since their independence, developing countries have continued to be plagued by the same major side effects: exploding populations on a horrendous scale, continuing backwash effects, and aggravated dualism. In the mid 1970s all these unfavorable impacts were exacerbated by world-wide recession.

We might conclude this analysis of the emergence and continuance of dualism at this point, were it not that the Dependency theorists violently disagree with this theory of dualism, and their views deserve careful consideration.

DEPENDENCY VERSUS DUALISM

In their attack on the theory of dualism, *dependentistas* make two major points:

1. The concept of dualism, with its division into "modern" and "traditional" sectors, suggests that there are two economic systems operating in (nonsocialist) LDC's, whereas in fact there is only one; international capitalism, which makes the decisions for the whole (nonsocialist) world and determines the outcome in social, economic and political terms.

2. Whereas standard or "Dualist" economists tend to suggest that the continuing poverty and growing gaps in developing countries reflect failure of development policies adopted by governments of developing countries, either because the wrong development models were chosen or because they were inefficiently applied, the truth is that the current situation in LDC's reflects the *success* of the policies imposed by international capitalism. The persistence of marginal groups of poor workers and peasants in developing countries reflects a consciously planned system, designed to protect profits by keeping peasant incomes and wages down and reserving for capitalists of advanced countries production requiring advanced technology.

In other words, there is sharp disagreement between the dependentistas and the Dualists with respect to the *intent* behind development plans and policies. Let us consider the Dependency theory, by examining the relationship between the Third World and the capitalist world today in terms of trade, foreign investment and foreign aid.

CURRENT TRADE PROBLEMS

There is a close link between growth and import capacity. The fast growers in the developing world have all operated with substantial amounts of foreign exchange; they have either received substantial foreign financing or they have enjoyed exceptional export opportunities for earning foreign exchange. Probably the greatest contributions thus far made by the industrialized countries to

TABLE 4.1 DISTRIBUTION OF THE WORLD TRADE

(In Percent)

	1965	1970	1971	1972	1973
World	100.0	100.0	100.0	100.0	100.0
1. Developed Regions	69.0	71.7	71.9	72.0	71.6
United States	14.6	13.6	12.5	11.9	12.4
Canada	4.4	5.2	5.1	4.9	4.4
Japan	4.5	6.2	6.9	6.9	6.5
European Economic Market	34.5	35.7	36.7	37.1	37.0
West Germany	9.6	10.9	11.2	11.2	11.9
France	5.4	5.7	5.9	6.3	6.5
United Kingdom	7.4	6.2	6.4	5.9	5.4
European Association of Free Trade	6.5	6.6	6.5	6.6	6.6
Other Countries of Western Europe	1.3	1.5	1.6	1.7	1.6
Australia and New Zealand	2.1	1.8	1.8	1.9	2.2
2. Developing Regions	19.3	17.3	17.2	17.1	17.7
Africa	4.1	4.0	3.8	3.7	3.6
Latin America	5.8	4.8	4.3	4.2	4.4
Other Countries of Western Hemisphere	0.9	0.8	0.9	0.8	0.7
Asia	4.7	4.1	4.1	4.1	4.3
Middle East	3.5	3.3	4.0	4.1	4.5
3. Centralized or Planned Economies	11.7	11.0	10.9	10.9	10.7

Source: Economic Commission for Latin America, *Estudio Economico de America Latina* (United Nations, 1973), p. 23. Figures derived from data provided by the *Monthly Bulletin of Statistics* (1968, 1973, 1974) of the United Nations.

international development in the 1950s and 1960s was the rapid and fairly steady growth in their own economies, which created a similarly rapid and steady growth of world markets. The developing countries have shared in this expansion of trade, but less than proportionately; since World War II the share of world trade going to the developing countries has decreased (See Table 4.1).

Foreign trade specialists usually trace the failure of foreign trade of developing countries to assure adequate development to one or more of five factors: concentration of exports in one or a few commodities, unstable markets, deteriorating balance of trade, deteriorating terms of trade, restrictions on international trade.

INSTABILITY AND CONCENTRATION

Developing countries suffer from violent fluctuations in both the prices and the volume of their primary exports, depending on cycles of demand, and bumper harvests or crop failures. This instability, augmented when there is a concentration of exports in very few items, results in violent fluctuations in foreign exchange earnings, and consequently in the capacity to import. Long-range programming of developmental investment is well nigh impossible under these circumstances.

Not only have prices been unstable, but during the postwar period, prices have tended to go down in relation to Third World countries' imports, leading

to the high controversy over deteriorating terms of trade, a condition to which
the dependentistas have attached great importance as evidence of capitalist
maneuvers.

DETERIORATING TERMS OF TRADE

During the 1950s the thesis was proposed that one reason for the continued
retardation of development in poor countries was an inevitable tendency towards "deteriorating terms of trade" for those countries. That is, according to
the argument, the prices of exports of developing countries have a tendency to
fall relative to prices of imports.

The theoretical explanation for the presumed historically deteriorating
terms of trade of underdeveloped countries rests partly on "Engel's Law":
i.e., in most countries the proportion of income spent on food falls as income
rises. Once a certain level of food consumption is reached, people will prefer
to spend increases in income on durable consumers' goods and services.
Imagine, for example, a typical underdeveloped country exporting petroleum
and plantation products; importing textiles, other consumer durable goods,
and luxury foodstuffs; and producing rice, fish, and handicraft products in the
rural sector. Favorable developments in the industrialized sector (improved
techniques, higher world market prices) will not increase proportionately the
demand for the output of the rural sector (the demand is "income-inelastic").
It may even fall, as the industrial workers substitute "superior" imported
consumer goods for local products ("income elasticity of demand is negative"). On the other hand, the demand for industrial products is elastic. Any
favorable development in the rural sector will increase the demand for industrial products imported into that sector (either from outside the country or
from the industrial sector of the same country) and again *reduce* the demand
for the rural sector's output. It seems very likely then, that there has been—
and still is—a trend toward deteriorating terms of trade between the *rural sector of underdeveloped countries* and the rest of the world.

It is also true that some underdeveloped countries have on occasion suffered declining terms of trade and that there has been a long-run tendency for
the terms of trade to turn against producers of raw materials and foodstuffs;
but one cannot establish a "law" from the evidence, particularly in the light
of changing world conditions. The empirical backing of this thesis was, in
fact, very thin. The original argument was based solely on trade of the United
Kingdom with the rest of the world. It is now clear that a "law" based on
nineteenth-century European experience cannot be generalized for late twen-
tieth-century Asia, Africa, and Latin America.[9] On the contrary, as societies
move through a spectrum of incomes per head which is still below nineteenth
century European levels, it is apparent that thresholds are reached where "in-

---

[9] For a recent and relatively cautious statement of the "terms of trade" doctrine by its origina-
tor, see Paul Prebisch, "A Critique of Peripherial Capitalism," *CEPAL Review,* first semester
1976, especially pp. 65–66.

come elasticity of demand'' (ratio of percentage increase in demand to percentage increase in income) is very high for *particular* foodstuffs, such as meat, wheat, sugar, and even rice. In any case, the assumption that advanced countries always import food and export manufactured goods, while developing countries do the reverse, is clearly wrong. Advanced countries are among the major exporters of foodstuffs, and it is the manufactured exports of developing countries that are most rapidly expanding.

In Latin America, however, the dependentistas argue that the tendency for the prices of exports from developing countries to fall to the prices of exports from advanced countries is related to the exercise of superior bargaining power of the advanced countries; developing countries sell in highly competitive markets they say, while advanced countries exercise monopoly power. It is true that the advanced countries have enjoyed superior bargaining power in the past, although their monopoly power may be waning, with more and more advanced countries (including Japan) coming to the fore. It is also true that advanced countries are transferring their own inefficiencies to the rest of the world through high prices. High costs require high prices if inefficient industries are to survive. And unfortunately, policy in most advanced countries is directed towards assuring that even inefficient industries should survive. Such measures are inflationary and ultimately tend to raise costs and prices of goods and services which are very efficiently produced as well as those which are inefficiently produced. In this fashion, the advanced countries export their inflation to developing countries, thus weakening the Third World's terms of trade through high export prices. This inefficiency is indicated in the slow rise of productivity (with the exception of Japan) in Table 4.2.

However, world shortages in primary products are raising prices; and as J. B. Clark predicted, as the Third World develops, the terms of trade are changing in favor of some developing countries. Indeed, the events of 1973 and 1974 have destroyed any remaining shred of credibility in the argument.

TABLE 4.2 GROWTH OF OUTPUT PER MAN-HOUR IN MANUFACTURING 1950–1974.

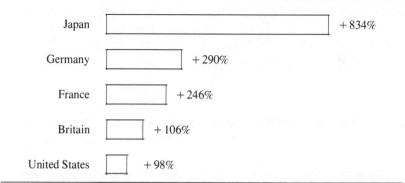

Japan	+ 834%
Germany	+ 290%
France	+ 246%
Britain	+ 106%
United States	+ 98%

Source: Norman Macrae "America's Third Century," *Economist,* October 25, 1975, pp. 17–25.

It is now clear that the foreign trade picture of developing countries is a good deal more complex, and cannot be described by any such sweeping generalization as was contained in the original versions of the "terms of trade" thesis. Many of the oil producing countries are still ranked as less developed; but it is obvious that for most of these countries the terms of trade have improved a good deal with the four- to sixfold increase in oil prices.

Of course, in the dependency analytical framework, the energy crisis of 1973 and since, arising from reduced exports and 400 percent higher prices of oil, is seen, not as exploitation of North Americans and Europeans by Arabs, but as exploitation of workers and peasants the world over by American, British, Dutch, French, and Arab capitalists working in unison to maximize their profits. Yet the high price of petroleum led in turn to price increases of 100% to 300% in a single year for vegetable oils, rubber and coconut products, indicating market action, rather than an omnipotent control of raw material prices on the part of the "center".

In other words, it is no longer meaningful to talk of "advanced" and "developing" countries where terms of trade are concerned. For any one country, the trend depends on the precise mix of its imports and exports; as an exporter of petroleum, bauxite, rubber, and palm oil, Indonesia is doing very well at time of writing; but neighboring Sri Lanka, as an exporter of tea and importer of petroleum, rice, flour, and sugar is doing very badly. Finally, terms of trade of less-developed countries with other less-developed countries, or of advanced countries with other advanced countries, are just as important as terms of trade between advanced and developing countries.

TRENDS IN DEMAND

Even if the terms of trade argument does not stand up as a general principle, there can be no doubt that many developing countries are hampered in their economic growth by balance of payments difficulties. The economically advanced countries are more than ever each others' best customers and primary producing countries do not benefit from expansion of world markets to the same degree as industrialized countries. The income elasticity of demand for major imports in a number of developing countries tends to rise more than the demand for their exports as world incomes rise. The faster increase in value of imports compared with exports has resulted in a reversal of the trade *balance* of underdeveloped countries in general.

TRADE RESTRICTIONS

The moral would follow that while the stronger position of primary exports improves their position temporarily, in the long-run, the ultimate answer to many development problems would seem to lie in the developing countries' present efforts to industrialize and to export manufactured goods. These efforts are adversely affected by restrictive policies of advanced countries, which impose barriers against the import of industrial goods in the form of tariffs and quotas. Certainly during the 1960s, we saw the first tentative movements towards reciprocal liberalization of international exchange, treating advanced countries and underdeveloped countries equally. During the 1970s advanced countries experimented with a system of generalized preferences without requiring reciprocity from the LDC's. But advanced countries still impose barriers by insisting on "voluntary" limitations of exports of developing countries.

As we shall see below, the capabilities of countries vary in the degree to which they can profit from a lifting of trade restrictions, but for a number of countries, it could make a great difference. Sri Lanka is a case in point. This small country has never had enough foreign exchange to operate at full potential capacity. At the present time, it has by Asian standards an excellent educational record (education is free through university) but a growing legion of educated unemployed and it would make a world of difference if trade restrictions were raised. It has been industrializing, and it has the potential to industrialize further, particularly in preparing agricultural products for export in a processed form.

Unfortunately commercial policies of the developed countries seem almost systematically rigged against such efforts of the underdeveloped countries to industrialize. The more processing involved in the production of a good, the higher the tariffs are likely to be. While the primary material may be let in duty free, the effective tariff on a semimanufactured commodity is often prohibitive. For example, Brazilian instant coffee entering the United States faces a 60% duty, compared with no-duty beans.

Since tariffs exist to protect domestic industries, preferential trade arrangements for developing countries confront the advanced countries with the challenge to expose some of their own industries to competition and, in some cases, to certain extinction. As a solution to this conflict, "plant transplants" were suggested some years ago as a smooth transition to a new international division of labor: enterprises in advanced countries that cannot compete with "cheap foreign labor" might be moved to the developing countries, thereby taking advantage of the low wages there. This idea mushroomed into the phenomenal growth of the multinational.

FOREIGN INVESTMENT AND THE MULTINATIONAL ENTERPRISES

The multinational enterprises (MNE's) have aroused a highly emotional debate. "For some," Wilfred Jenks comments (at the time Director General of the International Labor Office) "the multinational corporations are an invaluable dynamic force and instrument for the wider distribution of capital, technology and employment; for others, they are monsters which our present institutions, national and international, cannot adequately control, a law unto themselves which no reasonable concept of the public interest or social policy can accept." [10]

---

[10] International Labor Office, *Multinational Enterprises and Social Policy* (Geneva, 1973), p. ix.

The essential nature of the multinational or global enterprise lies in the fact that its managerial headquarters are located in one country (referred to as "the home country") while operations are carried out in a number of "host countries" as well. Not that MNE's are a new phenomenon. Multinational and multi-product enterprises existed already in the seventeenth century: the British East India Company and the Netherland East India Company were among the largest, most far-flung, and most spectacular; many of the plantation and mining companies of the nineteenth century, were also large-scale. These companies were mainly concerned with exploitation of natural resources, international trade, and international finance. Some of today's MNE's are similarly engaged. However, what characterizes today's version of the MNE's is a sharp shift away from such colonial patterns of investment, in favor of establishing *manufacturing* enterprise in the Third World.

The basic argument in favor of the MNE's is their efficiency. The multinational firms collect in their head offices, and quite often in their field operations and branch plants as well, the best entrepreneurial, managerial, scientific and engineering skills available. This battery of brains is then available for solving all manner of production, marketing and financing problems in any country, and in any line of economic activity, that offers interesting prospects. The highly skilled top management is backed up by large and high-quality research and development staffs. Together, these teams of highly qualified personnel produce a steady stream of innovations. When branch plants are opened, these technologies are transferred and, according to a study made by the International Labor Office (ILO), lead to a lively interaction of ideas, stimulating a two-way flow between home and host countries:

> The multinational corporation can usually set an example of enlightened and effective management in a developing host country. It can also have a direct impact on the development of national management cadres in the host country, by training national managers in the firm, who later go into local firms or government service.[11]

GROWTH OF THE MULTINATIONAL

At first glance, then, the concept of the "global factory" seems logical. The idea of at last pursuing true comparatage advantage on a global scale by pulling the vast labor force of the Third World into manufacturing would seem to set right the economic distortions of the past, and provide a means of spreading world wealth.

The move toward freer trade after World War II did, in accordance with neoclassical principles, stimulate a movement of capital and modern technologies into the Third World. High-cost producers in advanced countries, threatened with competition from cheaply produced industrial products (particularly from Japan) began to expand their production facilities into Asia, Africa, and Latin America. "Export platforms" were established in low-wage areas such as Hongkong, Taiwan, Singapore, and the United States-

[11] ILO, *Multinational Enterprises*, p. 62.

Mexican border area, where TV sets, cameras, calculators, stereo sets, and computers could be produced and then sold in advanced countries. Meanwhile, Japanese capital and technology was moving into Asia. Environmental considerations, the tightening supply of raw materials, combined with Japan's shift from standard manufacturing to knowledge- intensive industries, and the increasing reluctance of the Japanese to do factory work has been initiating what may prove to be a massive movement of Japanese capital into industry in neighboring countries such as South Korea, Taiwan, some of the Southeast Asian countries, and even into China. Meanwhile western producers have also established factories within the Soviet Bloc. Everyone was supposed to profit by this great new experiment. Bringing technologies that had already been developed at considerable expense at home, Western producers could apply them abroad with relatively little extra cost. On the other hand, the host countries would receive modern technologies, managerial expertise, jobs, finance capital, increase in earning from exports, and taxes from the global firm. Critics however deny these latter claims.

CURRENT CRITICISMS

Far from being a source of capital, the argument goes, the MNE's earn little foreign exchange, and by one device or another repatriate their profits. The MNE's, it is claimed, do not in fact provide significant amounts of capital to developing countries, and may even generate a net drain of capital and of foreign exchange. There is little doubt that the latter situation can occur. In the early 1950s a Brazilian Minister of Finance was heard to remark "If Brazil gets any more foreign investments, we are going to go broke." What he meant was that foreign enterprises were borrowing from Brazilian banks in cruzeiros in order to establish manufacturing and mining enterprises, making profits both in the domestic market and abroad, and then transferring these profits in foreign exchange. Moreover, large foreign enterprises like Exxon or General Motors are likely to be regarded by local investors and banks as better and safer investments than small local enterprises. (About 78 percent of the manufacturing operations of U.S. based global corporations in Latin America during the sixties were financed with local capital). Thus the presence of the MNE's in a developing country may attract local savings away from the investment in domestic enterprises.

It is also pointed out that the vertical integration which is characteristic of many MNE's permits swollen profit transfers and tax evasion. Vertical integration of the product from the extraction of raw materials through to the end product, opens the door to the creation of artificial "transfer prices." Profits can be transferred by overpricing imports from the parent firm for resale in domestic markets of the host country, or by overinvoicing raw materials and equipment obtained directly from the parent firm or another branch, so as to show a narrower profit margin in the host country. Thus, not only can profits be transferred beyond the agreed level, but taxes are reduced by the lower apparent profit. A study of U.S. based global corporations in Latin

America found that 75% conduct all export transactions with other sub-sidiaries of the same parent, and control prices to suit. They consistently charged on an average of 40% less for their exports than prices charged by local firms.[12] Guatemalan economist Gert Rosenthal, calculating the "financial contribution" of global corportion to the Central American Common Market countries found that while net inflows increased during 1960–71 by 344%, outflows rose by 982%.[13]

Critics insist that globals also like to maintain maximum control of their processes, marketing, and management. A study of 409 "transfer of technology" contracts, in Ecuador, Bolivia, Peru, Chile, and Colombia, shows that in almost 80% of them, the parent company totally prohibited the use of the transferred technology for producing exports. U.N. studies in India, Pakistan, the Phillippines, Mexico, and Iran indicate a similar widespread use of "restrictive business practices." In some cases, the local subsidiary was permitted to export to nearby markets too small to be of interest to the parent company, or to distant markets beyond its reach. Nor have they transferred key managerial responsibility. The International Labor Office study points out that while multinational corporations run courses for middle and junior management, relatively few of the local managers are promoted from the subsidiaries to top positions in the head offices in the home country.[14]

One of the most frequently voiced accusations against the MNE's is that they do not adapt their technology to the factor endowment of the developing countries. Despite the scarcity of capital and the redundance of labour, it is argued, they still use capital-intensive labor-saving techniques. That such techniques aggravate unemployment problems is well illustrated by agricultural modernization. Huge farms produce an average of four hundred times what small farms can produce, but they employ only fifteen times as many workers. Moreover, agricultural business is accused of affecting foodstuff distribution through its increasing control of land use. Agribusiness prefers to grow high-profit crops such as strawberries and asparagus for export rather than low-profit grains for local consumption. In Colombia, a hectare devoted to carnation cultivation reaps a million pesos a year, while wheat or corn brings only 12,500 pesos. Meanwhile local populations find local fruits and vegetables priced beyond their reach.

Multinationals are also blamed for introducing inappropriate life styles. Marshall Wolfe, Director of the Social Development Division of the U.N. Economic Commission for Latin America, maintains that the MNE's contribute to internal instability of developing countries, by accelerating the "revolution of rising expectation" to a point where no government of a developing

[12] Richard J. Barnet and Ronald E. Muller, *Global Reach* (New York: Simon and Schuster, 1974) p. 158.

[13] Gert Rosenthal, *The Role of Foreign Private Investment in the Development of the Central American Common Market,* Guatemala, 1973 (a study prepared under auspices of the Aldai Stevenson Institute of International Affairs, Chicago, and the Permanent Secretary of the Central American Common Market).

[14] ILO, *Multinational Enterprises,* p. 60.

country can hope to keep up with the demands of all the politically powerful groups within a society. In his view, this situation is particularly severe in Latin America:

> At prevailing per capita income levels, satisfactions of these taste for minorities that are much larger than the previous élites implies patterns of income distribution, patterns of distribution of public expenditure on services and urban infrastructure, and patterns of saving, investment and production that are just as remote from conventional conceptions of developmental priorities as they are from the publicly endorsed principles of social justice. The initiative for implantation of the new life styles has come mainly from the world center through the transnational corporations' mass media content . . .[15]

Finally, imported life styles threaten to stifle indigenous cultural creativity.

APPRAISAL

It is probably true, as the global managers claim, that the global corporations are the first in history with the organization, technology, and money to manage the world as a unit by integrating production on a worldwide scale. It is estimated that global corporations already have more than $200 billion in physical assets under their control, and that by 1985, two hundred to three hundred of them will control 80 per cent of all productive assets of the non-Communist world. A comparison of the annual sales of corporations with the gross national product of countries for 1973 reveals that in these terms, General Motors is bigger than Switzerland, or Pakistan; that Royal Dutch Shell is bigger than Iran, Venezuela, or Turkey; and that Goodyear Tire is bigger than Saudi Arabia. Moreover, by 1973, U.S. and Western European companies had already entered into more than twelve-hundred cooperative agreements with socialist governments. Finally, the average growth rate of the most successful global corporations is two to three times that of most advanced industrial countries.[16]

There can be little doubt that the introduction of the multinationals into the Third World has tended to aggravate the technological dualism inherited from the colonial regime, and that multinationals can be elusive of government control. In appraising the behavior of the MNE's, however, it is necessary to separate the responsibility of the multinationals from those of government, and to discern problems that have their roots in basic economic dilemmas. The problem of the Colombian carnations, for example, involves dilemmas of modernization often requiring government action to make necessary adjustments within the economy. Modernization, by displacing labor with capital, leads to a higher degree of specialization and thereby creates greater *dependence*. A shift from self-sufficient agriculture to producing crops for export is a case in point. If wheat and corn do not flow automatically through the market process to replace the wheat and corn which would have been

---

[15] Marshall Wolfe, "Approaches to Development: Who Is Approaching What?" *CEPAL-Review*, first semester 1976, pp. 151–152.

[16] Barnet and Muller, *Global Reach*, p. 15.

grown in the carnation fields, the government must insure that they are imported and distributed. Furthermore, displaced workers do not have the purchasing power to create a market for wheat and corn. If they do not find jobs through the employment market it is up to the government to devise alternative occupations for them. Through job creation the government can take care of a crucial responsibility for redistribution; it captures a fair share of the profits from the sale of carnations and channels them back into the economy. Wherever possible, however, the multinationals have a clear responsibility to adapt their technology to local conditions.

Certainly, rapid changes in technology can have adverse effects on local producers in a developing country. Replacement of artisan workshops and cottage industries by mass-production techniques can lead to unemployment and the squelching of potential indigenous enterpreneurial material. The question then arises as to whether or not there exists a *high productivity,* labor-intensive technology which can be applied over a wide range of manufacturing activities.

At first glance, the picture seems mixed. Two studies made in Indonesia suggest that the MNE's tend to transfer their technology to their subsidiaries intact.[17] On the other hand, a study made for the United Nations Institute for Training and Research (UNITAR) states that foreign firms operating in the Third World have investigated possibilities of employing more labor-intensive methods with reasonable care:

> Such successful modifications as have been made have resulted from disaggregating the production function and seeking out those operations that may be effectively modified, notably in the plant and in construction operations as well as in the simpler repetitive operations in technologically unsophisticated forms of food processing, pharmaceutical packaging and the like.[18]

A Japanese glass company, for example, operated a subsidiary in India which was about half the size of the company's plant in the home country, but employed three times as many workers, using manual methods for cutting sheet glass, materials handling, and crushing coal.[19] Years ago at the brand new, fully automated Standard Vacuum Company refinery in Bombay, more workers were observed outside, cutting the lawns with knives, than in the plant itself. But beyond such devices, which do not alter the total employment picture very much, UNITAR found little scope for replacement of capital-intensive with labor-intensive methods. One of the most thorough studies of choice of technology found substantial adaptations by MNE's to local conditions in Brazil.[20] Fixed capital per employee is markedly lower in the Brazil-

[17] Grant L. Reuber, *Private Foreign Investment in Development* (Oxford: Oxford University Press, 1973); Louis T. Wells Jr., "Economic Man and Engineering Man!" Choice of Technology in a Low Wage Country", *Public Policy* 21, no. 3, 1973, pp. 319–42.

[18] Walter A. Chudson, *The International Transfer of Commercial Technology to Developing Countries* UNITAR Research Reports No. 13 (New York, UNITAR, 1971.) pp. 25–26.

[19] Terulomo Ozawa, *Transfer of Technology from Japan to Developing Countries* UNITAR Research Reports No. 7 (New York, UNITAR, 1971) p. 13.

[20] Samuel A. Morley and Gordon W. Smith, "The Choice of Technology: Multinational Firms in Brazil," *Economic Development and Cultural Change* 25, No. 2 (January 1977) pp. 239–64.

ian plants than in the United States (as is value added per worker). The same firms use much more nonautomatic, general purpose machinery in Brazil than in the United States. For example, in the U.S., painting is highly automated in both the automobile and consumer durable goods industries; in Brazil only hand-held spray guns were found. However, the study makes the point that the adaptations were in response to the small size of the market rather than the abundance of cheap labor, and that the most important factor in choice of technology is scale of production, not the relative cost of labor and capital. While these studies suggest some flexibility, it seems that in general, technical coefficients (proportions in which factors of production are combined) are more or less fixed for most industries and for each scale of production.

As will be discussed in more detail in a later chapter, governments are beginning to find ways to curb and guide multinationals. In some cases, the host government is completely excluding foreign firms whose operations are deemed detrimental to the country. Guatemala, for example, decided to keep Sears Roebuck out of the country, because of its threat to small indigenous retailers. (This decision will be applauded by anyone who has searched in vain for an item, then looked vainly for a sales clerk in Sears' vast environs; or by anyone who has had the extraordinary good fortune to find a sales clerk, only to be told that the desired item is out of stock.)

When governments choose to accept the multinational, the objective is to curb and guide the multinationals through planning, legislation, regulation, and international codes of good behavior, in such a way as to dovetail the operation to the needs of the country—encouraging labor-intensive enterprises being a prime example. The ILO suggests that the right kind of contract is the key:

> Since the establishment, by a multinational corporation, of a subsidiary in a developing host country is preceded by months or even years of negotiation with the host government there is ample opportunity to plan, in direct collaboration with the government, for management development and training that will be of benefit both to the firm and to the host country, provided that such collaboration and planning are based on fairness and reciprocal respect for the aims of each party.[21]

But according to dependency theory, at least in its pure neo-Marxist form, such care in designing the contract would avail nothing because the multinationals exercise power on local governments and the local elite, and at the same time multinationals themselves form an exceedingly powerful club.

There can be little doubt that in today's world (as in the past) control of advanced technology is a source of power. If the management of MNE's, or at least the larger of them, are regarded as members of a species of "international club," and if, as Adam Smith maintained, such people cannot assemble together "even for merriment and diversion" without joining together in some new conspiracy in restraint of trade, the aggregation of the power of the MNE's can be awesome indeed. There is also no doubt that a meshing of interest among local governments, the local elites, and multinationals can exist—Cuba was a case in point.

On the other hand, the fact that the MNE's are scaling down their investments in the Third World (particularly in Latin America) suggests that they have *not* had the power to arrange things as they would like.

Present Trends in International Investment • While a great deal has been said concerning the misdoings of the multinationals, their managers in turn face a "hostile" climate in the Third World. Difficulties attending investment in the Third World include such problems as unrealistic profit limitations (hence the transfer prices), chronic uncertainty concerning tax laws, foreign exchange regulations, and possibilities of expropriation—not to mention being required in some cases to put money into the enterprises of ambitious generals or government officials. Multinational managers who really want to contribute to the development of the country (and there are many of these) do not relish it when the royalties and taxes which they do pay find their way into the Swiss bank accounts of politicians rather than being spent on development. Moreover, the climate has been deteriorating in *advanced* countries with regard to investment in the Third World.

It would appear that the amount of employment provided by MNE's in developing countries must be significant, if only because of the deep concern expressed by representatives of trade unions in advanced countries. According to the AFL-CIO, the U.S. Division of the Global Factory lost 900,000 jobs during the sixties. These losses were deemed largely due to industrial plants moving to Canada, Japan, Taiwan, Hongkong, and Mexico, reducing the United States to "a nation of hamburger stands." According to union spokesmen, this transfer not only reduced jobs, but exerted a downward pressure on wages by the demonstrated freedom of choice of location.

Whether from domestic pressure, or as a result of the hostile climate in some developing countries, patterns of investment are changing. Today the activities of the MNE's do not reflect primarily a transfer of capital from advanced countries, in order to exploit natural resources and cheap labour in the developing countries. Table 4.3 shows the changes in geographic distribution of American foreign investment in the fifties and sixties. Most striking is the

TABLE 4.3 PERCENTAGES DISTRIBUTION OF UNITED STATES DIRECT INVESTMENTS ABROAD, BY AREA, IN SELECTED YEARS, 1950–70

Area	1950	1960	1965	1970
Africa	2.4	2.8	3.9	4.4
Asia	8.5	7.0	7.2	7.2
Canada	30.4	34.2	31.0	29.2
Western Europe	14.7	20.4	28.3	31.3
of which: EEC	(5.4)	(8.1)	(12.7)	(15.0)
Latin America	38.8	28.3	22.0	18.8
Rest of world	4.3	7.3	7.7	9.0

Source: Survey of Current Business (Washington, DC, US Department of Commerce), Aug. 1963, pp. 18–19, Sep. 1967, p. 42, Oct. 1970, p. 31, and Oct. 1971, p. 32.

relative decline in importance of Latin America for United States direct foreign investment, and the relative growth of investment in Europe. (Some of the strongest attacks on MNE's, and on foreign investment in general, have come from Latin America). Asia also shows a slight decline in importance, Africa an increase. Table 4.4 indicates that the role of American direct investment in developing countries has declined substantially as a proportion of total activity, in favor of a significant increase in the relative importance of American investment in other highly developed market economies. Table 4.5 indicates that the United Kingdom as well as the United States is reducing the share of its direct investment abroad which is allocated to Latin America and the former British colonies (overseas sterling area) and increasing the relative importance of investment in Western Europe, North America, and the rest of the world. United States investment in Europe and European investment in the U.S. are growing simultaneously. Japan too is investing mostly in Europe, North America, and Australia.

Will this new trend in investment liberate the developing world from the advanced world at last? Once again the picture blurs. In comparing the mul-

TABLE 4.4 PERCENTAGE DISTRIBUTION OF UNITED STATES DIRECT INVESTMENTS ABROAD AS BETWEEN DEVELOPED AND DEVELOPING COUNTRIES IN SELECTED YEARS, 1950–70

	1950	1955	1960	1965	1970
Developed market economies	48.3	54.0	60.6	65.2	68.0
Developing countries	48.7	42.9	35.1	30.8	27.5
International, unallocated	3.0	3.1	4.3	4.0	4.5

Source: Survey of Current Business, Aug. 1957, p. 24, Aug. 1959, p. 30, Aug. 1963, pp. 18–19, Sep. 1967, p. 42, Oct. 1970, p. 31, and Oct. 1971, p. 32.

TABLE 4.5 UNITED KINGDOM NET DIRECT INVESTMENTS ABROAD[a] IN SELECTED YEARS, 1960–66

(Millions of US$)

Area	1960	1962	1964	1966
North America	124.6	51.5	97.4	171.1
Western Europe[b]	71.1	134.7	116.5	172.2
of which: EEC	(60.2)	(81.8)	(102.8)	(141.4)
Latin America[c]	40.9	38.9	50.7	31.4
Overseas Sterling Area	477.7	342.4	450.8	332.6
Rest of world	15.7	17.6	21.0	65.5
All areas	730.0	585.1	736.4	772.8

Source: European Free Trade Association: *EFTA foreign investment: Changes in the pattern of EFTA foreign direct investment* (Geneva, Mar. 1969), p. 32.

[a] Excluding oil and, for 1960 and 1962, insurance.

[b] Comprises members of the European Free Trade Association and the European Economic Community only.

[c] Listed as "South and Central America" in the source.

tinational to the colonial investors of old, there is one more significant difference; the volume of investment.

The astronomical statistics connected with the multinationals are somewhat misleading. It is seldom appreciated that in relation to the world economy, the flow of capital to the developing countries today is a trickle in comparison with the flood of capital to the developing countries in the nineteenth century, a torrent which helps to explain the takeoffs of the United States, Canada, Australia, New Zealand, and Argentina after heavy initial British investment. A. K. Cairncross estimated in 1953 that if the United States were to lend abroad on a scale equivalent in terms of per capita real income to that of the United Kingdom during the nineteenth century, the United States would have $600 billion of foreign investments.[22]

Today the figure would be closer to $2,000 billion. To match the *flow* of capital from the United Kingdom in the nineteenth century, relative to its per capita real income, the United States would have to carry out the entire Marshall Plan three times every year, which today would mean spending some $200 billion annually. Instead, there is only $50 billion of U.S. foreign investment at present in developing countries; and net transfers of capital, including foreign aid from all sources, run at some $57 billion per year (see Table 4.6). The predominant financial problem today in most underdeveloped countries is still the lack of foreign exchange. Developing countries lack equipment and expertise within the country to develop and do not have the foreign exchange to import them. Except for the few lucky countries with strong exports, imports have had to be curtailed, reducing development ef-

TABLE 4.6   NET FLOW OF RESOURCES RECEIVED BY DEVELOPING COUNTRIES

(Billions of Dollars)

	1970–72 Average	1973	1974	1975
1. Bilateral flows (total net)	16.9	23.5	29.1	39.1
—DAC countries	15.3	21.7	25.0	33.8
of which: ODA	6.2	7.1	8.3	9.8
other official flows + private	9.1	14.6	16.7	24.0
—OPEC countries	0.4	0.6	2.9	4.4
—Centrally Planned Economies	1.1	1.2	1.2	0.9
2. Flows from multilateral institutions, net [a]	2.1	3.3	4.6	5.8
3. Estimated Euro-currency, borrowing, net	2.1	8.5	8.0	9.5
4. Total I to III	21.1	35.3	41.7	54.4
IMF Oil Facility	–	–	1.1	2.4
Grand Total	21.1	35.3	42.8	56.8

Source: Organization for Economic Coperation and Development, *Development Co-operation, Efforts and Policies of the Members of the Development Assistance Committee, 1976 Review,* Pans (UECO) November 1976.

[a] DAC Members provided $3.8 billion to multilateral agencies as ODA in 1975.

[22] A. K. Cairncross, *Home and Foreign Investment 1870–1913,* (Cambridge: Cambridge University Press, 1953), p. 3.

forts. In sum the retreat of the colonial powers has left a gap which has not been filled either by foreign investment or by foreign aid.

FOREIGN AID

Foreign aid was supposed to fill the gap left by the departure of colonial investment and colonial administrations, until indigenous people could be trained and their economies could get going. However, this attempt in international cooperation has led to great disillusionment of both donors and recipients.

At first disillusionment arose from ill-founded expectations of "instant development." Later confidence waned in the light of waste and profiteering along with evidence of corruption in the countries concerned. Criticism ranged from complaints that aid has never met the agreed targets, has never been enough, has been too much in relation to absorptive capacity of country concerned, has had undesirable effects (such as food aid impeding the development of the agricultural sector of the recipient country) has been badly allocated; that a great deal of bilateral aid has gone for infrastructure such as roads and docks to service multinational investment.

It is true that equipment for industry and infrastructure—road building, railways, postal systems, power plants and telecommunication facilities improved beyond recognition in Asia and Africa. It is also true that installations such as power plants sometimes had disappointing results. They did not always create expected spin-offs because of lack of complementary resources to make use of the new power supply—lack of experienced entrepreneurs, engineers, technicians, lack even of farmers capable of taking full advantage of new hydro-electric possibilities. It is also true that multilateral aid, although characterized by error and consequent waste, furnished a great deal of useful technical assistance, that more than $100 billions have been transferred since 1960 of which about one-third took the form of loans. In this latter regard, many recipient countries found the price of aid too high.

Recipient countries have been alarmed by mounting external debt and "tied aid" which "forces" them to buy goods, often highly priced, exclusively from the donor country; they then pay interest on the loans that bought them. Moreover, terms have hardened, and since prices have risen, aid in real terms has been decreasing. Yet because of the pervasive disillusionment with aid on the part of the donor countries, aid is increasingly taking the form of loans. As one Canadian official commented: "Loans are easier to get through Parliament than a grant." Foreign indebtedness of the developing countries, resulting not only from development "assistance" but also from the large export credits many of them have contracted, has risen rapidly. Debt service has been growing at about 17% per year, absorbing much of the increase in export earnings. Finally, recipients point out that unexpected discontinuance of aid makes long-range development planning virtually impossible. For these reasons many countries would prefer "trade not aid."

CONCLUSIONS: NEW DIRECTIONS?

While this historical review identifies mistakes of the past it also casts light on current economic dilemmas. On the one hand, recent European and American economic history suggests that vigorous trade and investment in the developing world could trigger centripetal movements towards a robust global economy. On the other hand, the current destructive results of trade and foreign investment (in particular the loss of jobs) explain the recent talk in both the North and South of "uncoupling" from the global economy. The disappointment with trade, aid, investment, and technology transfers can be largely explained by the fact that such interchanges have usually been treated as global monetary flows among countries, and not as indigenous interactions between differing national structures. In standard macroanalysis, for example, additional investment always adds to the existing stock of capital; in reality, new investment of a certain type could render obsolete installations which are still productive. Certain kinds of foreign trade can destroy national industries, other kinds can import inflation; implantation of advanced technology might effectively reduce the indigenous capacity to develop intermediate techniques better adapted to the national reality. Here we begin to see the limitations of the macro economic approach noted earlier, and the need to more thoroughly consider micro economic aspects of an economy. Fundamentally, economic analysis has been so myopically directed toward money flows that it has not allowed for destruction by inadvertence and marginalization of economic activities. As a colleague, economist Jacques Henry, neatly sums it up, "know-why" is just as important as "know-how".

The mistakes and consequences of the past point to a number of areas to explore. Each country must seek its optimal pattern of trade and its optimal degree of interdependence within the global economy. Foreign investment and foreign aid must be dovetailed into the economy of the host country in terms of income and employment, impact on distribution of income, and last, but by no means least, social structures.

While entrepreneurs have long complained of employment problems arising out of sociocultural conditions—out of the "indolence of the people", their disinterest in increasing their incomes, their desire to "keep one foot in the village"—there is a school of thought that carries this idea much further. The sociocultural dualists contend that the troubles arising out of the era of international trade and colonialism were largely caused by sociocultural rather than economic conditions, that the problems arose from the clash of imported systems with traditional societies, the latter incapable of adaption to or inimical to Western style modernization. *Dependentista* extremists attack this idea, asserting that there are no traditional societies but only dependent peripheral ones. Yet Third World countries themselves attach great importance to their culture and traditions and are determined to preserve them, insisting that development patterns must be designed to harmonize with their physical and sociocultural environment.

5

Environmental and sociocultural determinism

Apologetic colonial theory maintained that the reason the people of the backward regions showed so little economic initiative was because they were different from Europeans. According to this view, the reluctance of colonial peoples to seek wage employment, their inefficiency when they did, and their general lack of response to opportunities for increasing their income reflected limited economic horizons and a preference for leisure. While unfavorable climate was accorded an important role in colonial theory, and the effects of undernutrition were sometimes noted, the carefree attitudes were believed to be the outcome of the whole system of social relations, institutions, and traditions of the societies. It was argued that there were no real possibilities for modernization after the European pattern; the colonial powers, reluctant to interfere needlessly in the local culture and traditions, extended their policies of laissez-faire to noninterference in social matters.

In the early postwar years, many development economists, reacting against colonial attitudes, were inclined to dismiss the idea that the people of the developing countries were essentially different from anyone else. They also tended to downgrade environmental conditions, including climate. These conclusions, however, were often arrived at by "armchair" economists: if they eventually went out in the field, they usually modified their ideas, realizing there was *some* basis for the colonial assumption that some countries were failing to develop because of environmental conditions or a hostile cultural "climate." A fast-growing body of research into the physical and sociological environment ensued.

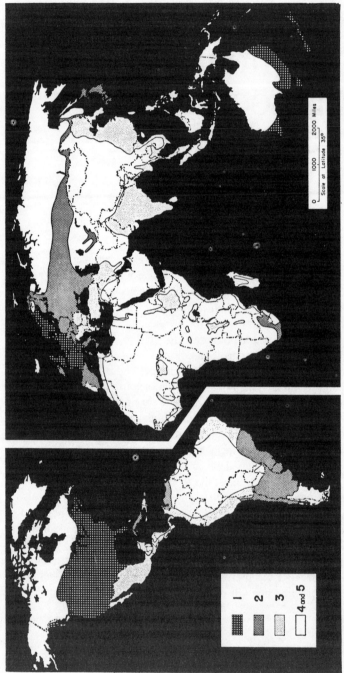

Figure 5.1. Kinds and Levels of Economic Development. (1) High level of productivity, predominantly exchange economy; (2) intermediate level of productivity, generally of exchange economy but with large sectors of subsistence economy in most cases; (3) low level of productivity, commonly of predominantly subsistence economy but in some cases largely in exchange economy; (4) almost completely subsistence economy, at a low level of productivity; and (5) largely undeveloped for production, with no distinction as to kind or level of the economy that does exist. (4) and (5) are not distinguished from each other on this map. SOURCE: Richard Hartshorne, "Geography and Economic Growth," in Norton Ginsberg (ed.), *Essays on Geography and Economic Development* (Chicago, 1960), p. 22. Reprinted by permission of the Department of Geography, University of Chicago.)

ENVIRONMENTAL DETERMINISM

A glance at the map (Figure 5.1), reveals the striking geographic concentration of economic development. The advanced countries are confined to North America, Australasia, Japan, and Europe (including European Russia). There is no developed country within one thousand miles of the equator. Except for Venezuela, the countries of intermediate development are all in temperate zones: Argentina, Uruguay, Chile, and southern Brazil; the union of South Africa; eastern Europe and Japan. In short, virtually all underdeveloped countries are either too hot or too cold. The lack of development in icy countries, such as Greenland, is easy enough to understand. The great majority of the less developed countries, however, are in the tropics, and no tropical country has as yet graduated into the ranks of advanced countries. Venezuela is the only tropical country to reach even the "intermediate" stage of development, but its oil wealth has not yet brought a high level of welfare to the majority of the people.

Faced with facts like these, it is necessary to ask: "To what extent is the level of development affected by the physical environment?" The question can be broken down into three major aspects of the physical environment: soil, climate, and natural resources in general.

TROPICAL SOILS

The lush vegetation of tropical jungle does not necessarily indicate rich soil; on the contrary, tropical soils are usually poorer and more fragile than those of temperate regions. The mutual support system between biotic life and organic material is disrupted with clearing of tropical vegetation. With this disturbance of the ecological cycle of growing and rotting vegetation the soil quickly becomes infertile. Monsoon rainfall alternates with high temperatures to create lateritic soils with the characteristic hardpan of aluminum and iron—a layer of soil so hard that a pickax may be needed to break it up. Poor soil is therefore an important factor in the low yields per acre in Asian and African countries. Only where rivers provide silt or volcanoes provide ash does one find rich, fertile soils in the tropics. The use of fertilizers is also difficult in the tropics. Not only are factory-produced fertilizers often beyond the means of the tropical farmer, but their use requires knowledge of the local soil, and the needs of a particular crop—facts still insufficiently known in tropical areas. Finally, when fertilizers are applied, they are often washed out to sea with the next rain.

In animal products, the average output per animal of milk and wool is much lower in tropical than in temperate countries, partly because of poor nutrition. Tropical grasses and other forage plants are frequently lacking in nutritive value. Raising livestock productivity may require importing feeds or developing new natural feeds, which again may be difficult in tropical conditions.

CLIMATE AND AGRICULTURE

Disease and pests thrive in the hot tropical climate and take a heavy toll of new projects. "The tropics are littered with the ruins of projects that refused to recognize the special problems of the tropics," writes Dr. Andrew Kamarck of the World Bank's Economic Development Institute.[1] He mentions a chicken-raising scheme in Gambia, which was wrecked by disease; a rice-growing project in Senegal where hundreds of thousands of weaver birds destroy each year's crop; and the Ford Motor Company's efforts to establish rubber plantations in the Amazon basin, which was defeated by disease. The famous Gezira scheme in the Sudan, for growing peanuts, which started full of promise, seemed destined for failure six years later when weeds and disease seemed insuperable, but eventually succeeded because of the ultimate effectiveness of the basic research that was carried out.

Finally, the effect of climate is obvious in a desert. In the hot arid regions of the world, lack of water is the major agricultural problem.

CLIMATE AND HUMAN BEHAVIOR

Before World War II, most of the diseases of temperate lands were rife in the hot wet countries, as were the terrible endemic and epidemic tropical diseases. This statement is much less clearly true today. Malaria is now being brought under control in many tropical countries, and the same may be said of yellow fever, bubonic plague, and other tropical diseases.

But there can be little doubt that disease still helps to explain the low productivity of many developing countries. Malaria has by no means disappeared, and other typical tropical diseases that debilitate rather than kill quickly undermine the capacity for work. One of these is bilharzia, a liver fluke transmitted by river snails, for which no effective cure has been found. There are several sources of blindness—onchocerciasis, trachoma, glaucoma. Many types of intestinal parasites sap the strength of tropical peoples, including hookworm, Guinea worm, and the filaria which causes elephantiasis.

The incidence of these diseases in some communities is unbelievably high. A study of six villages in northeast Brazil showed that most people had at least two parasitic infections, and the blood hemoglobin content was less than half of normal levels. On Ukara Island in Tanzania, only 0.6% of the population was free from parasites. A survey of villages in northern Nigeria showed 85% of the population over forty-five to have tuberculosis. Some 200 million people in Africa, Asia, and the Middle East suffer from bilharzia. In some villages of Upper Volta and Ghana, 15% of the population are blind from onchocerciasis (river blindness) and most of the population has impaired vision. In two villages of West Bengal, 72% of the Moslems and 89% of the Hindus had hookworm. Under these conditions it is scarcely surprising if the people "show reluctance to seek employment, and are unresponsive to opportunity."

[1] Cited by Andrew Kamarck, *Climate and Economic Development* (Washington, D.C.: Economic Development Institute, International Bank for Reconstruction and Development, 1972).

The direct impact of climate on human beings seems to be the least important of the various effects of tropical climate on productivity. While the pace of life is somewhat slower in the Australian north, the relaxed attitudes toward work, leisure, and income in Australia seem much the same from tropical Darwin to chilly Hobart. Arthur Lewis observes that a tropical climate does not prevent a farmer from grasping opportunities:

> It is . . . hard to get the farmers in tropical countries to work as many hours as industrial workers in temperate countries, but this does not prevent them from seizing opportunities to use better seeds, or fertilizers, or to plant more profitable crops. It has not prevented the Gold Coast farmer—who is said, no doubt erroneously, to be one of the laziest farmers in the world—from switching from subsistence production to creating the largest cocoa industry in the world over a short space of time; or prevented the farmers of Uganda or of Indonesia from taking enthusiastically to cotton and to rubber respectively.[2]

There *is,* however, a difference in capacity for work between healthy tropical peoples and unhealthy tropical peoples.

These observations are of considerable importance. In geographic terms it appears that the comparative advantage of advanced countries, with their better soils and climate, is greater in agriculture than it is in industry. The location of industries is less restricted by the constraints of the physical environment than is agriculture. Technology can be transported; soil and climate cannot.

Nevertheless, given a major research effort and the adaptation of technology to the needs of a tropical environment, many if not most of the problems of deficient soils, and of animal and human disease, can be overcome. At present, appropriate technology is largely lacking. Brazilian economist Celso Furtado writes of his own country:

> It is clear that available technology—largely developed in regions of temperate climate and for the combination of resources found in the Northern Hemisphere—is by no means readily adaptable to the Brazilian tropics.[3]

Consequently, Furtado continues, millions of acres of good soil with water go uncultivated in Brazil's impoverished northeast. Research and technology, concentrated as it has been in the advanced countries of the temperate zones, has still to be directed with full force toward the problems of developing countries.

NATURAL RESOURCES

Geographers have been exceedingly chary of tracing differences in levels of development to differences in the resource base. Certainly, in ancient times, development was easiest when agricultural conditions permitted sufficient food and raw materials to be grown to allow increasing numbers of people to do other things. Man's first great civilizations flourished in rich river valleys

[2] Arthur Lewis, *The Theory of Economic Growth* (Homewood, Ill.: Richard D. Irwin, 1955), p. 51.

[3] Celso Furtado, "The Development of Brazil" *Scientific American Technology and Economic Development Issue* 209 (Sept. 1963): 216.

because the Tigris and Euphrates, the Nile, the Mekong, and the Yellow River valleys provided conditions where men could grow food relatively easily freeing them to devote time to industry, the arts, and sciences. Geographers however argue that lack of material factors of production does not in itself preclude economic growth, since resources can be imported. The success of such countries as Switzerland (now the world's most prosperous country) and Japan are cases in point. However, *resources can be imported provided the country can produce sufficient surpluses of other products needed elsewhere.*

This qualification is significant because often underdeveloped countries cannot produce these surpluses. While indigenous resources are much less important to Japan and to other highly developed countries, with their large supplies of capital, skilled labor, technology, and entrepreneurial experience, they can be critical to the less developed regions. The possession of sizable natural resources is a major advantage to any country embarking upon a period of rapid economic development. Rapid rises in agricultural, forest, or mineral production can be a means to needed capital accumulation and thus to accelerating economic growth.

As the environmental crisis continues and countries with abundant resources become increasingly chary of sharing them with others, a solid natural resource base becomes ever more advantageous for any country. Countries with renewable resources such as forests, if conserved, may prove in the long run to be better off than countries presently rich in nonrenewable resources like petroleum. This kind of advantage is already becoming apparent in the good prices natural substitutes for petroleum have been enjoying, such as palm and coconut oils and various natural fibers. Moreover, in the light of the pollutive effects of some synthetics as well as the high costs of others, there is today a trend back to natural products: natural rubber for synthetic rubber, soap for detergents, hemp and sisal for nylon, etc.

Resource patterns can have a profound effect on a country's development, and not just in terms of their scarcity or profusion. Natural resources can bring problems or prosperity, according to how they are used and on the timing of their discovery. If, for example, someone had been asked two hundred years ago to predict whether Indonesia or Malaya would have the better economic future, Indonesia would undoubtedly have been the choice. Malaya consisted mainly of mountains and malarial swamps, with poor soils and few good known resources except tin, supporting a population of less than one million. The Indonesian islands were also mountainous, and some had swampy lowlands, and population was probably approximately six million; but the islands also had mineral resources, while the great wealth at that time seemed to lie in the "spice islands" and in the rich volcanic soils of Java's rolling lowlands, which were growing a splendid range of tropical products. In the following two centuries, Indonesia's range of known natural resources was extended, particularly in Sumatra where oil was discovered; rubber and tobacco plantations were added to the agriculture, but Java's rich soils also permitted the enormous population explosions of the eighteenth and nineteenth centuries.

Consequently, in spite of substantial development, Indonesia's per capita income has only recently crossed the $100 per year mark. On the other hand, Malaya's mountains, poor soils, and malarial swamps discouraged colonization and kept the population small. When the British did finally settle in the interior towards the end of the nineteenth century, establishing law and order, mechanizing the tin mines, and introducing the rubber tree, a very favorable population-resource ratio prevailed. Most of the population could accordingly be drawn into the modern sector (the plantations and the mines). Consequently per capita income now stands at over $700.

Diversity of resources as well as quantity facilitates development. The most advanced countries have not only had a lot of resources, but have also enjoyed varied resources. In the United States in particular, population movements and technological advance have been accompanied by the discovery somewhere in the country of new resources important to each new phase of development. On the other hand, no country dependent on a single resource—Senegal and the oil countries being obvious examples—has yet become highly developed. Yet the capital accumulated by a single easily exploited natural resource such as oil can, if properly used, spark the economic development process.

Not only diversity but also the geographic spread of resources is important for development. Of two countries with the same resource endowment per head, however measured, the country with resources spread throughout its length and breadth has a better chance of development than the one whose known resources are concentrated in one part of the country. This idea is related to the theory of the role of an ever moving frontier in the generation and regeneration of entrepreneurial activity.[4] Progressive movement of the frontier linked to resource discoveries and opening up of new farmlands, bringing settlement and urbanization to all major regions, was a feature of United States economic history. It was less of a feature of Canadian development, and virtually absent in Brazil; since in these countries resources are spread out but isolated.

A resource known to exist but not accessible at a cost which makes its exploitation worthwhile is not a "resource" in the economic sense. If a raw material necessary for some phase of industrialization does not exist locally and is unavailable elsewhere due to tariff barriers or transportation costs, modification of that phase is likely.

The environmental crisis is driving this last point home in developing countries. Government leaders, who have always thought in terms of scarce resources, and have long encouraged the use of local materials, are attaching even more importance to that policy, faced as they are with catastrophic increases in prices of imports. The Ministry of Culture in Indonesia, for example, has launched a large project to encourage and revive local arts and crafts using local materials, to substitute for goods otherwise imported. In the Pahang Trengganu Project in Malaysia, a government-financed tourist resort

---

[4] Discussed in Chapter 2.

recently incorporated local architectural modes adapted to the environment and local resources. It was built almost exclusively of local woods, no elevators were used, and few air conditioners; buildings are consequently one or two stories high, and built to take every advantage of sea breezes. The architects hope to influence local taste. For a long time it has been fashionable to build Western-style houses of concrete. Here the environmental crisis is lending a hand. Not long ago, houses of the beautiful local woods were relatively expensive. Today there is little difference in their cost from the cost of a house of brick or concrete. These interventions reflect the general interest today in fostering indigenous cultures in opposition to complete westernization, and a fresh awareness of the interaction between the physical and cultural environment.

PHYSICAL ENVIRONMENT AND CULTURE

It is obvious enough that the culture of a sedentary peasant will vary from that of a pastoral nomad, and again from a fisherman. Not only does physical environment shape a culture; it can protect and preserve a civilization.

There is an old saying in Indonesia: *agama manuk dari laut, tetapi adat datang dari buki*—religion comes up from the sea, but custom (*adat*) comes down from the mountains. During thousands of years migrants from China pushed the old inhabitants of Indonesia into the less fertile areas and into the mountains, which became a stronghold of the old animistic religions and custom. When later the Indians brought Hinduism and Buddhism, and when later still Islam swept the land, these religious invasions also penetrated unevenly. In some corners of the country, the older cultures survive to this day, protected by an undesirable environment, or by innaccessibility. One of the most extraordinary of such survivals is Bali's fourteenth century Hindu-Buddhist civilization.

The painter Miguel Covarrubias once described Bali as "a cluster of high volcanoes, their craters studded with serene lakes set in dark forest filled with screaming monkeys. The long green slopes of the volcanoes, deeply furrowed by ravines washed out by rushing rivers full of rapids and water-falls, drop steadily to the sea without forming lowlands."[5] The steepness of these slopes shaped Bali's history and culture. When Islam swept through Java in the fourteenth century, the Javanese court fled to Bali, taking the priests, intellectuals, and libraries, and in doing so transplanted the Hindu-Javanese culture to Bali. For a long time the refugees were protected from the Islamic invaders by the dangerous currents which swirl around the island, and by the steep slopes of the volcanoes which rise straight out of the sea, affording few landing places or safe anchorages. Later, when the Dutch finally subdued the island in 1908, they recognized the exceptional quality of the civilization, and did little to disturb it.

Until recently the civilization has remained virtually intact, nurtured by the rich volcanic soil and tropical climate. Most Balinese need work in the rice

[5] Miguel Covarrubias *Island of Bali* (New York: Alfred A. Knopf, 1956), p. 4.

fields but twenty hours a week: they can then devote the rest of their time to their religion and their arts. The exceptional scale of artistic life may be judged by that of the village of Ubud. This small village of a few hundred families supports two *gamelans*—i.e., two symphony orchestras, first-rate by any standard. Ubud has an art school and gallery, a school of music and dance. The cultural life centers around the Sultan's palace and the temples, but few households are without a painter, a sculptor, a musician, or a dancer. It is a rare evening when there is no performance of drama, music, or dance in the neighborhood. True, Ubud is an art center, but the same pattern of life pervades the island.

Not only has Bali proven a stronghold for the Hindu Buddhist culture, but also for the Indonesian *adat,* the ancient customs guiding human behavior, which still pervade Indonesian life, and which are highly valued as a continuing heritage. Because of the strength of Balinese *adat,* Bali has been called the ''land of *gotong royong''*, referring to certain principles of cooperation in village society.

When an economist encounters such a self-sufficient civilization, he begins to wonder about the standard economic approach to development, and whether societies like Bali should be left as they are.

SOCIOCULTURAL DETERMINISM

In the early days of the development effort, few economists had any doubts that economic development was a ''good thing,'' nor did they believe that sociocultural attitudes would pose barriers to development. Most economists assumed human nature to be much the same everywhere, and felt sure that all people wanted to raise their levels of production and consumption (to assume otherwise would be to slip into colonial patterns of thinking). Attitudes and motives were invariably considered to reflect rational choice directed towards maximizing satisfaction.

Economists also joined other social scientists in the idea of society as a *gestalt,* a closely interwoven pattern of social, political and economic characteristics, a ''seamless web'' in which fundamental changes in one sphere would bring ''harmonious'' changes in the other spheres. Without worrying much about specific mechanisms of social or political development, economists took it for granted that the process of economic growth would bring ''progress'' in the social and political fields as well. Other social scientists, without worrying much about the mechanics of economic development, also believed that ''modernization'' in the economic sphere would be accompanied by broader political participation, more ''advanced'' forms of social organization, improved health and education. Moreover, this process of overall development was thought to be much the same everywhere; industrialization was conceived as ''a relatively uniform, worldwide process.''[6]

---

[6] Wilbert Moore, ''Motivational Aspects of Development'' in Amitai and Eva Etzione, *Social Change: Sources, Patterns and Consequences* (New York and London: Basic Books, 1964).

A number of psychologists, sociologists, and anthropologists, however, warned of the folly of assuming all behaviour to be "rational" and of expecting "rational behavior" to mean the same thing in all cultures. They emphasized differences in values and aspirations in space and time, were "extremely reluctant to assume that Western experience can be used as a guide to behavior in Dahomey, Nepal or even Peru," and were inclined to pessimism about the consequences of economic change, having "a normal prejudice toward the view that bread or all purchasable goods and services are enough to satisfy human values."[7] Moreover, some economists returning from field missions declared that the sociocultural characteristics of many underdeveloped countries were insuperable barriers to economic growth and that these countries should be left alone. American economist Everett Hagen, returning from an economic development mission in Burma, was convinced that even if the barriers were not insuperable it would take several generations and profound sociological change before economic development can be attempted.[8]

The concept of a society as a gestalt, a "seamless web," led some sociologists and anthropologists to stress the delicacy of the equilibrium in any society, however primitive, and to warn of the grave dangers in heedlessly disturbing that equilibrium. In effect, they were querying the idea that changes in economic activity would automatically trigger harmonious changes in other spheres and were suggesting that economic development could prove highly destructive of the social fabric. Thus J. L. Sadie, writing in 1960 about the Bantu of South Africa, described them as an equilibrated society within which individuals are more or less content; with land held as communal property, and a built-in social security system, and a number of antidevelopmental attitudes resistant to change. He saw no way for economic development to take place within the traditional culture, and seemed to wonder whether the game was worth the candle:

> Economic development of an underdeveloped people by themselves is not compatible with the maintenance of their traditional customs and mores. A break with the latter is a pre-requisite to economic progress. What is needed is a revolution in the totality of social, cultural, and religious habits, and thus in their psychological attitude, their philosophy and way of life. What is, therefore, required amounts in reality to social disorganization. Unhappiness and discontentment in the sense of wanting more than is obtainable at any moment is to be generated. The suffering and dislocation that may be caused in the process may be objectionable, but it appears to be the price that has to be paid for economic development.[9]

In general, this group regarded economic developers as clumsy fools, who rushed in where anthropologists feared to tread, destroying an existing civilization without having another ready-made to put in its place, and leaving

---

[7] Ibid.

[8] Everett E. Hagen, *The Theory of Social Change: How Economic Growth Begins* (Homewood, Ill.: Dorsey Press, 1962), p. 22.

[9] J. L. Sadie, "The Social Anthropology of Economic Underdevelopment," in David E. Novack and Robert Lekachman, eds., *Development and Society, The Dynamics of Economic Change* (New York: St. Martin's Press, 1964), p. 213.

disintegration, demoralization, degradation and needless suffering in their wake.

In recent years, development economists have learned by hard experience the elements of truth in past warnings, and are now more inclined to take sociocultural considerations into account, and to ask themselves a number of pertinent questions before proceeding with an economic development program.

The first basic question is whether economic development should be introduced into a traditional society at all. Are people any happier in rich countries than in poor ones? If "development" means becoming like today's rich countries, may not the poor countries be better off as they are?

From the development economist's point of view, if people are happy within a traditional environment, and if their way of life is not threatened by population growth or resource exhaustion or both, there may be no need for change. Traditional agriculture, handicrafts, and construction techniques may be less pollutant than more modern methods and may use only abundant local materials. Often they produce results which are both beautiful and functional. Some governments have, in fact, taken the decision to leave some self-sufficient traditional groups largely outside the development stream. This decision, however, becomes more difficult when a society is "stable and equilibrated" simply because death rates are high and the people are illiterate, undernourished, and riddled with disease. Is it "right" to leave it alone, even if the people themselves are "content" or fearful of change?

Fortunately, this dilemma does not present itself to many governments. Few societies are so isolated that their members are "content" to be ignorant, hungry and sick. Fortunately, too, in concrete cases the answer often emerges from the facts. Within Malaysia, for example, is a small group of primitive people, about 50,000 in all, known as the *orang asli,* or "original people." This hunting and fishing civilization lives in the depths of the jungle, in an extraordinary symbiosis with nature and with a highly developed appreciation of natural beauty. At first sight the life of the *orang asli* seems tranquil, filled with beauty. Why not just leave them alone? The answer is easy. They are undernourished and malnourished, and consequently suffer low levels of health. Despite the establishment of reservations, their natural environment is shrinking, and there are not enough animals and fish to support them. The *orang asli* supplement their incomes with rattan gathering and the Malaysian government has been helping them expand their economies with fruit trees (which in some cases were destroyed by wild elephants). In the long run, however, there may be no alternative but to absorb the *orang asli* into the rapidly growing modern sector of the Malaysian economy.

If a society does not really have the choice of remaining as it is, if the population is growing or resources are depleting, there is no choice but to limit population growth (as even primitive societies have succeeded in doing) and/or to raise productivity, by opening up new resources, or by introducing better technologies. If a traditional society *must* develop its economy in order to survive, a government can proceed at once to the questions as to whether it can be done and how it can best be done.

For economic development to take place in most poor countries, people must be prepared to work harder and better, to save more and to accept technological and institutional change; entrepreneurs (whether socialist or non-socialist) must emerge to introduce new ideas. The third group of "actors" in development are the political leaders who must have the will and imagination to create a dynamic interplay between government, entrepreneurs, and people.

The next basic question, then, is whether or not people are willing and able to do these things in every society. Are there indeed insuperable sociocultural barriers to economic development? If not, what is the time required for social change? Is it possible to isolate the conditions necessary to create the right climate for economic development? Mindful of societies which wish to retain traditional modes and their essential values along with modernization, they next ask what is the degree of social change necessary? How can this change be brought about? What role—if any—must the political élite play in bringing about these changes and what is a viable political framework?

Sociocultural Characteristics: Barriers to Economic Growth?

The debate concerning sociocultural barriers to development resolves itself into two subquestions: are people different, or are societies different? The people of some traditional societies, such as those of nineteenth century Japan and seventeenth century Europe, have adapted and changed in the course of economic development. Today other traditional societies have begun to change in response to development needs, while some have shown themselves strongly resistant to change. Does this divergence arise from the fact that people are different? Does individual behavior—the aspirations, incentives, motivation, decision-making of individuals—differ from country to country, or does the social framework of countries differ, so that individuals who are basically the same nonetheless behave differently?

ARE PEOPLE DIFFERENT?

"Limited wants" and the "backward bending supply curve of effort" (working less rather than more when wages rise) are probably the most frequently cited barriers to development in primitive or peasant societies. From Malthus on (and probably before) social scientists have pondered why some people are "different" in that they prefer more leisure to more income—particularly if they are poor yet healthy.

Lack of incentive is clear enough in the case of peasants as tenants in large landholdings (such as the great latifundias of Latin America) where, often in debt to their landlord, extra effort avails them little. But questions are raised in situations where the opportunity to make extra income exists. This phenomenon is well illustrated by some black societies in South Africa. Melville Herskovits tells of the failure of a textile mill set up near the native reserves. Labor turnover was the most serious problem: ". . . a man will work long enough to meet the limited goal set by the needs of his family unit. When he has earned enough for this, he leaves, to return to a mode of life that is in harmony with an economic system that existed before industrialization was introduced into the area, whereby subsistence and prestige wants were satisfied without reference to pecuniary considerations." [10]

Herskovits also describes the ironworkers of Upper Volta, who for many generations have known how to make knives, hoes, and other iron implements. But the ironmongers are principally agriculturalists, working their forges only in the dry season when the fields are not cultivated. "One does not have to pursue the matter further," says Herskovits, "to perceive that motivations quite different from those obtaining in the economies of Europe and America are operative here. The question (is) . . . why these ironworkers do not take advantage of the obvious market at hand. . . . It is apparent that the answer lies outside the scope of economics as envisaged for our culture; that to reach a satisfactory explanation would require probing deep into what we know concerning the psychology of culture, as applicable to this particular situation." [11]

SOCIOCULTURAL DUALISM

One economist who did "pursue the matter further" for the better part of his professional life was J. H. Boeke. As Weber and Schumpeter described the favorable social conditions for development of Europe and North America, so Boeke sought to analyse the hostile social climate to development of traditional societies. [12]

Boeke was one of the many devoted and highly trained Netherlands East Indies officials who went to Indonesia during the period of the "ethical policy" (1900 to 1930), which was dedicated to raising the standard of welfare of Indonesians. His "dualistic theory" is therefore based mainly on the emergence of dualism in Indonesia during the Dutch colonial era, when mod-

---

[10] Melville J. Herskovits, "The Problem of Adapting Societies to New Tasks," in Novack and Lekachman, eds., *Development and Society: The Dynamics or Economic Change,* p. 281.

[11] Ibid., p. 281.

[12] J. H. Boeke, *Economics and Economic Policy of Dual Societies* (New York: International Secretariat of the Institute of Pacific Relations, 1953); cited as Boeke, *Economics;* "Three Forms of Disintegration in Dual Societies." Lecture given in the course on Cooperative Education of the International Labor Office, Asian Cooperative Field Mission, October 1953 and published in *Indonesie,* Vol. VII pp. 278–295, No. 4 (April 1954) cited as Boeke, "Three Forms"; and "Western Influence on the Growth of Eastern Population," *Economia Internazionale,* Vol. VII, No. 2 (April 1954), pp. 358–369 cited as Boeke "Western Influence."

ern Dutch enterprises operated side by side with traditional Indonesian activities; however, Boeke believed his theory had wider application in Asia and Africa.

In the preceding chapter we ascribed technological dualism to shortage of local technical skills, the labor-saving nature of modern technologies, and the limited scope of investment. Boeke saw sociocultural dualism as arising from values and motivations in Eastern society resistant to development. "Social dualism is the clashing of an imported social system with an indigenous social system of another style," Boeke declares. "Most frequently the imported social system is high capitalism. But it may be socialism or communism just as well, or a blending of them." [13]

An economist, Boeke saw this clash between East and West as arising out of differences in values and motivations concerning effort and risk-taking needed for modernization and development. [14]

> . . . anyone expecting western reactions will meet with frequent surprises. When the price of the coconut is high, the chances are that less of the commodities will be offered for sale; when wages are raised the manager of the estate risks that less work will be done; if three acres are enough to supply the needs of the household, a cultivator will not till six; when rubber prices fall the owner of a grove may decide to tap more intensively, whereas high prices may mean that he leaves a larger or smaller portion of his tappable trees untapped.

He ascribed this backward sloping supply curve of effort to "limited needs" (in contrast to the "unlimited needs" of Western society). Such needs as exist in Eastern societies are social rather than economic. If the Madurese values his bull at ten times the worth of a cow, it is not because the bull is ten times as useful to him in his business, but because the bull increases his prestige at the bull races.

A closely related feature, in Boeke's view, is the almost complete absence of profit seeking (except speculative profits) in an Eastern traditional society. Similarly there is no professional trading in the Eastern village community. Eastern industry is characterized by "aversion to capital" in the sense of conscious dislike of the risks of investing capital, only slight interest in finish and accuracy, lack of business qualities, and the absence of organization, discipline, and corrective local specialization. "There is no question of the eastern producer adapting himself to the western example technologically, economically or socially." [15] Where Western industry is dominated by common sense reason, Eastern society is molded by fatalism and resignation. Because of these great differences between Eastern and Western societies, Western economic theory is totally inapplicable to underdeveloped areas.

In general, Boeke's conclusion is that the best thing the Western world can do for underdeveloped areas is to leave them alone. Not only would the members of Eastern traditional societies not respond to development efforts, but moreover the introduction of Western systems—whether free enterprise or

[13] Ibid., p. 4.
[14] Ibid., p. 40.
[15] Ibid., p. 103.

socialist—would bring retrogression and finally destroy the indigenous culture, for which he had deep respect.

Boeke set great store by the political and social strength of the Indonesian villages—the "little republics"—where village councils reach consensus through open discussion guided by the *lura* (headman). Boeke believed that the Indonesian *adat* (traditional law and custom) provided a harmonious structure for everyday life, that the culture of the village community was "perfectly adapted to the environment" and that the methods of Eastern agriculture could hardly be improved upon. With the principles of cooperation—*gotong royong* (mutual assistance, solidarity) and *ramah tamah* (the family-like society)—guiding social relations, with a well ordered agriculture, with a lively indigenous theatre (which was the medium of the classical literature, music and dance and a vehicle of commentary, humor, entertainment and spiritual education) the culture seemed something that should be left alone.

Boeke's solution was gradualism. Any industrialization or agricultural improvement must be a low-key, small-scale process. New leaders with a strong feeling of local social responsibility must spring from the "small folk themselves." The sphere of action must be small, the time slow and the goal won by "faith, charity and patience, angelic patience."

THE BACKGROUND OF COLONIAL IDEOLOGY

The dualistic theory did not spring full blown from the head of Boeke. Dutch officials in general regarded Indonesia as incapable of development along Western lines; consequently, the conception of what was appropriate for Indonesians in the way of education, training, and industrialization was very limited. The gradualism of the "ethical policy" failed, however, to raise standards of living. "The only popular response to all these nostrums," despaired Boeke, "is an increase in numbers while foreign capitalists and foreign energy take out of native hands a rapidly increasing share of native activities." [16]

Although Boeke was so sharply aware of the relationship between "foreign energy" and "native activities," he seems to have failed to make the connection between the monopolization of economic activities by Europeans, and the indolence of the people. Indonesia had entrepreneurs and traders as lively as any in the fifteenth century. The transfer of entrepreneurship from the Indonesians to the Dutch in the course of three hundred and fifty years is an example of one of the most serious "backwash" effects of colonialism. Boeke is in tune with present day thinking that initiative should come from the "small folk" themselves. There can also be no question about the phenomenon of dualism, but it was the result of the course of events, rather than from the nature of the people and their society. The advent of colonialism, leading

---

[16] Boeke, "Het Zakelijke en het Persoonlijke Element in de Koloniale Welvaartspolitiek," *Koloniale Studien,* April 1927.

to the transference of entrepreneurship, the introduction of labor-saving technologies, new crops, health measures, followed by the enormous population explosion produced a pervasive inertia—a virtually static economy and society. What remains in question is a static society's degree of immutability, and whether the motivations of Eastern peoples are innately different from those of progressive societies, and what kind of development they wish to pursue.

THE BACKWARD BENDING SUPPLY CURVE OF RISK-TAKING AND EFFORT

In the first place, the backward bending supply curve of risk-taking is not exclusively a feature of underdeveloped economies. The consciousness of risk attending capital investment prevails everywhere. "Nothing is so shy as a million dollars," as a famous American financier once said. Leisure and security are valued in any society, and for people anywhere the rewards must seem adequate before people will wcrk harder or longer or assume additional risks. In the years following World War II in Australia, when shortages of goods still prevailed, the unions chose to offset the increase in the basic wage by a reduction in hours per week, leaving money income essentially unchanged. This backward sloping supply curve of effort also began to appear at the time in certain industries (such as coal mining) even in the United States and is more widespread today.

If contracting opportunity persists in a country, as during a period of increasing overpopulation, values and customs are likely to change. In a limited or contracting world, competition may in fact lower collective output more than if cooperation is stressed.[17] In the case of Java, as population and unemployment grew, cooperative work-and-leisure spreading devices became so deeply ingrained that people forgot the original reason for them and knew only that proper behavior required them. Once such customs are established, they are likely to prove resistant to change, particularly if they assume moral or religious status. It is said, for example, that the sacred cows of India originated from an edict against killing cattle in order to build up the herds as draft animals; this tradition has proven highly resistant to change.

On the other hand, what anthropologists take for "cultural resistance to change" often turns out to be good economic common sense. In the retarded Greek region of Epirus, the peasants were given cows in order to start dairy herds, as part of a "pilot zone" regional development project. But instead of seizing this opportunity for economic advancement, the peasants slaughtered and ate the cattle. There was no lack of armchair anthropologists in Athens ready to explain this "noneconomic" behavior in terms of cultural resistance to a change in the peasants' pattern of life. But on-the-spot investigation revealed that the Epirus peasants' behavior was rational even in the narrowest economic sense of the term. The number of cattle provided to each family was too small to make any real difference in their level of living. The pilot zone

---

[17] David McClelland and John Winters, *Motivating Economic Achievement* (New York: Free Press, 1969), p. 94.

was extremely isolated, and feed and equipment had to be brought in over a winding and rutted mountain track. Finished dairy products had to be taken out to market over the same track, which became impassable in bad weather. In any case, no marketing channels had been established. Thus the cost of feeding the cattle and processing dairy products was high, and the price of final products net of transport and marketing costs was low. The failure of the Epirus scheme was not due to the planners' neglect to "probe deep into the psychology of culture" but to their failure to make dairying profitable to the peasants. Meanwhile, what could be more sensible under the circumstances than to kill the cows and eat them?

A subsequent study of the farmers of Epirus confirmed them as rational decision makers. Tests revealed that in assessing the alternative cost of labor, the Epirus farmers decide to hire or not to hire a tractor for the autumn ploughing by considering the opportunity costs of their labor; to hire out their own services or to employ men to assist them; to migrate seasonally, or quit agriculture to work in industry in the cities. It was concluded that they were indeed rational, profit maximizing decision-makers within the present technological and market context.[18]

The main point is that peasants living close to the subsistence level cannot afford to take risks; a poor decision may mean the extinction of the tribe. Peasants know that their traditional techniques work, and will as a rule protect the family, village, or tribe from starvation; before they will try something new they must be convinced that it will work. A "demonstration effect" is necessary for technological change to be accepted, and sometimes, traditional wisdom proves superior to the imported technology. In Mexico, for example, over the resistance of the local peasants, a foreign expert used heavy equipment to build dikes. During the annual floods the dikes washed away, and the topsoil which had been scraped up to form them was lost. On the other hand, when a demonstration is clearly successful, peasants respond briskly to opportunity, as in the terracing of the Bio-Bio River in Chile. The terraces (built to prevent erosion) survived a downpour of flood proportions, which caused heavy damage to neighboring fields that were not terraced. This demonstration led to many requests for similar assistance, and to the ultimate establishment of a soil conservation department in the Ministry of Agriculture.[19]

Examples such as these make an economist wonder about Herskovits's ironmongers in Upper Volta; was the marketing of iron products really organized, and was it clearly profitable? Might there not have been transport problems? Did they live in villages where the incidence of impaired vision was high? A number of economists has in fact made careful statistical and econometric studies of peasant economic behavior which prove that peasants in developing countries are just as rational and as powerfully motivated by the

[18] Pan A. Yotopoulos, *Allocative Efficiency in Economic Development: A Quantitative Approach* (Athens: Center of Planning and Economic Research, 1967).

[19] Charles Erasmus, *Man Takes Control* (Minneapolis: University of Minnesota Press, 1961), pp. 23–25.

desire for gain as farmers in advanced countries.[20] It is fair to say that in its extreme form, the theory which suggests that *people* must be changed before development can take place, is now generally discredited.

SOCIAL FRAMEWORK AND DEVELOPMENT

While people may be basically much the same the world over, no one can deny that societies differ. For example, while *all* major societies in Indonesia have proven capable of generating enterprise since independence, there is a marked difference in the scope of entrepreneurial performance from one region to another. The mountain people of Sumatra—the Minangkebau, the Bataks and the Atjehnese—provide political and economic leadership far out of proportion to their numbers, particularly in the fields of trade and business.

"The Bataks are everywhere," Mohammed Hatta (Indonesia's first Vice President) commented soon after independence. "With a capital of one million they raise forty million from a bank, secure a manager from abroad, and create an enterprise."[21] Their success has been attributed to the fact that their contact with the Dutch was short-lived and shallow. Inimical mountainous and swampy terrain made the region easier to defend and discouraged the Dutch from economic penetration for nearly three hundred years, so that the long process by which entrepreneurial and labor incentives were undermined in Java never took place in Sumatra. Hatta also emphasized that the Minangkebau and the Bataks are good businessmen because they are nomads. "A nomad has to take a daily risk. A businessman has to take a risk too. [On the other hand] the Javanese waits for his crop. He has the indulgence to wait. The Javanese are very bound by tradition."[22]

In discussing peasant societies, anthropologist Raymond Firth makes substantially the same point: it is not that people differ widely in their individual motivation from one society to another, but that the institutional framework must be taken into account.

> Putting it bluntly, peasants on the whole would probably prefer to make a profit rather than not, and to go into business for profit if they see a clear way to do so. But the definition (of a peasant society) has more meaning. A peasant economy is one that links purchasers and consumers, resource allocation and product allocation, in a network of ties which are more personal, more directly perceptible, than in a more developed, complex economy.[23]

[20] T. W. Schultz, *Transforming Traditional Agricultures* (London and New Haven: Yale University Press, 1964), p. 37; Jere Behrman, "Supply Response and the Modernization of Peasant Agriculture: A Study of Four Major Annual Crops in Thailand," in Clifton R. Wharton Jr., ed., *Subsistence Agriculture and Economic Development* (Chicago: Aldine, 1969), p. 240; Merril Bateman, "Case Study: Supply Relations for Perennial Crops in the Less Developed Areas," in Clifton R. Wharton, Jr., ed., *Subsistence Agriculture and Economic Development*, pp. 243–56.

[21] Elizabeth Clark Pelzer, *Batak Entrepreneurship* (Cambridge: M.I.T. Center for International Studies, 1959), p. 36.

[22] Ibid., p. 36.

[23] Raymond Firth, "Social structure and Peasant Economy: the Influence of Social Societies," in Clifton J. Wharton Jr, ed., *Subsistence Agriculture and Economic Development* (Chicago: Aldine, 1969) p. 25.

Membership in a community implies constraints upon resource use as well as stimuli:

> The rewards for economic effort may lie to a great degree in the fulfillment of social obligations and social roles, and patterns of decision are regulated accordingly.[24]

Social structures may even impede development, such as, for example, restrictions imposed on a free market for land by patrilineage or matrilineage systems, or the dissipation of savings for ceremonial and ritual purposes.

Firth also confirms that members of peasant societies are more wary of investing in the macroeconomic field (where large-scale investment in new ventures would have to be made to further modern development):

> In the microeconomic sphere peasants are well aware of the possibilities of rational economic actions and make strong endeavours to better their economic position. . . . In the macroeconomic field they have not shown the same perspective, primarily because of lack of an understanding of how large-scale commodity markets work and the existence of external competitors with differential advantages.[25]

This point is well illustrated by a study of the limited scale of operations in village entrepreneurship in east and central Java. These Javanese entrepreneurs are mainly upper middle-class Moslem reformists and to a lesser extent skilled craftsmen, the same sort of religious, highly serious, petty businessmen who have appeared in the earlier phases of economic revolution in many countries, from the New England Puritans or the Dutch Calvinist reformists who believed in the virtue of hard honest work and saving. "All (I do) is work and pray: and it only takes a few minutes to pray," one of them said. "Those who are poor are poor mainly because they are lazy, stupid or sinful . . . while those who are rich are rich because they work hard and are clever." Their activities, however, were essentially small-scale. The smaller enterprises were expansion of craft activities, the larger ones usually development of trading activities, still linked to the *pasar* (bazaar), and operating within trading patterns that were "individualistic, speculative, marvelously intricate," but limited in foresight and scale of operation. There would seem no easy route by which these Javanese enterprises could grow gradually into modern large-scale industries; such a change would need a long step forward in education and experience.[26]

Indeed, the peasants and small-scale entrepreneurs described here were behaving rationally within a given social framework. They were responding to change—in prices, costs, techniques—within an existing system. They were not introducing the fundamental changes which development sometimes requires—changes in the system, as in technology, in organization, in scale of operations, in education, and changes in values and institutions.

---

[24] Ibid.,
[25] Firth, "Social structure and Peasant Economy, p. 26.
[26] Clifford Geertz, *Peddlers and Princes: Social Change and Modernisation in Two Indonesian Towns* (Chicago: University of Chicago Press, 1963), pp. 147–56.

DEVELOPMENT FROM WITHOUT?

Because of the gaps in education and attitudes to be bridged, a number of social scientists believe that development must be introduced to primitive or peasant societies from the outside, through foreign private investment or through financial and technical assistance agencies. In this way the cart is put before the horse, in that economic changes will generate social revolution. Some adherents of this view, however, believe that such a process involves serious social disorganization.

It is no doubt true that the equilibrium of primtive societies may be delicate, and that disturbing them can be dangerous; witness the decimation of the Australian aboriginal and American Indian populations by white man's diseases, drink, firearms, and disturbance of the ecology. On the other hand, there is evidence that cultural change can come with great rapidity, even to a primitive society, and apparently with little suffering on the part of the people involved, where the magnitude of the "outside shock" is great enough. The Manus society, for example, was transformed as a consequence of the occupation of the island by American troops during World War II.[27] The demonstration effect of having on the island a number of American soldiers considerably greater than the local population resulted in the Manus' culture jumping two thousand years in ten.

The experience of the Manus, anthropologist Margaret Mead declares, points up the completeness with which the people may *want* to change rather than merely submit to being changed. She also suggests that rapid change may well be less upsetting than gradual change: "It is easier to shift from being a South Sea Islander to being a New Yorker—as I have seen Samoans do—than to shift from being a perfectly adjusted traditional South Sea Islander to a partly civilized, partly accultured South Sea Islander." Each human culture, like each language, is a whole, and is capable of being learned. The term learned is the keynote; where culture is learned, it can be changed by reeducation.[28] Few countries, however, could mount such a large-scale vehicle of change as the Manus example, even if they wished to do so. Some societies are determined to retain indigenous modes.

DEVELOPMENT WITHOUT SOCIAL CHANGE?

It seems clear enough that development with no social change whatsoever is extremely unlikely. But there is also evidence that entrepreneurship can be generated, and development can ensue without a wholesale transformation of the society, even when the society has long been both traditional and stagnant. The spectacular industrialization of Japan after the Meiji restoration of 1868

[27] Margaret Mead, *New Lives for Old* (New York: Morrow, 1956).
[28] Margaret Mead, "From the Stone Age to the Twentieth Century," in David E. Novack and Robert Lekachman, *Development and Society* (New York: St. Martin's Press, 1964), pp. 204–205.

was accomplished, not by scrapping the feudal structure, but through the transfer of the feudal system from farm to factory. Feudal loyalties, commitments, rewards, and methods of leadership were rephrased in the setting of modern industry, allowing a relatively smooth transition to industrialization.[29] Even today, remnants of the feudal system contribute to the extraordinary discipline of the Japanese industrial organization. The history of Japanese development also includes instances of modifying change by encouraging improvement of traditional technologies alongside modern technologies. While Japanese development did not take place without some disruption, it suggests the possibility of designing a relatively smooth transition to modernization.

"WHAT NEED CHANGE AND WHAT NEED NOT"?

The idea that society is not a seamless web but a patchwork quilt, in which some patches can be changed without changing all or even most of them, is both good news and bad news. On the one hand it indicates that there is no need to change everything at once in order to get on with the job of raising productivity, output, and incomes. On the other hand, the enormous question emerges concerning what changes to make. There is plenty of evidence that economic modernization alone cannot be counted upon to bring a satisfactory pattern of social and political development; and at this point warnings concerning interference with the equilibrium of a traditional society become pertinent; an indiscriminate "replacement of patches" can lead to regression in other spheres.

Replacement of traditional by modern forms in one sector of society (such as technology) may bring stagnation in some sectors and breakdown in others warns sociologist E. S. Eisenstadt, (a former adherent to the theory of integrated modernization). Feudal regimes may be replaced by other forms of despotism rather than by democracy. The social security system of the village, tribe, or extended family can be swept away by a change to a monetary economy, without an adequate social security system taking its place. Not all undesirable traditions will disappear with modernization. Some, like the Indian caste system, may prove highly durable. Planned changes may not have expected results: Marxists have discovered that abolishing private ownership of the means of production does *not* automatically create a classless society. The process of modernization may introduce undesired life styles. Indonesian college students for example used the occasion of the visit in 1974 of President Tanaka of Japan to register violent protest against the pattern of modernization, invasion of foreign investment and foreign ways—by smashing massage parlors and night clubs in Djakarta. The blend of modernization and preservation of tradition, of rational and planned change with unexpected resistance to change, or even with reversion to "lower" forms of social orga-

---

[29] James C. Abbeglen, *The Japanese Factory* (Glencoe Ill.: Free Press, 1963), pp. 129–134.

nization, will vary from country to country in accordance with historical and cultural background.

Nor does past experience indicate any clearly defined "best" pattern of social and economic development. Eisenstadt has concluded from the experience of developing countries since World War II that there is no uniform pattern of development or modernization. It would be wrong to assume, Eisenstadt writes, that once the forces of modernization have impinged on any society, they naturally push toward a given, relatively fixed "end plateau."[30] What then, can a development economist do? How can he determine on which variables to work? Some pioneering work has been done in discerning strategic variables in the development process, but so far it offers only limited guidance.

SOCIOMETRIC MODELS

One of the first of such quantitative studies was carried out in 1960 by the United Nations Research Institute for Social Development (UNRISD). With the objective of defining and measuring levels of development, economic and social data were analyzed in terms of the importance of the correlation of each variable with all the others, reducing the original seventy-three variables to a group of 18 key indicators which had the highest scores (shown in Table 5.1). Nearly all of the more purely social variables dropped out in the course of eliminating the variables with low average correlation coefficient.[31] The highest scores (apart from newspaper circulation) were obtained for proportion of the labor force employed outside agriculture and output per agricultural worker, themselves highly cross-correlated (raising agricultural productivity is largely a matter of getting rid of farmers). Moreover, the average correlations for all countries in the sample hid wide differences in the correlations from one country to another. For example, in Ireland the social development indicators were high relative to the degree of urbanization and industrialization, while in Venezuela the reverse was true. Beyond confirming the hunch concerning the importance of "getting rid of farmers," the study indicated that the number of possible permutations and combinations of these elements of economic development and social change is virtually unlimited.[32]

Irma Adelman (economist) and Cynthia Morris (economic anthropologist) attempt to find generalities applicable to groups of countries. In effect, their studies try to plot the harmony or disharmony of changes within a society, with a view to selecting strategic variables to work on.[33] Their "factor analy-

[30] E. S. Eisenstadt, *Tradition, Change, and Modernity* (New York: John Wiley & Sons, 1973), p. 358.

[31] All of the measures of level of health services, except life expectance (which is an end-result of many developmental factors); most of the demographic variables and indexs of levels of education facilities; all of the measures of housing standards and transportation facilities. Even GNP per capita does not figure among the high correlation variables.

[32] D. W. McGranahan, C. Richard Proust, N. V. Dovani, and M. Subramanian, *Content and Measurement of Socio-Economic Development*, Report No. 70.10 (Geneva: UNRISD, 1970).

[33] Irma Adelman and Cynthia Taft Morris, *Economic Growth and Social Equity in Developing Countries* (Stanford: Stanford University Press, 1973).

TABLE 5.1 AVERAGE CORRELATION OF EACH CORE INDICATOR WITH
ALL OTHER CORE INDICATORS

(Adjusted Data, 1960)

Indicator	Average Correlation
1. Expectation of life at birth	.744
2. % population in localities of 20,000 and over	.730
3. Consumption of animal protein, per capita, per day	.791
4. Combined primary and secondary enrollment	.777
5. Vocational enrollment ratio	.788
6. Average number of persons per room	.783
7. Newspaper circulation per 1000 population	.823
8. Telephones per 100,000 population	.762
9. Radio receivers per 1000 population	.737
10. % G.D.P. in electricity, gas, water, etc.	.769
11. Agricultural production per male agricultural worker	.839
12. % Adult male labour in agriculture	.809
13. Electricity consumption, kwh. per capita	.687
14. Steel consumption, kg. per capita	.765
15. Energy consumption, kg. of coal equiv. per capita	.760
16. % GDP derived from manufacturing	.752
17. Foreign trade per capita, in 1960 US dollars	.737
18. % Salaried and wage earners to total G.D.P.	.750

Source: United Nations Research Institute for Social Development.

sis'' (a type of statistical method to measure the relative importance of various factors) of forty-one social, political and economic variables for seventy-four countries of development isolates significant differences in relations among variables at three levels of development. Of particular interest to this inquiry is the conclusion that the early stage of development is characterized by growth of the market sector and increasing dualism as the modern sector emerges, and that incentives for social transformation at this level of development are provided by economic forces.

While such sociometric models add to the understanding of the development process and may yet lead to a theory of social development, they do not offer a clearly defined plan of action. Yet governments must, in the meantime, find a basis for making policies. Anthropologist Clifford Geertz has suggested that a wide range of cultures is capable of generating entrepreneurship and economic growth, and that the problem is to recognize in each culture those forces that are conducive to growth and those that are not, and design economic development plans accordingly.[34] This concept of asking "what need change and what need not" demands individual case studies. There is simply no escape from the need to study each society in all its aspects. As these studies accumulate and actual experience is examined, certain uniformities will no doubt appear, and may eventually be woven into a general theory of development. This process has already begun.

[34] Clifford Geertz, *Peddlers and Princes* (Chicago: University of Chicago Press, 1963), Chap. 5.

OPERATIONAL EXPERIMENTATION

While there is still a long way to go, governments are widening their view of the things they ought to know. Increasingly, sociologists and anthropologists are included on planning teams to investigate special problems, such as the feasibility of migration and the possiblity of modernizing existing institutions. In the case of the preparation of an integrated development program for the region of Petit Gouave-Petit Trou de Nippes in Haiti, for example, development projects were limited during the initial phase of planning to "risk-less"[35] measures such as preventative health-delivery systems (balanced by a vigorous family planning campaign), rodent and pest eradication, repair of existing irrigation channels, and antierosion measures, while largescale projects involving new social organizations awaited the outcome of both anthropological and technical studies.

Pioneering work is also being done in integrating agro-industry into sociocultural environments by a team comprised of two organizational science specialists, a community development planner, and an economist. They are developing procedures to help community decision makers in Pahang Tenggara, Malaysia to choose technologies and the type of organizational design (patterns of work-sharing and decision-making) appropriate to local social and human requirements.

At the operational level, many governments—either consciously or unconsciously—are deciding "what need change and what need not" and devising policy accordingly. Two extreme approaches are emerging to the problem of changing people's overt behaviour so as to accelerate development. The more prosaic approach assumes that there is nothing wrong with people's basic motivation and that individual behaviour is responsive to new opportunities. The second approach sets out to change people's motivations so that they react differently to a given situation. In this view only the objective setting—including institutions—need be changed.

USING EXISTING INSTITUTIONS

With the more prosaic approach, measures are taken to overcome such barriers as fear of risk, of insecurity for the family and tribe by supporting technological change with "packages" consisting of credit and marketing arrangements, crop insurance schemes, training and demonstration. These measures are either channeled through existing institutions or new ones are created. The Commila Institute in Bangladesh, for example, has been introducing agricultural improvement by using an existing institution teaching local government officials how to conduct rural development by means of cooperative action. They have had some successes: savings institutions have displaced the moneylenders; cooperative use of pumped irrigation water showed an early

---

[35] The term "riskless" is used in the double sense that the projects could not prove a mistake in terms of subsequently acquired knowledge, and did not require discontinuous change in social organization.

payoff, while the introduction of tractors and transportation equipment along with draft animals proved profitable within the cooperative context.

Motivating Economic Achievement • On the other hand, some government institutions in India are experimenting with educational training courses designed to motivate economic achievement by psychological means. In the small city of Kakinada, conventional means of promoting technological advance—demonstration of new methods, business and technical training organized through SIET (the Small Industries Extension Training Institute) —were supplemented by motivational training courses conducted by the Center for Research in Personality at Harvard University.

The SIET Institute is oriented towards encouraging small factories in small cities. Frequently, wealthy Indians are neither interested in nor competent in business. In cities such as Kakinada, much capital is tied up in prestige possessions such as gold or jewelry and in moneylending to farmers at high rates of return. A key problem for SIET was to draw this "frozen wealth" into productive investment; the Harvard training scheme offered a possible solution.

These courses were conceived with the idea that investment should be supplemented by psychological education. It was argued that while vigorous economic activity may be successfully encouraged by improved economic opportunity, it can only succeed if the "target population" (entrepreneurs, managers in public enterprises) have the appropriate interests. Men naturally seek to maximize their satisfaction, but exactly what are they trying to maximize: income, growth of the firm, leisure? A fisherman of Kakinada who is trying to maximize leisure may choose to work shorter hours; a businessman may prefer to keep tight control of his company, rather than to expand its capital base; a moneylender may choose to lend funds at 24% annual interest to finance elaborate wedding ceremonies rather than manage a productive enterprise. In order to understand and predict action, one must know the interests, strategy, time perspective, and perceived environment of the man. If a businessman does not have an appropriate outlook, it must be changed so that he will respond to new situations in certain ways.

The achievement motivation course, designed for self-development, presented methods for achieving a self-directed change in motivation. The participants learned to view job situations, problems, and possibilities in terms of achievement. A continuing theme was that participants could initiate and control change by setting reasonable goals for change in themselves, in their firms, and in their area. They were encouraged to understand the needs of others and to help them in solving their problems. A major feature of the course was group discussion; the idea was that businessmen should work together to develop their city. It was assumed that the source of creativity is the desire to do a job well, to satisfy self imposed standards rather than a lust for material gain as such.

A review of subsequent activities of the participants revealed more active business behavior; they worked longer hours, made more definite attempts to start new business ventures, made more specific investments in new fixed productive capital (compared to moneylending) and employed more people (almost twice as many new jobs per entrepreneur during the subsequent two-year period after the course than did the controls). Small groups helped each other: since the original group included a bank manager and a moneylender, different combines were arranged to provide capital; in certain instances small groups combined to start new enterprises, something that was almost nonexistent in the control group. Finally they tended to have relatively large percentage increases in the gross income of their firms. Thus, by measures of all the basic aspects of the entrepreneurial function they had become improved entrepreneurs, and much more cooperative in spirit.

TO PATCH AN ISLAND

In Bali, where much store is set on absence of change, the question "What need change and what need not" is posed, not in terms of individual behavior (which is assumed to be responsive to new opportunities) but rather in terms of what *institutions* need change, in what part of the island. What might be described as a deliberate dualism has been attempted.

Until recently Bali had been largely left outside the main development stream by the Indonesian government, along with other "outer islands" whose economies seemed reasonably self-sufficient. However, a process of change began, reducing levels of living. Bali is changing, because the physical environment is failing to support the increasing population. Bali's 5,620 square kilometers supports 2.1 million people, making the island one of the most densely populated areas in the world. There is already a telltale decrease in forest lands, a steady and dangerous drop from 23% of total area around 1950 to less than 14% today. The decrease is not only dangerous because building costs are soaring and wood has to be imported for Bali's famous wood carvings; encroaching on the forest lands of the steeper slopes of the mountains runs the risk of erosion as is now happening in Java. (When forest land had been cleared for agriculture on the higher slopes, the earth eroded, not only rendering the land useless but also silting up the irrigation channels further down the mountain). There has been some emigration to Kalimantan, but the effect has been reduced by immigration into Bali from Java.

The predominant "patch" being added to stem this economic regression and reverse the trend toward economic development is an enormous expansion of the tourist industry, mainly through foreign investment. It is expected that by 1984, close to one million tourists will be visiting Bali annually, about ten times the present flow, and the main issue today is how to use the tourism bonanza without destroying the Balinese civilization.

An invasion of tourists on such a large scale could play for Bali the role that the invasion of GI's did for the Manus, a service which is not desired. The master plan for tourism therefore recommended that tourism should be "contained" in one area—a dry, infertile area with sparse population on the Bukit peninsula. Certain roads through the rest of the island have been designated as tourist circuit roads with convenient stopping places. To avoid disruption of religious ceremonies, special performances of dance and drama are to be provided for the tourists. The central government is acquiring the land in the tourist complex, providing the basic infrastructure, with a view to making long-term leases to foreign and domestic investors, and exerting some control. No casinos or nightclubs are allowed; architecture must have a Balinese flavor—a regulation which the Balinese Department of Public Works is enforcing with some effect.

The most serious threats, however, are the economic forces being set in motion. Isolating the tourist industry on a peninsula concentrates the main spill-off of the tourist industry in a small corner of the island, and a form of localized dualism is emerging. Possible economic spread effects to the rest of the island are diluted by Javanese immigration. Contracting firms report that not only must they recruit their technical staff from Java in order to assemble the necessary skills; but even unskilled labor is sometimes imported in order to have permanent staff *not subject to frequent absences on account of desa duties.*[36]

Here appears the "clash" of which Boeke spoke. The Balinese village is the epitome of the traditional Indonesian village which Boeke so admired. *Not* "keeping one foot in the village" endangers a very efficient system of cooperation. At present, the twelve-hundred traditional village units of Bali—the *desa adat*—are still very powerful. Primarily religious units, the *desa adat* can also make and enforce their own laws while across the interterritorial lines operate the *sekehe*—groups of people who cooperate to carry out a task, or to practice some art or craft. The most important of these autonomous organizations from an economic point of view are the *subak*—the irrigation societies. Decisions made by the *subak* may include not only the division of water supplies and maintenance of the irrigation dams and channels but also determination of the crops to be sown, the order of sowing and harvesting. Because they are so effective, the government in many cases uses the *subak* as channels for credit or as administrative vehicles for village subsidy projects. In general Balinese agriculture is efficient, but as it is now organized, depends on everyone's cooperation.

The Governor of Bali has taken a number of steps to counteract disruptive pressures. In 1972, he requested the *kabupaten* (district) Badung, which receives the bulk of the tourist receipts, to divide them among other *kabupaten*. To stem the influx of immigrants he issued a regulation that no non-Balinese were to be allowed to enter Bali unless employment and housing were already provided. Negotiations are under way to extend the scope of Bali's Udayana University. It has also been stipulated that proceeds from dance and drama performance be paid directly to the theatre *sekehe* rather than to individual performers. But the final solution will greatly depend on how the tourist receipts are used.

[36] For a more detailed treatment, see Ruth Daroesman, "An Economic Survey of Bali," *Bulletin of Indonesian Economic Studies,* Australian National University, Canberra, vol. 9 (Nov. 1973).

The crucial extra "patch" needed is the development of the other sectors of the economy. Promoting agricultural development might take care of population growth and take advantage of the excellent market the increase in tourism will offer. It could also ensure that food prices remain within the reach of the local population; the price of fresh eggs in the tourist areas has already risen so steeply that the Balinese complain that they can no longer afford them. Modernizing agriculture would also free labor to move into the tourist complex and into light industry. It is possible that agricultural development could take place within the cooperative structure; moreover, employment opportunities in tourism involve only a small percentage of the work force; tourism is expected to create only about one hundred thousand jobs, at best, both directly and indirectly in the foreseeable future. Relatively few Balinese, therefore, may need to change their way of life. If an adroit economic development plan is designed and carried out, Bali's traditional culture may be saved while levels of welfare are improved.

It can be questioned whether the enormous dimension of the "tourism patch" was well advised. A smaller "patch" might have sufficed, combined with agricultural modernization, light industrialization, and a vigorous family-planning campaign. But the decision has been taken, and people who know the island well believe that Balinese culture is strong enough to survive the onslaught through its long capacity to absorb new cultures into the old.

THE NEW CHINESE MAN

By contrast, Chinese policy during the Cultural Revolution was directed toward uprooting tradition with the ambitious objective of the creation of a new Chinese man with motivations in keeping with the new order. The reason behind the Maoist attack on the "four olds" (old culture, old traditions, old politics, old economics) was the unwelcome continuance of a Chinese middle class, a phenomenon which had not been foreseen in Marxist theory.

According to Marx, the *base* of a social system provides a foundation for its *superstructure,* which consists of the pattern of institutions, organizations, chains of authority, traditions, and habits of thought of the society. The base of capitalism is private ownership of the means of production; and its superstructure is characterized by untrammeled individualism, a social hierarchy based on wealth, leading to a predilection for rank, status, and power, and resulting in inequality of consumption. Marx seems to have assumed that changing a capitalist base to a socialist base involving state ownership and control of the means of production would lead to a classless society. However, according to the Maoist view, a capitalist-type superstructure can grow up on a socialist base, and may eventually—if not checked—transform the socialist base back to a capitalist base.

Chinese Marxists point out that although the old Russian middle class was almost completely wiped out, a new class developed afresh. In China, a large section of the middle class welcomed the victory of the communists over the corrupt Kuomintang regime. However, although many "turned over" and became socialists, the change had not always gone deep; furthermore, many of the peasants and workers who were given positions of authority swiftly assumed undesirable bourgeois attitudes. The "Party persons in authority taking the capitalist road" were accused of carrying out their work in an authoritarian manner, assuming a superior attitude to the workers, forming cliques to protect each other and taking advantage of their position to gain privilege and amenities for themselves. Not only were class prerogatives persisting, but showed signs of becoming hereditary; power and privilege could be passed on, not only through influence, but also by means of education, since the children of the old middle class, coming as they did from literate family backgrounds, had a natural advantage over the children of peasants and workers, particularly in entrance examinations. Worse, Chinese Marxists saw a potential danger in the economic incentives and market relations being introduced by "revisionists." Although they recognized the difference between using profits as a criterion of success in an enterprise and relying on profits as a motive for activity, they believed that the first would inevitably lead to the second, and finally back to capitalism.

But what to do? To develop a modern socialist state needed coordination and a unified command, requiring a bureaucratic apparatus. Mao Tse-tung's solution was based on the simple idea that power should pass to the people— that workers and peasants should participate in decision making. Leaders there must be, but they should be chosen for their identity with the people, and to prevent leadership degenerating into rulership, cadres must merge with the people, through the "three togethers"—eat together, live together, work together. True democracy could be achieved by imbuing the whole nation with a selfless spirit of "serving the people." Mao decided that this cultural revolution should be carried out by the people themselves.[37]

Mao advocated the formation of cultural revolutionary committees and groups whereby the rank and file could criticize the cadres with whom they had been working. Such committees and groups, might be formed not only in government and other organizations, but also in factories, mines and other enterprises, in urban districts and villages. In colleges and schools, students (along with sympathetic teachers) could form similar groups and engage in constructive criticism of the education system. "The methods to be used in debates is to present the facts, reason things out and persuade through reasoning."

In the subsequent months the Cultural Revolution raged, with violence along with the "reasoning"; at the end of it, the bureaucracy had been thoroughly shaken up and simplifications of procedures had been made. A number of institutional devices were introduced to encourage social fluidity and discourage marked distinctions either of prestige or income. Educational reforms have included a new system of selection to overcome the handicaps of workers' and peasants' children, and a new system of examinations emphasiz-

---

[37] For a more detailed account of the 16 points see Joan Robinson *The Cultural Revolution in China* (Harmondsworth, England) Penguin Books 1970.

ing practical work rather than memory. To "merge school with society" high school graduates work for at least two years before they can be considered for university admission.

Within enterprises, participatory management and the chance to participate in innovation was believed not only to effect a social leveling, but also to evoke creative potential in individuals. Opportunity was created for the development of a free flow of information and decisions both to and from workers—a feedback mechanism that is supposed to bring initiative from below into full play. Mass participation in decision making takes place by means of worker membership in the Revolutionary Committees which now govern all organizations. Rapid promotion of factory workers to leadership positions took place during and after the Cultural Revolution; at the same time, the expert, the technicians and the managers spend frequent periods of time in manual labor. "Three in one" teams consisting of managers, technicians and workers engage in industrial research and development, and in general group discussion is encouraged. Material incentives are deemphasized; managers are paid little more than skilled workers, while profits go to the state; people are expected to work well from social conscience. (Since Mao's death there appear to have been modifications in these policies. Some material incentives have been resumed.)

The above examples of social engineering were chosen to provide a variety of situations in various settings, and with various objectives. It was only noticed later that they had two uniformities: cooperation (either to foster it or to preserve a cooperative tradition) and vigorous and imaginative leadership. Moreover, while emphasis on goals vary widely, in both the Chinese and Indian cases, encouragement of cooperation was accompanied by vigorous encouragement of individual initiative, emphasizing self-satisfaction rather than self-interest, by encouraging "the will to succeed not for the fruits of success, but for success itself . . . the joy of creating, of getting things done, or simply of exercising one's energy and ingenuity." This description of the spirit of entrepreneurship from Joseph Schumpeter fits objectives of both the Chinese and Indian experiment.

Finally from all these examples emerge the importance of political leadership in launching such experiments. While the emphasis today is placed on devising ways to allow individual initiative full play, yet all these examples suggest that development requires not only entrepreneurship but an interplay of creative entrepreneurial activity and encouragement by the political power elite. Which brings us back to our third group of actors in the development process: the leaders and the political framework within which they operate.

THE POLITICAL FRAMEWORK OF DEVELOPMENT

A great deal of economic development theory simply assumes a political system within which development can take place. The truth is that lack of an appropriate political framework is the most common cause of failure to develop. In this regard the shortcomings of the "seamless web" concept and of traditional political theory become glaringly obvious.

Traditional theory assumed a general pattern of "political development" which would accompany technological progress, social modernization, and economic development. There would be a natural progress from feudalism or despotism to full fledged parliamentary democracy with universal adult suffrage and active political participation by all social groups. This process would be accompanied by diffusion of individual freedom and civil rights, rule by law and enlargement of the political unit from village or city state to nation state. As already outlined, Marxist thought predicted a series of conflicts ending with the rise of the masses and revolution, and an eventual withering away of the state.

Experience in the last thirty years particularly has shown that economic development does not guarantee greater freedom, democratic institutions, or broader political participation. As noted above, feudal or semifeudal regimes may be replaced in the course of "modernization" not by democracy but by other forms of despotism, such as military regimes. Meanwhile a rise of the masses and revolution has indeed taken place in some countries, but communism has not always been the choice and nowhere has the state "withered away". Instead most Third World countries are trying to forge a political system which suits their own history and culture, their own social institutions and economic potential.

In light of these explorations, the essential elements of a political framework conducive to continued economic development may be suggested:

1. There must be a political power elite committed to development.

2. The government must have a substantial measure of popular support.

3. The government must have sufficient strength and stability and competence in public administration to permit policies and programs to be formulated and carried out.

4. There must be a mechanism for the expression of regional and local needs and the government must be in some measure responsive to these needs and changes in them.

5. There must also be a means of changing the government, without violence or disruption, when it becomes too far removed from the needs and aspirations of the society.

6. Finally, and fundamentally, development requires also a widely shared ideology or religion of a kind that is not inimical to development. Where necessary political leaders must reinterpret the country's ideology to heed the needs of development, creating new institutions and adapting old ones where appropriate.

A DEVELOPMENT-MINDED POWER ELITE

Nothing reflects more accurately the nature of a society than the sort of people it puts or permits in positions of political power. The sociocultural framework not only determines who gets political power, but also affects the views of those in power as to just what is feasible by way of economic and social reform. Since a traditional society may engender social pressures tending to thwart innovation and change, the forces that disrupt it must be powerful ones.

It is obvious that economic development will not take place in countries where the political power elite likes things as they are. When land was the only source of wealth in Latin America, for example, the owners of the great *latifundia* had little incentive to initiate a process of economic development. Nor did their ideology prompt them to do so. In much of Latin America in the early days, the ideology rested on Christianity and a large residue of intellectual adherence to liberalism. The liberal philosophy with its emphasis on the natural harmony of things brought no effort to promote development and the *latifundista* interpretation of Christian ethics (with its emphasis on divine right of property) brought no effort to reduce the extreme inequalities of wealth although it did bring a feudal style of social security to the peasants. In the case of Mexico the "powerful force" which disrupted the *status quo* was revolution and, as will be discussed later, the revolution was followed up by vigorous economic leadership.

Alternatively, an outside shock or threat may jolt the elite into taking the lead in initiating economic development, as did the threatened elite of Meiji Japan, who responded to their fear of colonial domination by modernizing Japan. A dominant social group may also respond to the challenge of withdrawal of status from a social group, a change in the power structure, contradiction among status symbols, or derogation of institutional activity without change in the power structure.[38] When, for example the Balinese sultans were demoted as governors for the Dutch after Independence, losing handsome yearly allowances, they turned to small industry and hotel keeping to replenish their income.[39] Another milder shock might come from changes in export prices for a traditional product. If, for example, an elite depends on sugar and the price falls drastically, traditional landowners may move their money into industry. When some industrialization takes place, as it has in the Philippines, Chile, and Brazil, and the balance of political power shifts from the landed aristocracy to the industrialists, the role of the middle class increases opening up further possibilities for change.

POPULAR SUPPORT

Even if a society produces a development-minded political elite, the people may not give their support to economic and social development policies, if they themselves do not fully understand what is involved. "Reform" governments that prove unable to introduce truly effective reforms are all too familiar a phenomenon in developing countries. While the people may want economic development and the government they elect may reflect their wishes, it

[38] Hagen, *The Theory of Social Change.*
[39] *Ibid.*

is a long step from there to passing and enforcing the stiff legislation which would be required to launch the country into economic development. Government leaders must make unpalatable decisions on land reform, educational reform, tax reform and patterns of spending. A well-intentioned government may fall, or the reform may not come to pass if the population is not sufficiently sophisticated politically to support its government in its political efforts. The Wilopo government, the most development-minded and efficient of all Indonesian governments of the 1950s, fell when it tried to move illegal squatters from plantations to good rice land elsewhere, in order to grow the export crops badly needed to earn foreign exchange for development.

A UNIFYING IDEOLOGY

Often the trouble with reform governments lies in the fact that they are undecided as to the means by which the reforms should be made. A fundamental requisite for successful development is a generally held ideology which will at once unify the people behind their political leaders and permit effective decisions to be taken and implemented. Countries which decide to choose what is best from other systems and evolve their own brand of democracy to suit their indigenous culture patterns can suffer long delays in economic development in the course of reaching this synthesis. Imported systems (whether socialist or private enterprise) have to be adjusted to local conditions, and vice versa. Enormous disagreements may arise; Indonesia is again a case in point.

When Indonesia attained her independence at the end of 1950, several favorable sociopolitical conditions were present. There was no entrenched landed aristocracy, no ingrained tradition of corruption. The multi-ethnic composition of the population posed a potential problem, but Sukarno—a brilliant, charismatic leader—was welding the many ethnic groups into one nation, and moreover, the revolution had already begun to unite Indonesian society, galvanizing energies which could be directed toward economic growth. The elite, which had led the four-year fighting revolution included a number of brilliant men eager to tackle the problem of development; they were, however, in disagreement as to what the new Indonesian democracy was going to be. Their lack of accord was mirrored by the 469 registered political parties.

While everyone was agreed that the best elements of Western systems should be chosen and fashioned into an Indonesian socialism based on the values of village cooperation, there was indecision concerning the type and degree of socialism. What role should the government play in production and in distribution? Should everything be done by cooperatives? Should foreign enterprise be allowed to continue? Should Indonesian private enterprise be given its head? Problems in designing various institutions as vehicles for change arose in the translation of village democracy to the national level. At the time, a haggard foreign expert was heard to expostulate: "Yes, by all means let us build on village democracy, but tell me, how do you launch a multimillion dollar hydroelectric power project as a village cooperative?"

While the initiative of governmental entrepreneurs, was largely frustrated, through indecision, the prevailing nationalism stifled going private concerns. Not only were the Dutch (and eventually the British and Americans) driven out of their plantations, mines and banks, but local Chinese were forced out of the countryside and collected in ghettos in the cities where they could be more easily restricted, and finally even the burgeoning Indonesian entrepreneurship was crushed as a threat to Indonesian socialism. There was not enough constructive effort towards alternative modes of production. When inflation assumed serious proportions, eventually reaching an annual rate of price increase of 1500% in the last months of 1966, Sukarno's solution for the economic crisis was to tell his government to find the people responsible for it and shoot them.

Yet the later Sukarno years also offered an interesting example of concrete ideological definition. Sukarno finally realized the need for positive action concerning economic development. The fall of the Wilopo government had signified the difficulties of parliamentary democracy, and Sukarno decided the country needed a political organization closer to tradition. He achieved some success in mobilizing the country through his "guided democracy," modelled on village democracy with himself as *lurah* (head man).

The Eight Year Plan merits attention because it was not merely a design for economic development; it sought to crystallize the concept of Indonesian democracy and to define the sort of society the Plan was expected to produce. The Indonesian national identity, the Plan stated, was to be sought in the traditional culture; the goal must be "a just and prosperous society" to be based on the Pantja Sila, the five pillars of Indonesian social and political philosophy—nationalism, internationalism, democracy, social justice, and belief in God. This "familylike society" would reproduce at the national level the spirit of village organization. More concretely, Indonesian socialism should guarantee every citizen adequate food, clothing, and shelter; appropriate public health and education facilities; support in old age; and freedom to develop his spiritual and cultural life. The plan also sought to define the roles of government and private enterprise. Since the government could not carry out all activities, private enterprise should have a limited role in production and transport, but no role whatsoever in the field of distribution. If government activities must be supplemented in that sector, it should be done by cooperatives. Ownership of house and yard was permitted, and the peasants were guaranteed that they would own their own land (it was stressed that this was contrary to Soviet doctrine).

Economists roundly criticized the Plan on technical grounds, but it proved a rallying point and a basis for making some decisions. Some new institutions were designed, cooperatives launched, adaptations to existing institutions made. Where necessary (as an Indonesian economist explained) "we dress modern institutions in traditional costume." Some joint enterprises, for example, were presented as a *"gotong royong,"* where government cooperation with foreign enterprise was arranged. Tragically, energies and resources thus mobilized were dissipated in supporting Sukarno's military confrontation of

Malaysia. Indonesia's economy, which had stagnated since independence, began to regress.

After an abortive communist coup was followed by Sukarno's deposition, the subsequent military-technocratic government took the decision to accept large amounts of economic assistance from the West and to permit large amounts of foreign investment. Indonesia now has a combination of private enterprise and central control with considerable responsibility for development accorded to regional and local authorities, including cooperatives and traditional institutions.

The earlier Indonesian experience thus provides an example of a sometimes, irresolute, sometimes irresponsible, political power elite inhibited by memories of colonial domination, rather than an example of the impossibility of adapting a traditional society to modern life. Taken as a whole, the post-revolutionary Indonesian experience represents a continuing imaginative seeking after and evolution of an indigenous democracy.

TOWARDS A UNIFIED APPROACH

While this inquiry seems to have raised more questions than it has answered, some conclusions may be drawn. Virtually any society or culture is capable of economic development *if it wants it*. As the UNESCO conference on social prerequisites to economic growth has concluded: "There are no social prerequisites which must be fulfilled *first* in order that economic development may take place afterward.[40] A traditional society may not need to change, and once development has been decided on, drastic cultural change is not always necessary. At the same time, there is nothing we know for certain which suggests that a well thought-out development program of sufficient scale will fail, or that it need be particularly painful to a society, if it is supported by massive efforts in education and reeducation, not only in the new technologies, but in understanding of what is involved in development. If well-designed, such a program may provide the "sharp stimulus" Rostow asks for, the "impetus for growth" to which Hagen refers, and the "purposeful change" which Margaret Mead advocates. To ensure the success of such a program, however, economists now realize that sociocultural factors must be taken into account. This awareness has led to the emergence of an integrated system of development, now officially designated as the "unified approach", which will be described in more detail later.

First officially called for at Stockholm in 1969 by the United Nations Expert Group on Social Policy and Planning in National Development, the unified approach treats the problem of development as a total societal process. The concept of development now includes all elements of human life that con-

[40] Raymond Firth, *General Working Paper,* UNESCO Working Group on Social Prerequisites to Economic Growth, UNESCO/SS/WP, March 22, 1963. See also UNESCO, *Social Prerequisites to Economic Growth* (Paris: UNESCO, 1964).

tribute to human welfare, including nutrition, health, shelter, employment, the physical environment, the sociocultural environment, (quality of life) and such matters as participation in the decision making process, a sense of human dignity, of belonging—anything pertaining to the "style" or pattern of development most appropriate to a country's values and circumstances. In practice, economists are now building these considerations into all stages of development planning. What becomes important is to include the relevant sociocultural factors in the development planning process, both as objectives and as instruments of change. The art of unified planning is to recognize within the culture those dynamic elements that contribute most to a raising productivity and incomes, and to discern in each case the optimum mix of social change wanted for its own sake, institutional and cultural changes needed for or likely to follow measures to raise productivity, with the changes in technology and occupational structure that will bring higher productivity; and family planning. Assuredly, some mix can be found in every society that will bring significant improvements in overall welfare and start a process of sustained development. However, while sociocultural considerations must be taken into consideration, they must be built into a *solid economic framework*.

6

Formulas
for development

We can now focus on our ultimate objective: to design policy for economic development. In doing so we must examine more purely economic reasons for past failures in development. First of all we shall ask: is there anything wrong with the standard formula? Is a new formula needed?

In Chapter 3 we noted that the basic formula of development—"getting rid of farmers"—involves the successful transfer of an agricultural (or primary) surplus (along with the farmers) to the industrial sector, and the generation of mutually stimulating interactions between the sectors:

1. Agricultural production increases.

2. The farmers sell their surplus food and raw materials to the industrial sector, buying industrial goods and services. They may invest their profits in industry, thereby creating new industrial employment.

3. Agricultural workers move into the newly stimulated industrial and service sectors, attracted by the higher wages and lighter work.

4. Industrial consumer goods are sold to workers and peasants and better equipment is sold to farmers and industrialists; Farmers and industrialists can produce a further surplus with better equipment. The interaction continues.

5. As labor becomes scarce, wages rise, and consumption increases, banking institutions and other services emerge in response to need.

There are variations to this basic formula. Malaysia, for example, has succeeded by moving large numbers of farmers into modern agriculture as well as into industry. It is also conceivable that a country could simply modernize agriculture, thus *keeping* farmers (depending on population growth and trade). Occasionally the impetus has come from the tertiary sector, such as tourism in Bali and Morocco. In future, surpluses are likely to move more and more into the tertiary (particularly marketing) and quartenary sectors as world technologies improve. It is a matter of strategy to chose the right variation, a process of choice which will be discussed in the following chapter.

In this chapter, we are concerned with isolating forms of inertia impeding the application of any of these formula, and finding a way around the largest single stumbling block: population growth. Countries have begun such a process of development; they have produced and transferred a surplus, but development has slowed down or come to a grinding halt through failure to keep pace with population growth. When supplies fell behind population growth, prices of food and raw materials rose; wages then had to be increased to offset the higher cost of food; profits were squeezed, investment fell, and stagnation set in.

These interactions and reactions are very clear in India. At the local level, a bumper harvest is followed by industrial expansion and a movement of rural labor into the towns; a poor harvest is followed by industrial unemployment and a return of city workers to the villages. At the statistical level, the effects on wages and food prices are also very clear. Food grain output stagnated between 1961 and 1964, then a good crop was followed by two years of drought. The price of food rose at an average annual rate of about 19.8% between 1962 and 1968; wholesale prices generally rose by 10.7%; industrial production suffered from the shortage of agricultural raw materials and money wages rose because of the rising prices of food. The growth rate of industrial output of about 9% in 1965–66 turned to a rate of decline of 9.8% in 1966–67 and 0.7% in 1967–68. Then, as a result of the high-yield grains, food grain output rose sharply by 28.4% in 1967–68 and the consequent demand for consumer goods from the farm sector led to a recovery of industrial output which rose by 6.4% in 1968–69. The seventies have continued the same pattern of "boom or bust" according to good or bad harvests.

For the development process to continue, not only must agricultural production increase, but also technological progress in the industrial sector must offset rising wages. Since innovations are likely to be labor-saving, the scale of investment must grow continuously if transfers from agriculture to industry and services are to outrun growth of the agricultural population—*unless population becomes stationary*. Since agricultural populations are seldom stationary but usually burgeoning in developing countries, it is at this point that the formula again breaks down. Labor is not made scarce. On the contrary; ever increasing amounts of rural labor move into the cities, but the work is not there. Some drift back to the villages, but increasing numbers find their way into the urban slums and shanty towns. Most sought after is an economic model designed to strike at the central problem of unemployment. While population growth has created the enormous dimensions of the unemployment problem, are there other reasons for the insufficient scale of investment?

DEVELOPMENT OF THE LABOR SURPLUS ECONOMY

Unemployment is the end result of a number of "lags," or inertias, which arrest the dynamic interaction among the sectors. Most developing countries, whatever their endowment, and however appropriate the formula applied, are threatened by one or more of these lags. Economists have been isolating these underlying reasons for inertia and consequent unsatisfactory sectoral interactions prevailing in poor and stagnant countries in order to *alter* the interactions so that the necessary movements of labor, food and raw materials and capital are achieved. Unsatisfactory interactions are due to:

The Agricultural Lag: lack of an agricultural surplus or (in some cases) failure to transfer surpluses due to lack of transport, marketing facilities, etc.

The Industrial Capital Lag: lack of savings for industrial investment, or occasionally failure to transfer saving into industry.

The Industrial Employment Lag: the consequent lag in employment opportunities in the secondary and tertiary sectors, leading to failure to transfer sufficient agricultural labor into industry.

Population: a rapid growth in population can swallow up an agricultural surplus and limit savings.

THE AGRICULTURAL LAG

Of all the conditions on the list, the most important is the lack of an agricultural surplus. Lagging agricultural production has been a problem in the Soviet Union, Yugoslavia, Cuba, Brazil, Indonesia, Algeria, and indeed in most of the underdeveloped countries attempting a takeoff. These failures to achieve potential increases in productivity in agriculture are known as the "agricultural lag."

By the "agricultural lag" we do not simply mean low agricultural productivity, although productivity is obviously related to the problem. The phenomenon of the "lag" is best understood in the context of a development plan. A development program may call for an increase in food production; steps are taken to raise productivity, yet the expected increase does not take place. In certain cases, total production has actually fallen rather than increased. China provides a spectacular example in the Great Leap Forward which was supposed to double agricultural production in a single year, but in fact production dropped. India provides another example: in spite of a considerable proportion of national income allocated to agricultural improvement during the first three Plans, (as will be discussed below) food grain output increased very slowly (except for bumper harvests with good monsoons) and finally stagnated in the early sixties. In some socialist countries, collectivization has sometimes proven a disincentive to the peasants, who preferred to work their own land. Land reform sometimes has similar effects, as in Mexico. But quite apart from such specific setbacks, a built-in, little understood inertia in agriculture has become strikingly evident in developing countries as a group. The high yield grains have changed the picture somewhat, but the success of the Green Revolution itself is threatened by some of these inertias.

The "ag lag" resolves itself into three main questions: why do countries with idle land fail to achieve an agricultural surplus? In countries where there is a labor surplus in the agricultural sector, why should agricultural production go down when a development program is mounted and some of this surplus labor is transferred to industry? Why is an overall increase in supply of food-stuffs necessary when a development program is mounted?

LAND SURPLUS COUNTRIES

In many countries, low agricultural output per man-year reflects over-crowding on the land. This phenomenon is still relatively rare in Latin America, where, more than any major developing region, the gap between ac-tual and potential agricultural productivity with existing population densities in agriculture seems needlessly great. Yet in some countries where idle land exists, increased requirements for food and agricultural raw materials are met less by expanded domestic production than by imports, increasing the burden on the industrial sector.

Why indeed import food rather than open up more land? This particular inertia often lies in the land-holding systems. As Malthus perceived, large landholders may not wish to go to the expense of opening up new land while their returns from their land already under cultivation are high. The idle land provides them with a reserve for the future, permitting more intensive cultiva-tion of the land already in use. They are also reluctant to face the managerial problems of operating still larger units. It is in their interest to *create* an ar-tificially "land-poor" country. In such situations the peasants working on the land suffer lack of incentive; often in debt to their landlord, working harder is of little advantage to them.

DOES A LABOR SURPLUS REALLY EXIST?

Part of the agricultural lag arises from what now appears to be the false as-sumption that if workers are moved from the agricultural to the industrial sec-tor, agricultural production will not fall. In the course of implementing devel-opment plans, governments have moved labor from rural occupations to industry, assuming that because of agricultural unemployment the transfer could be effected without reducing total agricultural production. But often ag-ricultural production has gone down. Some observers have long pointed out that the early optimism concerning development by absorption of "disguised unemployment" from agriculture is unfounded.[1] Rural unemployment in un-derdeveloped countries is neither cyclical nor chronic, but underemployment that arises mainly from seasonal variations of agricultural operations. It is therefore not possible to transfer large numbers of workers permanently and full time from peasant agriculture to industry without a drop in agricultural output, for during planting and harvesting seasons, which altogether amount to several weeks per year, the entire labor force is occupied. It may even be

[1] Technically, disguised unemployment consists of those who are employed, but in a situation where hours worked are so few and productivity is so low that they could be completely and per-manently withdrawn without a drop in output, and without new investment or technological prog-ress.

necessary to bring back members of the village who have gone off to take casual jobs in the industrial sector. Even in so densely populated an area as Java with 1,500 people per square mile, there are still labor shortages in planting and harvest seasons. What one finds is seldom chronic underemployment, but extreme seasonal variations, combined with work-sharing devices and short hours during the off-seasons. No country has a "reserve army" of agricultural workers, completely unemployed, who can be transferred the year around with no rise in industrial wages, no investment in the agricultural sector, and no drop in agricultural output.

THE NEED FOR INCREASE IN FOODSTUFFS?

Yong Sam Cho explains the need for increased footstuffs during a development drive in terms of malnutrition.[2] In certain very poor countries, the caloric intake is too low for the number of hours of work put forth to be increased. His analysis relates to societies where agricultural incomes are so low that only an increase in agricultural wages rates will permit the increase in caloric intake necessary for a man to work additional hours. His analysis, therefore, applies to those very poor countries of Asia, Africa, and Latin America where land is already scarce, with special reference to South Korea.

Cho defines a "technical wage" as the minimum wage needed to sustain an employed worker in a biological sense. He divides the supply of labor into the number of hours worked per man, dependent on the wage level (i.e., nutrition) and the number of workers. With a higher wage rate, each man works more hours, because he will be better nourished. Thus, given a fixed amount of land, or a fixed total of output to be produced, the aggregate number of workers required to accomplish the task decreases as the wage rate rises.

In a traditional society, open unemployment is not acceptable; a system of work-sharing is in effect, so that all workers are absorbed. Limitations are imposed on the level of total output and consumption by the necessity of providing savings (in the form of seed for example, for next year's cultivation), and the limited amount of land available. In other words, work-sharing ultimately means food-sharing, and the amount of food available limits production.

By the same token, this analysis explains why economic development requires an overall increase in foodstuffs, not only for the agricultural workers but for the industrial workers as well. One obstacle to development in the past has been that nutritional requirements for the industrial sector are usually greater than for the agricultural sector in many underdeveloped countries.[3]

For a man to do a full day's work in a factory, he needs an improved diet. He could survive on a lesser diet in agricultural work simply because he did not have to work all day. If a development program moves some of the agri-

[2] Yong Sam Cho, *Disguised Unemployment in Underdeveloped Areas With Special Reference to South Korean Agriculture*. (Berkeley: University of California Press, 1965).

[3] In some thinly populated African countries, where land is abundant but poor, peasants are both able and required to work long hours. In these cases, nutritional requirements may not rise much with a transfer to industry.

cultural labor force into industry, the agricultural workers left behind also require an increased diet if they are to accomplish their increased work load.

Sometimes even modernization of agriculture may be difficult without an initial food surplus. In Mauretania, for example, the key element in development over the next ten years will be irrigated, modern agriculture based on the Senegal river and its tributaries. But the new technology will require considerably more labor-intensive operation than the present traditional agriculture. At present levels of nutrition, the peasants are simply incapable of working harder and longer. For the new system to succeed, additional food will be needed until the more advanced agricultural technology begins to bear fruit.

Mauretania also illustrates another biological, rather than cultural, explanation for "inertia" or "indolence": ill health. The majority of the Mauretanian population suffers from one or more debilitating diseases, such as malaria, bilharziasis, river blindness, and intestinal parasites. Not only will the irrigation projects fail if health standards do not rise, the same situation exists for industry; for industrial enterprises to compete successfully in world markets, costs must be low, and that means continuous operation at a high level of efficiency. These requirements cannot be met with a labor force suffering simultaneously from malnutrition and assorted diseases.

Virtually all the underdevelopment theorists cite an agricultural surplus as a key prequisite to a takeoff, but their theses are mainly devoted to the mechanics of structural change, without enough thought as to how this increase in agricultural production is to come about. The key to success in the Japanese, American and European cases was that an Agricultural Revolution went hand in hand with their Industrial Revolution. Any country that neglects agricultural improvement in the course of industrialization does so at its peril, as one socialist country after another has learned.

The importance of the Green Revolution in this context is obvious as a means to producing this crucial agricultural surplus. However, it is not just a matter of better seeds. Considerable capital investment is necessary in fertilizers, insecticides, irrigation systems and training, along with extra storage facilities and transportation. Eventually, if the agricultural surplus is to keep up with, or even catch up with, population growth, and if the desired transfer of agricultural labor is to be made to the industrial and services sectors, mechanization must follow. It is therefore important to examine more closely the reasons for the past lack of agricultural investment.

THE ABSENCE OF AGRICULTURAL MODERNIZATION

Let us return briefly to our coinciding sectors and regions: the modern industrial sector and the agricultural traditional sector coincide with the rich and poor regions. If we rephrase the statement and say instead: the modern industrial sector is rich and the traditional sector is poor, the answer to the development problem seems simple: modernize agriculture and it should become rich too. Why has there not been a modernization of agriculture? Or more specifically, why has there, in the past, been so little capital movement, either from the industrial sector or from the agricultural sector, to invest in modernizing agriculture?

Returns to capital are higher in the rural sector in some countries than in the industrial sector. Why then has not industrial capital flowed into agriculture, if returns were higher than in the mines, the oil fields and the plantations? Some local urban capital has indeed moved into agriculture, but it has usually been a matter of businessmen, lawyers, and doctors buying land and becoming absentee landlords rather than agricultural entrepreneurs. In any case, industrial capital in the past has been predominantly foreign capital; the failure of foreign capital to flow into peasant agriculture was due mainly to the fact that the men who launch, finance, and manage the foreign enterprise know little of peasant agriculture and village life. The high returns to agricultural capital came from high rents, moneylending, and middleman activities. The rural capitalist relies for this success on his personal and firsthand knowledge of the villagers with whom he deals; he lends to them, sells to them, buys from them. This is knowledge of a sort the foreign capitalist does not have and does not wish to acquire; moreover, there were other more familiar avenues for investing capital rather than the alternative formidable undertaking of modernizing peasant agriculture.

But why did not the rural capitalists promote a shift to mechanized commercial agriculture as their counterparts did in the United States and Canada? The middleman of the Asian type, selling consumers goods, advancing seed and simple tools on a sharecropping basis, and lending money, was by no means unknown in North America. Such middlemen were also buffers between the small farmers and the advancing technology of the big cities. The difference is that a time came when manpower became scarce in the agricultural sector, making it profitable for the North American middlemen as a class to take over the land altogether, to foreclose on their tardy debtors, and to amalgamate small holdings into units large enough to permit large-scale, extensive, mechanized and commercial agriculture. From there on the advance of technology spread to agriculture as well as industry. Likewise, progressive individual farmers increased the size of their holdings and used more capital-intensive methods.

The barrier to agricultural improvement in the underdeveloped countries has been that labor never became scarce in the rural sector. In Asia and Africa, the middleman has continued to play his traditional role, directing his efforts to maximizing his share of the output obtainable through labor-intensive methods. As for the farmers themselves, there was no incentive to introduce labor-saving innovations, even if they knew about them, and could finance them.

The Green Revolution is, in some cases, breaking these deadlocks by initiating changes in agricultural investment and in certain situations leading to amalgamation of plots. The status of the tenant, seems liable to drastic change, and with it the longstanding dependency relationship will disappear. In some of the land reform zones in the Philippines this relationship has already become contractual, involving leasehold arrangements. All in all, the

Green Revolution is bringing about social change along with a substantial increase in agricultural productivity in a number of countries.

THE INDUSTRIAL CAPITAL LAG

What, then, could prevent this improved agricultural technology from having the desired cumulative effect of continuously rising productivity? Let us consider several possible models.

1. The Farmers Are So Poor That They Consume the Increased Output Themselves • As pointed out in Chapter 4, backwash effects are already emerging in the wake of the Green Revolution; the richer, better educated farmers can best exploit the high-yield grains; the poorest farmers dare not take the necessary risks, nor can they afford enough fertilizers. Moreover, the high-yield grains can only grow in irrigated areas; more than three-quarters of the cultivated area in India, for example, has neither irrigation facilities nor assured rainfall. For various reasons, then, some farmers who introduce the high-yield grains may produce so little or may be so poor that they simply consume the increased output themselves. The increased demand for fertilizers, insecticides, or various other services by the richer farmers may stimulate the secondary and tertiary sectors somewhat, but there is no substantial agricultural surplus which can be transferred into the industrial sector. All in all, there is a once-over improvement in welfare but no cumulative effect; the farmers may simply have more surviving children, or may deliberately have more children to deal with the increased work that the high-yield grains entail. In this case the initial improvement in welfare will be dissipated, and the population will remain caught in the "low income trap."

2. Landholding Is Concentrated in the Hands of a Few Rich Landlords Who Do Not Transfer the Agricultural Surplus to Industry • Even if an agricultural surplus is achieved, it may fail to reach the industrial sector if land is concentrated in the hands of a few landlords. If the country is politically unstable, they may send their profits abroad into Swiss banks, or into investment in more stable areas. Even if the country is politically stable, the landlords may be afraid to invest in industry—about which they may know little—particularly if a skilled industrial work force does not exist. While there has been some transfer of agricultural profits into urban investment in Latin America, the overall lack of capital movement into industry and the consequent economic stagnation in some Latin American countries has been blamed primarily on the large-scale landholding systems called the *latifundia*. Through high concentration of rural property in a few hands a great deal of the capital has either been sent out of the country or spent on luxury goods.

Certainly, in areas where they have been successfully introduced, the high-yield grains have directly stimulated the industrial sector. The demand for fertilizers, insecticides, and other imputs have led to the development of secondary occupations, while the increased needs for transport, storage, and other services are generating some increase in the tertiary sector. If the workers and peasants manage to get some share of the surplus (sharecroppers, for example, would gain something), welfare will rise. Not only do they stand to improve their nutrition, but their increased spending power may stimulate the local town's commerce. However, if the main proceeds are invested abroad, the overall increase in domestic investment may be too small to have any cumulative effect.

If the landlords sell the agricultural surplus abroad, and buy jewelry, gold, or other assets, such as existing apartment houses, *at home,* rather than abroad, inflation is likely to follow. The domestic price of gold bars, jewelry and apartment houses will tend to rise; the domestic money supply will expand through repatriation of profits, generating an inflationary tendency. If existing apartment houses are bought, this investment may stimulate the building trade, but once again, the large-scale investment in industry essential to stimulate cumulative development in the whole economy may not take place, leaving the country with a highly concentrated expansion in building trades only, as in Lebanon during the fifties.

In India, an important factor delaying the development of indigenous industry has been the high returns on investment in agricultural credit. Interest rates on loans in the rural sector range from 16% to 100%. In addition, the rural capitalist, who usually makes loans on a sharecropping basis, is frequently in a position to earn a handsome profit on speculative investment in stocks of crops. In comparison, industrial investment is less lucrative and less certain because here again, the traditional landlord is more familiar with local matters than with urban possibilities.

3. The Landlords Sell Abroad and Invest in Industry at Home • Obviously, the transfer of the agricultural surplus is easiest if there are "dualistic" landlords who operate in both sectors as in nineteenth century Japan: they exist today in the Philippines, in Malaysia, in Brazil, Mexico and other countries but there are not yet enough of them. Dualistic landlords usually prove to be modern landlords for whom investing in industry is not such an unknown quantity. Often they are large plantation owners who, when profits are squeezed by adverse movements in world prices and adverse trends in world demand, are interested in shifting their capital to industry.

If these landlords sell their agricultural surplus abroad and invest at home, using their foreign exchange to buy capital equipment and raw materials, a process of development can begin.

4. The Land and the Agricultural Surplus is Largely in the Hands of Peasant Proprietors and Small Farmers • In the case of a nation of peasant proprietors and small farmers, the pattern of development is a little different, although some problems are basically the same. Small farmers may not buy gold bars or Rolls Royces, but if they buy imported watches and radios or jewelry, the immediate effect is the same. Moreover, peasant proprietors do not ordinarily buy shares of new industrial enterprises, or even put their savings into banks. However, they are much more numerous than the ''few rich landlords'' and consequently have a big potential spending power. Not only will they buy fertilizers and transportation services; after a bumper harvest, they will go into the towns to buy household goods and clothing. In response to this new market, the merchants may invest *their* profits in factories to manufacture clothing, furniture, etc. The creation of a *mass* market for radios, may induce some entrepreneur to start producing them at home.

It is true that the merchants may simply put *their* profits into frozen wealth—gold bars, jewelry, or put them out to finance weddings at high interest rates because they, too, are inexperienced in industry, as were the merchants of Kakinada. In such cases the government must intervene at this link in the feedback system in order to keep it going.

5. The Government Does the Investing or Directs Private Investment • In the case of rich landlords, or smallholders, or merchants who do not save and invest profits accruing initially from the agricultural surplus, the government can achieve the same effect by taxing the landlords and doing the investing for them, or the government can design an incentive tax program to encourage private individuals to invest in industry, reducing risk of failure through entrepreneurial and technical training programs.

TRANSFERRING AGRICULTURAL LABOR

Once the agricultural surplus has been produced and invested, a transference of agricultural labor to industries and the services should follow. The success of this stage of the process of development depends greatly on the magnitude of the unemployment problem and on the resources of the country; Malaysia, a well-endowed country, with a relatively small population of 10 million people is at the present time succeeding with this type of takeoff.

THE MALAYSIAN EXPERIENCE

Malaysia's takeoff originated in a stimulus from the primary sector in the form of plantation rubber and palm oil, tin and timber. Expansion of these industries allowed a transfer of some 50% of the labor force into the modern sector, including advanced technology production of food and raw materials, plus finance, trade, transport, processing, etc., linked to them. However, the unemployment problem was never solved and was aggravated when the postwar population explosion began to pour school leavers into the labor stream in the sixties. Today, a program of expanding plantation production combined with vigorous promotion of industry, has finally resulted in a scarcity of qualified labor and rising wages, although there is still a serious scarcity of jobs considered suitable by high school and university graduates.

The investment gap was closed by a combination of foreign and domestic private investment, foreign aid, and government investment. Government investment included the opening up of new land for settlers, planting rubber and oil palm, investment in infrastructure, and participation in new manufacturing enterprises. Recent settlements have not only provided opportunities for Malaysian peasants to move into modern agriculture; unified planning has also built in opportunities for employment in industry and services.

As with so many success stories, there was an element of luck; the energy crisis boosted rubber and oil palm prices (oil palm prices quadrupled, rubber more than doubled) and at the same time, oil was found off the Malaysian coast. This timely swelling of foreign exchange earnings gave a final boost to the takeoff.

Rates of growth have been high, and it may be questioned whether today Malaysia, with a per capita income over $800, should still be regarded as a less-developed country. Inequalities of wealth remain marked, but there has been substantial sharing of the new prosperity by a wide spectrum of the society.

THE INDUSTRIAL EMPLOYMENT LAG

In less well-endowed and overpopulous countries, where massive unemployment still exists, "making labor scarce" is much harder to achieve. Even if an agricultural surplus is created and successfully transferred, a chronic gap may exist between capital available and the investment needed to achieve full employment. The problem is to achieve full employment in occupations affording acceptable productivity.

One temporary escape valve is the fact that the cultivation of the high-yield grains has been *creating* high-productivity employment, rather than freeing farmers. Mechanization can and does substitute capital for labor, particularly in large-scale land cultivation; however, the type of mechanization associated with the agricultural improvement consistent with prevailing conditions in most developing countries may raise the demand of labor, initially at least. Some early results of the Green Revolution in the Punjab showed that an increase in output of 100% led, in spite of mechanization, to an increase in employment of 22.6%. Terraces for irrigation and soil conservation, wells and tanks, country roads, afforestation, require few resources to complement labor beyond those locally and inexpensively available.

The construction industry also offers efficient labor-intensive techniques; the same can be said for low-cost methods for improving sanitation and water supply. A much quoted example is the use of fishponds for disposing of garbage, a natural method which is labor intensive and provides a valuable source of protein.

In industry, technologies requiring little capital but achieving acceptable productivity are glaringly rare. Some opportunities lie in combining more labor with *existing* capital equipment through multiple shifts, gearing factories to three eight-hour shifts or four six-hour or even six four-hour shifts. As national incomes rise, work-sharing in urban as well as rural activities may be the final answer, and one the Asians understand very well. In one prosperous Filipino village, for example, there are so many passenger "jeepneys" (small busses) that they go out only on alternate days in order that everyone may have a chance to earn. In very poor countries, however, this kind of work-sharing can only go so far, since what is obviously and urgently needed is an overall increase in production.

A great deal of surplus labor has found its way into the tertiary sector but often into very low-productivity occupations. While the Green Revolution and expanding industrial activity has stimulated some high-income services such as banking, modern transportation, insurance, and storage, the unemployed have drifted into the low-productivity services—such as peddlars, domestic servants, peddicab operators. Governments are now trying to channel the unemployed into intermediate services, such as paramedical services, along with the high-productivity services such as education, recreation, the professions, the arts, and research. The Chinese government, which has eliminated unemployment under particularly difficult circumstances, has used this device together with most of the others discussed above.

THE CHINESE EXPERIENCE

Chinese leaders since the revolution have attached more importance to the agricultural sector than is usual among socialist planners. Of peasant stock himself, Mao always clearly recognized the economic and political importance of the agricultural base. Even in the early fifties, when Chinese development planning followed the usual socialist bent of a major allocation of investment resources in heavy industry, it is generally agreed that agriculture was not so tightly squeezed as in most socialist countries.

Producing the Agricultural Surplus • However, agricultural output was still deemed inadequate; it was planned that it should be doubled during the Great Leap Forward in 1958. The subsequent crop failures were partly due to underinvestment, to bad weather, and to the psychological and organizational upheaval of collectivization.

Originally, it had been planned to follow moderate agrarian policies during the First Five Year Plan (1953–57) rather than disrupt the agricultural sector by rapid and radical socialization. Only a third of the peasants were to be organized into cooperatives, and they were to be lower level, semisocialist cooperatives to which the peasants would contribute their lands, draft animals, and farm equipment. The peasants would be reimbursed through dividends, according to their respective contributions. Mao, however, speeded up the process; by the middle of 1957 most peasant families had been organized into higher-stage cooperatives in which the peasants contributed their land, animals, and implements without reimbursement. The following year, the three-quarters of a million cooperatives were amalgamated into some twenty-six thousand rural communes, and their lands were declared nationalized. However, adequate skills for managing the large collectives had not been accumulated; moreover, some of the moves towards full communism, such as abolishing private plots and distributing food according to needs rather than the basis of work points proved premature. In the subsequent reorganization, such extreme policies were dropped, and a period of consolidation of the gains began.

Greater emphasis on agriculture in the 1960s led to expanded irrigation and other water-control systems; more multiple cropping; heavier applications of fertilizer; increased supply of farm machinery; and large, modern state farms, increasingly engaged in reclaiming wastelands. Incentives have included pricing modern imputs close to cost of production; moderately higher government procurement prices for major crops; moderate agricultural taxation (at present about 6% of gross agricultural output), lower prices for manufactures, thus improving agriculture's terms of trade. It has been estimated that agricultural production is now increasing at the rate of 3% per year while population is increasing at about 2%, giving a small margin for improved diet.

The Capital Lag • Since the beginning of the Chinese communist regime, capital formation appears to have been rapid. The planners first gave industrial development priority, investing nearly 60% of total capital in industry, most of which went on modernization and expansion of extractive and heavy industry. The USSR helped by building 156 key productive units, including the integrated steel works at Anshan and Wuhan, electric power stations, tractor and lorry factories, cotton mills, and coal mines. In the first years, a major stimulus also came from the land reform, which redistributed income among the peasant population; the government then captured much of this income through tax and price instruments and redirected it towards capital formation. Since that initial impetus, various estimates and guesstimates indicate an increase of 20%–25% per annum. However, this increase started from a very low base, and a large gap has appeared, to the extent that industry has not been able to absorb desirable amounts of the increase of agricultural labor. Indeed, it appears that so far, the industrial sector has achieved little more than absorbing the natural increase of the urban population.

The Nontransference of Agricultural Labor • Since the 1953 census, when some 13% of the population were living in urban settlements, the urban population has slowly increased to about 20% at which it is holding steady–in response to deliberate Chinese policy.

As in most countries, farm workers in China are attracted to the cities, where work is lighter, wages higher, and educational and cultural amenities better. However, to avoid urban drift and urban unemployment, the Chinese government has controlled population movements by a variety of means. A would-be rural-urban migrant must first have a job before being allotted an apartment by the city housing control. The municipal employment bureaus try to utilize the labor supply from the existing urban population before assigning employment opportunities to rural-urban migrants. Lengthy paperwork is involved in changing a migrant's "ration book location," and it is changed only for good reason. By these means the Chinese have avoided the rural exodus and urban unemployment prevalent in most developing countries. Moreover, if the cities cannot absorb their own natural increase of labor, unemployed school leavers may even be despatched to the country for farm work.

What happens, then, to the increase of the labor force bottled up in the rural areas? In the first place, agricultural improvements in the form of greater use of fertilizers, improved irrigation systems, etc., by allowing a shift to double cropping, provide increased employment. The expanded production of fruit and vegetables, poultry, dairy products, and livestock has also created labor-intensive work. Moreover, not all rural labor engages full time in agriculture. Farm workers have been diverted into building roads, schools, public buildings, and housing. The communes are industrial as well as agricultural producing units. Their activities include agricultural machinery repair shops, fertilizer plants, water pumps, as well as brick kilns and cement plants. They also produce some consumer goods for local sale and sometimes even for export. Excess labor is also absorbed into the services sector. The communes have numerous medical and paramedical staff, large administration staffs, and education is very labor intensive. These sectors are not entirely divorced from each other. Administrative and industrial workers may help with the harvests, while roads and housing and other construction work may be off-season occupations for farm workers. All in all, the Chinese leaders declare that not only is rural labor fully employed but that labor is scarce in the countryside.

Rising Wages? • According to the standard formula, when agricultural labor is made scarce, wages should rise. Chinese wages are holding steady, with occassional, entirely discretionary raises in wages for the lowest-paid echelons. However, rising wages in the standard model (based on wage and price movements in a market economy) indicate rising levels of living, which is the ultimate objective. From available estimates, the Chinese have achieved modest improvements in levels of living. The city price of food grains has remained unchanged since the early 1950s; the prices of cloth and other necessities also remain stable, removing upward pressure on the wage structure, and prices of manufactured goods are falling slightly. These prices bear out the estimated 3% increase in agricultural output and 4% increase in output of manufactured consumer goods, while educational, health, and other public services have increased. On the assumption that population has grown at no more than 2% per year, it can be assumed that per capita consumption has been rising at 1 to 2% per year.

While this control of wages and prices hides the increases of welfare it also hides the labor surplus. Labor is not truly scarce in the usual analytical sense. China still has a labor surplus economy in the sense that her full employment includes some very low-productivity work, such as creating new land by carrying earth in baskets from elsewhere. Such employment has enabled a better spread of wealth and a better nourished population which can form a firm basis for further development and eventually full high-productivity employment activities. The chances will be improved if China can continue to slow down population growth.

Restraining Population Growth

The preceding analysis underlines again and again the fact that the race towards prosperity is still finally the race against population growth. While the ultimate success of the new agricultural improvements can be swamped by another population explosion, a reduction in the population growth rate of any country by 1% is tantamount to raising the growth of agricultural output by 1%, and is much cheaper. While a decline in fertility rates would have little influence on the size of the labor force in the underdeveloped countries for nearly a generation, its impact of the number of consumers would be immediate. There would be fewer children to support, freeing capital for investment in production rather than consumption.

As already observed, history indicates that structural change discourages fertility; the whole process of development including education and women's emancipation, wider horizons, all tend toward smaller families. At the purely economic level, modernization and mechanization of agriculture and industry mean that farmers no longer need large families to work the farms; the same may be said of labor-intensive cottage industries. Even in a socialist country, where this kind of home economics may not have such a strong influence, the influence of structural change still seems to hold. According to observers, it is believed that in China birthrates are falling quite rapidly in the cities but slowly in the countryside.

The Basic Needs Approach

The dilemma posed by the fact that in a very poor country raising productivity and employment together is extremely difficult, (whether investment is made in agriculture or industry or both) has led to increasing emphasis in both theory and practice on a third approach, which lies outside the standard two-sector model. This approach consists of launching the cumulative process of development by working directly on human resources (improving health, nutrition, education) and in raising productivity by simple devices such as reducing waste and improving the efficiency of present techniques rather than introducing drastic changes in technology. Now called the ''basic needs approach,'' this solution has been used for many years in countries where poverty of resources precluded major structural change or modernization.

In Libya, for example, when the first United Nations team went there in the early 1950s (before the discovery of oil), the country was very poor in physical resources. Rather than introduce sweeping modernization, it was decided ''to help Libyans do better what they were already doing.'' The tanners were taught how to flay hides without spoiling them; on the basis of a survey, the fishermen were advised to cast their lines further out at sea (where they caught more fish) and were provided with better boats to do so; wool growers were trained to shear, scour, sort, grade, and bale wool so as to get better prices in the Rome market; and, at the agricultural level, sand dunes were turned into olive groves and citrus fruit orchards.

Sometimes very simple forms of intervention can bring quick results. Thus, in Haiti it is estimated that half the crops are lost to rats, birds, and insects. Accordingly the Canadian team working in the Petit Goave to Petit Trou des Nippes region planned a campaign to eradicate the rats and construct a system of birdproof and insectproof storehouses. These facilities could double the real income of peasants in a single year, eliminating of the prevalent malnutrition and thus permitting further increases in productivity. Together with a system of credits against crops in storage, they will also improve income distribution by allowing the peasants to hold crops for higher prices rather than being forced to sell immediately after the harvest when prices are low, and to buy back the same foodstuffs at high prices when food is scarce.

An important aspect of this approach is the multipurpose role of employment. More and more countries are making full employment a major developmental instrument, not only to increase national income, but as a departure point for a system using improvements in human resources as positive feedback loops to create more productivity and increasing welfare. Employment creation is regarded as the most effective instrument to get this feedback system underway; full employment provides one of the simplest, most direct ways to effect a more equitable distribution of income, and consequently of human welfare. Workers and their families are more likely than non-workers to be adequately fed. Better health and nutrition thus underpin not only employment, but education as well. Malnutrition, of course, hampers a child's ability to learn. Ensuring that all families receive incomes from steady employment makes it more likely that the children will actually get to school, and once there, will be able to learn something; also that they will stay in school, rather than being taken out prematurely. Improved health and nutrition make better workers. Several countries, including Algeria, Tunisia, and Morocco, have instituted "food-for-work" programs, in which the unemployed are hired for public works projects and are paid partly in well-chosen foodstuffs, thus improving nutritional standards at the same time that useful projects are completed. The Canadian team in Haiti also planned to use "food-for-work" programs. The idea was to organize the work along the lines of the traditional "combite" institutions, under which a farmer would invite his neighbors to spend anything from a few hours to a few days on a particular project and provide them with food and drink. Under the Canadian scheme, peasants hired in their spare time to build access roads, anti-erosion terraces, and simple irrigation systems would be provided with well-balanced meals for themselves and their families.

All the Haitian tactics cited were part of what was essentially a "basic needs" approach designed by Canadian economist Pavel Turcan, and Haitian agriculturalist Raoul St Clerc. The strategy involved little structural or technological change and no great outlay of capital. The basic idea was to increase agricultural output through a better infrastructure (preventing erosion, building access roads and silos, improving, repairing or installing small irrigation systems), using local materials where possible and local technical capabilities. An important part of this rationale was to give full rein to the entrepreneurial initiative of the people, using local traditional cooperative institutions as vehicles for change, along with vigorous encouragement from the *animation sociale* team.

A rough translation of *"animation sociale"* would be "community development." But this essentially French approach (also utilized in the Canadian province of Quebec) has a scope and method of its own embodied in professional courses which train *"animateurs sociaux"* who are awarded special diplomas. As the term suggests, the objective is to involve the concerned population in the development process, including decision making, and to smooth the way to social change. Supporting this move for change are improvements in the physical and cultural environment. A city plan is being prepared for Petit Goave and community centers are being set up with films, educational, and training programs. This project is supported by a strategic public health program run by a Harvard Medical School team which combines *preventive* medical services with education in nutrition and family planning.

The official basic needs approach acquired its formal shape during the International Labor Office (ILO) World Employment Program (WEP) and particularly at the World Employment Conference of 1971. The ILO worked its way, step by step, from a direct concern with employment creation, through a consideration of the special problem of the educated unemployed, to a recognition that the basic problem in developing countries is not unemployment but low-productivity employment (hence, the working poor). The major resolution of the World Employment Conference calls for a basic needs approach to development planning. The background report for the conference defines basic needs as follows:[4]

1. Adequate food, clothing, and shelter.

2. Education and health.

3. Basic human rights.

4. Employment as a means and end.

5. Improved quality of employment (improving the work place, and individual and group relations within it).

The report rejects a strategy of "growth followed by filtering down" in favor of "growth with distribution". It suggests that projects should be chosen with a view towards fulfilling basic needs rather than maximizing national income. For example, food grains might be grown rather than export crops.

[4] International Labor Office, *Employment, Growth, and Basic Needs: A One World Problem*, Report of the Director General, Geneva 1976, p. 32.

At the same time, the report underlines the fact that growth is still necessary if the basic needs of poor countries are to be met by the year 2,000.

AN INTEGRATED DEVELOPMENT PROGRAM

How, then, does the standard model stand up? Essentially, it stands up well. In any country, agricultural or primary surpluses must increase to keep pace with population growth and to keep prices down (or waiting lines short and rations adequate); agricultural and industrial technologies must advance in order to raise productivity and thus continue to raise welfare levels. Whether it is termed "profits" or not, the difference between total national income and wages after tax must increase to permit the capital accumulation necessary to raise standards of living. To assure continued progress, labor must be "made scarce"; full employment is the most reliable means of raising incomes, spreading welfare more equitably, and providing a further stimulus to technological progress.

The Chinese experiment suggests that labor can be retained geographically in the agricultural sector, and absorbed in the agricultural industry and para-medical and other services, thus forming a basis for an industrial sector. The basic needs approach indicates a major switch in thinking. In the 1950s, governments assumed that development consisted of a more rapid growth of GNP (gross national product) and while all governments had on their official list of goals better distribution of wealth and improved welfare, health and education, planners counted much too heavily on a rapid growth of the GNP to fulfill these goals by a trickling down process. Planners now realize that the achievement of these goals must come *first* in order that GNP will grow as a *result*. These modifications are stepping stones towards the basic model rather than its renunciation (although a society may chose *not* to industrialize once basic needs are achieved).

However, what comes out of this review is not a refutation of the basic model, but rather the discovery that failure results from inputs insufficient to enable it to function, bringing us back to an essential aspect of *the unified approach*. While it overlaps the basic needs approach in many aspects, the unified approach may be said to begin where the basic needs leaves off. The basic model is needed for very poor countries; *the unified approach comes into the picture when a country is ready for, and wants, structural change*. In this context, the unified approach stresses inclusion of *all* the necessary inputs—not only quantities of capital, labor, and resources, but also inputs such as research, education, and nutrition. The latter will improve the quality of both physical and human resources at each stage of the process resulting in a robust development system with all desired interactions.

If we construct a model for an integrated development program and if we spell out how our "system" would work in a country where a period of expansion is triggered by introducing high-yield varieties of grain, we can see the importance of a unified approach. Leaving out any items listed in the

Employment in the industrial sector depends on:
· the stock and quality of capital;
· the quality of human resources;
· the wage rate in the industrial sector.

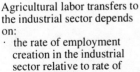

Agricultural labor transfers to the industrial sector depends on:
· the rate of employment creation in the industrial sector relative to rate of growth of total labor force

Wage rates in the industrial sector depend on:
· productivity and incomes in the agricultural sector.

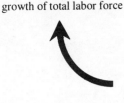

Productivity in the agricultural sector depends on:
· the ratio of capital (including land) to labor force;
· the quality of the capital and human resources;
· output per head raised by transferring workers to the industrial sector.

FIGURE 6.1

model meant risking failure. Permanent increases in output *per head* in the agricultural sector, as a result of once-over improvements such as high-yield grains, then requires transferring workers to the industrial and services sector, or the modern agricultural sector. Employment in the modern (industry and services) sector depends on the level of technological advancement, worker skills, and the wage rate; wages, in turn, depend on productivity and incomes in the agricultural sector, which will rise once again with *further* technological advancement, and new agricultural skills. Meanwhile, the increased agricultural output should further improve nutrition and general health.

For this feedback to continue, technological progress in agriculture must be matched by capital accumulation and technological progress in industry. Scientific and technical progress depends on the amount and pattern of spending for research and development, and on the requisite formation of skills. Even borrowing technology from abroad requires adaptation to local conditions, and the capacity to borrow depends on local investment in research and development. Reduced population growth will clearly help as well. Achieving these ends depends on the people themselves, on their willingness to forego a certain minimal percentage of income (consumption) and on whether they are willing to undertake family planning.

This analysis also indicates that launching underdeveloped countries into economic growth is a matter of *scale*. It requires certain critical minimum effort and investment in both industrial and agricultural sectors if the development effort is to be great enough to outstrip population growth (in an over-populated country) by eliminating unemployment and sustaining growth until fertility rates fall. Some countries may prove too poor to get out of the low-income traps by themselves. To be sure, an "up-by-the-bootstraps" approach is easier if the boots are provided by foreign aid, as was the case with the food used in the "food-for-work" programs in North Africa. In both of our case studies, Malaysia and China, timely aid helped to close gaps. At the very least, a "minimal effort" will depend on *how* the surpluses are invested, which is the concern of strategies.

7

Planning development: strategies

Recently an industrial economist was telling a group of friends about the Pahang Tenggara Project in Malaysia. In describing the plan for opening up some empty territory, he mentioned that the farmers would be settled in the cities rather than in the country, and would be bussed out to the palm oil and rubber plantations. "But why put them in the towns when they could live near their work in that beautiful countryside?" queried one of the group. "Why shouldn't the towns be beautiful?" countered the economist.

This reply reflects the revolution which is taking place in developing planning. Ten years ago, the planner might have replied in terms of maximizing efficiency; moreover ten years ago the planning team for opening up this territory would have included agricultural economists, and a forester or two, rather than an industrial economist. In fact, the team included all these and, as well, architects and physical planners, who brought their tradition of the "City Beautiful" to the problem along with a knowledge of how to handle such subtle variables as "enrichment of life." The project was also served by a team of sociologists who made studies of a number of *kampongs* (villages) in neighboring areas whence new settlers might be expected to come. Among the items on their copious questionnaire (designed to ascertain the life styles of the settlers and their idea of welfare) were inquiries as to preferences for easy access to city amenities. There was a nearly unanimous opinion among those who had been exposed to city amenities; they would consider rural occupations only if they could still have access to the resources a city offers.

While "development" is essentially a matter of raising the overall productivity of an economy, so as to permit continuing and widespread improvements in general welfare, each society has its own concept of "welfare." The concept of "development" must be broad enough to take these differences in values into account. Preservation of cultural traditions, protection of the environment, national security, city amenities—all these are a part of welfare, and thus of development, if they are valued by a particular society. If a society prefers more dance performances or more sculptures or temples to more automobiles, "development" may entail producing more dance performances, more sculptures or more temples. If a society chooses to utilize its increased productive capacity to increase leisure, welfare improves just the same, and so "development" takes place.

Given all the pitfalls noted in the previous chapter, it is clear that successful development will seldom be a "natural state of affairs." At every turn the need is apparent for informed foresight and analysis of trends, to be made either by government or private enterprise. The concept of *planning* development, then, instead of just letting it happen—or not happen—implies the existence of some group of decision makers who believe that the present situation is not satisfactory and that intervention is needed in the economic and social process. These decision makers must have power to influence overall productivity in such a way as to improve welfare, and the will to use it for development; otherwise what will really be planned will not be development but something else—maintenance of the power and privilege of the political elite, for example. In most situations the "group" that has the power is the central government, although it may be influenced and assisted by state and local governments, business groups, trade unions, farmers' organizations, and, one hopes, by the professional planners who do the basic analysis and present the fundamental options to the government.

Implementation of a plan is easier if a government has direct control of all investment decisions, as in a centralized socialist system; however the possibility of planning is not related to the relative size of the government sector. So long as a government has a single instrument of control—a budget, a central bank, a tariff system, a foreign exchange control system—it can plan for the use of that instrument to influence private decisions so as to promote development. These observations might seem redundant to people living in nonsocialist countries; but not many years ago the socialist dogma was that planning is impossible in a nonsocialist country. This skepticism sprang partly from Marxist political theory, according to which governments of advanced capitalist countries are mere creatures and tools of the monopoly-finance-capitalists. That bankers and industrialists have an influence on government decision making in such countries as France and Japan no one would deny: but planning takes place just the same, and most socialists today would admit it, although some would still question the motives and the efficacy of nonsocialist planning.

By definition, then, the purpose of development planning is to intervene to increase productivity, i.e., raise output per man-hour, and to improve the uses to which the increased productivity is put. How can this best be done? Finding the answer to this question in each country, for each plan period, is the essence of determining *development strategy*.

Raising Output per Man-Hour

There are only half a dozen ways in which output per man-hour can be raised:

1. Improved Resource Allocation • Obviously output per man-hour can be raised by moving resources from low-productivity to high-productivity uses. Historically, the most important form of such improvement has been the shift of manpower from agriculture to industry and then to services. In today's developing countries, with the services sector already so important an employer, it is rather a matter of shifting manpower from agriculture and low-productivity services to industry and high-productivity services.

2. Increase the Amount of Resources Used per Man-Hour • The most obvious way of providing manpower with more resources is by capital accumulation—more plant, equipment, and tools per worker. Some land-rich countries may still be able to increase the amount of arable agricultural land per worker, by jungle clearance, irrigation, reclamation, etc. (Malaysia for example). A third way of providing more resources is through resource discovery; a fourth way to achieve increased resources per head is through effective family planning, so as to restrict the rate of population growth. In an extreme case a government might conceivably plan for a falling population.

3. Technological Progress • A government may seek to improve the quality of plant, equipment, tools, and raw materials used in industry; and better seeds, better fertilizers, improved livestock, and machinery in the agricultural sector.

4. Improve Human Resources • A government may plan to improve human resources directly through education and training, public health, and better nutrition.

5. Reduce Unemployment • In terms of pure arithmetic, a simple way of increasing output per member of the labor force is to put idle people to work (without reducing the output of others) so that total output, and thus output per member of the labor force, will go up. In most situations, moreover, the increase in number of productive workers will increase the productivity of land, capital, and previously employed workers as well.

6. Improve the Pattern of Foreign Trade • Through planning, a country may be able to improve its terms of trade; that is, to raise the average price of goods and services it exports relative to the average price of its imports. It might do so by improving the mix of its exports, or by "import replacement" (producing at home relatively expensive products previously imported). A country might also plan to increase the total volume of exports, so as to import more equipment and raw materials for developmental purposes. Finally, government might seek to improve its balance of trade (total exports minus total imports). A so called "unfavorable balance of trade" means that a country is consuming more than it produces; and so long as a poor country can finance import surpluses through foreign aid or investment, it may be very helpful. Ultimately, however, every country must be in a position to finance its own imports by its own sales of goods and services.

THE BALANCES

These six elements of a strategy to raise productivity can be translated into six balances.

The first balance is between capital accumulation and increased consumption. If any society tries to save and invest too much out of its own resources, not only may the improvement in welfare be so restrained as to dishearten the population (or fall short of adequately nourishing it), but there may not be a sufficient market for the final product of the new plant and equipment once in place. This balance can be expressed in terms of a "growth path," or the rate at which total output expands in each period. Up to a certain point, allocating more resources to capital accumulation (plant, equipment, transport facilities, energy) will accelerate economic growth. Beyond that point, at least in a private enterprise society, capital accumulation itself will be inhibited, because consumption does not expand fast enough to absorb the output of final products. Socialist countries can continue longer to produce machines to make more machines (capital accumulation), because the capital goods industry need not be immediately profitable; but as one socialist country after another has found out, even in the most enthusiastic of socialist countries the population will eventually bring political pressure to bear to persuade the planners and politicians to use the growing stock of capital to raise current living standards.

The second balance to be struck is between sectors and regions. We have already seen that any country that neglects either the modern industrial sector or the agricultural sector is likely to run into trouble. Since in developing countries the modern sector tends to be concentrated in one or two regions and the traditional sector in other regions, sectoral balance also implies regional balance.

With respect to technological progress, the most obvious balance relates to the amount of resources to be allocated to research and to scientific and technical training, as opposed to utilizing existing technology to expand current production. But there is a more subtle balance to be considered between technological progress and unemployment. Technological innovations are usually labor-saving. They may be capital-saving as well, but since no developing country has too much capital, that is something devoutly to be desired.[1] Most

---

[1] Most innovations are "capital-saving" in the sense that they reduce capital costs per unit of output; but they may raise the capital-labor ratio at the same time.

underdeveloped countries, on the other hand, have idle labor. If technological progress merely adds to unemployment, there may be little net gain. Each government encouraging technological progress must consider the country's capacity to absorb labor elsewhere when it is displaced by innovation.

Every country faces, sooner or later, the need to shift emphasis from natural-resource-based to human-resource-based development if high rates of growth are to be sustained. The planning problem is to discern when, where, how, and at what speed this transfer should be made. The answer clearly depends on diversity, quality, as well as quantity of natural resources available. Oil countries like Kuwait or Libya, with little in the way of natural resources except oil, have little choice but to use oil as the leading sector for development. But by the same token, they must prepare to shift to human-resource-based development; there is little to do with the 95% of the population engaged outside the oil sector except to train it, educate it, and make it healthy, so that it can be employed in undertakings (such as electronics, optics, scientific instruments, sophisticated services) which do not depend on domestic resources. In resource-poor countries like Mauritania or Niger the need to develop through improvement of human resources is even more pressing and much more difficult. Venezuela, which has recently added iron, hydroelectric capacity, and other resource discoveries to its petroleum, can depend more on natural-resource-development for the next decade or so. Indonesia, with her enormous variety of natural resources (including volcanically renewed soil and abundant rainfall) can depend mainly on natural-resource-development at this stage. But countries which get stuck in a particular type of natural resource development are likely to stagnate—witness Cuba, (sugar) Argentina, Uruguay (beef)—or even Australia and Canada, whose exports are tied in large measure to their mines, forests, and soil.

Foreign trade policy is also a matter of "balance." It is not really a question of "export promotion or import replacement," but rather of arriving at a judicious mix of the two which reflects the country's endowment of natural and human resources, and its potential for change.

Since the economy is a system, it is only to be expected that these six balances will be interrelated, with feedbacks among them. The balance between import replacement and export promotion obviously depends on the balance between human-resource-based and natural-resource-based development, and vice versa; the balance between industry and agriculture is affected by, and also affects, both of these balances. The potential for technological progress influences, and is influenced by, all the other balances; and so on. It is precisely this "feedback" or "system" character of the economy that makes the planner's task so difficult. For while all the balances are interrelated, it does not follow that every government can or should give equal weight to all of them in the preparation and implementation of a development plan. In making these choices, "perspective planning" offers a useful device.

PERSPECTIVE PLANNING

A perspective plan is designed to determine a set of targets which are socially and politically acceptable, mutually consistent, and technically attainable. It puts together a reasonable and satisfactory picture of what the country might look like in ten to twenty years in terms of total population, national income, income per capita, income distribution among regions and social groups, occupational structure, distribution of the population among regions and between cities and countryside, employment and unemployment, structure of international trade, and levels of education and health. In putting together such a picture, one naturally begins with the current situation and recent trends. These trends can be projected, and if the results in ten to twenty years are not satisfactory, or if they are inconsistent with other projections which are satisfactory, the planner can ask if and how the trends can be changed for the better.

Take, for example, the balance between capital accumulation and consumption. One might find that the picture looks very attractive except that the required investment greatly exceeds potential domestic savings, resulting in dangerous inflationary pressure (savings gap). Then ways must be sought to encourage savings, or to increase taxes without discouraging investment, or to attract foreign investment and foreign aid. If none of these approaches works, there is no solution but to lower targets and reduce investment. Alternatively, it may prove that potential imports greatly exceed potential exports (balance of payments gap). So back to the drawing board; foreign aid and investment might provide more foreign exchange, or ways of promoting exports or replacing imports may be found. Failing all means of cutting the balance-of-payments gap, once again targets must be lowered. During the past decade, this kind of "two-gaps analysis" has played a major role in perspective planning, and also in foreign aid policy.

In the case of the Pahang Tenggara Regional Plan in Malaysia, (discussed in detail at the end of the next chapter), the initial perspective plan was fundamental in determining the character of the plan. At the time the major strategy of development in Malaysia was export promotion through land settlement, with modest amounts of industrialization, improvement of agricultural techniques, upgrading of human resources, and extension of the transport system thrown in. The planning team began by looking at the Malaysian economy as a whole, as it might be in twenty years, if the stated and quite reasonable overall objectives of the government were achieved. The team next asked, "What should the Pahang Tenggara region be like in such a Malaysia?" The answer, accepted by the government, was that per capita incomes in the region should be close to the national average in the first years of settlement, and should rise at the same rate as per capita incomes in the country as a whole.

Innocent as these conclusions may seem, they revolutionized regional planning in Malaysia. For with further study, it became abundantly clear that this objective for the region was totally inconsistent with the patterns of land settlement previously adopted by the Malaysian Government: two to three thousand people settled in isolated villages and working on the same rubber or oil palm plantation for the rest of their working lives. Instead, a much more urbanized pattern of settlement was adopted, with settlers commuting to their work on the plantation, and with provision of considerable mobility, not only as between oil palm and rubber (which have complementary employment requirements) but as between agricultural and urban occupations. As a consequence of this revelation of inconsistency as between the ultimate plan targets and the earlier pattern of short-run planning, the Malaysian government is now reviewing and overhauling its approach to land settlement, regional development, and thus—given its basic strategy—to national economic development.

BALANCED OR UNBALANCED GROWTH?

In the course of achieving the second balance—among sectors and regions—a planner may find himself caught up in the issues underlying the "balanced or unbalanced growth" controversy. Some economists advocate a wave of capital investments in a number of different sectors at once to create an overall enlargement of the market, while others advocate a strategy of judiciously unbalanced growth.

As originally presented, the "balanced growth" doctrine was related to the theory of the "big push." The development effort must be large-scale, it was argued, because of three indivisibilities: indivisibilities in the supply of capital, and especially of "social overhead capital" such as power, transport, and education; indivisibilities in savings; and indivisibilities of demand. One cannot build half a power plant, or stop building a road or railroad half way between one city and another, and make any contribution to higher productivity. Roofless schools or hospitals and schools without teachers, doctors, and nurses are not much use. There is for each of these kinds of investment a minimum scale which is efficient and effective, and this scale must be attained if productivity is to be raised.

Similarly, savings do not increase continuously with income. Instead, certain thresholds of income are reached where consumption requirements for a particular standard of living are met (adequate nutrition, for example); when incomes rise beyond these thresholds, savings rise steeply, permitting a still larger scale of development investment. Thus the scale of the development effort at each stage must be large enough to bring income above one of these thresholds. Otherwise savings will be little affected and development investment will be inhibited by the "saving gap." (See Table 1.4.)

The "indivisibility of demand" compels investment in a variety of industries. One might conceive of a big push concentrated in one sector, or even one industry—boots and shoes for example. Such concentrated investment may be all very well for a country with an assured export market for the output, or a large internal market. But if there is no export market for boots and shoes, and the rest of the population is unemployed or underemployed, the industry will fail because only a very small fraction of the increased income generated by the industry will be spent on boots and shoes; the bulk of the output will remain unsold. In order to build up an expanded market for boots and shoes, there must be a wave of investments in a number of industries and farms, as well. The output of a wider variety of commodities can then be met by an adequate increase in *effective* demand for all of them. Mexico's takeoff provides an example of balanced growth—a "big push" in agriculture, infrastructure, and industry.

BALANCED GROWTH OF AGRICULTURE AND INDUSTRY: MEXICO

Before the 1910 revolution Mexico was just another example of a stagnant, 80% agricultural society "in the apparently closed circle of poverty resulting from the narrowness of the local market, lack of big social capital, lack of savings and monopolistic advantages possessed by foreign enterprises exploiting local natural resources".[2] (Ninety-eight per cent of the mines were in the hands of Americans.) The revolution of 1910 ushered in sweeping agricultural reform, which abolished the feudal system of land ownership and distributed the land in a manner permitting modernization of techniques. Improved farming methods, irrigation, extension work, and better farm implements helped to raise agricultural productivity.

Meanwhile "balanced growth" proceeded on several fronts. In the early stages of development the government invested in the infrastructure, including railroads, highways, power, and housing along with reorganizing education to meet the needs of development. Some export industry was already established, such as the mining and petroleum industries. The expropriation of foreign-owned petroleum and railroad investments in 1937–38 led to an international boycott of Mexico, but once the Mexican economy began to move and new opportunities for profitable investment appeared, foreign capital flowed back into the country, accelerating the rate of economic expansion. World War II gave the final thrust to Mexico's takeoff. There was considerable excess capacity in industry and in overhead capital at the beginning of the war, which permitted substantial increases in output without much new industrial investment.

The result of this constellation of policies, measures, and events has been an extraordinarily high rate of growth, accompanied by an equally rapid structural change. Between 1939 and 1945, total output increased at an average rate of 8% per year. Since then the rate of growth has tapered off somewhat, to an average rate of about 6% per year. In 1930, some 70% of the labor force was engaged in agriculture, producing only 21.6% of the gross national product. By 1959, less than 56% of the labor force was in agriculture, but it was still producing nearly 23% of GNP, indicating a significant increase in man-

---

[2] Alfredo Navarrete, "Mexico's Growth: Prospects and Problems", in Eastin Nelson, ed., *Economic Growth: Rationale, Problems, Cases* (Austin: University of Texas, 1969), p. 127.

year productivity. Today Mexico is presumably over the watershed with respect to the employment structure, with more than half the labor force engaged outside of agriculture. Thus "balanced growth" in this sense does not mean proportionate growth of employment in agriculture and industry. The "balance" refers rather to the effort to raise productivity in both sectors at once.

UNBALANCED GROWTH: INDIA

Unfortunately, balanced growth strategy fails to come to grips with the problem of most underdeveloped countries: the shortage of resources. "Think big" is sound advice to underdeveloped countries; but "act big" is unwise counsel if it spurs them to attempt more than their resources permit.[3]

For many of the really poor countries the combination of "big push" and "balanced growth" is a counsel of despair. If the scale of the effort in each industry and sector must be large and the effort must be made in a large number of industries at once, how is a country with little by way of natural resources and low levels of education and health ever to escape the "vicious circle of poverty"? In order to get something going in the way of development, such a country may be compelled to concentrate on one sector at a time, in hopes of increasing the responsiveness of the economy and the society to development opportunities that may appear in later stages of growth.

As we have already observed, the industrialized countries did not get where they were through "balanced" growth. If we compare the economy of the United States in the 1970s to the economy in the 1870s we find that many things have grown, but not everything grew at the same rate throughout the whole century. Development proceeded as growth was communicated from the leading sectors of the economy to the followers, from one industry to another, from one firm to another, and from one region to another.

Moreover, the balanced growth doctrine assumes that an underdeveloped country starts from scratch. In reality, every underdeveloped country starts from a position that reflects previous investment decisions. At any point in time there are highly desirable investment programs that are needed to offset existing imbalance. And once such an investment is made, a new imbalance is likely to appear that will require still another "balancing" investment, and so on.

Some proponents of unbalanced growth therefore insist that deliberate unbalancing of the economy, in accordance with a predesigned strategy, is the best way to promote development.[4] They focus attention on motivation; the basic idea is that in most societies there is a latent capacity for investment; by undertaking a "big push" in strategically selected sectors or industries, tensions, pressures, and incentives are set up to correct the imbalance. If the pro-

[3] Hans Singer, "The Concept of Balanced Growth and Economic Development: Theory and Facts", in Eastin Nelson, ed., *Economic Growth: Rationale, Problems, Cases*, p. 80.

[4] See especially Albert Hirschman, *The Strategy of Economic Development*, (New Haven: Yale University Press, 1958).

cess begins, for example, with public investment in power or transport, there will be a tendency for private investment to take place subsequently, in order to make use of the new capacity. If the big push begins in the private, directly productive sector, scarcities will appear in the public, social overhead sector, necessitating investment in power, transport, ect. in the next period. India, another 80% farmer economy, and one of the poorest countries in the world, has of necessity followed a strategy of this nature.

When India drafted her first five year plan in the early 1950s, the per capita income was only $60 per year and had been rising very slowly. Over 80% of the population was rural, yet only 48% of the national income was produced in the rural sector. Much of India is arid and a great deal of the soil poor; increasing acreage and raising yields per hectare both require substantial investment. The proportion of per capita income derived from manufacturing, mining, and public utilities, remained just under 17% despite considerable industrial investment. The long-run prospects for Indian agriculture were less bright than the outlook for industry, but so long as three-quarters of the active population were engaged in agriculture, increased agricultural output had to be achieved to sustain a growing population and to permit some labor to be shifted to industry.

The first plan therefore followed an essentially basic needs approach. Emphasis was on agriculture and social overhead investment. Agriculture and community development took 15.1% of the budget, irrigation and power 28%, transport and communications 23.6%, and 22% was allocated for industry and mining.

This development brought useful increases in output. National income rose 17.5% and per capita income 10.5%. Despite the emphasis on agriculture, the biggest percentage expansion occurred in mining, manufacturing, and transport.

For their second phase of planning, the Commission shifted the balance to an emphasis on rapid industrialization with particular emphasis on the development of basic and heavy industries. Overall expenditures were more than doubled. Investment in industry and mining increased to 18.5%, investment in power and irrigation was reduced to 19%. Agriculture and community development dropped to 11.8%, while transport and communications increased to 28.9%. Social services dropped to 19.7%.

By the time the third Plan was drafted for 1961–66, India's course toward industrialization was firmly set, and the budget involved no sharp changes in the structure of investment. The proportions allocated to power, large industry, and mining were slightly increased. Transportation, communications, and social services were reduced to a smaller proportion of the total, while nonetheless increasing in absolute amount of investment outlays.

Since the Third Plan, the balance between sectors has not changed substantially, in terms of percentages of the development budget; however, in the Fourth Plan and thereafter, attention has turned to other balances within the sectors in response to the results of the first three plans. Faulty choice and formulation of projects had resulted in a number of imbalances: the actual output, for example, of the steel plants and heavy industries projects developed during the second plan were still below capacity at the end of the Third Plan period; various bottlenecks had emerged, such as inadequate managerial talents and skilled personnel, and limited foreign exchange. Review of the product mix sought a new balance between food grains and export crops; among capital goods, import replacing industrial products, and export industrial goods. Planning has since emphasized maximization of national efficiency in project selection. At the same time planners have been encouraging a dynamic agriculture. In other words, India has graduated to a more balanced pattern of growth.

APPRAISAL OF BALANCED AND UNBALANCED GROWTH

The experiences of Mexico and India indicate that the conflict between the "balanced" and "unbalanced" growth strategies is more apparent than real. The "unbalanced growth" strategy is simply a means of achieving long-run (*ex-post,* end-of-the-planning-period) balance by the device of creating short-run (*ex-ante,* start-of-the-period) imbalance, which is expected and designed to prompt a reaction. How much of the development effort can be concentrated effectively in a few sectors or industries depends upon a country's international trade relations, the richness and variety of its resource endowment, the quality of its human skills—indeed, on all the "balances" outlined above. In the final analysis, each country must decide at each point of time how best to allocate its development effort—in terms of investment, of land use, of manpower, and of enterpreneurial, managerial, and scientific talent—so as to maximize its rate of development.

BALANCE AMONG PROJECTS

The first wave of industrialization in many countries has been followed by a realization (as in India) that not only must an optimal balance be found between the agricultural and industrial sectors and regions; a more complex balance must be sought amongst individual projects. It has become clear that in many countries, the projects have been chosen without full regard to the range of possibilities. Export crops have sometimes been favored to the detriment of food grains, capital goods production selected without adequate consideration of other industrial possibilities. Even among the capital goods industries, there remains a choice in the timing and type of capital goods to be produced or to be imported.

When seeking an appropriate balance of investment among particular industries and projects, the ideas concerning imbalance become even more useful. A deliberate unbalancing may yield "extra dividends" of induced, easy-to-take, or compelled, decisions resulting in additional investment and output. If for example, a textile factory is built, it may encourage the establishment of a clothing factory, and may stimulate cotton raising. The planning problem is to determine the *sequence* of expansion that will maximize *induced* decision making, to find the projects with the greatest total linkage. Any particular investment project may have "forward linkage"—may encourage investment in subsequent stages of production, or "backward linkage"—may encourage investment in earlier stages of production.

Albert Hirschman has observed that underdeveloped countries are weak in interdependence and linkage.[5] Agriculture, especially peasant agriculture, is short on linkage effects. Primary production is low in backward linkage effects by definition, but agriculture and mining are low in forward linkages too. Here is the intuitive source of the grudge against the "enclave" type of development, because the output of mines, oil wells, and plantations can slip out of a country without leaving much trace in the rest of the economy.

This grudge, however, may mislead nationalistic governments into concluding that to go on producing raw materials for export is tantamount to preserving a colonial pattern of trade. Thus, they may fail to give enough support to peasant exports and concentrate too much on industrial development, as did the Burmese government in the first years of independence. There is a close link between growth and import capacity. The fast growers in the developing world have all operated with substantial amounts of foreign exchange needed for development; the only way to earn more foreign exchange in the short run is by expanding traditional exports; therefore export drives are very important. For these reasons, the first moves towards industrialization in some countries may be paradoxically to build up plantation exports or other raw material exports.

EXPORT PROMOTION

International trade can prove profitable if a country ascertains the products where it has true comparative advantage. This classical principle provides useful guidance if properly applied; it is excellent business to produce rubber if a country's soil and climate are ideal for growing it, *and if other countries want to buy it.* Comparative advantage can change because of changing international market conditions or internal change. Each country must constantly reassess its current true comparative advantage, to predict when and whether to add another export product, when to abandon cultivation of an export product, and when to begin processing the raw materials produced at home.

DIVERSIFICATION OF PRODUCTS: CUBA

Excessive dependence on one export may prove catastrophic, as in the case of Cuba's dependence on her sugar industry. The Cuban experience provides a curious example of dependence on sugar, then a period of diversification, followed by a return to building up sugar as a strong lead export.

As we have seen, the economic stagnation in prerevolutionary Cuba and the

[5] Hirschman, *Strategy of Economic Development,* pp. 109–110.

attending poor conditions could be explained largely in terms of the stagnation of the sugar industry. Because of its dominant position in the economy, stagnation of the sugar industry virtually meant stagnation of the economy as a whole. Sugar accounted for 40% of the country's total industrial production. It provided employment for one-quarter of the labor force, or for half of the active agricultural population. Sugar output provided 20% of Cuba's gross national product. Its impact on the economy, however, was even greater than these figures suggest. When we reckon the secondary income and employment through financing, storing, transporting, insuring, and otherwise handling sugar; when we consider the effects on the government budget, banking operations, and the multiplier effects of the respending of the income created in the sugar sector; it is clear that the Cuban economy was uncomfortably close to a monoculture and a dangerous monoculture, as the record shows.

The 1950 World Bank Mission to Cuba suggested a strategy designed to seek forward linkages for sugar and other primary products, and to introduce new industry bringing its own linkages. The Mission suggested four major objectives:

1. To make Cuba less dependent on sugar by promoting additional activities, not by curtailing sugar production.

2. To expand existing, and create new, industries producing sugar by-products or using sugar as a raw material.

3. Vigorously to promote nonsugar exports such as minerals and a variety of crude and processed foodstuffs.

4. To make further progress in producing in Cuba for domestic consumption a wide range of foodstuffs, raw materials, and consumer durable goods.

Five years later the United States Department of Commerce made essentially the same recommendations; after another four years had passed with little change, the Cuban revolution took place.

In the first years of the Castro regime, economic strategies paralleled the broad lines of the World Bank's recommendations. Diversification was promoted with the objective of producing more foodstuffs and raw materials for domestic consumption. Cooperatives began producing rice, tomatoes, henequen, potatoes, and charcoal. At the same time, raising more chickens, pigs, and cattle was encouraged. According to the 1962–65 plan, sugar mills and textile factories were to be repaired, with some additional capacity in such established fields as textile manufactures, foods, mining and metal products. Hydroelectric capacity was to be raised; the foremost infrastructural project would be further electrification. Radical departures in industrial investment, however, were scheduled only for the period after 1965.

As the foreign exchange needed for the purchase of industrial equipment dwindled, strategy changed from diversification back to an emphasis on sugar production and increased cattle raising. In 1963, it was announced that for some years agricultural development must receive first priority, that agriculture would be the basis of Cuba's economic development. Sugar was to be promoted to the fullest extent; Castro set a target of 10 million tons of sugar to be produced during 1970.

While at first glance such a program might appear to follow much the same pattern as the pre-Castro economic policies, the Cuban planners emphasized two main differences. Cuba had an assured and growing market for sugar in the socialist bloc countries which held out the possibility of sugar being a "strong primary export" capable of earning the foreign exchange needed for launching development. The other difference lay in the spending of the foreign exchange the sugar would earn. Rather than buying luxuries for Cuba's elite, the foreign exchange would be used primarily to promote economic development.

In 1970, Cuba came close to the 10 million ton sugar objective with 8.5 million tons, but at the expense of labor diverted from other objectives. Today Cuba has again deferred the decision to swing to heavy industry "The Russians talked them out of that," comments a European economist who spent some months in Cuba. Cuban development continues to be slanted heavily toward the expansion of agriculture involving some diversification into citrus fruits, and into agricultural processing industries. Considerable emphasis remains on sugar; the economy received strong stimulus from the high sugar prices in the early seventies, but slipped back again after the boom. Small exporting countries need a stable world where markets can be counted on. Their vulnerability to market changes is one of the reasons why countries strive to broaden their base by fostering import-replacing industries.

DIVERSIFICATION OF PRODUCTION: PROCESSING RAW MATERIALS

A considerable degree of economic development is sometimes possible without dramatic changes in the general composition of foreign trade if export industries provide opportunities for forward linkage. Canada still has one of the highest standards of living in the world, despite limited change in the general composition of Canada's exports. In the course of the last three generations, Canada has moved toward further processing of its agricultural and forest products; but today the farms and forests are still the major sources of Canadian exports. Yet the economy as a whole shows the same general structural change that took place in other advanced countries. Economic growth has been generated by diversifying *production* more than exports by further processing of local raw materials, and by effecting some import replacement. Single strong exports—furs, fish, wheat, flour, pulp and paper, newsprint— have done much to sustain Canada's economic development at various points in Canada's economic history. Yet, as seen above, Canada is now paying the penalty of excessively natural-resource-based development and is losing out, in terms of levels of per capita income to more human-resource-based countries like Sweden and Switzerland. Most countries need to diversify exports to permit continued growth and to reduce vulnerability to market fluctuations.

REPLACING ENCLAVE IMPORT INDUSTRY

While enclave industries often have great difficulty in breaking out of the enclave situation and producing "forward linkage" effects within the country, such need not be the case with enclave import industries. Much of the recent economic history of some rapidly developing poor countries, observes Hirschman, can be written in terms of industrialization working its way backward from the "final touches" stage to domestic production of intermediate materials and finally to that of basic industrial materials.[6] He mentions Brazil, Colombia, and Mexico as examples; he might also have included Japan.

To foster a domestic market, Hirschman suggests protection or subsidizing of import-replacing industries, but at the right stage of development. There is some reason to believe that investment will take place in any industry where demand reaches a certain "threshold." While that threshold is being reached, it is a good policy to leave the market to importers. Thus, foreign trade should go through clearly defined stages with respect to any one industry. In the "prenatal" stage Hirschman envisages a kind of "jacking-up" process for the economy, using imports to create the market and then jumping into the production of the import itself when the market becomes large enough. When the "threshold" is reached, protection or subsidies for imports-replacing industries becomes good policy. Tax concessions are an apt instrument for such protection. This strategy implies a plentiful supply of capital to create the threshold. Certain countries, such as the oil rich nations, may be able to use such strategies.

The chief problem in oil rich economics is to design a development program using the present abundant capital and abundant supply of foreign exchange to accumulate productive domestic capital outside the petroleum sector. This stock of capital should eventually create a self-sustaining economy that can remain prosperous when oil supplies wane.

If the country has no strong industrial base other than oil, it must find other export industries. With the foreign exchange which the oil earns, this task is not particularly difficult; capital equipment can be purchased, raw materials can be bought abroad or a search may be made for additional raw material within the country's own borders. Often the crucial scarcities are the entrepreneurial and technical abilities needed to bring these resources into play. Here again, oil revenues can finance technical assistance, but acquiring enough human resources will probably also require a liberal policy toward immigration of scientists and technicians and an enormous push on the education front.

DEVELOPMENT THROUGH HUMAN RESOURCES: MAURITANIA

It is relatively easy for a rich oil country to change to a human-resource-based economy. It is much more difficult for a poor country to do so; yet some

---

[6] Hirschman, *Economic Growth: Rationale, Problems, Cases*, p. 122.

countries are so short of known natural resources that the only possible strategy is improvement of human resources. Mauretania is such a country.

Mauritania's president Ould Daddah has spoken of his country as the potential "Switzerland of Africa." The president was, of course, thinking of human-resource-based development, with sophisticated industries and services requiring high levels of human skill but needing only limited amounts of imported materials and equipment. To compete in a world market, the products must be of a type that requires little outlay for transport; transistors, other electronic components, scientific instruments, optics an the like.

Does this scenario seem too fantastic for a country like Mauritania? The answer is that the country has little choice. The copper mine and the iron mine, the sole sources of growth in the past decade, are expected to close down within a few years; a few more jobs could be created if the fishing industry were to become a domestic venture, rather than the foreign concern that it is at present. During the next two five-year plans the development of the Senegal valley will offer the most chance for launching a chain of "easily taken decision" by modernizing both the product mix and the technology of agriculture; but even on the most optimistic projections, these projects will not absorb a number of families much in excess of the natural rate of population growth in the valley itself. Nor can the nomadic livestock sector absorb a continuously increasing population. There is no long-run solution other than the absorption of the bulk of the population increase outside of agriculture altogether. The government has perhaps ten years to effect this changeover. What are the chances?

Mauritania's major resource is its people, a resource which has been relatively neglected in the past; the level of unemployment and underemployment combined is extremely high, and the levels of health and literacy are abysmally low. Moreover the population (about 1¼ million) is so scattered and isolated that there is no dynamic interaction among sectors. At present, little is bought or sold from one sector or region to another. The "grand nomads," roaming the deserts, living within a camel economy, are virtually self-sufficient; the cattle graziers drive their herds across the Senegal river to sell them in Senegal, and buy household goods there; the agricultural sector is virtually self-sufficient. The modern sector, consisting of the capital city, Naouakchott, the two mines, and the fishing industry is scattered, and is particularly isolated economically—a typical "enclave," selling nothing to the rest of the country and buying virtually nothing from it.

Two major interlocking strategies were recommended for the Third Plan: full employment to be supported by vigorous health and educational campaigns; employment-creation projects, in turn to be chosen and located so as to forge links among sectors and regions, so that expansion in one would have favorable repercussions on others.

The first linkages are to be established between the farming and the livestock sectors. Instead of selling their cattle on the hoof in Senegal, the graziers can fatten them in the agricultural zone and have them slaughtered in the zone's modern abbatoir in Kaédi. With higher productivity and incomes the farmers themselves can buy some of the beef mutton. The livestock raisers in turn can buy farm products. Some of the meat can be shipped to industrial workers in the cities, and the rest exported to Europe, perhaps by air if the airport at Kaédi is improved. More prosperous farmers and livestock raisers can buy at least some of the output of the new industrial sector; and the exports from this sector will permit increased imports of other consumers' goods to contribute to higher standards of living, plus raw materials and equipment to carry overall development to a still higher level. The weak link in this chain is obviously the "exports" from the industrial sector; they may have difficulty finding a market.

AGREED SPECIALIZATION

Small countries such as Mauritania trying to switch to a human-resource-based economy usually suffer limitations in the size of their own market, and have difficulties in breaking into overseas markets. For some of them, the solution may lie in agreed specialization. Both the West African and the Southeast Asian countries (mostly with limited markets) have been exploring the idea of agreeing to specialize in certain industries and marketing the products to each other. Groups of African and Latin American countries have also been investigating these possibilities. Intercontinental groupings have also been suggested, such as Brazil's proposal for a Portugal-Brazil-West Africa grouping. Since neighboring countries often produce the same products, limiting trade possibilities, this more varied grouping offers more scope for international trade.

REGIONAL INTEGRATION WITHIN COUNTRIES

Once the product mix has been determined, the question arises of where to put the new enterprises within the country. Should the footloose industries be established in the leading or the lagging region? Should scarce capital be invested in the modern or retarded region? The geographic distribution of economic activity becomes a major instrument of regional integration.

The problem of regional integration within countries takes two forms. In retarded countries like Mauritania, there is a task of regional integration in the sense of establishing linkages among isolated regional economies, each of which is still poor, as described above. Most of the large underdeveloped countries, such as Brazil, Indonesia, India, and Nigeria, face a different kind of regional problem: despite substantial interregional trade, migration, and capital movements, there are vast and growing gaps between rich and poor regions. Even smaller countries such as Thailand and Malaysia face similar problems. In all these cases the regional disparities act as a drag on the development of the entire economy, rich regions as well as poor.

There are two main strategies for reducing regional imbalances: to invest in the modern region, creating opportunities for migrants from the poor region; the alternative is to modernize the poor region by implanting therein elements of the modern sector, and creating new linkages with the rich region.

The powerful agglomerative pull of leading regions usually reflects genuine advantages in training and skills, social overhead capital, and access to raw materials, finance, and markets. In many cases, if not in most, additional investment in the already progressing sector and region will add more to national income than in the short run an equal amount of investment in the stagnant region. But while the best short-run solution—almost by definition—may be to invest in the leading region, long-run healthy growth of the national economy as a whole requires reduction of regional gaps. In any case, a decision may be made to rescue the lagging region for the sake of political unity or for humanitarian reasons. Brazil has faced a choice of this nature.

BRAZIL

Brazil has an enormous regional problem; the modern sector consists of the south, and especially the southeast central region with the two major development poles, São Paolo and Rio de Janeiro. The traditional sector consists of the north and the northeast. In the northeast, nearly half of total production and two-thirds of employment are accounted for by the agricultural sector, compared with about one-third and 40% for the rest of the country. The spreads in per capita income between the traditional and the modern sector are enormous—of the order of 400%.

The northeast has been an area of "calamities." Except for small parts of it the average rainfall is very low. Recurring calamities of flood and drought have set a limit to development of the frontier. Good land with more or less assured rainfall is already suffering from overcrowding, and population densities in the coastal areas near Recife are more than 300 per square kilometer. It also suffered the economic calamity of a "boom and bust" in sugar.

The northeast might have been in an even worse state were it not for migration, which assumes a triangular pattern. The larger share of the outmigrants from the northeast go directly to the east central region, where they move into the plantations, filling the jobs left vacant by workers moving into the nearby southeastern cities. The northeast has in fact been a fountainhead of people; *Nordestinos* have panned gold in Minas Gerais, tapped rubber in the Amazon, planted coffee in São Paolo; they have built Rio de Janeiro, São Paolo, and Brasilia, as well as providing great national leaders.

These facts suggest that Brazil's northeast problem might be solved in the south and east center, until one studies the statistics. Nearly 30% of Brazil's population lives in the northeast and another 6% in the north. Moving some 30 million people out of the area is out of the question. Any plan must have a strategy for northeast development as well. Brazil has in effect, adopted a combination of the two main strategies.

Regional planning for the northeast has attempted to create a resurgence of the area by promoting new industry. Public investment programs have been designed to attract and orient private investment from within the country, particularly investors in the center-south, and from outside the country. High priority has been given to electric power and transport facilities to incorporate growing areas of the region into the development process. National planning efforts for the northeast have included such measures as moving the head office of Petrobras (the nationalized petroleum company) to Bahia, and improving connections between the northeast and the center-south of the country, particularly the building of the great Belem-Brasilia road, the opening up of the north itself with the Trans-Amazonian Highway, and the Perimetral Highway which will almost encircle the country. Meanwhile, the recent vigorous expansion of the national economy has kept the traditional migratory routes open. Recently, Brazil's national growth rate has been estimated at 10% and the growth of the northeast at 13%.

The Brazilian tactics included not only the classical measures of providing infrastructure with a vigorous attack on the "boom and bust" problem by the ambitious road network; they also included the "development poles" approach.

PÔLES DE CROISSANCE—DEVELOPMENT POLES

The idea of *pôles de croissance,* or development poles, grew up originally among a group of French economists led by François Perroux, and has since interested development economists everywhere. This approach was developed at a time when economists, dissatisfied with the results of planning in terms of growth of national income, were seeking a more disaggregated approach to planning, subdividing up the economy into sectors, industries, or projects. The development pole concept offered the attractive alternative of subdividing the economy *in space,* permitting attention to sociocultural differences among regions as well.

In effect, the development pole theory translates into geographic space the concept of unbalanced growth. Schumpeter's ideas concerning innovating enterprises, and the classical emphasis on movements of men and capital. As do the proponents of unbalanced growth, these economists point out that growth has not proceeded at the same rate everywhere. Rather, in each period, it has been concentrated in certain leading sectors and propulsive industries. Since these sectors and innovating industries tend to be clustered in certain areas, national economic growth is also concentrated in particular regions in each phase of development. Moreover, the leading sectors and propulsive industries—*sui generis* enterprises which have a major impact on the growth of other sectors and industries—tend to cluster in a few large metropolitan centers. These centers then become development poles, generating "spread effects" (favorable impact on investment decisions or linkage) throughout the whole region which they dominate.

A distinction is made between development poles and "growth centers." The economies of the development poles are dominated by true propulsive enterprises, generating spread effects through investment which is not to any significant degree a reaction to investment previously made elsewhere in the system. They are Schumpeterian innovating enterprises; investments are made in anticipation of future success of the innovation, not because of past success of a routine operation. By contrast the economies of "growth centers" are dominated by "growth industries" (akin to Schumpeter's "clusters of followers") which *react* to the economic energy being generated by the poles. Thus in our earlier example, Montreal is a development pole, while Quebec City and other towns in the Province of Quebec are "growth centers," reacting to Montreal's propulsive industries.

The policy implication is that when a particular country or a retarded region of a country lacks such development poles, it is necessary to create them. Brazilian planners, for example, selected San Salvador and Recife as development poles for the northeast. Since they were the old capitals of the northeast they were an easy choice. The growth pole approach tackles the more difficult question of *where* to create development poles in a retarded region if they do not already exist.

In attempting to create development poles and growth centers where they do not exist, François Perroux emphasizes that new urban activities, no matter how dynamic they may be, do not automatically generate *effets d'entraînement* (spread effects) to the peripheral region. "A growth pole or development pole is a growth industry coupled with its surrounding environment"[7] he says; attention must be given to the "reactors" and the "transmission lines" as well as to the "generators." Thus, in the Mauretanian case, Kàedi, with its abbatoir and airport, is "coupled" with the needs of the agricultural and grazing zones. Likewise, when the time comes in Mauretania to locate the footloose industries, Nouadhibou may be the choice, since it already has the makings of a pole—the modern fishing industry, a good port (servicing the iron mine), an international airport, together offering a small, useful nucleus of expertise and infrastructure, which could attract both capital and men.

Where it is a matter of encouraging private enterprises already established in the dynamic region of a more mature economy (such as Brazil) to open new branches or establish new enterprises in the retarded region, the problem resolves itself into two main questions:

1. What are the manufacturing and services enterprises that we can hope to lure or push into urban centers of various sizes in the retarded regions, and what is the net cost in terms of subsidies or inefficiency?

2. What will be the impact on income, employment, income distribution, etc., within the region, and what will be the impact outside the region?

These considerations require studies of interurban and interregional flows—migratory flows of people, of capital, and of goods and services, of the sort analyzed by neoclassical theory. Here, once again, the development

---

[7] François Perroux, "Multinational Investments and the Analysis of Development and Integration Poles." Reprint from *Economies et Sociétés,* Cahiers de l'I.S.E.A., Series F. No. 24, pp. 842–44.

pole approach puts these forces into geographic space. In addition, in development pole theory stress is laid on flow of technology, and on systems of cities as mechanisms for diffusion of technology.

A distinction is also made between centers of attraction and centers of diffusion. That is, expansion of a pole (or center) may raise the level of per capita welfare in the peripheral region by attracting people to the pole, reducing the population pressure in the peripheral region, permitting larger holdings of land per family, improvements in agricultural techniques, etc. On the other hand, investment in a city which is a "diffusion center" may increase population density in the peripheral region.

The development poles approach has been an important influence in shifting the emphasis from planning in terms of national income as a whole to planning in terms of smaller, more visible subdivisions of the national economy. Thus the idea of using development poles as building blocks for regional plans has extended to using them as a basis for national development plans. Both politicians and planners are increasingly attracted to an urban-based approach to national development planning, proceeding from a planned urban structure to the consequent pattern of regional development, and aggregating regional plans to obtain a national plan. The result may then be compared with national goals, and if there are discrepancies either the planned urban structure or the national goals might be modified.

Another important outcome of experience in regional integration is the conviction that efforts to reduce regional disparities do not only have a humanitarian justification; investment in the retarded region is proving to be of overall advantage to the economy in the *long run*—including the *leading regions*—as has been the American experience, the European experience, and seems to be proving true in the Brazilian experience.

DECENTRALIZATION

But experience also shows that to change centrifugal forces into centripetal movements may require a prodigious effort. Planners dislike putting themselves *against* economic forces; they prefer to find a natural impetus and encourage it. While some of the above tactics take the form of a forced decentralization, other natural impetuses to decentralization are beginning to put feedback systems in motion in smaller cities and rural centers.

Some poor regions are already receiving the required impetus from a variety of needs for decentralization. Indian planners have been encouraging development of smaller city centers to discourage the massive urbanization around the big cities, such as Calcutta and Bombay, and to encourage transitional industry. Industrial decentralization in China was motivated by recognition of the limitations of Soviet-style central planning, by a desire to save on transport costs (transport being one of the economy's weakest links), by a wish to disperse pollution, and by a long-run objective of modernization of agricultural production. Local industry is expected to impart attitudes to the peasants appropriate to a technological environment. In countries where the

Green Revolution is making an impact, efforts to integrate agricultural and urban development at the regional level include building up the small agricultural towns. The other interlocking strategy underlying all these efforts at decentralization is employment creation, which introduces another balance.

BALANCE BETWEEN INCOME MAXIMIZATION AND EMPLOYMENT MAXIMIZATION

Achieving full employment involves one of the most difficult of all balances—between technological progress and employment. It is easy enough to put people to work, the problem is to employ them in socially and economically useful occupations. New technologies may be more productive, but they may displace labor, leading to bitter choices. If a country's capital and resources are limited, should these scarce resources be allocated to highly productive, capital-intensive, labor-saving technologies, or to less productive labor-intensive technologies?

This conflict is less apparent in agriculture than in industry. As we have seen, many agricultural improvements require using labor with relatively little capital and even less foreign exchange. In industry, unfortunately, all ambiguity disappears: with rare exceptions, the more capital-intensive techniques are so much more efficient than labor-intensive ones that not only output per man-hour is higher, but *output per unit of capital as well*. There are, however, significant differences in the ratio of capital to labor that can be efficient from one industry to another. It would seem then that countries with a surplus of labor and a shortage of capital would be well advised to give priority to those goods and services which intrinsically permit efficient operation with labor-intensive techniques. Unfortunately, even this choice is not always feasible. The country's resource pattern may be such that its comparative advantage in international trade may lie in industries requiring capital-intensive techniques—oil, tin and bauxite mining, for example. There is no sense in recommending to Libya, Kuwait, or Venezuela that their oil should be left in the ground because it can be efficiently mined and refined only with capital-intensive operations. The balance of payments situation may strongly favor the development of import-replacing industries of a capital-intensive nature, or the "linkage" factor may be higher for heavy, large-scale capital-intensive industries.

The successes and failures of the Great Leap illustrate the nature of the choice. The basic concept of the Leap was to fully mobilize China's enormous human resources for development. Tens of millions of people worked on labor-intensive water conservation projects, such as the huge Ming Tombs reservoir near Peking, which was completed in six months. The Chinese experience in such work projects proved an efficient substitution of manpower for capital equipment. On the other hand, the campaign to raise industrial output included the establishment of over six hundred thousand "backyard foundries," which produced metal of such poor quality, that it could not be used for industry. Modern large-scale foundries would have been the more economical technology.

Certainly the most useful discovery of all would be a broad-gauged industrial technology, applicable over a wide range of manufacturing activities, that would use less capital and more labor *while raising productivity of both labor and capital*. After centuries of invention of labor-saving devices, it is not easy for Western-trained engineers and scientists to think in terms of new techniques that will use more labor rather than less, while raising output per man-hour and per unit of capital. Yet this is the sort of "Green Revolution" needed in industrial technology and the possibility becomes brighter now that the advanced countries, too, are eager to find capital-saving techniques.

In the absence of an efficient labor-intensive industrial technology, planners search for labor-intensive industrial techniques with acceptable productivity levels. A rewarding inquiry is being made into "transitional" industry.

TRANSITIONAL ENTERPRISES

Planners, particularly in India and China, are searching out transitional regions and industries and small entrepreneurs. The kind of entrepreneur they like to find is the Indian manufacturer of truck drive shafts who tired of waiting for a 2,500 rupee forging hammer from Germany. He invested 200 rupees in locally available capital equipment and started producing the shafts by hand. The shafts are somewhat higher in price than imports but of acceptable quality, and provide a straight gain to the economy by eliminating delay, and creating employment.

The technologies used in these transitional enterprises tend to be much more labor-intensive, and less education-intensive than in modern enterprises. At the same time, these operations are sometimes large enough, while still using these traditional labor-intensive techniques, to move more closely to the modern entrepreneurial mode of operation and to provide transitional training. The idea is to start with labor-intensive, technologically primitive production methods and gradually modernize as these plants acquire more capital reserves and their workers absorb greater technical knowhow through on-the-job training, buttressed where necessary with supplementary training.

Encouraging smaller factories has been a major feature of policy in China in recent years. "Gigantism" characterized China's first Five Year Plan and continued into the late 1950s. However, this approach was very expensive and was only possible with Russian foreign aid. In 1956, Mao stated that while the large-scale modern enterprises would serve as the mainstay of the industrial system, the majority of enterprises would in future be small or medium-sized and economically built, making use of the industrial base left over from the past.[8] This change of emphasis was given further impetus when the Soviet government withdrew its technical assistance and blueprints in 1960.

[8] Jack Chen, "Taking off on a Tricycle," *Far Eastern Economic Review*, Sept. 4, 1971, p. 26.

Since then thousands of new small factories have come into being, operating with discarded machinery or on-the-spot contrivances devised by the workers themselves, who also design most of the products. In other cases, the large factories provide raw materials, technological expertise, and markets to the small operators, as happens in the electronics industry. In this way, handicraft workers in Tientsin are producing semiconductors, a small Nanking umbrella factory turns out transistors, and a cooperative established to make straw rope now produces magnetic elements.[9]

It is important to note that what has worked in China—as in the United States or Yugoslavia—is not a system of small enterprises, but a highly organized system of large, medium, and small enterprises, with much of the technology, management, and marketing coming from the large enterprise, thereby reducing both responsibility and risk. Initiative of workers and small entrepreneurs is useful, but it is most useful within a framework that permits its effective use by providing the other elements essential to efficient production.

While the transitional enterprises may sometimes be economically inefficient, the creation of an experienced work force is considered worth the price. This strategy works well in India, with a huge potential market of 450 million people, or in an essentially closed market of 800 million people (as in China). The same "up-by-the-bootstraps" approach might not work in small countries.

EMPLOYMENT TACTICS FOR SMALL COUNTRIES

Few small countries can permit themselves the luxury of relatively inefficient industry, because their market may be small, and they may depend on export products which must compete in the world market, as in the case of Columbia and Sri Lanka.

Two reports on unemployment made by the International Labor Office (ILO) on unemployment in Colombia and Sri Lanka[10] come to grips with choosing maximization of employment or income. The argument for income maximization is that a higher national income provides more opportunity for job creation, because there is more capital available to invest in further projects or in jobs in high productivity services. (Where this breaks down is when the surplus is *not* directed towards such projects or services.) The argument for employment maximization is that it is the best vehicle for improved redis-

[9] Jonathan Unger, "Mao's Million Amateur Technicians," *Far Eastern Economic Review,* Apr. 3, 1971, p. 115.

[10] Prepared by the International Labor Office, in collaboration with other United Nations agencies, they are the first two of a series of pilot country missions to study the unemployment problems in particular countries, and to make recommendations to alleviate it: International Labor Office, World Employment Programme, *Towards Full Employment: A Programme for Colombia* (Geneva: ILO, 1970). International Labor Office, *Matching Employment Opportunities and Expectations: A Programme of Action for Ceylon* (Geneva: ILO, 1971).

tribution of income and the increased spending power stimulates further employment creation. The two reports confront the dilemma, reaching right into the whole economic and social framework, suggesting far-reaching reorientation of institutions and economic framework to release capital and to achieve full employent.

COLOMBIA: MAXIMIZING EMPLOYMENT

The Colombian report places much of the blame for unemployment on the concentration of income in the hands of the few (the proportion of pretax income in the hands of the top 5% is about 30% or 40%) who spend their money largely on imported goods and foreign travel. The ILO team respond with a set of proposals, which taken together in the Colombia context, really amounts to social revolution. The proposals include steep increases in taxes on income and wealth of the rich; limitations on foreign travel; antimonopoly legislation and regulation; land reform to make land available to landless peasants and agricultural workers; a thorough overhaul of the educational system to make education and training more widely available, particularly in rural districts, and to direct it toward development needs; and subsidized housing for the lower-income groups.

These proposals are linked with a strategy of decentralized industrialization, slowing migration to the towns and revitalizing rural areas. The report proposes a large share of public investment to be shifted to the rural areas, and a major emphasis on rural education for both children and adults.

The authors of the report then choose a clear bias toward maximization of employment. The proposals are designed to accelerate growth of national income and consumption, while reducing unemployment, but reduction of unemployment remains the "queen" objective throughout. The rate of growth of national income *would be less high* than it would be with the same level of investment and an income-maximizing strategy.

The proposals give virtually unqualified support for introduction of labor-intensive technology where possible. The authors of the report feel that there is a Colombian "bias" towards advanced techniques. The degree of mechanization above the average for advanced developing countries (3.3 vs. 3.0) and industry is more capital-intensive than it need be. The proposals include special assistance to handicrafts and small industries, and incentives to accelerate growth of those modern, large-scale industries that happen to be labor-intensive, such as metal processing and machinery workshops), while discouraging expansion of relatively capital-intensive industries. Expansion of the construction sector is recommended, particularly for housing, since construction offers wide flexibility of techniques, and the housing shortage is so severe. They suggest a system of carrots and sticks to impel builders to choose the more labor-intensive methods. The authors recognize that such policies will retard the growth of man-year productivity of those employed; but they expect such an increase in employment that the growth of total output will nonetheless be accelerated.

They also recognize that in the field of labor-intensive industries, the existence of export markets is the chief basis for success; "large foreign markets" must absorb any surpluses arising from the distorted structure of the economy. They realize that their approach requires marketing studies which they themselves have not made. Here is the Colombian Achilles heel—in contrast with the Chinese and Indian situations, where large internal markets can absorb labor-intensive, less-high-productivity items, the Colombians would have to depend largely on foreign markets, facing world competition.

Other questions arise regarding the total impact on the society of the policies outlined above. Capital-intensive industries are more modern as a rule; discouraging them may retard technological change. Beyond a certain point in a country's development, there is some danger of converting a "developing society" into a "backward society." Colombia may be close to the point where the shift from a natural-resource-based to a human-resource-based strategy of development is called for. The report states that there is at present no general shortage of persons with middle or higher levels of education. There might be a case for building on these human resources and creating needs for university and high school graduates through a more ambitious program of industrialization and urbanization.

In sum, when a country is approaching the transitional stage, the ideal solution is to meet the employment problem through increasing the *scale* of economic activity rather than by restricting its pattern to relatively low-productivity activities. While any useful opportunities for using labor-intensive methods with acceptable productivity should certainly be seized, they should fit into an overall development program aimed at *raising productivity*. How raising productivity may be combined with achieving full employment is discussed in more detailed in Chapter 8 below.

It is worth noting Raul Prebisch's views concerning the dangers of primarily employment-oriented programs.[11] The central theme of his solution for a stable and peaceful Latin America is a better income distribution (best achieved by redistributing *high increases in income*) and full employment, which is the basic condition of equality of opportunity and social justice. Achieving these objectives requires a high internal rate of growth.

Prebisch emphasizes that insufficient capital formation and insufficient savings in the past have resulted in unemployment, bad income distribution, and insufficient growth. He sees three possibilities. The first is a "distribution of poverty," sacrificing the increase in income in order to increase employment by large-scale subsidies to small farms and handicrafts, making integration into the world economy (or even into regional Common Markets) impossible. The second alternative would be to adopt a "compulsive" (communist) system, which would at least provide for a high rate of growth and full employment. The third alternative would be to achieve a "critical rate of growth" which would lead to full employment in a growing nontotalitarian economy. Prebisch appeals for the third solution.

[11] Raul Prebisch, *Transformacin y Desarollo, La Gran Tarea de America Latina*. (Report presented to the Inter-American Development Bank, April 1970.

Whatever system prevails, the answer is the same: to solve the welfare and employment problem requires high increases in national income, which requires a very high *scale* of investment, which in turn requires for a number of years, as Prebisch puts it, a very high "discipline of development": a voluntary—or compulsory—forgoing of increases in consumption.

SRI LANKA: MAXIMIZING INCOME

If a country follows this rule of creating as much employment as possible with acceptable productivity, but with an overall objective of maximizing national income, it follows that more income will be available to finance further industrial projects and to employ people in the services, especially in *high-productivity services*. The ILO employment report on Sri Lanka suggests an overall strategy closely aligned with these principles; it aims at maximizing national income with an ambitious fiscal policy to support adroitly meshed wage, educational, and employment policies.

One of the marked differences between the Sri Lankan and the Colombian case is that rather than requiring employment as a means to spread welfare as in the Colombian case, the problem in Sri Lanka is to find ways of continuing to support far-reaching social welfare services already there. Social progress has outdistanced economic progress.''

By comparison with Colombia, Sri Lankan income distribution—not only in terms of money income but also of welfare services—is much closer to that of an industrialized country. As compared to Colombia's 40% of pretax income in the hands of the top 5%, in Sri Lanka it is about 20%. Sri Lanka has relatively heavy direct taxation, and extensive food subsidies and welfare services including free education; the rate of population growth is also falling. However, Sri Lanka is still suffering the effects of a spectacular population explosion which followed a particularly successful campaign to eradicate malaria; the economy has so far failed to expand and diversify fast enough to support both the growth of the population and the consequently increasing burden of social services.

Sri Lanka depends heavily on the export of tea, and suffers the usual problems attending a narrow-based export economy. Sri Lanka has been attempting to industrialize to negate these drawbacks, but she has suffered a sharp deterioration in her terms of trade. She has a chronic balance of payments deficit, running at over 5% of GNP in spite of tight exchange and import controls. And here is a vicious circle—the lack of foreign exchange keeps industry short of materials and spare parts, and these shortages in turn hold back industrialization, employment creation, and ultimately the capacity to earn the needed foreign exchange. All in all, Sri Lanka's employment problem could be most readily solved by an increase in international trade and a lowering of tariffs which would allow her to earn the extra capital she needs to expand industrialization.

Meanwhile the report advocates a big drive to develop new exports—both industrial products and more highly processed forms of traditional exports—

in order to raise national income and to create jobs. The report points out that Sri Lanka has an overvalued exchange rate for capital goods, interest rates which are too low, and tax treatment too generous to investment; and so suggests an increase in the premium paid on imports of goods other than food-stuffs, so as to remove hidden subsidies on capital equipment and nonessential consumer goods. In direct sacrifices the team suggests increased taxation of the rich and restraints on salaries; they hint at the reduction of the rice sub-sidy, and suggest lower differentials and fringe benefits for clerical and ad-ministrative jobs to reduce the fascination of the white-collar job. Land re-form is also recommended.

The report then turns directly to the problem of unemployment, which runs at about 14% with high correlation between the level of education and unem-ployment. The team reports that unemployment is staggeringly high in the younger educated groups; manual jobs are available, especially at harvest time, which these young, educated unemployed refuse to take. Yet the econ-omy cannot provide the jobs these young people with secondary education ex-pect—mainly office jobs. White-collar jobs pay salaries several times as high as what is offered for manual work; they provide greater security, and incom-parably higher status. Rather than risk missing a chance for a white-collar job by taking even temporary manual work, young secondary-school graduates will wait years (a wait made possible by the free rice ration which makes it possible for their families to support them).

The report recommends a large-scale rural public works scheme to support the proposed land reform. Not only estate workers and landless peasants would find jobs in it, but also smallholders would be given firm offers of employment under the scheme if they agree to rent out their land, which would, in turn, be incorporated into viable farming units. Moreover, some of the young unemployed with secondary-school certificates could be absorbed into the paraprofessional labor force in education and health programs, back-ing up the agricultural expansion.

The team suggests a national youth service, designed not only to expand youth employment, but to effect a general leveling, and to prepare the way for introducing lower salary scales in some fields. During their first three years of employment, young people would be paid at a rate related primarily to their *age* not their *educational achievements,* whatever they were doing, whether working in an organized youth camp or in the civil service, or for a public cor-poration or private employers. In the latter two cases, the employer would pay the difference between their rate and the going wage into a fund, which might be used to finance employment creation schemes (a device used in Algeria).

Several changes are suggested in the educational system, particularly a reform in the primary school curriculum. At present primary school prepares pupils for secondary education rather than farming work; since most of the children will be farmers when they leave school, and since there is a high rate of dropouts from the present program, the team recommends more emphasis on practical work and on aptitude tests. They also suggest that young people break their education with productive jobs, especially in the period between leaving school and entering university. Everyone would be able to *apply* for a period at a university, then return to their work after graduation.

Thus, the scheme proposed for Sri Lanka, while taking advantage of opportunities to generate new employment opportunities in agriculture and in public works, emphasizes productivity and income rather than make-work projects. The proposal builds on Sri Lanka's already high level of education and training, and recommends raising it still higher, while directing it more closely toward the country's technical requirements in both agriculture and industry. The differences between the Sri Lankan and Colombia reports of the World Employment Programme reflect differences between the economic and social situations of the two countries; Colombia is already more advanced economically than Sri Lanka; the scope for sacrificing income for employment is greater. On the other hand the Sri Lankan report recognizes that the "conflict" between income and employment is not of the simple "either or" variety. It is possible to allocate the great bulk of the available scarce resources in the most efficient manner possible, so as to maximize output, and still to find useful ways of employing any labor left over.

Summary

The precise nature of the development strategy chosen by each country, to be effective, must vary with the stage of development, the resource endowment, the supply of human skills, the pattern of foreign trade, and the political and social framework; on the other hand, there are some features that any strategy must have if it is to work. First, it must create a dynamic interplay of industrial and agricultural development. Second, it must eventually provide for a shift from natural-resource-based development to human-resource-based development. Finally, and closely related to the first two pillars of a sound development strategy, over the long run regional disparities must be reduced by measures designed to turn centrifugal into centripetal movements. Translating these broad strategies into detailed tactics, determining the optimal allocation of scarce resources among sectors, regions, and—ultimately—among individual projects, is the concern of programming.

8

Planning development: programming

Some years ago in Greece, three isolated mountain villages had no schools. On the other side of a mile-deep gorge was a larger town with exceptionally good educational facilities that were not being fully used. It was decided to build a *téléférique* across the gorge, thus solving an educational problem with a transport project. Today, one of the most effective ways of raising the level of education for girls in rural Haiti would be to pipe safe drinking water into the mountain villages. It is the responsibility of the young girls to fetch the water for the household's daily needs. Often the source is miles away along steep mountain tracks. A girl can carry only so much water in a jar on her head, and may need to make several round trips a day. As a consequence she seldom gets to school. These situations illustrate the integration necessary to the programming process, a dove-tailing of projects which must be effected from the community and regional levels to the national level.

To achieve this integration, a battery of techniques and tools is used to evaluate and compare each project in order to arrive at an optimal allocation of the resources available. Socialist and nonsocialist planners have perfected these techniques and tools between them, and today the tool kit of both groups of planners is essentially the same. Nonetheless, there remain differences between what a member of the Polish Planning Commission might do in his office all day and what a member of the United States Council of Economic Advisers might do, or even between what an Indian or Indonesian planner might do and what a Brazilian planner might do. These differences reflect variations in the degree of reliance placed on the market and on particular techniques and in the extent of centralization of planning and implementation.

SOVIET-STYLE "BALANCE PLANNING"

The elaboration of a Soviet plan starts with the determination of the scope of development and the rate of growth of the key sectors (discussed in Chapters 2 and 3). These main links are selected by what is essentially "cost-effectiveness analysis" (although the Russians do not call it that), measuring the costs of development projects and determining the benefits in terms of the established national objectives. Soviet bloc planning, however, has long concentrated on "balance planning."

In balance planning available material, manpower, and financial resources are related to anticipated requirements for achieving objectives by means of a system of balances. *Material balance* coordinates and correlates the production and consumption of individual products or groups of products. Resources (including those locally produced or imported) are balanced against distribution of products for individual consumption, products used for further production, and exports. *Manpower balance* coordinates and correlates human resources with production requirements and sociocultural activities. *Financial balances* are concerned with the generation and distribution of the national money income. Demand elasticities are calculated to balance demand and output.

By confronting supply and demand, resources, and requirements, disproportions are detected and shortages and bottlenecks identified. Solutions are found to eliminate imbalances; adjustments may be made in supply (production increase, substitution of materials, new technological imports) or demand (postponement of certain needs). These alternatives are weighed and the best balance chosen to achieve the proper linkage between the various elements of the expanded production process.

The balancing method makes use of special quantitative ratios, called norms, which cover both production and consumption. They establish quantitative standards for input in terms of materials, manpower, and finance required per unit of output, (for example, the materials, manpower, time, and finance needed to produce a pair of shoes). For consumption goods or social services, norms are calculated on the basis of existing relationships and proportions; they are changed in response to technological advance, the increase or diminution of available resources, and rising incomes with accompanying shifts in the structure of wants. With regard to the latter, socialist planners have learned the great convenience of leaving to the market a large proportion of decisions about how much to produce of what commodities.

THE MARKET ECONOMY

In advanced private enterprise societies, a basic device used for the economy's management is a gigantic financial balance, with objectives similar to those of the Russian financial balance—equating effective demand and output. The capitalist planners make their balances in highly aggregative terms:

total money income is equated with total products at current prices, with the objective of avoiding inflation while creating favorable conditions for entrepreneurs to generate full employment at the national level. This balance is effected mainly by using the Keynesian formulas quoted earlier: easy money and budget deficits to expand the money flow and reduce unemployment, tight money and budget surpluses to check inflation.

On the eve of World War II there was still a lively debate on "Plan or No Plan". Planning was associated with socialism, capitalism with a laissez-faire economy. During the war, however, the advanced private enterprise countries did a good deal of planning, and none of them has since reverted to a pure laissez-faire system even as an ideology, let alone as a method of economic organization. All advanced nations engage to one degree or another in some type of economic planning.

Central government planning in countries where the basic ideology is to minimize government intervention may be limited to so called "indicative planning"; forecasting is an integral part of the planning operation. In Japan for example, the major contribution of central government planning is to improve the accuracy of private forecasting by making careful econometric and policy determined projections for major sectors of the economy as a whole, hence encouraging private investment by reducing uncertainty. In any country it is a good idea to look ahead, on the basis of the best available knowledge regarding quantitative relationships among strategic variables, and to see what troubles or deviations from targets may lie ahead in the absence of appropriate government measures to prevent them. Even in the Soviet Union, a development plan is always a mixture of agenda for government action and forecasts.

Once these forecasts and projections have been made in countries relying on indicative planning, subsequent decisions concerning allocations of investment will be mainly made by private enterprise, and consequently will be substantially decentralized; however, for major investment decisions, such as whether to build an automobile plant or a shipyard, consultation with government usually takes place. The government also uses subsidies, taxes, tariffs, and other incentives and disincentives to influence entrepreneurial decision. Nevertheless, the underlying philosophy is that the best resource allocation is achieved by giving entrepreneurs their head, leaving it to the market to guide them as to what they should produce, and to allocate scarce resources. Finally, a share of their gains is recaptured through taxes and redistributed among the population by expenditures on education, health, etc.

Macroeconomic balancing and projections are far from being a development plan. A complete plan includes the analysis of individual projects to establish priorities for allocation of scarce resources. Few advanced private enterprise countries make detailed plans for the allocation of scarce resources, mainly because they feel they are unnecessary; they either have sufficient resources at home, or can earn the foreign exchange to buy them abroad, and they have faith in the market as an allocating device. (A notable exception occurred during World War II when the Allied Nations used a species of balance planning to husband resources in short supply.) Moreover, in these countries rising national income has—as the classical economists expected—brought with it widely diffused improvements in human welfare. While some programming is usually done for education, health, and social security, it has neither the scale nor the depth needed for an underdeveloped country.

PLANNING FOR UNDERDEVELOPED COUNTRIES

By contrast, virtually all Third World countries make official development plans. Even countries so firmly commited to the private enterprise system as Brazil, Malaysia, Mexico and the Philippines do so. The scope and degree of detail of their plans tends to increase as one descends the ladder from richer to poorer countries.

Developing countries make plans for a number of reasons. Our analysis has already indicated a need for attention at the microeconomic level. Detailed plans can ensure that small industries have the necessary inputs to get started, that a power plant does not fail in effectiveness for lack of complementary resources and capacity to use its output, and that large scale projects are dovetailed into the economy. Planning may be needed to initiate a green revolution, to acquaint peasants with its possibilities, to devise a framework within which traditional institutions can apply new techniques, and to mobilize all the inputs needed for successful execution. Success may require a concerted effort in research and training and related efforts in the fields of health and nutrition.

Developing countries which have resolved to carve out their own indigenous democracy may use their plan as a vehicle to crystallize their ideology and goals, and as an instrument both of social change and of preservation of certain traditions. In some cases, development planning can itself become a unifying ideology. In Latin America *desarollismo* (literally—"developmentism"), meaning in this context planned development, has become a middle-of-the-road philosophy in its own right.

THE PLANNING PROCESS

The process of formulating a development plan is a continuous feedback system. It can be divided into aspects or phases, but in practice these go on more or less continuously and simultaneously. As in the case of Petit Goave, preliminary programs may be started while larger, longer term projects are reviewed, and, at the same time, anthropological studies may be under way to ascertain the peoples' wants and caapacities. The outputs of each phase of activity then become inputs for the other phases. As individual projects and studies are completed and knowledge accrues, plans may be revised and goals changed. Indeed, no plan is really finished, even if it is officially published as a legal document. Long-term perspective plans with "horizons" of ten to twenty years, must be continuously translated into intermediate–term plans of three to six years, and these in turn into one-year plans or development budgets. Meanwhile, preparation of the next long-term plan begins. In what follows, the various aspects or phases of planning in a certain logical order will be presented; but this order should not be interpreted as a strict sequence in time. One could break into the planning process at almost any point, and be led from there to a consideration of the other phases of the entire operation.

1. Target Setting (Selecting Goals or Objectives) • Any government begins with an idea of what is wrong with the economy and the society for which it is responsible. If nothing is wrong, there is no need for development and no need to plan. For the most part, the maladies are highly visible and much the same in all developing countries: poverty, unemployment, malnutrition, ill health, grossly unequal distribution of income among regions and social groups, and poor human and physical environments. The diagnosis of these maladies leads simply and directly to a statement of the general goals of development: to raise the income of a target group, create employment, improve nutrition, and the environment, and to enrich life. What is possible depends mainly on the natural and human resources available and on savings-investment capacity.

2. Natural and Human Resource Surveys • In any actual planning operation a large share of the total time and energy absorbed goes to finding out what the economy has to work with. Soil surveys, hydrological surveys, geological surveys, aerial photography, forestry inventories, manpower studies— these are the grist for the planner's mill. On the basis of these elements, he can take a second look at the targets and see whether or not they seem reasonable. If they do not, they must be revised downwards; on the other hand, if the resource surveys show that targets are too modest, the sights can be raised.

3. The Two Gaps • Various other balances besides resources–targets must also be considered. Particularly important are the balances between saving and investment requirements, and the balance between foreign exchange earnings and foreign exchange requirements. Once again, if the targets are too high in terms of these gaps means must be found to fill the gaps or the targets must be revised. When determining how much national income is to be invested and how much is going to be consumed, use can be made of the incremental capital-output ratio (ICOR); that is, the relationship between investment and consequent increases in output.

4. Project Evaluation • On the basis of the established targets, individual development projects (roads, mines, manufacturing enterprises, agricultural programs, schools, clinics) can be evaluated in terms of their contribution to the targets, and compared in terms of their contribution to all goals per million dollars worth of expenditure.

5. Weighting Goals • When the cost-effectiveness analysis is done it becomes necessary to weight goals. One project may contribute more to employment, another more to nutrition; if a choice is to be made, it is necessary to relate additional calories to additional jobs. This weighting is essentially a political process in which the people, politicians, and planners are all involved.

6. Involving the People • The current approach to development planning sets great store in involving in the decision-making process those who will be directly affected by the plan. The ordinary machinery of government, whether in parliamentary democracies, peoples' democracies, or other political systems, is generally regarded as inadequate for this purpose and many devices are being used to supplement this machinery. In the case of *animation sociale,* specially trained experts work continuously with the people (target populations) to help them determine, define, and formulate their needs and aspirations. Community centers and village councils afford the public opportunities to discuss the plan as it affects them directly with each other, with local political leaders, and with government officials and planners. Increasingly, a planner's major task is help to interpret the aspirations of the people to the politicians.

In some countries, for example Indonesia, more responsibility is being assigned to local government for planning and executing development projects and programs. India has used a number of such devices to involve its citizens. Each local government and each state government prepares its own development plan, which is then submitted to the central planning commission for integration into the national effort. A massive attempt at community development has been undertaken, which involves planners working at the village level with the local population. Economists outside of government also contribute to plan formulation in a formal way. Trade union organisations, farmers' cooperatives, and employers' organisations are consulted. The plan framework is published before the plan itself is adopted and given wide publicity through press, radio, public meetings, and the like, in order to give the general public a chance to react to the plan before it becomes law. And since the process of consulting the people is a continuous one, the goals of development are themselves under continuous review. Thus we have come full circle in the feedback of the planning process.

Within this process, the planner's role is to stimulate systematic interaction among planners, politicians, and the people, in order to reveal preferences outside the market mechanism. He puts price tags on various items, indicates the trades-off—the nature of the choices to be made—and offers advice on the choice. Providing these facts and analyses to the politicians enables them to exercise informed judgment with respect to the final weighting of objectives. Assessing the costs and effectiveness of possible projects is therefore the major task of the nonsocialist planner.

EVALUATING PROJECTS: COST-EFFECTIVENESS ANALYSIS AND SHADOW PRICES

It is easy enough to cost a factory or a power plant and measure its returns in terms of profits. It is less easy to measure effectiveness in terms of contribution to the various objectives retained in the welfare function. If a power plant, for example, permits rural electrification, not only will people in remote villages be brought into contact with modern technology, but they will also be linked with the outside world through radio, television, films, etc. The real value of the power plant can be expressed by a shadow price.

There are two kinds of *shadow prices*. In the original, and more technical, sense a shadow or accounting price is designed to make allowances for imperfections in the market. Market prices do not reflect "external economies" (the new power plant reduces costs of other outputs), and "diseconomies" (the pulp and paper mill pollutes the river). This type of shadow price is also used for costing items in a project where market prices do not reflect the true scarcity of factors of production. For example, in a country with both a minimum wage rate and protracted unemployment, the "shadow wage" of unskilled labor would be lower than the minimum wage, since unskilled labor is not scarce but superabundant. The true "opportunity cost"[1] to society is zero, since no other output is sacrificed in employing otherwise unemployed labor. One of the most notorious forms of imperfection in the market are monopolies, which may result in overestimation of social benefits if market prices are used as the measure. "Patching the market" in this case might consist in setting a shadow price below market. Both socialist and nonsocialist planners sometimes use a shadow price for foreign exchange, because the official rate does not measure accurately the relative cost of importing or producing at home.

Shadow pricing has also sometimes been used to mean weighting targets in terms of social values. Virtually all governments assign shadow prices to education above the market value, i.e. governments are willing to spend more for education than people are willing to pay in fees. Thus shadow pricing can estimate feedbacks within the system as in the case of education and health.

Education and health programming are at once much desired consumption items and crucial components of development. Along with social security and housing programs, they have special interrelationships within the economy, illustrating a basic tenet of the unified approach: a society in the process of development is like an organism in the course of growth and evolution—a biological feedback system in which distinctions between ends and means disappear. Education, nutrition, health care, transportation, employment, environmental care, and enrichment of life are ends as well as means of development. There are interactions among them in all directions which must be taken into account in program design.

PROGRAMMING EDUCATION

Education should produce the system of values and quality of civilization that are desired by a society and at the same time make sure that manpower

---

[1] "Opportunity costs" are the satisfactions foregone in using scarce resources to produce one good or service rather than another.

requirements are met. Once the goals are established and technical data accumulated, planning becomes a matter of establishing the appropriate programs and related budgets.

Since educational programming must serve a number of objectives, a programmer has a host of questions to answer, and simultaneously, problems to solve. To furnish the government with the appropriate information to make decisions concerning the size of the education budget, the programmer must make a cost-effectiveness analysis of primary, secondary and higher education, of technical and vocational training, of agricultural extension services and of adult literacy. At the same time, he must find a way to correct the chronic imbalance between rural and urban schooling, and to solve special problems, such as reaching nomadic children, at viable cost.

Because of past inadequacies in solving these problems, educational planning has recently been undergoing a revolution. To understand this revolution, it is necessary first to take a look at traditional techniques; the field of educational planning provides a museum of implements for planning inherited from the past, unfortunately still frequently used without adaptation to the real needs of today.

The Demographic Approach • Most outworn of all is the traditional demographic approach, still in wide use, which attempts merely to respond to "social demand for education." As one minister of education in a small Asian country outlined his "programming technique" to the author: "The children are there, they've got to be educated." Thus the social demand or demographic approach consists mainly in finding out how many children are there, and how many are likely to be there in the foreseeable future, in various age groups. This approach is based on the hypothesis that a certain amount of education is a "human right"; and once the exercise of making demographic projections is done, these governments usually try to provide enough school to give some primary education to children in that age group. If funds are left over, an allocation is made for secondary and university education. Obviously this approach might mean, in some cases, that nothing but primary education could be offered.

Education as a Factor of Production • Some planners have long been attempting to relate education to the economy. They have been treating education both as input and an output in the "input-output matrix" of the economy as a whole. The value of education as an end in itself is treated as an output— a part of national income. In addition, investment in education is considered as an input, together with inputs of labor, raw materials, and capital equipment, in the production of goods and services.

They have also been relating educational inputs to the choice of technology. Some products are inherently more education-intensive (electronics) than others (rice). Textiles, on the other hand, can be produced with more or less education-intensive techniques; higher degrees of skill can be substituted for more raw materials, capital equipment, or unskilled labor.

The Manpower Planning Approach • The manpower planning approach is used in conjunction with this analysis. This approach is based on the assumption that the main feedback of education into economic development is the knowledge and skills it produces in the labor force. It implies that if the educational system produced qualified people in the right numbers and the right places, the major part of the economic and social contribution of education planning is achieved. It therefore seeks to determine the relation of manpower requirements to the level and composition of gross national product, and to translate these manpower requirements into needs for education and training.

The Econometric Approach • The econometric approach carries this method further. It relates the stock of educated people, and the flow of students completing education at the different levels, directly to the national output of goods and services without passing through the intervening stage of making forecasts of manpower requirements. It is possible to set up a series of linear equations that relate the stock of persons who have completed a given level of education, and the number of students at each level, to the aggregate volume of production. These equations suggest how the structure of the educational system should change with different growth rates of the economy.

Cost Benefit Analysis • Unless the budget is unlimited, costs must be related to benefits. Choices must be made according to where the educational investment will have the greatest effect. Measuring the costs of education is relatively simple, so long as they are cast in terms of classrooms, teacher's salaries, equipment, etc. Measuring costs in terms of income foregone by being in school rather than in the labor force is a bit more complicated. The real difficulties, however, arise in the effort to measure benefits or returns to investment in education. Just how much does primary education contribute to the economy, compared with additional years of secondary and higher education, for example; and how many doctors should be provided, as compared with engineers? The income approach provides some of the answers.

The Income Approach • The income approach assumes that differences in personal incomes are a close approximation to differences in individual contribution to aggregate social welfare. It assumes that differences in lifetime earnings are primarily the result of differences in educational background, and correlates personal incomes with the amount and kind of education received by individuals. Putting these two assumptions together, a rough measure of the contribution to aggregate social welfare of additional pupil years of education of various kinds can be obtained.[2]

What cost-benefit analysis can contribute is illustrated with a study done on Indian education. In India, unemployment of engineers grows (reportedly

---

[2] There are two obvious defects to this approach: income is not a perfect measure of contribution to total output (questions of monopoly power, parasitism, and special privilege arise) and differences in income depend partly on native intelligence. However, methods of taking account of these factors have been explored with some success.

50,000 unemployed engineers at the time of writing) and there is much "disguised unemployment" among doctors and lawyers. As Indian economist Amartya Sen declares, such unemployment among highly educated people involves a "maddening waste of resources."[3] This comment was based on a cost-benefit analysis by M. Blaug, P. R. G. Layard, and M. Woodhall.[4] They found that the average cost of educating one undergraduate in arts and sciences for one year (in India) to be the same as educating twenty-two students in the primary school; one year at M.A. level to equal that of schooling forty-one primary students. The rate of return of primary education for an illiterate was found to be 15% on investment in education, middle school about 14%, and secondary school 10.5%; bachelor's degrees in arts, sciences, or commerce a little less than 9%.[5] The United Nations Research Institute for Social Development (UNRISD) indicators also show a higher intercorrelation with other development indices for primary, secondary, and vocational schooling than for university education. Both these measures show that more university graduates are being turned out than can be effectively used.

FROM QUANTITATIVE EXPANSION TO INNOVATION AND QUALITY: SYSTEMS ANALYSIS

While the foregoing approaches provide useful methods for integrating education into the development process, they assume implicitly that the existing types of education will meet the needs of economic development. Many countries, however, inherited a colonial system of education, which was seldom adequately revised to fit the needs of the day. Indeed, some educators have insisted that making investment in education more productive is a matter of educational reform, especially innovation in teaching methods and curricula, rather than continued expansion of the traditional educational system. Latin American educators, for example, declare that "through intelligent use of technological innovations and the elimination of irrelevant subject matter and outdated teaching routine, the basic task of the schools could be accomplished in less time and expense per pupil."[6]

In order to make the farreaching qualitative changes needed, many planners are turning from the principle of planning uniform education on a national scale and on the basis of equal opportunity to the idea of individual solutions for different sectors and regions of the country; they are also turning to systems analysis as a tool.

Essentially the systems approach does *not* base projections on past experience as does the econometric approach, but selects according to future needs. Thus the "scenario method" envisages the "final scene" in educational terms

[3] Amartya Sen, Lal Bahadur Shastri Memorial Lecture, 1971. Montreal, McGill University, 1972.

[4] M. Blaug, P. R. G. Layard, and M. Woodhall, *Causes of Educated Unemployment in India*, (London: Allen Lane, the Penguin Press, 1969).

[5] Ibid., p. 206.

[6] Economic Commission for Latin America, *Population Trends and Policy Alternatives in Latin America*, Conference Document, Santiago, Chile, 1971.

and then elaborates a plot for getting there. Moreover, the systems approach examines the interactions and feedbacks within the system, how education is related to other development objectives, and other aspects of the society and the environment, as was done in the Sri Lanka report of the ILO World Employment Programme.

These interactions are obviously easier to discern at the regional or local level than at the national level. Consequently, there has been increased interest in deriving education plans from studying economic and social requirements of relatively small communities, analyzing their socioeconomic needs, and determining educational requirements within the context of these needs. Thus, in Mauretania, not only did the University of Montreal team recommend that educational content be revised to suit the needs of agriculture and the industries of the future, but itinerant schools and radio were suggested as a means for reaching the nomad children. Sometimes a relatively small administrative adjustment can make a big difference; one of the reasons for the high rates of dropouts in rural schools is that the children are taken out of school to help with the harvest, and often they do not return. In some schools in India, harvesting time even coincides with examinations. These problems could be corrected relatively easily by coordinating rural school timetables with agricultural activities.

Planners are also looking beyond the current student population to the educational needs of the current work force. Not only do they continue to promote on-the-job training and agricultural extension. "Recycling of adults" is being proposed; that is, "recurrent education" for adults who want to resume their education, previously interrupted. In its extreme form this approach might mean sending adolescents into the fields and factories to permit adults to return to school—and bringing the adolescents back to school after some job experience. It has been suggested that every citizen might be provided in effect with "tickets" for, say, sixteen years of education, to be used at any time between the ages of six and forty.

In the immediate future, educational programmes will probably avail themselves of whatever is most useful in all the approaches. It is no doubt a good idea to begin with an analysis of the educational system and its relation to the economy and society, so as to permit the design of a simple "system" for analytical purposes. The system may be further broken down into subsystems for particular states or provinces, regions, or even cities, and finally into educational *projects* for individual evaluation in terms of national objectives.

In estimating educational requirements for development, the manpower approach might break with the econometric methods and adopt the "systems" approach. Instead of deriving relationships between level and composition of output and educational requirements from statistics showing relations in the past, it would be better to rely on engineering data, questionnaires or interviews with employers relating to *future* relationships, with as much allowance as possible for technological change.

In calculating the contribution of specific educational projects to per capita income or consumption, there is no avoiding some variant of the "income approach." However, if information is available on productivity or value added, it might be a closer approximation to true social returns than income earned. Estimating an educational project's contribution to national income also requires a forecast of future employment, which may be derived from the employment opportunities expected to be created by the overall development program.

PLANNING SOCIAL SECURITY AND HOUSING

Social security programs and housing differ from other aspects of social development in that they are not so obviously part of a "feedback system." Both are desirable in their own right, and can be used to help stabilize the economy and the society; but their impact on *other* goals, or on productivity in general, is not clearly established.

Social Security • There is no very clear relationship between the degree of social security and either individual income or national income. There is even some doubt, at the present state of knowledge, as to whether protection against the insecurity of unemployment, ill health, and old age makes people work harder and better, or, whether such protection makes people less concerned with providing for themselves, so that they work less hard or less well. It is likely that the reactions will differ from one culture to another, and each country may have to do its own research to find out.

Meanwhile we are left essentially with the "social demand" for social security. If we trust the political process, we can say simply that social security schemes should probably be included in development programs because people seem to want them.

Given the social demand, we can meet it in various ways with differing feedbacks into the economy. With a young population and an immature system we can make it pay for itself by turning the social security system into a means of financing other development projects, reducing rather than increasing current consumption and thus releasing real resources for investment. Or we can use the system to redistribute income from rich to poor as well as from young to old, well to sick, and employed to unemployed. The financing and administration of the system can be designed to achieve this redistribution with aggregate consumption unchanged, increased, or diminished, according to political choice.

Housing • People all over the world want improved housing; it is therefore an important part of economic development in itself. We know little about the impact of housing on productivity; improved housing may create a better human environment and better health, and so contribute to productivity. Yet in most developing countries it is by no means clear that standards of housing (as distinct from sanitation) are so low as to be a menace to health. In terms of incomes and profits generated, it is true, returns may be quite high. In a

Korean project, it was estimated that there was a return of 18.2% on the capital cost of housing, as reflected in the direct and indirect (multiplier) increases in income. This figure compared well to some manufacturing sectors where the rates of return run about 16.6%, according to the study.[7] However, the situation may differ from one country to another; costs of housing vary enormously, and each country will have to design and conduct its own investigations in order to assign appropriate priorities to the housing sector.

Some governments arrive at the housing budget by using the housing sector as a "balance wheel" in the economy; that is, new housing can be retarded for some years, if need be, in periods of prosperity and high levels of employment, or in periods of heavy investment in other sectors. (People can get along with less housing temporarily but people cannot put off eating). Conversely, during periods of recession and unemployment, housing construction can be stepped up, with governmental support, to provide employment and to catch up on housing requirements.

Public Health Programming • Feedbacks between health and the rest of the economy are illustrated by the story of a health program made for an Asian country. The chief economic planner of this country was eager to have a good health program in order to attract foreign aid, so he asked the World Health Organization (WHO) to design the program. He made his request to a highly placed WHO official, who, in turn, inquired what the budget was to be. The government planner replied by asking for a cost-benefit analysis in terms of the health program's contribution to economic development.

The WHO official returned to the government planning office a few weeks later, and stated blandly that any health program WHO could design could not be justified in terms of contribution to economic development. Nutrition and health levels were relatively high; therefore the planner should recommend to the government that no allowance should be made for public health in the development plan. The planning chief, scandalized, then asked WHO to make a plan based on a modest increase over last year's budget.

The WHO official returned a few weeks later with an excellent health program. He handed it to the planning chief, remarking that the plan was guaranteed to obtain the desired technical assistance from WHO, to justify the Ministry of Health budget, and to attract capital assistance from the World Bank and bilateral donors. But, he added, "this plan will not raise the health standards of your country." The planning chief, again scandalized, asked why. The WHO officer then pointed out that without roads and other support needed from other sectors, nothing effective could be done for the majority of the population. "If you have to choose between a road and a clinic, build the road," he said. "If you build the clinic without the road, the people can't get to it. At least with the road, the doctor can get to the people".

---

[7] These studies are part of the United States Agency for International Development (AID) sponsored International Housing Productivity Study. See *Report on Productivity in Relation to Housing Conditions and Community Facilities in Hamback, Korea* by B. Khing Tjioe, with the assistance of Leland S. Burns.

The WHO official was making two points. First of all, health cannot be justified entirely in terms of contribution to economic development. He exaggerated somewhat to make his point, since a healthy population is a basic ingredient of development. However, health programs are desired for their own sake; the aged, for example, cannot be left uncared for merely because they are economically unproductive. Health programs, as such, must receive their allocation largely on the basis of a value judgment on how much can be spared from the budget for this human need.

The second point made was that levels of health depend heavily on investment in other sectors. Malnutrition is at the root of many maladies in developing countries, and solving this problem requires investment in agriculture. In richer developing countries, adequate diet may be brought about by education and rising incomes. In the very poor countries, government action is often required to bypass income differences. But this action may, in turn, depend on cooperation with the private sector, as in the case of the Indian government's nutritional program involving the fortification of wheat bread with synthetic lysine, vitamins, and iron. In other countries, the key may be found in better housing for urban migrants or in improved roads so that health services may reach those in need of them.

There are several other characteristics which make public health programming particularly difficult. It is the only sector where there seems any likelihood that increased investment may actually retard the growth of per capita income and possibly even prevent "take off." The reason, of course, is that increased investment in public health tends to reduce death rates and accelerate population growth. Thus, health programs often now include vigorous family planning efforts. At the same time, higher levels of expenditure for public health are not necessarily associated with increased "quantities" of health. A healthy population necessitates less monetary outlay for medical care than an unhealthy one. A study of six countries (Sri Lanka, Chile, Czechoslovakia, Israel, Sweden, and the United States) shows little relationship between per capita outlays on health and the level of health as measured by crude death rates. Sri Lanka, with the lowest level of expenditure ($5.60 per capita annually as compared to $133.70 for the United States) had death rates lower than any of the six countries except Israel. And Israel, with the lowest crude death rates, had the second lowest level of per capita outlays on health.[8] These findings seem to indicate that once public health has been raised to a certain level, it becomes less expensive to maintain.

This fact, if heeded, might solve the problem of the reluctance of the medical profession to think in terms of priorities, even within the public health sector itself. Health, like education, has thus far been regarded as a "human right"; the medical profession, tied to its oath of Hippocrates, has been reluctant to abandon the concept of curing everyone who is sick, and keeping well everyone who is not sick, as the only acceptable goals. Yet any public health

[8] Brian Abel Smith, *Paying for Health Services,* World Health Organization (WHO) Public Health Paper No. 17 (Geneva, 1963); and United Nations Department of Economic and Social Affairs, *Provisional Report on World Population Prospects* (New York, 1964).

budget must have a cutoff point, and priorities are in fact set within each public health system. For one thing, nearly all developing countries—if not all—are spending far more on curative medicine than on preventive medicine. An enlarged health program enabling intensive drives in both curative and preventive medicine could raise public health levels to the point where considerably less outlay might be needed in future years.

Health planning has followed somewhat the same progression as educational planning in terms of tools. The first Development Decade brought linear expansion of health activities, with little attention to priorities within the health field in particular developing countries. Some health planners are now turning to systems analysis, such as the WHO team developing a new Project Systems Analysis to study management of the planning, programming, implementation, and evaluation of WHO assisted projects. Out of this research and field testing has come a "technology-cost matrix." Essentially, this is a matter of identifying in minute detail public health "tasks," their grouping into "activities," translating these into inputs so as to get a "cost-per-minute" of activities and tasks.

The system was tested in a proposal for the design and implementation of health services in the Jengka Triangle project, a land settlement scheme in central Malaysia. The overall objective was to improve the quality of health services in land settlement schemes such as Jengka without large increases in the expenditure of manpower and monetary resources. More concretely, in cooperation with the Ministry of Health, the objectives are stated as: to assist the National Family Planning Board in reducing the rate of population growth in Jengka to 2% per annum by 1985 (compared to the current rate of 3.6% per annum in rural areas); to reduce the infant mortality rate (IMR) in Jengka to 42 thousand by 1980 and 38 per thousand by 1985 (compared to the current IMR 59 per thousand in rural areas) for the fourteen most important disease groups, to reduce mortality by 50% between 1974 and 1985, to reduce morbidity (new cases) by 30%, and temporary disability by 40% in the same period. An estimate is made of the number of disability days saved at the current level of demand, and on the assumption that demand will double with population growth.

The report then proceeds to analyze current health services in Jengka, and to make detailed proposals for reorganization of these health services. A capital expenditure budget for these services over the next five years, and an operating cost budget are presented. There is a detailed list of "health problems" with numbers of cases of each for 1968. Figures are also given of changes in reported cases between 1960 and 1968 per thousand population, and of numbers of hospital beds. Projections are then made of a number of cases for each problem for 1971–75, 1976–80, and 1981–85. Out of this comes "an estimated community demand for specified conditions." In short, what we have here is a rather sophisticated estimate of "the social demand for public health services."

There are also projections of morbidity, disability and mortality for the periods 1971–75, 1976–80, and 1981–85 for each of the "problems" or objectives. (Objectives being relief of problems). There are estimates of the numbers of disability days saved. Next comes an analysis of constraints, including transportation, distance from hospitals and clinics, and the like. Finally, the "condition" or "problem" is translated into "tasks" and the tasks into manpower requirements in terms of time. These figures, in turn, permit a translation into costs, which can be compared with effectiveness in terms of reductions in mortality, morbidity, and man-days of work lost through disability.

This cost-effectiveness analysis is a part of the "unified approach" which seeks to accommodate all objectives. When all the information is in, the implications of various possible weightings of objectives in terms of the public health program that emerges can then be analyzed and demonstrated. Confronted with these options, the Ministry of Public Health and later the entire Cabinet, can then make the final decisions regarding weights, projects, and programs.

CONFLICT BETWEEN GOALS: MAXIMIZING EMPLOYMENT VERSUS MAXIMIZING INCOME

Once the first selection of projects is made, certain conflicts among goals must be resolved. None appears so strong as the conflict between maximising employment and maximizing income, although the conflict may prove more apparent than real.

In most countries, over some range of increase in developmental investment income and employment will increase together. But at some level of investment, a conflict between maximizing increases in income and maximizing increases in employment will appear; the technology and product-mix that are best for one goal will not be the best for the other. However one can plan to maximize income, recognizing that choosing techniques in terms of income maximization may limit the number of jobs in the primary and secondary industry, but that maximization of national income will provide more wherewith-all to create high-productivity jobs in the services sector.

The planner must first cost labor appropriately, using a shadow price equal to the true opportunity cost to society of employing more people. Usually this cost is slightly above zero; improved nutrition and clothing are probably necessary if idle people are to be employed, but the unemployed are normally fed, clothed, and sheltered in any case. This shadow price will automatically accord a strong bias toward labor-intensive techniques.

As he begins to put together the development plan, the economist can then choose projects which will make the most contribution to achievement of stated objectives other than employment. If a labor-intensive technique offers the same efficiency as any other, then the labor-intensive technique will be chosen. Labor-intensive techniques of acceptable productivity should be sought and introduced wherever possible, with capital-intensive techniques used where clearly advantageous. At this stage "quality of employment" can be built into the program.

When all scarce resources are fully utilized, all avenues should be explored to find useful projects using resources which are not scarce (usually local materials), and to initiate socially profitable undertakings in the services (health, the arts, research, environment). If a country runs out of such projects with some people still unemployed, it can expand the educational system. In Indonesia, for example, planners combined school-age children not in school, unemployed primary and secondary school graduates, and some unemployed university graduates as well, into various patterns to form educational units. For such ventures scarce resources need seldom be used. Most villages have a mosque or a church or some other structure that could be used for a school at odd times. Otherwise, the unemployed themselves can often build one with local materials. In the tropics, bamboo poles and a thatched roof is schoolroom enough. Books and materials might be provided through foreign aid, or by longer runs of textbooks through the government printing office. Real costs are unlikely to be high.

Putting everyone to work in this way, while utilizing *scarce* resources so as to maximize *their* productivity should bring substantial increases in income in most countries. How income and employment goals may be reconciled in practice, along with other goals, is illustrated by the Unified Approach of the Pahang Tenggara Project.

THE UNIFIED APPROACH: PAHANG TENGGARA

The Pahang Tenggara project set out to develop an almost empty region on the east coast of Malaysia, with the idea of giving Malays a chance to participate more fully in the commercial and industrial life of Malaysia, to equalize opportunity, and to create more employment.[9] The team decided to adopt a "unified approach" that would combine social, economic, and environmental considerations.

The plan's basic aim was to achieve an average per capita income equal to the average for Malaysia as a whole, rather than the much lower incomes typical of earlier Malaysian resettlement schemes. The plan spans a twenty-year period, essaying to encompass the entire development process, beginning with agricultural development and processing industries and working toward large industry as the population grows. Not only will the children of the farmers have industrial jobs waiting for them as they reach maturity, but even in the first years of the plan, opportunities will be provided for some of the original immigrants to participate in industrial and service activities.

At first glance the main strategies seem orthodox enough. Based on surveys of future market prospects, the backbone of the first years of development will

---

[9] Heretofore, the Chinese Malaysians, and to a lesser extent the Indian Malaysians, have had a predominant control of the modern sector of the Malaysian economy. The indigenous Malays are mainly in the agricultural sector or in government administrative positions.

be large-scale planting of Malaysia's traditional export products (rubber and oil palm) along with encouragement of Malaysia's highest foreign exchange earner—the timber industry. However, in line with the government's wish to diversify agricultural production, fruit growing on a commercial basis is planned, along with other crops such as tapioca and sago. A beef cattle unit will in turn require the growing of animal feeds. Linear programming techniques tested the economic viability of mixed cropping systems for smallholders (ten to fourteen acres) and analyzed the best combination of crops. Tourism is also being promoted, since Pahang Tenggara has long stretches of magnificent tropical beaches, offshore islands (where most of *South Pacific* was filmed), as well as mountain and hill jungle country abounding in wild life.

A major aspect of the strategy of the project, however, falls in line with the government policy of geographic dispersal of industry and of modern industrial techniques. The development of the region provides obvious immediate industrial opportunities for small and intermediate-sized local plants producing construction materials from local materials and with local labor and entrepreneurs. Processing of the resource-based projects will involve rubber- and palm-oil-processing factories, a fruit-canning plant, sawmilling, plywood and particle board plants, furniture making and prefabricated housing. The beef industry will require a slaughterhouse and later a beef by-products industry. Other small industrial opportunities will lie in the need for consumer durable goods; clothing, radios, and bicycle shops. Financial and organizational support (such as industrial sites and training programs) are planned for the immediately relevant industries; later, with expanding local markets, and with good communications, larger-scale industries may be established.

By far the most interesting feature of the strategy, however, is the immediate urbanization of the farmer. Rather than living on the land they cultivate, the farmers will inhabit towns and will be bussed to the plantations. They will settle in an urban environment of some ten to twenty thousand people, *avoiding the problems of inadequate rural educational and health services.* The scheme essays to provide the farmers not only with an enriched urban life which the larger towns can afford to provide, but also the chance to engage in urban employment as well as rural work. (The first seven years of a rubber plantation's growth offers little employment after the initial planting, and little income; the rubber tappers would hopefully find work in the town in the meantime). The size of the centers was chosen on the basis of research, which confirmed the relationship of town size to level of public service, education, and manufacturing activities. The size-structure was also confirmed by UNRISD indicators, showing the relation of city size to occupational structure, diversity of occupation, and movement toward a modern society. Not only does a center of ten thousand to twenty thousand people allow better community welfare facilities, but also statistics indicate that the higher figure is a threshold for light industry.

Suggestions for maintaining the Orang Asli (the forest people) in their traditional environment (as distinct from bringing them into the modern sector) were three: immediate action should be taken to protect the permanent crops from the invading elephants; building of fishponds to improve their dietary intake; encourage poultry farming.

Final Selection of Projects • The real crunch comes in the final selection of projects for inclusion in the plan, according to all the goals, because the goals may conflict. In the final selection of projects for inclusion in the plan, goals had to be stated in such terms that they could be translated into criteria for evaluating individual projects. In this regard the project profited from being led by a physical planner H. van Ginkel. Physical planners are in some ways well equipped to follow a unified approach, since in the course of fulfilling their contracts and coming up with a plan for a client, they are compelled to reach decisions about both objectives and means of attaining them, and they have learned to deal simultaneously with quantified and nonquantified objectives. The goal-setting techniques used on the project bear a useful imprint of their approach.

The team agreed first of all on four major objectives, i.e., four components of the "welfare function" for the development of the region:

1. Maximize the growth of per capita income over the planning period, while at the same time improving its distribution, particularly as between Malays and non-Malays.

2. Maximize the contribution to reduction of unemployment over the planning period, with particular emphasis on creation of employment opportunities for Malays.

3. Maximize the contribution to the ecological harmony of the region.

4. Maximize the contribution to the cultural enrichment of the people living in the region.

These four objectives were not regarded as mutually exclusive. On the contrary, it was assumed that all four would be given some weight in any conceivable development plan for the region. However, the team experimented with different weighting systems by giving each objective in turn priority, in order to determine how and how much the outcome differed according to which concept or objective was given top priority. The Malaysian government could then decide which result it preferred. The final system of weighting, in other words, was left for the government to determine.

The Income Objective • Since the government was interested in having some "bankable" projects (projects which the World Bank might agree to finance), the planners were required to present figures of current net worth of projects from a strictly market point of view. Projects would therefore be evaluated in terms of internal rate of return on investment.[10] The government was also interested in total income generated, particularly income of lower-income groups, and, above all, of Malays. The team therefore decided to

[10] Internal rate of return is the rate of discount which equalizes the present value of the stream of returns to the stream of costs.

measure the income from each project in three ways: the internal rate of return; net value added per man-year; and net present value per acre of income generated.

Employment • Employment is the most straightforward of the four objectives. It could be measured in terms of number of jobs created per million dollars of investment.

Ecology • Since contribution to ecology and cultural transition cannot be measured directly, they have to be estimated by "proxy variables," that is, measurable factors closely related to the objective. For example, the contribution of flood control could be measured by increase in agricultural production and employment. The measure might on the other hand be the cost of offsetting erosion or pollution. There is no yardstick for ecological or cultural excellence and in some cases "dummy variables" may be used, as described below.

Since the settlement of a largely empty region involves clearing land, and thus a violent disturbance of the existing ecology, it was clear that the plan must take into account the ecological impact of alternative patterns of development. Carelessness in this respect could destroy large tracts of land, kill fish and wildlife, and pollute air and water. In other words, the projects or programs might be poorly meshed with the existing ecological pattern and so prevent an optimal utilization of the resource potential over time. On the other hand, the development of the region offered opportunities for improvement of the ecology, such as flood control and irrigation; also a possibility of resorting to existing natural processes in such a way as to improve the ecological balance.

There were two possibilities with respect to measurement of impact on ecology. One was to use a "dummy variable": perhaps to score a project as "2" if it brought "great improvement" in the ecology, "1" if it brought some improvement, "0" if it brought no change, "−1" if it brought some deterioration, "−2" if it did serious harm. The other possibility was to measure the costs of preventing any deterioration in the ecology (stream pollution, for example) and to measure both costs and benefits of improvement in the environment (through flood control and irrigation schemes, for example).

Cultural Enrichment • There is a close correlation between the complexity, sophistication, and diversity of daily life and the degree of urbanization. Indeed the availability of a wide range of opportunity and choice is well summarized by the word "urbane." A simple approach to the concept of cultural enrichment, therefore, would be to use the impact of projects and programs on the degree of urbanization as a proxy variable. However, the team did not wish to rule out the possibility that a high degree of urbanization might prove impracticable for the region, while at the same time a relatively satisfactory pattern of social and cultural life could be created within a structure of small towns and villages. An alternative measure, therefore, might be the amount of employment created in "rare" services (education, research, professions, recreational and cultural activities) plus administrative, scientific, and technical activities in industry.

A smooth transition to the new and richer way of life was also considered important. Here it was not merely a question of creating a more complex, diversified, and sophisticated mode of life but also of designing institutions to facilitate the departure from the old sociocultural pattern to the new one. Some of these "institutions for transition" may be familar, such as schools, community centers, recreation facilities, transport; others might be new. In new settlements in central Malaysia, for example, people have been able to remain involved in the social life and built-in social security system of the villages whence they came because of a good local transport system, made possible by good roads. They kept "one foot in the village," returning home, not only for feast days, but also in times of sickness and to have their babies. The new roads linking Pahang Tenggara with the rest of Malaysia will probably provide a similar transitional link between traditional and modern living. However, since the Pahang Tenggara project is somewhat isolated by distance, the plan also calls for the settlements to be designed in "steps"; approximating *kampong* life in certain areas (each house to have a quarter of an acre plot to cultivate) to permit gradual adjustment to a more urban life style.

The Priority Formula • Given these four "concepts" or objectives, together with the proposed measures for each, flexible priority formulas could be constructed that would permit giving major weight to each of the four objectives in turn, and comparing the resulting patterns of programs of development. The basic idea is that projects are ranked in order of priority by classifying them in terms of contribution to each of the four objectives.

Some Results • To no one's surprise, the technical and economic studies combined indicated that the best use for most of the land was for rubber, oil palm, and forestry complexes. Smaller scale projects for cattle, tea, and sago were also included in the master plan. Table 8.1 shows the results of the analysis with respect to income and employment for "representative firms" in the fields of rubber, oil palm, and forestry. As is readily apparent from the table, a clear-cut conflict appeared as between maximization of income (on any of the three measures used) and maximization of employment per 1,000 acres in year ten; rubber was clearly best for employment and forestry complexes clearly best for income. However, the time-pattern of employment creation was quite different for rubber and oil palm; rubber requires considerable labor for planting, and then very little for the next seven years while the trees mature; oil palm needs intensive application of labor throughout the first five years. Since the government was clearly more interested in employment-creation during the next ten years than in employment-creation ten years hence, we applied the same discount factor to employment as we did to income. When that was done, oil palm emerged as slightly superior to rubber for

TABLE 8.1 MACRO COST-EFFECTIVENESS MATRIX

	INTERNAL RATE OF RETURN			NET PRESENT VALUE			VALUE ADDED YEAR 20			EMPLOYMENT PER 1,000 ACRES YEAR 10		
	Worst	Best	Probable	Worst	Best	Probable	Worst	Best	Probable	Worst	Best	Probable
Oil palm	8.3[a]	17.0[b]	15%[c]	−$186	$1,103	$686	$7,024[h]	$9,552[i]	$ 8,500[j]	60[m]	67[n]	65[o]
Rubber	10.4[d]	16.0[e]	13.0[f]	69	1,287	511[g]	5,461	8,590[k]	7,000[l]	96[p]	146[q]	146[r]
Forestry	30.0[s]	34.5[t]	32			677[t]			30,711[u]			8

[a] Class III soils; present high-yield seeds.
[b] Experimental seed.
[c] Best minus 1 standard deviation.
[d] Present clones, no stimulant, limited soils.
[e] Experimental clones, best soils, stimulants.
[f] As in "3". With limited soils, new clones, stimulants, IRR = 14.3% ± 2.5
[g] As in "3". With limited soils, new clones, stimulants, NPV = $854 ± 608.
[h] Present varieties.
[i] Present varieties, new methods.
[j] Average.
[k] With mechanization, stimulated present clones, best soils.
[l] Average.
[m] Present varieties.
[n] Future varieties.
[o] Guess.
[p] Present clones new techniques, Class 1 & 2 soils.
[q] Present methods, present clones, limited soils.
[r] Employment year 5:

	Worst	Best	Probable
Oil Palm	84	92	96
Rubber	36	66	60

[s] Bukit Ibam.
[t] Lesong.
[u] Lesong: $18,675 at year 10, assumed increase of 5.1% per year.

employment. In terms of the four major objectives, the ultimate ranking were as follows:

Strategies:	N	Y	C	E[11]
Maximize rubber	B	D	D	C
Maximize oil palm	A	C	C	C
Maximize forestry	C	B	B	A
Maximize forestry plus incentive for manufacturing	D	A	A	B

The government's task of choosing among strategies, given these results of the study, was facilitated by technical considerations. Some land was suitable for one of the four uses and not for the others. The final plan therefore ended up with a judicious blend of all four strategies, with a different mix of the four main types of economic activity in each sub-region.

INPUT-OUTPUT ANALYSIS

When all major projects have been studied, it is useful to undertake some form of "balance planning," which in the Western version is usually called input-output analysis. An "input-output" or "inter-industry matrix" shows the interrelationships among all the industrial sectors in any economy, broken down into as many categories as statistics and computing facilities permit, showing purchases of each industry from all others, and sales of each industry to all others. Table 8.2 shows a fairly simple input-output matrix for India. Such matrices provide a picture of the flow of goods and money through the economy at a point in time. With such pictures for two or more years, it is also possible to project these relationships to some target year of the development plan, although there are dangers in assuming that the relationships remain constant over time.

An input-output table serves to remind planners of the interrelationships among expansion of some sectors and expansion of others, thus preventing failure to provide for simultaneous growth of all interrelated industries, which must by their very nature grow together. Since one sector in a complete matrix is imports, it can also warn planners of the import implications and the consequent need for a specified and effective program for providing foreign exchange.

While input-output analysis was originally developed to measure flows of goods (and possibly services) among industries, conceptually it can and should include all elements of the development process. Thus, health, education, nutrition, environmental protection, transport, power research, and technology, could all be put into the matrix, to show who produces them, what producers buy from others, and to whom they sell their product.

[11] Use "Y" for income, "N" for employment, "E" for impact on the ecology and "C" for the smooth transition to an enriched social and cultural life.

TABLE 8.2 INDIA: ABRIDGED INPUT-OUTPUT TABLE, 1960/61 *

(ten million rupees, 1959/60 producers' prices)

From \ To	Agriculture	Food Industry	Textiles	Chemical Fertilizer	Transport and Electricity	Manufacturing and Mining	Construction	Sub-total	Consumption	Gross Fixed Capital Formation	Net Exports	Output
Agriculture	604.7	795.0	371.0	–	11.0	143.1	68.9	1,993.7	5,412.6	83.6	–113.0	7,577.0
Food industry	55.0	48.4	5.6	–	–	12.9	–	121.9	1,072.2	102.3	26.6	1,323.0
Textiles	3.9	6.6	25.3	0.9	0.4	18.8	–	55.9	713.9	10.8	144.8	930.0
Chemical fertilizer	30.3	–	–	–	–	–	–	30.3	–	1.3	–10.7	20.7
Transport and electricity	8.0	5.8	25.5	0.3	13.4	37.0	–	90.0	302.9	175.5	–68.7	1,164.0
Manufacturing and mining	49.4	22.2	62.2	5.5	264.1	555.4	630.4	1,589.2	687.2	499.6	–631.2	2,164.1
Construction	–	–	–	–	–	–	–	–	104.0	1,360.0	–	1,617.0
Sub-total	751.3	878.0	489.6	6.7	288.9	767.2	699.3	3,881.0	8,292.8	2,233.1	–652.2	14,795.8
Value added	6,752.0	271.2	325.6	9.2	750.1	905.5	636.6	9,650.2	860.0	–	–	13,734.2†
Margin	44.4	67.4	36.8	1.7	31.6	201.2	281.1	664.2	4,646.8	276.0	164.8	–
Value of output	7,577.0	1,323.0	930.0	20.7	1,164.0	2,164.1	1,677.0	14,795.8	13,984.9	2,509.1	–457.6	–

Source: "Interindustry Transactions (India), 1960/61," Planning Commission, India. From United Nations, *Economic Survey of Asia and the Far East, 1964* (Bangkok, 1965), p. 35.

Agriculture: Plantations, animal husbandry, food grains, other agriculture, forestry products and rubber.
Food industry: Food industries.
Textiles: Cotton and other textiles, and jute textiles.
Chemical fertilizer: Chemical fertilizers.
Transport and electricity: Transport equipment, motor transport, railways and electricity.
Manufacturing and mining: Electric equipment, non-electrical equipment, iron and steel, iron ore, cement, other metals, other minerals, leather and leather products, glass, wooden and non-metalic mineral products, petroleum products, crude oil, rubber products, chemicals and coal.
Construction: Construction, urban and industrial, and construction, rural.
† Gross value added.

An input-output matrix provides a "snapshot" of the economy in operation; with matrices for several years, the planner has a moving picture of the economy. The pictures provided by input-output analysis reduce the risk that vital elements will be overlooked, or that bottlenecks will appear because key components of the system have been left out.

PROSPECTS OF SUCCESS?

What could go wrong, then, if a plan is well designed? To begin with, a plan could gather dust on a shelf if the government is not really committed to the program suggested by their hired hands in the planning department. If it is to be effectively implemented, a plan needs a number of supporting government policies. Even if an adequate number of doctors are educated for a country's needs, and if medical facilities are provided for them in the villages it may still require a government regulation that new M.D.'s must spend the first years of their practice in the countryside—a regulation enforced in a number of countries today. If it is decided to upgrade education through innovation and revision of the curricula, competent educators will have to be attracted by an acceptable wage, which will probably be determined by the government. If a plan is designed on the assumption that a certain level of national savings will be attained, an appropriate tax system must be designed and enforced. In sum, for a development plan to succeed, much depends on government action to persuade and guide people to carry out the plan.

9

Policies for
development

There is an old Brazilian saying that Brazil grows at night while the politicians sleep. While some economies can grow despite the shortcomings of politicians, successful execution of an economic development plan requires an integrated design of legislation and regulation, with efficient public administration to ensure smooth implementation. Measures must be designed to encourage and channel investment, to influence individual economic decisions as to what to produce where, what job to take, what to buy, what sort of education and training to seek. Even skillful neglect of a private enterprise economy requires some original political action. Furthermore, the government may have to protect the environment, negotiate favorable trade agreements, promote regional integration with neighboring countries, control inflation, and finally, to take a hand in distributing the opportunities and the fruits of development more evenly.

Governments of socialist and nonsocialist countries alike have at their disposal a wide range of instruments to influence individual economic behavior and to alter income distribution: taxes, subsidies, interest rates, tariffs and quotas, commodity agreements, foreign exchange controls, wage-price regulations, manpower allocation, licensing of building and other investment, government lending and grant programs, and control of land use. Intervention regarding the institutional framework may cover an enormous range—from birth control programs to land reform; from eliminating feudal or caste privilege to preserving certain traditional institutions. These measures have overlapping impacts, and for optimal results must be woven together into an articulated system.

Choice of instruments varies a great deal from one country to another. In large measure, the choices reflect differences in the operating ideology of governments, particularly ideologies about the extent and nature of government intervention that is considered desirable in principle. Except in crisis situations when a whole nation feels threatened, as in time of war, great depression, or hyperinflation, drastic and sudden changes in the nature and extent of government intervention are politically difficult. However, once a plan is set in motion, initiating new situations and new possibilities, a government can channel the new drives and induce further changes. Politics has been described as "the art of the possible," and discerning which policy measures are both possible and effective constitutes the true art of economic development.

In this chapter, then, we shall look at some of the more common measures of development policy, examine some of the differences in the manner in which they have been used, and finally consider the relative merits of different economic systems for development purposes.

THE HIERARCHY OF GOVERNMENT INTERVENTION

Real differences between socialist and nonsocialist approaches to development appear in the degree or nature of government intervention in the implementation of a development program. From a purely economic viewpoint, there is a whole hierarchy of degrees of government intervention, all consistent with the preparation of some kind of economic and political development program, and two main criteria for judging the degree of government intervention. The first is the *relative size of the public sector,* the hierarchy of which may extend from less than 1% to 100% of national income or investment. The second criterion is the extent and tightness of control over the private sector, whatever its size; that is the degree to which intervention in the market is used to control the private sector. Government intervention may range from complete centrally planned decision making and public ownership, through the various degrees of intervention and public ownership of mixed economies, to the other extreme of complete *laissez-faire.*

Implementation of a plan is easier if a government has direct control of all important investment decisions through the dominance of the public sector, as in a centralized socialist system; however, the possibility of planning as such is not related to the relative size of the government sector. So long as a government has a single instrument of control—a budget, a central bank, a tariff system, a foreign exchange control system—it can plan for the use of that instrument to influence private decisions so as to promote development. In mixed economies, a development program will consist partly of investment budgets for the public sector and partly of sets of policies designed to encourage and direct private economic activity.

If any government has sufficient knowledge of the characteristics and behavior of demand on the one hand, and of costs of production and supply on the other, it can always design policies to achieve through the market any objective that can be attained by direct government action. These government measures, undertaken to effect private decisions, may be monetary, fiscal, or foreign trade policies, direct wage and price controls, regulation of monopolies, selected subsidies and similar measures. In an essentially private enterprise economy, a whole battery of such policies may come into play.

In degree of intervention in the private sector, one might rank development policies in the following order: reliance on monetary and fiscal policy alone; reliance on monetary and fiscal policy *plus* foreign trade policy (tariffs and quotas can be used to influence the pattern of private investment, to encourage investment in import-replacing industries and the like); reliance on monetary and fiscal policy plus foreign trade policy plus exchange control. With this combination of instruments, a country could exert powerful effects on the pace and pattern of economic development. The highest degree of control would be all the foregoing *plus* direct controls. With this degree of intervention, a country would have in effect, a "war economy," but with economic development rather than winning a war as the objective. The direct controls might include price controls, rationing, wage fixing, licensing investment, control of new capital issues, and manpower allocation.

Since a government can plan economic development even with no public sector whatsoever, and conceivably even with no intervention beyond monetary and fiscal policy, it becomes clear that the choice of the nature of government intervention must rest on political philosophy or matters of administrative convenience. However, even societies that set high value on the initiative that private enterprise unleashes will accord to government responsibility for action in some areas where private enterprise may not wish to enter.

AREAS OF INTERVENTION

Government intervention falls into six main overlapping categories: improving resource allocation; improving distribution of wealth, income, and opportunity; improving the "style" of development; improving the "mix" of public and private sector activities; and improving economic relations with the outside world.

ALLOCATION OF RESOURCES

In private enterprise systems, governments may largely confine their intervention in allocation of resources to tax incentives and subsidies to attract private enterprise into key sectors and retarded regions. The basic reason for resorting to direct government investment is that certain projects may not be profitable as private undertakings, or may be too long term, or too large-scale for private action; yet such projects may significantly increase gross national product, or social welfare, or both.

Projects most commonly relinquished to government are communication systems, roads, airlines, railroads, public health, hydroelectric projects, education, and some areas of research. These activities yield large external economies and support other, directly profitable enterprises; in some cases, government enterprise can open up entirely new possibilities, such as the construction of Brasilia and the great road system which will eventually link the regions of Brazil.

Since economic development is more a matter of creating new firms and industries than it is of encouraging expansion of existing ones, governments may sometimes create new enterprises that are both desirable and profitable where private enterprise fails to do so for lack of foresight. A government may also intervene if a set of individual private investment decisions each seems unattractive in itself, whereas an investment program undertaken as a unit may yield substantial increases in national income, as in the case of the Vanoni Plan (1954–64) in Southern Italy.

Originally the Italian government had hoped that industrialization could be achieved in the retarded south by giving incentives to private enterprise, mainly in the form of financial and fiscal facilities, and by establishing the necessary infrastructure: transport, communications, water, electricity. For example, the National Electric Power Corporation brought considerable benefit to the south by establishing uniform electricity tariffs (which previously had been at higher levels in the south than in the north) and promoted rural electrification schemes. The plan also provided various incentives to encourage private enterprises to locate in the south. These included a ten-year exemption from income tax and related taxes; a 50% reduction of the turnover tax on machinery and materials; exemption from customs duties imposed on machinery and materials; "soft loans" for expansion of existing plants or establishment of new ones. In addition, there were loan guarantees, state participation in the share capital of new industries, outright grants as contributions to construction costs, and preferential rates on state railways for materials and supplies. Government agencies were required to place one-fifth of their orders with southern firms, apart from "normal" orders, which southern enterprises could obtain on a competitive basis. Government-owned enterprises were also established in the region.

However, once it became clear that the policy of establishing general infrastructure and offering special conditions was not leading to a corresponding increase in entrepreneurial activity, the government decided to take over directly major entrepreneurial responsibilities. Consequently public undertakings were called upon to play a steadily increasing part. A law was passed obliging undertakings with state shareholdings to locate 60% of investment in new projects in the south, and 40% of total investment.

The final outcome of the plan somewhat disappointed the plan's architects. They had hoped to reduce the absolute income gaps between north and south. That has not occurred. The plan did succeed, however, in bringing the percentage growth rate in the south up to that of the north, and later to slightly exceed it.

Today, governments are paying increasing attention to protection and conservation of resources and the environment. Measures range from pollution control and energy conservation by means of persuasion, regulation and taxes, to limitations on fish harvests. A government can conserve resources by heavy taxes on luxuries or even forbidding the manufacture of nonessentials such as electric toothbrushes. Another effective way to make resources go further is to curb population growth.

FAMILY PLANNING POLICIES

Not much faith is placed in family planning programs in themselves to curb population growth. Studies made in many countries indicate that women want smaller families than they have, and the importance of education in family planning is indicated by a recent story of a peasant husband and wife who took the trouble to get a rubber contraceptive and then nailed it firmly to the front door to scare off unwanted conceptions. However, family planning policies, by and large, address themselves to preventing *unwanted* births; the difficulty remains that many parents *want* large families for valid economic reasons. When child labor contributes substantially to family income, as it does in many peasant societies, and when parents are dependent on a large family for protection and security in old age, there are few incentives to reduce fertility. In these cases, access to family planning information and facilities may make little difference, and indirect government action to change peoples' attitude towards family size may be more influential.

Indirect government action can take a variety of forms. As noted earlier, promoting development itself brings powerful social change; mechanization of agriculture and modernization of industry means that large families eventually become a heavy burden rather than a source of labor for the family farm or handicraft. Compulsory education, automatically precluding parents from using their children as full-time income earners at an early age, can—as it has in the past—act as a strong incentive for smaller families. Compulsory education for girls in particular is likely to delay their marriage and reduce the number of their childbearing years. Once such measures have initiated the desired change, institutional devices can cushion the transition, particularly social policies which reduce the dependence on the family as the sole source of security, such as old age pensions, public health schemes, and unemployment insurance.

REDISTRIBUTION OF WEALTH AND INCOME

There is an old Asian saying that it is difficult to persuade the tiger to part with his fur. A Western economist might reply that there is more than one way to skin a cat. A government ready and willing to redistribute wealth has a variety of ways of doing it; the problem is to choose the most efficient and acceptable way. The two main avenues for equalization are land reform and fiscal policy—using tax and spending powers to improve distribution of income.

LAND REFORM

The idea of land reform arouses deep emotions, yet, above all, redistribution of land must be approached pragmatically. Land reform has not always proven successful; for the best results, the political, sociological, and economic aspects must all be taken into account.

Usually the term "land reform" conveys the concept of breaking up large estates and dividing them among small farmers: "the soil to the tiller." Agricultural economists are quick to point out that in many developing countries, splinter holdings and scattered fragmented holdings are at least as great a problem as concentration of land ownership in few hands; they would encompass action to reassemble *minifundia* into farms of efficient size as well as subdivision of *latifundia* in the concept of land reform. They point out that plantations are usually a highly efficient form of agricultural organization, heavily capitalized, and responsible for the bulk of agricultural exports. Breaking them up into smaller units might result in a decrease in production. They cite Mexico's experience: the immediate result of land reform was a decline in the production of staples, and it took more than two decades for the total output of corn, wheat, beans, and rice to regain its 1920 level. The appropriation of large estates by peasants in Bolivia in 1952 reduced production by one-third.

Such land reforms, however, have been deemed worthwhile by some economists in terms of the social improvement achieved. The land reform in Mexico, for example, has been considered a success, because even if it reduced agricultural output for the time being, it combined with the expropriation of the oil fields and nationalization of public utilities to set the stage for subsequent rapid growth. Some governments, however, give first priority to maintaining an optimal size of farm to ensure raising agricultural productivity; and achieve a leveling up by other means. Even in Cuba, the holdings permitted by the postrevolutionary agrarian reform were decided on a pragmatic basis—for unirrigated land, sixty-six acres per family was considered to be the "vital minimum."

Some economists are very skeptical of the concept of "optimum size of farm," feeling that the concept may be used to justify traditional patterns of land holding and thus delay economic and social progress. Edmondo Flores has said that trying to decide the optimal size of a firm is like trying to decide the optimal size of a bikini; it depends on your point of view and the particular case in question. He emphasizes the difficulties in establishing the precise optimum size for a particular crop of a given country at a particular time, and recommends a politically determined minimal unit to be left to present landowners.[1] He maintains that successful land reform requires expropriation of all land above this minimum without immediate compensation (otherwise no redistribution of wealth is involved). It must proceed rapidly and massively, and it must be accompanied by vigorous development policies both within the agricultural sector and elsewhere. Flores instances the Mexican land reform. He also cites the land reform in Japan, beginning in 1947, which not only increased the share of owner-operated land from 54% of the cultivable total to 92% but also transferred technology and capital from the industrial to the agricultural sector, raised agricultural productivity, and expanded the market for industrial products.

[1] Edmondo Flores "The Economics of Land Reforms." Paper for the Eighth Regional Food and Agricultural Organization Conference, Vina del Mar, Mar. 1965.

Many governments would have difficulty in enforcing all the stringent reforms Flores suggests. On the other hand, there are other ways of achieving the ultimate objective—redistribution of wealth. If the size of farm is to be determined on the basis of total output, a government willing and able to carry through a program of redistribution of land can redistribute wealth and power in other ways—an effective progressive income tax, or a progressive land or capital tax, combined with vigorous industrialization and social development programs, for example. Solving the social and political problems in other ways would leave each government free to determine the size of farm for each type of agricultural enterprise in the country on technical grounds and then seek to establish tenure in parcels of optimum size.

There is also a number of forms of compensation. In Taiwan landlords were compensated, partly by shares in government enterprises and partly in commodity bonuses; the peasants, in turn, bought the land on easy terms. American aid made this type of reform possible. In Venezuela, the land was paid for at market prices, in cash up to about six thousand dollars and in bonds after that. These countries, however, had ready access to foreign exchange, through grants or strong exports. Such compensation would be difficult in countries with severe shortages of capital. But in some countries, land reform without compensation is so contrary to the views and interests of the dominant political elite that it could scarcely occur short of revolution.

Countries striving to bring social justice by evolution rather than revolution may seek changes which set further change in motion. More recent land reform measures in the Philippines involved only moderate change, and were therefore easier to introduce. The reform involves a change from share-cropping to leasehold, with lease considerations based on the average normal harvest during three agricultural years immediately preceeding the establishment of the leasehold. The owner receives 25% of the net production after deducting the costs of seeds, harvesting, threshing, loading, hauling and process. He no longer has obligations to his tenants to provide credit or irrigation; their relationship has become strictly contractual. The new system is less paternalistic, and could open the door to further change; but thus far its scope of application has been very limited.

The most practical way to land reform will vary from country to country, even from region to region; each government must find the best solution to fit the local situation.

EQUALIZING DISTRIBUTION OF INCOME BY TAXATION AND SPENDING

Equalizing distribution of income is a cherished avenue toward social justice. Yet here the measures may not only be obstructed by the self-interest of politically powerful groups, but in certain situations, equalization may conflict with increasing national income. An efficient redistribution must reconcile social justice with maximization of income. There is a trade-off here, which runs in terms of the health of the labor force, of incentives for work and risk taking, and of the volume of investment.

When incomes are very low, and the population suffers from malnutrition and disease, a greater equality of income may not only be dictated by concern for social justice, but may also be a condition for more rapid growth. At the same time, not even a socialist system has yet attempted to draw forth the best capacities of its people on a basis of income equality. Even in China, the average level of rural incomes is substantially below that of urban incomes, which range from 30 to 40 yuan a month for an unskilled worker and as much as 400 yuan for a top civil servant or university professor. The most competent and responsible efforts in any field evoke special rewards in any system; while higher wages may be required to attract workers into less desirable jobs, and to attract professional people into strategic sectors, such as education.

In mixed economies, the rewards will be largely determined by the market; but how unequal rewards will remain depends on the tax structure. Governments can and do reduce inequalities of income distribution through such measures as progressive taxation combined with public expenditures on health, education, housing, social security, and equal employment opportunities for women. Pricing systems and subsidies can favor basic food and clothing items.

There has, however, been a great deal of controversy concerning the relationship between income distribution and the volume of investment in private enterprise and mixed economies. One view holds that unequal income distribution mobilizes capital for investment. Japan's prewar economic growth, for example, took place under conditions of very unequal income distribution, as did the earlier growth of Western Europe. Since the Japanese and European capitalists invested their incomes to good effect, it has sometimes been argued that carried too far, equalization of income can result in demobilization of capital and its dissipation in consumption, thus bringing economic development to a grinding halt. Argentina's problems in the forties and fifties have been blamed on this kind of equalization.

On the other hand, despite glaring disparities in income and wealth, the rate of savings and investment during the 1950s in the Philippines was very low relative to national income. While some families reinvested profits to advantage, there were many in the upper incomes groups who assigned considerable prestige value to conspicuous consumption, while in some cases savings melted away in flight of capital. Significantly, in the sixties, when income distribution seems to have been better, the savings ratio was substantially higher. In situations where reinvestment by private persons does not seem to be the rule, a government would be well advised to mobilize capital for investment in development by heavy taxation, effecting equalization in the process. This capital can then be channeled into upgrading of human resources, and into development investment which further equalizes incomes by increasing employment.

EQUALIZING OPPORTUNITY: FINANCIAL INSTITUTIONS

Government can improve opportunity for small-scale undertakings through supports such as new credit facilities combined with demonstration and training. New credit facilities in India, for example, were designed to equalize opportunity and reduce regional imbalances by combating "gigantism" in the form of the big, increasingly powerful business houses. When the Indian government examined the structure and policies of financial institutions with a view to providing small entrepreneurs with credit facilities, it was found that the existing institutions were serving the credit needs of the big business houses, and that the regional imbalances and concentration of economic power were partly due to the operations of the financial institutions. Subsequently, fourteen major private commercial banks were nationalized in 1969, their structure and policies changed to accommodate the credit needs of farmers, small entrepreneurs, and merchants—who have relied in the past on moneylenders and middlemen. Each bank was assigned backward districts in which to play a "lead-bank" role by pursuing liberal credit policies and other measures to stimulate the development of the districts.

EVENING REGIONAL DISPARITIES

When it comes to evening up regional disparities by monetary or fiscal means, a government can do something tantamount to cracking the seemingly impossible problem of having tight and easy money at the same time. As observed earlier, inflation is normally generated in the leading region while unemployment is concentrated in the lagging region. With a steeply progressive tax system, the antiinflationary impact of tax increases will be strongest in the region where incomes are highest. On the other hand, increased government investment in infrastructure and incentives to private investment will be most effective in reducing unemployment in the lagging region. Thus through astute fiscal policy a government may approximate "tight money" in the leading region and "easy money" in the lagging region.[2]

EDUCATION

Where total budgets for education are severely limited, one of the worst tasks faced by governments is providing equality of opportunity in education. In the most affluent countries, relatively large educational budgets and the wide range of opportunity to "work one's way through college" means that virtually any capable person can have a university education if he sets his mind to it. In most countries, however, only a certain number of university places or even secondary school places can be provided; the agonizing question as to who will get them unleashes enormous social pressures.

In some cases, the children of the privileged (the rich or leading party members) gain these precious educational opportunities. More democratic govern-

[2] A recent study by the Economic Council of Canada has shown that uniform increases in taxes reduces disposable income and spending in rich regions more than in poor regions; while uniform increases in government spending reduces unemployment in poor regions more than in rich regions. Thus even a *balanced* increase in the budget will do something to reduce regional disparities. *Living Together: A Study of Regional Disparities* (Ottawa: Economic Council of Canada, 1977).

ments resort to various ways of making the choice; some countries rely on common nationwide examinations, despite wide differences in quality of teaching from city to countryside, and from region to region. Others try to modify the examination system to compensate for the difference. There is no truly satisfactory way of solving the problem except by increasing the education budget, as most developing countries are doing, and will continue to do as national incomes rise, at which time education will become particularly important in determining the style of development.

STYLE OF DEVELOPMENT

Focusing *only* on the best allocation of resources and a more even spread of basic material needs may lead to what has been described as the "zoo paradox"; the country takes on the aspect of a zoo where food, shelter, and veterinarian services are provided for all the residents but where individual expression is severely circumscribed. Modernization has tended to convert societies into the managers and the managed; even if the much vaunted freedoms of private enterprise societies prevail ever-larger-scale operations have reduced opportunity for individual expression.

Measures to assure the wider development of man cover a wide scope. They include measures such as those described above to encourage individual initiative through finance and education, measures to encourage indigenous arts and crafts, or even discouragement of undesirable imported life styles. Governments can—and usually do—guide consumer spending; a number of countries are working out their consumption patterns with a judicious mixture of taxes, regulations, and import controls.

And what if the society is content yet the government foresees that productivity must increase in order to sustain present levels of welfare? And if the government introduces new technologies, yet the benefits are dissipated in increased leisure or more beer, as in the case of the Kakinada fishermen? If a government decides that the very survival of the people requires the tough decision to "unbend" the supply curve of labor, the new technology can be introduced and the people can be taxed so that they must produce more in order to meet their basic needs. The proceeds can then be spent on better education and other means to raise productivity and afford a wider range of opportunity, if not for the "contented" fishermen themselves then at least for their children. As Arthur Lewis has observed: "The advantage of economic growth is not that wealth increases happiness, but that it increases the range of human choice." [3]

Whether such hard-line maneuvers as taxing Peter to educate Paul will bring a better life to the majority of the population will depend heavily on the adroitness of fiscal policy. In particular, governments must assure that the desired spending for development can be financed without destructive inflation.

[3] Lewis, *Theory of Economic Growth*, p. 420.

FINANCING DEVELOPMENT WITHOUT INFLATION

Once the development program has been formulated and the financial implications determined, the Governor of the Central Bank and the Finance Minister must translate these into a detailed monetary and fiscal policy designed to bridge any gap between current voluntary savings and investment requirements. An adroit monetary and fiscal policy can stimulate development; a maladroit one can create inflation. What is the difference?

CAUSES OF INFLATION

In Chapter 1, it was observed that world inflation results from too much money chasing too few goods, which in turn reflects the pressure of too many people on too few resources. But how does "too much money" come into being?

In most monetary systems of the world, money supply is increased in one or all of three ways:

1. By exports;

2. By private investment financed by bank credits; and/or

3. By government spending financed by borrowing from the banking system, or by printing currency or both.

Exports earn foreign exchange, which can be spent on imports by the government or private entrepreneur. On the other hand, the private exporter may hand over the foreign exchange he has earned to the government to hold in reserve for potential importers. The government will then issue to the exporter the corresponding value of the foreign exchange in local currency. Moreover, the foreign exchange then enters the basic reserves of the banking system, increasing its power to expand the money supply by lending.

No country need ever be short of its own currency. In the past, governments in need of money simply printed it. Today, nearly all developing countries have government-controlled central banks, which are the modern equivalent of the government printing press as a source of money. These banks can with the stroke of a pen create money to lend the government for development spending, or lend to private enterprise (usually through other banks) if the government gives the "go ahead". The printing press still comes into play, since some of the money created originally in the form of credits to bank accounts will be withdrawn in currency, and legitimate demands for currency must be met.

Money supply is reduced by three opposite factors:

1. By imports;

2. By repayment of private debts to banks (which results in cancellation of deposits); and/or

3. By collecting taxes and repaying government debts to the banking system, which also results in cancellation of deposits.

Thus money supply will grow on balance if exports exceed imports, if bank loans to private enterprise exceed repayment of debts to banks, and if government spending exceeds tax collection, and government indebtedness to banks increases.

From this somewhat oversimplified but essentially correct explanation, one thing should be clear: no country need have inflation if it does not want it. The Central Bank can force interest rates up to the point where no one wants to borrow and everyone tries to repay whatever debts he has. The government can limit spending and raise taxes, generating budget surpluses and reducing its indebtness to banks. The government could also, if it wished, encourage imports and discourage exports, although this particular antiinflationary device is seldom used. Through monetary and fiscal policy the government can always reduce the money supply to the point where prices will fall.

But if fighting inflation is so simple, why should world inflation continue? The answer is obvious: raising interest rates, reducing bank lending, cutting government spending, raising taxes—all these antiinflationary measures tend to reduce the volume of economic activity, slow down economic growth, and reduce the number of jobs. Stagnation, unemployment, or recession can result. No government wants to raise the level of unemployment, and no government of a developing country is eager to retard the rate of growth. So the "classical medicine" for excessive wage-price increases—cutting total demand so that sales fall off, and prices fall, forcing wage-cuts or unemployment or both, and perhaps bringing on some bankruptcies as well, is usually renounced. The renunciation is valid because an adroit monetary policy can promote development with monetary expansion yet avoid harmful inflation. What should be renounced is *inefficient monetary and fiscal policies*.

How? Money, after all is said and done, is a medium of exchange; it should represent goods in existence, or goods and services that are *going to come into existence*. If a government creates money to finance development, and if the development takes place and additional goods come quickly into existence, they can be bought and the extra money mopped up as described. However, if more money is created, and by inefficiency, chicanery, or delay, enough additional goods are *not* quickly created, then inflation will ensue, unless, once again, the money is mopped up. (In socialist countries with controlled prices, if the goods are not created, queues will grow longer or rationing will be tightened rather than open inflation ensuing).

DEVELOPMENT WITHOUT INFLATION

Let us suppose that a country initiates a program of development consisting of a mixture of private investment in directly productive enterprises and government investment in infrastructure. Faced with high unemployment and inadequate private investment in some areas, the government may also make some direct investment in development projects. Development may be financed by some outside capital in the form of loans, foreign investment, and foreign aid, the balance made up with expansion of local currency in the form of credit expansion to private enterprise and to government.

If development investment results in rapid expansion of exports, as in the case of Venezuela or Libya, imports can expand quickly, debts can be repaid, mopping up increases in money supply, and the economy can grow without serious inflation. In this way, in the fifteen years following World War II Venezuela had the highest rate of growth of all Latin American countries, yet enjoyed stability of currency for most of the time. The same can be said of investment which results in a rapid expansion of production of consumer goods for the local market. Wages and profits can be spent on the goods and services. The private enterprises and the government can pay back the banks. The government can also tax private enterprise and the consumers to pay for the infrastructure and thus repay the central bank; and the whole process can continue.

CAUSES OF INFLATION IN DEVELOPING COUNTRIES

Few developing countries, however, are so lucky. Usually, the increased investment does not bring quick and proportionate increases in output, because of bottlenecks of all kinds—lack of specialized capital equipment, transport, management, entrepreneurial or technical skills, and inefficient public administration. These bottlenecks may mean that only simple projects of low productivity can be executed quickly, and that there will be little increase in the flow of goods to offset the expanded flow of money. If more ambitious projects are undertaken—large-scale dams and irrigation schemes, for example—there may be long delays before any additional output reaches the market, and meanwhile money flow swells. If destructive inflation is not to ensue, excess purchasing power must be mopped up by taxation or other means until goods are available.

It is not always recognized that the main purpose of taxation in promoting development is to restrict consumption so as to permit developmental investment and provision for free government services without inflation. While a well-designed tax policy can create incentives to save and to undertake high-risk investment, improve distribution of income and wealth, and direct resource allocation, it must at the same time offset development spending to the degree necessary to avoid harmful inflation, until goods become available. Often, governments have not applied this unpopular part of the process with sufficient vigor, sometimes because they have not fully recognized this particular function of taxation, or because adequate fiscal machinery was not yet available. Failure has also been caused by tax evasion.

Ways can be devised to bypass inefficiencies until the institutional framework improves. One country, for example, may have an incompetent or corrupt internal revenue service and a capable and honest central bank; if so, foreign exchange control may be more effective in controlling resource allocation than tax policy. For example, an effective tax system was not available to the newly independent Indonesian government in 1952. To control a threatening inflation, the government resorted to a species of monetary "gadgetry," a system of advance payments for foreign exchange. Under this system, importers were compelled to make rupiah payments when the foreign exchange licence was granted instead of waiting to take up foreign exhange grants when goods arrived in Indonesian ports. The system of advance payments proved to be a powerful offset to forces tending to increase the money supply. At their peak at the end of 1952, the advance payments withdrew enough rupiahs from the money supply to stabilize the domestic price level and bring a hardening of the rupiah in the foreign exchange markets of the world.

HOW MUCH DEVELOPMENT SPENDING?

At the other extreme, a country may cramp the development effort because of fear of inflation arising from an overestimation of the investment-savings gap. Some governments do not realize the extent of the slack that exists in their economies, and the potential for mobilizing human and physical resources. They also forget that if production and income are increased, savings can also be increased by restraining consumption through such means as limitations on imports and production of luxury goods, exchange controls, savings campaigns, and steeply progressive taxes. Enlarging the gap between production and consumption in order to accumulate capital is good Marxist and classical economics for which Russia and China provide examples. The wartime experience of such advanced countries as Australia, Canada, the United Kingdom, and the United States provides a nonsocialist example of the extent to which huge government expenditures can be made, and unemployment converted into labor shortages without unwanted increases in prices.

The wartime problem, like the development problem, was essentially one of achieving a swift large-scale transformation of the economy, involving rapid and substantial reallocation of resources. Indeed, the reallocation of resources involved in the war effort was much greater than would be required for the structural change implicit in development. During the four years when the war effort was at its peak, all of the countries mentioned above were devoting more than half of their gross national product to the war. Yet all of these countries, after having deliberately permitted some rise in wages and prices in the first year or so to facilitate the transition to a war economy, succeeded in completely preventing inflation during the last five years of the war.

The important thing, in fighting a war or initiating development, is to assure that the necessary investment is undertaken. A moderate inflation rate, which is the price of successful execution of a large volume of investment for development, is often acceptable. On the other hand, inflation produced by deficit financing of current expenditures rather than development projects, or by careless expansion of bank credit to the private sector, is likely to hamper economic growth.

CREATING "EFFECTIVE DEMAND" INSTEAD OF DEVELOPMENT

Some governments (such as the Sukarno regime in Indonesia and a succession of Chilean governments) have expanded the money supply, hoping to stimulate the growth of the economy by increasing total spending, not always for development programs:

As stated earlier, the Keynesian formula of increasing the spending stream, works if there is excess plant capacity, and managers, engineers, technicians, and skilled workers as well as unskilled workers and peasants stand idle. In advanced countries during the late 1930s, extending credit to private enterprise and spending on current governmental activities or "makework" projects created effective demand and expanded general economic activity because the "development projects" were already in place ready to go. In developing countries, where the components for rapid expansion of production are not present, careless monetary expansion can result in bankruptcies, misallocation of scarce resources, and prolongation of "shared poverty" and inflation.

MISDEVELOPMENT

Commenting on such mistakes, the dean of Brazilian economists, Eugenio Gudin, was fond of saying that the trouble with many Latin American countries is not underdevelopment but "misdevelopment." There is a kernel of truth in his remark, and it applies to other parts of the Third World as well. Not only have some countries made bad selections of projects, but they have succumbed to the temptation of allowing government enterprises to operate at a loss in order to provide low-cost transportation, or housing, or energy, or food. A good case can be made for doing so if greater additions to gross national product are thereby generated in the long run, and if the enterprises are efficiently run. However, subsidizing public enterprises, housing, and foodstuffs frequently goes far beyond such justified cases. The Sri Lankan government at one stage operated every single public enterprise at a loss, while stating that the profits from these same enterprises would be used to finance development! In Brazil, a World Bank team estimated in the mid 1960s that the number of employees on the government railways was four times as great as was needed, and in government coastal shipping the number of employees was five times what was required. Such repeal of the law of supply and demand, by ignoring the price-cost relationships as an index of efficiency, adds further to deficits and to monetary expansion.

In sum, there is an enormous difference between an approach which first makes sure that the developmental investment takes place and then does what is possible to offset undesirable inflationary effects, and a policy of straightforward monetary expansion through easy money and deficit financing of current expenditures in hopes that the price increases themselves will generate developmental investment. The latter approach seldom works, whereas the former almost always does.

COST PUSH INFLATION AND INEFFICIENCY

In many countries, the inflationary spiral begins, not with deficit financing of current expenditures or abundant credit to the private sector, (pure demand-pull inflation) but with a "cost push" in the form of wage increases or higher import prices. No advanced country has embarked on pure "demand-pull" inflation since World War II; but no country, advanced or underdeveloped, has escaped "cost-push inflation." The process begins with negotiated wage increases, or a rise of prices of imported raw materials, energy, or equipment. It continues with the raising of administered prices by monopolistic enterprises, to regain their share of the pie. Then the government, fearful of retarded growth and unemployment, steps in and expands the money supply sufficiently to permit the new and higher level of wage and prices to stick, without contraction of output. The government, in short, supplies the demand-pull" to make the "cost-push" effective after the event. This process can be dangerously inflationary even if the total "pie" is growing fairly fast, but when the wage-price battle is fought over division of a slowly growing pie, with inefficient workers and managers sharing in the higher wages and prices, the process can be disastrous.

If trade unions achieve higher wages through long strikes rather than increased efficiency, and corporations raise prices, practice elaborate tax evasion, and indulge in massive advertising campaigns to maintain their profits rather than improving productivity, if they prevent competition from more efficiently produced imports by successful pressure for protective government measures, or obtain subsidies for inefficient industries, stagnation rather than development is likely to appear. For then, free markets cannot fulfill their function of rationing scarce resources, determining prices, wages, and profits, and squeezing out inefficient enterprises. Tax evasion denies governments sufficient resources to provide essential infrastructure. Money creation serves to negate efforts to redivide the pie, and to permit continuing economic inefficiency rather than stimulating higher productivity.

In sum, if government policy is directed toward making sure that no price and no wage need ever fall, that no firm and no farmer need ever shift to another line of production no matter how inefficient he may be, there is no way in which the price system can do its job and inflation be avoided. Lord Keynes himself described this sort of policy as "Keynesian economics gone sour and silly." Keynes did not believe that a free market would guarantee steady growth, with full employment and stable prices; but he also did not believe that an efficient allocation of resources and steady growth can be obtained together if price-cost relationships in individual markets are ignored. He remained too much of a neoclassical economist for that.

Ironically, monopoly power, combined with subsidies and protection, have destroyed the chief attribute of the market economy—mobility of factors of production. The paradox is that today factors of production may move more freely in some socialist countries than in some "free" private enterprise economies.

With the recognition of the influence wielded in the economy today by groups rather than individuals, we are brought up short with the fact that rewards of the factors of production are largely determined, not by the market, but by trade unions, corporations, employers' associations, cooperatives and other producers' associations. Is the solution then a return to the market to determine prices and wages? This question introduces the continuing search in mixed economies for the best mix.

IMPROVING THE MIX

All in all, a return to an entirely free market in order to make capitalism work better is unlikely. A government may make the market function more effectively by discontinuing subsidies and protective tariffs for inefficient industries. And it may change the mix by nationalization, particularly in the case of inefficient corporations providing essential public services such as transportation, communications, and power. A government may ascertain which conglomerates are, in fact, performing more efficiently than its component firms, with a view to breaking up clearly inefficient giants. It may prosecute firms conspiring in restraint of trade under anti-trust laws. But it is hard to imagine an electorate which would agree to eliminate all corporations, all unions, and all cooperatives with any power. True, employers might like to see trade unions smashed and consumers might like to see farmers' cooperatives smashed. It is less certain that trade unions want to see monopolies smashed; they have learned the advantages of sharing monopoly power with their employers at the expense of nonunion workers, the unemployed, and the consumer. With the trend toward group negotiations so strong, and the economies and achievements of large-scale production so obvious, the solution chosen will probably be to leave these institutions much as they are. The trick will be to adapt the institutional framework to conform to the liberal philosophy, maximizing freedom of choice, and, at the same time, achieve true efficiency for the economy as a whole.

A Simulated Free Market • For example, there have recently been calls for some form of flexible wage-price surveillance to make the mixed economies work better without putting them in a straightjacket. One approach in this regard is a "simulated free market," to determine what wages and prices would be in a purely competitive market and then regulate them accordingly. First, the structure of prices and wages which would emerge in a purely competitive market is determined. This step would require a knowledge of demand and supply curves, which is reasonably easy to acquire given today's statistical techniques and computers. All prices are set equal to marginal cost (cost of producing an additional unit of output) and wages at value of marginal product (value of increased output through adding one more man-day to the labor force) for all products and all kinds of labor skill. It should be noted that from this formulation wage-price controls are not the same thing as wage-price ceilings; wages and prices must change in response to changes in taste or technology and thus in demand and cost. Labor and business would then be expected to accept these wages and prices, including any adjustments required by considerations of social justice. They could be accepted by agreement, or they could be imposed by controls. Thus, rather than the "straitjacket" approach, an alternative is negotiated agreement among government, labor, and management, using the findings of the simulated market model to establish the rules of the game.

It should be emphasised that the proper role of government is not simply to arbitrate between labor and management, but to represent the people as a whole. Both unions and management represent only a minority of any society, and an agreement must be reached in which the government participates to achieve consensus in the best interests of the entire nation.

Would a well run simulated free market solve all development problems? Probably not. The kind of "self-interest" that Adam Smith admired related to such things as choosing between beer and wine and for such choices the market works reasonably well. Self-interest may also stimulate risk investment and research, thereby increasing productivity. But today's self-interest also relates to choices for which the market seldom serves: choices regarding resource conservation, pollution, health services, education, research, transport systems, full employment, income redistribution, and development without inflation. In fields such as these, relations between prices and marginal costs cannot be the sole considerations. Here the difficulty of integrating a mixed economy emerges.

An economic system is a highly articulated affair. It cannot be divided in two, with a private sector operating on one set of principles and the public sector on another. Holding back an invention, for example, may make sense in terms of maximizing a company's profits in the short run, but may be inefficient in terms of national income and the general health of the country's economy. But since in the long run a healthier national economy will contribute to the prosperity of individual firms and workers, *common* goals should be built into economic planning along with the narrower objectives of bigger profits and higher wages. The entire economy—even a mixed system—should be operated as a single entity. It need not necessarily be government that "operates" the system; it can be a combination of private enterprise and the effort of individuals joining with the government to achieve national goals in a variety of ways.

Large corporations with their own planning processes could include national goals in their corporate decision making. So far has the "managerial revolution" gone in the late 1970s, so divorced is management from ownership, so concentrated is decision-making, that it is not absurd to think of large corporations taking account of national goals in their own planning. A number of major banks in England and Canada have long heeded the directives of the Bank of England or the Bank of Canada; government and major corporations plan together in France and Japan as well. "Privatization" is another variant. It involves a government formulating projects and programs to improve social welfare, then turning them over to the private sector for execution. In this way, the government can continue the direction of economic and social development, while at the same time reducing the number of government officials directly engaged in development and government's portion of the GNP. Wherever possible small companies could be chosen to do the job rather than conglomerates in order to stimulate a competitive economy.

In sum, achievement of a truly efficient system may require a transformation of Adam Smith's idea that the common good will result from actions taken in the cause of self interest to the concept that out of goals set for the common good will emerge individual welfare. If turning liberalism upside down in this fashion seems unworkable in a nonsocialist society, it should be recalled that there are historical precedents. Governments of advanced capitalist countries have, in the past, operated economies with a good deal more centralized planning and many more controls than would be required today to set an advanced country on a healthy developmental path. During World War II, decisions regarding prices and resource allocation in individual markets were made in terms of widely shared national goals, rather than in response to hosts of individual decisions—and with marked success. Despite the allocation of more than half of the GNP to the war effort, consumption of goods and standards of living actually *rose* during the war in Australia, Canada, and the United States; and even in the United Kingdom and France, which bore the brunt of battle, consumption levels were higher than during the interwar period. Moreover, during the war, real-income inequalities among social groups and regions were substantially reduced, resource allocation was improved, technological progress accelerated, and full employment maintained without inflation. It was the combination of Keynesian policies and a unified approach, with controls, that did the trick; it was *made possible because both the people and the leaders had made up their minds they wanted to do it.*

Today, a democracy could accord its government similar powers to achieve development; however, the trend seems to be toward decentralized planning. Official central plans have never been popular in advanced mixed economies. In the United States, for example, the senior vice-president for corporate strategic planning of General Electric, Dr. Charles Reed, specifically rejects a "planned society" and calls instead for a "planful society" in which planning is decentralized and diffused throughout the system, although common perceptions of ends are shared. He suggests planning sectors of the economy where "severe problems exist: energy, utilities, construction, plus areas that cut across industry lines and which call for aggressive joint business, labor, and government action" such as urban renewal and employment policy.[4] Third World governments are already devising various forms of decentralization. They include arrangements for corporations to take on certain responsibilities (which will be described in the next section) and decentralizing decision–making according to local political and geographic conditions.

DECENTRALIZATION

Governments may decentralize decision making by administering through smaller and more easily managed units—regions, communities, industries, individual enterprises—and by relying more on the market. Efficient centralized decision making may require more trained administrators, better communications, and more reliable information than is available at the center. In most developing countries, efficiency is limited by the number of people with training, experience, and talents suitable for managing a centrally planned economy. An all too common situation in less developed countries is that

[4] Charles E. Reed, "Toward a Planful Society", The Planning Review 1977 pp 5–20.

there is a thin layer of well-trained and highly competent people in the upper echelons of the civil service, but no properly trained or experienced civil servants in the middle and lower grades, and no civil service tradition to guarantee honest, orderly, and efficient procedures in the implementation of policies and programs. Lower-grade civil servants in developing countries are often grossly underpaid as well as ill-trained. It is therefore not surprising that the morale and standards of performance do not come up to those of long-established, well-paid civil services in advanced countries, and that corruption exists. In such situations, market decisions may be preferable to government decisions.

Deciding what can be *better* controlled by government and what to leave to the market is one of the most difficult aspects of economic management, and there is no simple formula to be applied across the board. Some socialist countries have decided that profit maximization of the individual firm, or maximum growth of the firm, provides fairly simple rules of the game. Yugoslavia has found it more efficient to operate on the basis of "free public enterprise"—giving much freedom to the management of individual enterprises, which are publicly owned, but separately managed, with labor playing a major role in management. Poland has established a small free market for luxury and semiluxury goods, for guidance with respect to price trends and changes in taste. Some less developed countries which started independence with highly regulated market economies (some of them certainly overregulated) have reverted to greater reliance on the market. Indonesia, for example, inherited a highly regulated economy from the Dutch, and the Indonesians were at first inclined to add more and more controls of their own, with inadequate administration to carry them out. Indonesia now has a combination of private enterprise, central control, increased responsibilities for development by regional and local authorities, and cooperatives. Brazil has had a long and discouraging experimentation in regulation and finally turned back to a relatively free market. Herein may lie the truth of the Adelman and Morris findings that in early stages of development, expansion of the market sector is an important positive force, because at this stage there are many more people capable of making appropriate decisions with regard to individual purchases and sales and management of small firms, than there are who can think in terms of managing a national economy.

A number of countries—particularly far-flung countries such as Russia, China, Canada, and Indonesia—are turning to various forms of geographic decentralization. Some societies prefer a federal constitution, which makes centralized decision making and control more difficult, but permits closer attention and more effective response to regional differences through the regionalization of development policy. Canada is currently engaged in a program of decentralization by scattering Federal government activities among regional offices, because the government feels that such a system will contribute to the sensitivity and responsiveness of government to the wishes of the electorate. Similarly, the sheer size of the economy as well as the geographic and ethnic differences among regions has led to decentralization in the case of

Russia. China too has made "downward transfers of authority" to combat bureaucratic overcentralization and to encourage local initiative; lower levels of government have been accorded major responsibilities; the bulk of industrial activity and all agricultural activity is directed by the provinces, counties and communes. Indonesia has conducted a highly successful experiment in assigning more responsibility for planning and executing development projects to provincial governments and to towns (*kebupaten*) and villages (*desas*).

In sum, the trick is to discover the optimum mix of public enterprise, government control, and free market, given the preferred political system, and given the supply of managers capable of making good decisions at various levels of aggregation.

Once a government has done what it can to use local resources to their best advantage and to close the gap between investment requirements and local savings, the government must turn to closing the gap—between foreign exchange earnings and foreign exchange needs.

FOREIGN ECONOMIC POLICY

From the end of the post-Napoleonic War depression, to the beginning of World War I, governors of central banks, ministers of trade and commerce, and others concerned with formulating foreign economic policy led a relatively uncomplicated life. Free movement of men, materials, and money was the accepted basic principle of international economic relations, from which only exceptional departures could be justified. The minister of trade thought about which infant industries might justify temporary tariff protection, and the governor of the central bank about whether interest rates should be raised to attract foreign funds or lowered to frighten them away. Otherwise "the market" was expected to regulate matters satisfactorily in international economic relations just as it did at home.

Today's monetary, foreign exchange, and foreign-trade authorities face a host of complex and interrelated decisions with regard to the regulation of the country's economic relations with the rest of the world. Will the structure of interest rates most conducive to stability in domestic markets equilibrate foreign exchange markets as well? Should the foreign exchange value of the currency be fixed, or should it be set free to "float" in response to changes in supply and demand? If fixed, at what level? With a single or a multiple exchange rate? If floated, within what limits, if any? What structure of tariffs is optimal for development? Should the same rates be applied to all trading partners, or should preference be given to some? Should the country participate in certain international commodity agreements? Should it go further and join some association of countries seeking internal free trade, common tariffs against third countries, agreed specialization, and coordinated development planning? Should foreign capital be admitted freely, or only for some types of investment and under certain conditions? What kind of foreign aid should be sought and from whom?

This contrast with the free-trade epoch bespeaks a much more complicated world today, where, compared to the monolithic control of the imperial powers on nineteenth century world trade, power today is much more dispersed. It also reflects a herculean attempt to correct the distortions caused by nineteenth century "free trade," and in certain cases a trend towards isolationism. However, meddling with the market has to be expertly done to bring required results, and it is useful in this regard to review the catastrophic mistakes of the isolationist "beggar thy neighbor" policies of the interwar period.

BEGGAR THY NEIGHBOR

The move toward economic isolation began when Great Britain found herself with much of her foreign investment liquidated to pay for external costs of World War I. Without the income from foreign holdings, she was in constant difficulties with regard to balance of payments, and tried to protect her industries so as to reduce unemployment. Americans were so revolted by the horrors of war that they also turned in on themselves; isolation was translated into higher tariffs and tighter immigration restrictions.

Isolation intensified with the onslaught of the Great Depression of the 1930s, when all pretense of favoring a free international market was thrown to the winds. Instead, the major powers vied with each other to restrict imports, prevent flight of capital, and limit immigration. Commodity agreements sought to limit output and raise prices; exchange controls were used both to limit imports and to prevent an outflow of capital. Currencies were devalued in an effort to raise exports and reduce imports. When imports trickled in over the tariff walls, quotas were slapped on to stop them. Quotas reached absurd proportions, such as the French prohibition on import of spotted cattle spending more than three months of the year at an altitude of more than five-thousand feet, a thinly disguised barrier to import of Swiss cattle. But it was soon found that these were games that everybody could play, and every move by one country led to retaliation by others: tariff increases led to tariff increases, quotas to quotas, exchange control to exchange control, devaluation to devaluation. By the time World War II began, the world economy had almost ceased to function.

The story of German reparations and hyperinflation exemplifies the folly of these policies. Germany had been expected to pay reparations, yet she faced tariff walls against her exports, which had to earn the foreign exchange to pay the reparations. Flat on her back, crushed with the impossible burden of reparations, Germany resorted to monetary policies which led to hyperinflation. When prices reached 1,261,600,000,000 times their 1913 level and the German monetary system collapsed, the Allies capitulated, reduced the reparations, and lent Germany money to help her pay what was left! During the 1930s the Allies gave up trying to make Germany pay altogether, having learned the basic lesson that Germany could pay only by exporting German goods to the Allies so as to acquire the foreign exchange to make the payments. And with deepening unemployment at home the last thing the Allies wanted was German imports.

During this period there was one constructive set of policies: the protection of infant industries behind high tariff walls, which fostered industrialization in countries such as Australia and Mexico.

"COOPERATE WITH THY NEIGHBOR"

Partly because of the disastrous experience of the 1930s, most Ministers of Trade and Commerce today understand perfectly well that no country becomes rich through "beggar-thy-neighbor" policies. Negotiations begin from the simple premise that if some countries want to export, other countries must be able to export too, in order to acquire the necessary foreign exchange to permit them to import.

Not that the infant industry argument has disappeared; far from it. Today, it is called "import replacement" and is regarded by most economists, planners and politicians as a basic aspect, and a perfectly respectable aspect, of development policy. There can be no doubt that a policy of import replacement, if used judiciously and sparingly for cases where it is sure that the infant can some day attain robust adulthood, works. Thus in the early 1960s Brazil built up an automobile industry behind an extremely high protective tariff wall which effectively prevented automobile imports of any kind. In the early years costs and prices were high—Brazilian Volkswagen, Renault, or Mercedes Benz cost three to four times as much as their counterparts in the home country. Yet within five years the prices (in foreign exchange) of these same Brazilian cars were competitive with those in the home country, and automotive products had become one of Brazil's major *exports* to other Latin American countries, and more recently to Africa.

In other words, import replacement is justified by efficient use of the opportunity created. By the same token, if a currency is clearly overvalued, it will make sense to devalue, rather than to attach an unreasonable value to stable exchange rates; but the ultimate solution to failure to compete in world markets is to increase efficiency at home.

In today's world of international negotiation and agreement, policies to protect new or small industries are usually introduced only after discussion with trading partners, and devaluation is undertaken after consultation with the International Monetary Fund. Here, the basic difference between the beggar-thy-neighbor approach and today's approach emerges. The emphasis is not on reducing imports in general, but in stabilizing national economies by encouraging a wider spread of economic activity. At the same time world trade and every nation's share in it as both exporter and importer is expanded by means of forecast, planning, and cooperation at the international level.

Indeed, despite the presence of isolationist factions in both the advanced and developing worlds an international framework for management of the global economy is taking shape. Today most countries are likely to send representatives to a host of international assemblies, including those sponsored by the World Bank and the International Monetary Fund, the United Nations Conference on Trade and Development (UNCTAD), the General Agreement on Tariffs and Trade (GATT), the World Bank Consultative Groups, the Organization of Economic Cooperation and Development (OECD), the various Regional Economic Commissions of the United Nations (ECLA, ECA, ESCAP) as well as to meetings of particular interest groups such as OPEC.

While developing countries continue to negotiate *en masse* through international agencies, and unilaterally with other countries, they are increasingly moving to negotiate as well through small groups of countries with certain limited objectives in mind. For example, the OPEC group negotiates the sale of one product—oil; the African and Caribbean Associates negotiated on trade agreements concerning a number of products with the European Common Market; the Group of twenty-four central bankers represent the Third World. Another form of such specialized cooperation is regional integration.

REGIONAL INTEGRATION

Countries attempting regional integration (as economic cooperation among neighboring countries has come to be called) may coordinate their planning according to the degree of integration.

1. Coordinated Planning and Agreed Specialization • Development plans of neighboring countries may be coordinated to some extent even without an international agreement regarding the pattern of development in each country. As a minimum, governments may exchange advance information on the content of their plans, so that each government may take account of what the other countries intend to do in its own planning. Through continuous exchange of information in the course of the planning process, together with occasional discussion among planners and representatives of governments, the countries can arrive at a set of final plans for each country which reflect fully the final plans of the others. The discussions may result in some agreed specialization—"If you do the steel mill let us do the petroleum refinery"—without formal agreements. A further step toward closer integration would be an "indicative plan" for the region as a whole, in which targets for the whole group of countries are set forth, with an indication of what types of economic activity might take place in which countries, but without any formal commitments, and with each country carrying out projects entirely within its own borders.

2. Joint Projects • Further economic integration may be achieved through joint projects, undertaken by two or more governments, through an international agreement. Major rivers passing through several countries, such as the Mekong in Southeast Asia, the Senegal in West Africa, and the Paraguay in Latin America, provide excellent opportunities for this kind of international collaboration, with irrigation, flood control, hydroelectric power, and transport as common objectives. International roads like the Pan American Highway or the Asian Highway provide other examples.

3. Free Trade Areas • With or without agreed specialization in advance, neighboring countries might agree to eliminate barriers to trade amongst themselves. Competition within a free market would tend to bring some degree of specialization on the part of each country, each being left ultimately with those economic activities where it has some comparative advantage. Within a free trade area, agreed specialization becomes an effort to foresee what the results of unfettered competition in a free market would be, so as to avoid wasteful investment in enterprises that are doomed to lose out to competitors in this kind of market, and limit the scope of investment accordingly.

4. Common Markets • The common market arrangement goes farther still. It requires not only the elimination of trade barriers among members, but also the establishment of identical barriers, in the form of tariffs, quotas, etc., against trade with nonmembers. When freedom of migration of the labor force and freedom of capital movements are added, as in the case of the European common market, the countries come close to having a common economy. All that remains in order to create a single economy for all member countries is to establish a single currency, a unified money and banking system, and an integrated monetary and fiscal policy.

THE ANDEAN GROUP

An example of successful cooperation among neighbors, despite limited complementarity of resources or economic activity and sharply differing political regimes, is the Andean Group. This group, consisting originally of Colombia, Chile, Ecuador, and Peru, was established by the Cartagena Agreement in May 1969. Venezuela became a signatory of the agreement in February 1973. While the Group was set up "within the framework of the Montevideo Treaty" which created the Latin American Free Trade Association (LAFTA), it is in large measure a reaction to the failure of LAFTA to resolve the conflicts between major and minor powers in Latin America and to get something useful done. Not that the accomplishments of the Andean Group are spectacular; as one observer puts it, "the Cartagena Agreement sets a leisurely and uncertain pace for the achievement of free trade within the area." [5] But the point is that progress has been made, and the leisurely pace continued. The fable of the tortoise and the hare may hold some lessons where economic integration among neighboring countries is concerned.

The ultimate goal of the Agreement is complete economic union. Toward this end, a schedule has been established for elimination of tariffs or other

[5] Andrew B. Wardlaw, *The Andean Integration Movement*. A Report Prepared under Contract for the United States Department of State, Washington D.C., Sept. 1973, Department of State Publication No. 8719.

trade restrictions among members, the definition of a common trade policy towards third countries, the harmonization of economic policies, and the coordination of development policy. The Group is also working towards standardization of legislation regarding foreign investment, trademarks, royalties, and the like.

An interesting and admirable feature of the Agreement is that it accords preferential treatment to the two weaker members of the Group, Bolivia and Ecuador. All duties on imports from members were scheduled to disappear by December 31, 1980; but whereas reductions of tariffs against imports from Colombia, Chile, and Peru were to be cut gradually from 1970 to 1980, exports from Bolivia and Ecuador were to be completely exempt from duties by December 31, 1974, while liberalization of duties against imports into Bolivia and Ecuador from other members of the Group were to start only on December 31, 1976. This special treatment for Ecuador and Bolivia also appears in the industrialization policy, which is designed to establish specific industries in these countries while opening up the Andean market to their products in general. Multinational corporations are being promoted within the Group, to distribute industrialization among member countries. A long list of commodity sectors is being studied to decide what might appropriately be produced where within the Group.

The general schedule of tariff reductions set forth in the Agreement is as follows:

Tariff as % of Initial Rate Year:	Country of Origin	
	Columbia, Chile, Peru	Bolivia, Ecuador
1970	100	100
1971	90	60
1972	80	30
1973	70	0
1974	60	0
1975	50	0
1976	40	0
1977	30	0
1978	20	0
1979	10	0
1980	0	0

The Agreement is administered by a permanent junta with a small secretariat in Lima. There is a Consultative Committee, an Economic and Social Advisory Committee, and an Andean Development Corporation with an initial capital of $100 million.

The Group is not without its problems. When it was established intraregional trade was a tiny fraction of the trade of its members with the United States and Western Europe, and a small fraction of its trade with Japan or the rest of Latin America. Even Argentina—not a member—took more of the Group's exports than did the Group itself. Differing political ideologies and approaches to economic development make true economic union extremely difficult. A lagging agricultural sector, where per capita output is only 36% of that in the industrial sector, hampers industrial expansion itself. Yet the Group perseveres. It is still too early to make an appraisal of the impact of the Agreement on economic development itself, but it is not too early to conclude that it is a remarkable example of effective political cooperation among diverse though neighboring countries, simply because those countries want to work together in harmony to raise living standards in all of them and particularly in the poorest of them.

Success in such industrialization requires mobilization of capital, expertise, and technology; some of these inputs must still be sought abroad.

FINDING CAPITAL AND EXPERTISE ABROAD

Governments may seek capital in the form of foreign aid as grants, loans from donor countries, or from the World Bank Group; technical assistance can be furnished from the battery of United Nations Specialised Agencies. Governments can also sell securities in the international money markets, and then import technology, expertise, and equipment. The other alternative is to obtain the whole package in the form of foreign direct investment.

Foreign Aid • Governments can arrange loans from the World Bank group which has amassed considerable experience in applying development capital productively. Set up in 1944 to finance postwar reconstruction in Europe, it turned in the 1950s to financing development of underdeveloped countries. The "World Bank Group" includes the International Finance Corporation which finances private enterprise in developing countries, the International Development Association which provides "soft loans" (low interest, long term) for development to countries with incomes below a certain level. Regional development banks service special groups of countries. When economic integration among countries becomes necessary to form common markets and to agree on specialization, the regional banks usually play a major role.

The "soft loan window", however, cannot handle all financial needs. Developing countries would like to link foreign aid to the Special Drawing Rights (SDRs) of the International Monetary Fund to permit larger temporary trade deficits arising from imports for development purposes. Here once again the countries of the Third World are acting in unison through the Group of 24, consisting of eight central bankers from each of the three relevant continents; a group which commands enough votes to veto an "unsatisfactory" IMF reform.

In the absence of adequate loans from the World Bank, rather than resort to foreign direct investment, many countries prefer to assemble the package themselves, seeking "portfolio investment" from abroad and then shopping around for the necessary equipment and expertise which they are unable to provide themselves.

INTRODUCTION OF FOREIGN INVESTMENT AND TECHNOLOGY
INTO HOST ECONOMY

However, Third World countries' capabilities to "shop around" in world markets for technology and management skills are limited by the fact that the sellers of these inputs are often monopolists or oligopolists. When a country cannot initiate an enterprise entirely independently, either because outside financing cannot be found, or unattached expertise cannot be acquired, foreign direct investment may be invited. Today Third World countries usually take a positive approach, avoiding the pitfalls of the past, carefully designing contracts with foreign firms, and integrating foreign private investment into the total development effort of the host country.

A sovereign country can use its own corporation law, tax legislation and monetary system, foreign exchange regulations, etc., to control and direct investment. Certainly big business tends to exert an influence on government policy in any country where it exists; but this fact is no less true when the big business is owned by nationals than when it is owned by foreigners, and the foreigners are often easier to handle just because they are foreigners, with less influence on the local electorates, than nationals would have. This control is even stronger when—as many countries are doing today—investment is invited from several foreign sources rather than allowing one foreign country a virtual monopoly of investment.

Various types of "partnership" between the host country and foreign investors can be designed to furnish developing country's needs: immediately available capital, technology and experience, along with the opportunity for nationals to acquire experience while retaining control of their economies. Management contracts are one such device. A foreign concern can contract with the government of an underdeveloped country to set up and manage a new plant for a limited period, say for ten years. The foreign concern may either make a direct investment for the period agreed upon, or may enter into a joint project with the state or an indigenous firm. However, insistence on local private participation in ownership of foreign enterprises may increase the influence of private enterprise in the host country by creating a dependent *rentier* class which will tend to support the interests of the foreign investors, interests which they share.

In the case of established enterprises, control introduces the issue of nationalization. Large-scale expropriation has taken place in several developing countries, including Mexico, Iraq, Egypt, Indonesia, Brazil, and Libya, with varying degrees of success. It seems to have worked well in Mexico; in Indonesia, it seems to have delayed a takeoff because of the severe loss of expertise entailed. Government leaders have based their decision to expropriate foreign enterprises on the high cost of servicing foreign private indebtedness, and, in the case of Castro, on regaining control of the economy. While such action obviously inhibits further foreign investment, at least for a while, these leaders have concluded that, if the reduction of profits transfers abroad exceeds any potential influx of new capital (assuming that exports can be redirected so as to maintain total earnings), expropriation of foreign enterprises can be a means of adding to the net flow of foreign exchange.

Alternatively, an incoming foreign firm may abstain from ownership and provide a fixed-interest-bearing loan for the duration of the management contract. Properly designed, such a scheme can meet mutual interests. The foreign concern receives a predetermined management fee, the return at a fixed date of any capital provided, as well as a normal profit on its capital until then. The host country gains the needed technology and management, employment and training of personnel from the country itself, preparatory to the takeover of the plant either by the government or by a selected group of its own nationals. This arrangement also helps to allay mutual fears. The host country need not fear foreign control of its economy, and the foreign firm may profit from selling management and technology, while binding up capital abroad for only a limited period, or perhaps not at all. These conditions provide the needed encouragement and assurance for foreign investors.

Governments that decide to seek a large flow of foreign investment can also structure their tax systems to encourage investment and reinvestment by foreign firms, and in general can maintain stability in their laws and regulations affecting foreign investment, so that foreign investors know where they stand.

Governments of developing countries can also integrate foreign investment into their national economies by directing its flow. They can indicate the branch of industry and the sector where foreign enterprise would be welcome; they may request foreign investors to support the host country's goals for employment creation rather than adding to unemployment by pushing domestic industries off the market. Foreign investors may be required to use more labor-intensive production processes wherever feasible, and to organize linkages to domestic industries and services. They may also be asked to assume a more supportive and stimulating role in research in encouraging local initiative. In Peru, for example, Japanese investors were asked to permit, and agreed to, worker participation in management decisions. In Brazil, global corporations have been requested to conduct more of their research and development activities inside Brazil. Finally the home government of the investor may also take a hand in creating proper conditions for development investment by means of bilateral aid.

Three conditions are making this bargaining feasible. First, there is increasing competition among the advanced countries (U.S., Western European countries, and Japan) to invest in the Third World. Secondly, background knowledge is increasing. The Japanese have long demonstrated how to acquire foreign technology without losing control of the advanced industrial sectors, how to obtain not only manufacturing know-how but, as well, basic design and engineering knowledge. And today socialist countries such as China, Hungary, and Rumania are also setting precedents: how to refuse dividends or profits participation but instead to offer royalty payments for patents or know-how, engineering fees, management fees, interest, selling commissions; how to offer a management contract without equity ownership. Thirdly, information gathering of the globals' activities is also paving the way for better control of transnational enterprises.

In the past, host governments have been at a disadvantage in the lack of knowledge of the internal operations of multinational guests. Third World countries are now pioneering their own systems of information and analysis of the flow and effects of foreign investment. The Andean Pact countries and Mexico, for example, are developing a central data collection unit which pools information from all these market countries. The Andean Common Market also exchanges information with the East African Common Market. A center for the study of five hundred leading global corporations was established at the Algiers conference of nonaligned nations in 1973. These measures might be regarded as steps towards an international monitoring system of the multinationals.

There is little doubt that wherever possible developing countries would do well to exploit their own resources. However, where this alternative is impossible, in light of the better bargaining position Third World countries enjoy today, cooperation between foreign investors and the host governments could prove to everyone's advantage.

CONCLUSIONS: THE BEST SYSTEM

We have seen that government plays a large and increasing role in today's development process. Finally, then, we must ask: are some systems of government better equipped than others to deal with these problems? Economists have largely abandoned the search for Utopia, the ideal system with harmoniously integrated political, social, and economic institutions bringing a maximum rate of widespread and comprehensive development. However, given that countries will each seek their own system, can we point to any general guidelines for efficiency, for success or failure in development? Healthy development has been defined by John Galtung as security, well-being, identity, and freedom. We can therefore approach this question in the following terms: What are the requisites for healthy economic development? What is the best degree of control of the country's economy? How important is ideology?

REQUISITES FOR HEALTHY DEVELOPMENT

We have found that at the purely economic level the differences between socialism and capitalism tend to disappear. All theories of development, from Adam Smith or Marx to Myrdal and Mao, have strategic elements that are identical: capital accumulation, enterpreneurship, technological progress, structural change, acquisition of skills, reduction of inequalities, achieved within a sociocultural and political framework that allows the economic system to work.

Certainly much depends on the legacy of the past, in terms of education, spirit of enterprise, political attitudes and institutions. The fact that Japan was at the top of the list in Table 2.1 and Cuba at the bottom (in terms of growth rates) does not necessarily indicate that private enterprise economies are good and socialist states are bad. It does reflect the difference between competence and long experience as opposed to shortage of expertise and inexperience in a newly established system. Japanese history also illustrates the fact that some social institutions and cultures are more conducive to development than others; the inherent discipline of Japanese society offers obvious advantages in launching development. The sense of being one nation for thousands of years helps China in comparison with new countries freshly formed from former colonies. However, there is little reason to believe that any society is incapable of development *provided that both the people and the leaders are genuinely consecrated to development.*

This study indicates again and again the importance of imaginative leadership, whether it be the head of the Kakinada Institute for Small Industries, the leader of a cooperative in the Comilla Academy, the Director of the Economic Planning Unit in Malaysia, the Governor of Bali, the Director of SUDENE (the planning organisation for the Brazilian Northeast), or private business leadership. Generating healthy development depends heavily on leaders at all levels putting concrete and detailed content into each of the strategic variables listed above, in a fashion that conforms with the preferences and the potential of their society with regard to political framework, social justice, and "style of development," and thus translates the society's basic ideology into concrete and functioning institutions. Whether they succeed or not depends not only on their perception and initiative but also on *the degree of their control of the economy.*

WHAT IS THE BEST DEGREE OF CONTROL?

The advanced countries of Western Europe, North America, and Australasia went through their periods of industrialization with little government direction or control, but with vigorous entrepreneurial leadership and strong private control of the economies. Experience has shown that highly centralized governments such as that of the Soviet Union, with a strong revolutionary tradition, willing to use force where considered necessary, and responsible to the general will of the "masses" (as interpreted by the leaders) rather than to the wishes of individuals (as expressed at the polls or at the market place) can promote economic development at a rapid rate. The same is true today in vigorous private enterprise countries such as Japan, Taiwan, or South Korea, where government has a close association with leaders of private enterprise and where there is a strong tradition of obedience on the part of the people. Especially in Japan, this tradition made possible the mobilization of the energies of the country and contributed to one of the fastest rates of economic growth the world has ever known. Where the government does not exert strong centralized control, but where it commands the support of the people within a democratic framework through a broadly representative political party with a clear majority, as has been the case in India, it can also make progress. However, where sharply differing interests exist and the emphasis is on persuasion, as in the Indian case, progress on the economic front is likely to be slower than in the "hard states."

At this point it is important to distinguish between the official social philosophy, and the degree of state control. Despite the emphasis on planning and the announced socialist philosophy (which in India really means a social welfare philosophy), India is one of the least regulated economies in the world. J. K. Galbraith, well-known economist and President Kennedy's ambassador to India, once pointed out that by almost any test the Indian economy is less responsible to public guidance and direction than that of the United States. In the aggregate, Galbraith says, there can be little doubt that the United States is both much the more manageable and the more managed economy. "India has, in fact, superimposed a smallish socialized sector atop what, no doubt, is the world's greatest example of functioning anarchy".[6]

As a matter of record, economic development appears to have most chance of success in predominantly socialist or predominantly private enterprise economies. Successful economic development has occurred with a ratio of public investment to total investment ranging from about 10 percent to about 35 percent (capitalist countries) or from about 70 percent to about 95 percent (socialist countries). In a mixed economy, the incentives that motivate either socialist or private enterpreneurs seem to become diluted. "Socialist" Sweden with its mixed and managed economy might appear to be an exception; but here again, it is important to distinguish among the official social philosophy, the degree of state control, and the extent of public ownership. In Sweden some 70% of the means of production were privately owned. There is no clear case on record of successful economic development with a ratio of public to total investment between 40 percent and 60 percent over long periods. Brazil may soon give us a case, but there remains too much mass poverty and inequality for Brazil to be considered a success today.

People of any society, however, will have views regarding their political system for its own sake. For each stage of development, each set of problems, and each range of potential development, some political systems may prove more "efficient" than others; but the political framework and "style" of development are matters of importance in themselves and no society choses a political system in terms of economic development alone. There may sometimes be a trade-off between freedom from government intervention and achievement of other development goals. In the authors' view, every society should be free to choose its own form of political and social system in accordance with the will of the majority, and development should be sought in combination with complete freedom of political, artistic, and scientific expression. Political tastes will vary from country to country, and from time to time within each society, and it largely falls to a country's leaders to interpret these changes.

[6] J. K. Galbraith, "Rival Economic Theories in India," *Foreign Affairs* 36 (July 1958).

Leaders must reconfirm or reinterpret the existing ideology, or create an integrated new ideology, according to need, and then design institutions to fit. Even highly socialist or highly capitalist countries have introduced new interpretations from time to time, such as Russia's increasing use of the market, and the switch to managed economies in capitalist countries after the Keynesian revolution. Failure of leadership in market economies in the recent past to provide realistic and convincing ideological reinterpretations goes a long way towards explaining the relatively unimpressive performance of these economies.

By its very nature, liberalism sets freedom in a top position, and in so doing opens the door to conflict among political parties, social groups, ideas, and policy proposals. Moreover, "liberalism" has long been beset by misapprehensions, misinterpretations, confusion and "contradictions" and by the sheer difficulty of finding a workable diffusion of power.

Ideological Confusion • Because of the very nature of liberalism—its inherent trust in things taking care of themselves,—leaders have tended to lag behind in reinterpreting the ideology in terms of current events, conditions, and changes in the economic situation. Behind the long economic stagnation in a number of Latin American countries lies the transplanting of the European ideologies to a situation where they simply did not work. When land was the sole source of wealth in Latin America, the liberal philosophy and the *latifundista* interpretation of Christian ethics brought no effort to promote development or to reduce the extreme inequalities of wealth. Where and when landowners were displaced by industrialists and financiers as the political power elite, there was little improvement. While the business world did promote economic growth the *liberal philosophy* was used to justify neglect of the *moral responsibilities* imposed by a strict interpretation of the Christian ethic. This point is made by Daniel Cosio Villegas, one of Latin America's leading intellectuals:

> The old landowning oligarchy . . . certainly availed themselves of [power] to promote their own interests; but at the same time they did assume the attendant responsibilities. The new industrial and banking oligarchy wishes to influence governmental decisions, and actually does so, but without shouldering the responsibilities that such decisions necessarily involve. . . . In the course of time, the old landowning oligarchy reformed itself from within; . . . learned to understand general problems which had nothing to do with the farming of their land. . . . The new oligarchy is still unduly crude and coarse, smacks unmistakenly of money because it thinks of nothing else, and does not seem to understand anything that has no direct bearing on its business affairs.[7]

---

[7] Daniel Cosio Villegas, "Programmed Economic Development and Political Organization," in Egbert de Vries and José Medina Echavarria, eds., *Social Aspects of Economic Development in Latin America*, Vol. I (Paris; UNESCO, 1963) pp. 243, 250, 251.

The result has been a good deal of dissatisfaction, with liberalism, leading to efforts to change the mix. During the 1950s and 1960s, as we have seen, there were ill-considered efforts to "repeal the law of supply and demand" and rather blind efforts at dirigisme (Chile, Brazil) or creation of superwelfare states (Argentina, Brazil). Government intervention with no guiding principles and no calculus superior to the discipline imposed by even an imperfect market (indeed sheltered from the discipline of the market) failed to bring improvement. The private enterprise system was sufficiently hampered and incentives sufficiently diluted to prevent the system from working well, while no efficient system of public enterprise was put in its place. Yet out of continuing efforts and experiments has evolved the concept of planned "Desarrolismo" (or in Brazil Desinvolvimentismo)—a system of planned development as an economic, social and political philosophy in its own right.

POWER DIFFUSION

Even in countries where a strongly defined ideology exists, power diffusion can slow up the development process. India is a case in point. India's leaders have not lacked an ideology; Mahatma Gandhi's teachings, based on peace and love and on the precept that *the means are as important as the ends* provided a powerful and unifying social philosophy, not only for India, but for the entire neutralist bloc. Nor has India lacked imaginative leaders and dedicated planners; but they have never resolved the problem created by the awkward combination of socialist philosophy and the great concentration of wealth and power in an essentially free private enterprise system.

The dynamic private sector is hampered by the socialist ideology, by the constant need to justify its decisions to government authorities, and by cumbersome regulations and controls, too often confused with genuine socialism. A colleague once remarked that he had already spent three years trying to get a *foreign-aid* import through customs, and it wasn't through yet. These inherent problems of wide diffusion of decision–making power are compounded by provincial loyalties within a federal constitution. Largely for these reasons, India's leaders have not yet dared to endanger national unity by making the drastic reforms needed to establish a true Indian social democracy.

It is only fair to add that India's leaders have had to deal not only with a huge and increasing population, extreme poverty, bad harvests, and a multilingual community, but also with a number of crippling external events; absorption of millions of Pakistani refugees at Independence; savage blows dealt to the economy by war with Pakistan, border skirmishes with China, and finally the oil crisis. In light of these handicaps, it says something for the strength of her ideology that India has held together so long. This stability is no doubt partly due to the efforts of the planning commission. With the prime minister as chairman, it has provided a cohesion, continuity, and discipline to government operations which have survived shifts in the political power structure.

In any case, ideological confusion and awkward power diffusion are by no means unknown phenomena in the Western world. But conflicts and inefficiencies were, for a long time, hidden by expanding markets and plentiful resources. However, with natural resources becoming scarce and worldwide "slumpflation" rampant, ideologies at once more coherent, more convincing, and more pragmatic are at last being sought.

TOWARDS NEW IDEOLOGICAL REINTERPRETATIONS

Today, the increasing concern in both advanced and developing nations with inefficiences in mixed economies is evoking fresh ideological reinterpretation. Feelers for change are being put out in the United States, for example, by senatorial committees, business leaders and the media. The Humphrey–Javits bill (S. 1795) aims at the establishment of national economic planning. It would involve an expansion of statistical information services to create bigger and better economic models and to designate targets and objectives for the economy using an input-output matrix as a tool. Richard J. Barnet and Ronald Muller call for a plan for the U.S. which could be a good development plan for any Third World country.[8]

A particularly explicit presentation of the continuing quest for development plus freedom was made in an article in the July 14, 1975 issue of *Time Magazine,* America's leading news weekly, which posed the question "Can Capitalism Survive?"

Time suggests two criteria for judging the relative merits of socialism and capitalism: "Which system can make the most efficient use of manpower, materials, and money to create the greatest opportunities for free choice, personal development, and material well-being for the greatest number of people? And which system is more just and satisfying in human terms?" Time conceded that socialism offers stability, security, relative equality, full employment (although not always high productivity employment), and stable prices. *Time* also observed that to many idealists, giving primacy to the profit motive seems to be a sanctification of selfishness that produces a brutalizing, beggar-thy-neighbor society. However, the editors declare that capitalism encourages innovation, and the market "functions as a superbly adaptive, supercomputer that continuously monitors consumer tastes."

True, they add, the market has its shortcomings; while it is an excellent short-term indicator, it does not give the necessary guidance on such long-term issues as energy use, conservation, and development. Moreover, *Time* is

---

[8] The plan calls for: reduction in waste and pollution; full employment; control of inflation; major improvement in availability of public services—major investment in reconstruction if cities and towns, decentralization of political authority; a debate concerning new forms of public ownership, control for strategic industries, how priorities should be set— "In a time of resource scarcity and worlwide famine, many things that should not be made by anyone"; restoration of consumer sovereignty, more worker sovereignty, citizen sovereignty, more real participation in political process; a development of alternative technologies (particularly those which are cheaper, more resource-saving and simple); investment in job-creating rather than job displacing-technology; U.S. self-sufficiency. Richard J. Barnet and Ronald E. Muller *Global Reach* (New York: Simon and Schuster, 1974), pp. 376–77.

not wholly satisfied with the decisions or the behavior of businessmen, particularly those running large corporations; "a special set of problems" is recognized in the growth of the multinational corporations, which while being "the most creative international institution of the 20th century" also have "a unique freedom to escape from any country's regulation". While capitalist economies undoubtedly benefit from powerful corporations, large companies can set prices more or less independently of demand, produce what they rather than consumers want, and in effect ram the products down consumers' throats by the power of advertising. The broad solutions are to make the market work better; where the market falls short, the government should plan to improve productivity.

Time quotes prominent American businessmen who are calling for planning in a form which sounds like a combination of French or Japanese style forecasting and indicative planning with Russian balance planning. Ford Motor company Chairman Henry Ford II is quoted as calling for the creation of a federal planning body to examine cost-effectiveness and set timetables; to take a look at population growth, usages of raw materials and their availability, and what the price situation is going to be over a long period of time. Investment banker Robert V. Roosa, United Auto Workers' president Leonard Woodcock, and economist Wassily Leontief demand the establishment of a U.S. Office of National Economic Planning which should include several hundred scientists and technicians (and a few economists) who would study the future of the U.S. economy "much as a savvy company studies the market." They would: try to estimate the economy's future needs for developing supplies, expanding industries and raising capital; attempt to project how many cars, houses, and tons of wheat, steel, paper and other products the economy would demand; aim to identify the industries that should expand fast in order to avoid shortages, to calculate where the supplies are likely to come from, what exploration, research and development investment would be required to produce them, what conservation steps and recycling programs may be required to stretch supplies, and what substitutes might be used in a pinch. They would propose tax and investment incentives as well as broader monetary and fiscal policies for attaining those goals, and would estimate the effects of major legislation on prices and jobs. In sum, *Time* declares, government can do more to help private enterprise—not by setting up inflexible five-year plans, but by employing "the best of its fallible methods to give early warnings of what raw materials and investments will be most needed," meanwhile private businessmen must make the detailed decisions.

To improve businessmen's decision making, the market should be made to work better. Governmental "propping up" should be eliminated in some areas by the repeal of a number of laws, regulations, and practices that support prices for the benefit of special interests. To prevent unions and corporations from "using their muscles" to force outsize increases, the government should adopt some form of flexible wage-price surveillance. They call for "another Smith or Keynes" to devise restraints that are effective but not coercive.

Recommendations for governmental action to improve productivity include: enhancing the skills and mobility of labor by both private and government means; reviving manpower training programs such as those under which private businessmen, with federal financing, hire and train the hard core unemployed; the setting up of the long-discussed computerized "job bank" that would list employment opportunities throughout the country, and subsidize the moving of needy workers who want to take distant jobs (a method that has kept Swedish unemployment consistently below that of the U.S.).

Time winds up by concluding that in spite of all the drawbacks, the freedom of a capitalist society at its best must be prized above all. Capitalism demands by definition that the individual be free within broad limits to spend and invest his money in any way he pleases, to own private property, and to enter any business or profession. Moreover, "much of the demand for greater equality is really a protest against the injustices that a capitalist society could perfectly well remedy—while remaining capitalist. . . . If democratic leaders choose the correct policies *and explain them forthrightly*—a distressingly big if—the prospects are not at all bleak."

These essays in reinterpretation of the capitalist ideology makes good sense. The ideas are not new—they can be found in any good text book on development economics. The significance is, of course, that they are now being explored by leaders of industry, labor and the media. And, as E. M. de Windt, chairman of the Eaton Corporation once remarked "men like Ford and Sloan can and did make things happen." [9]

As for the Third World, when the great majority of developing countries, confronted with the choice between socialism and capitalism, replied, "A plague on both your houses," they seem to have been right. Neither North American–style capitalism nor Soviet–style socialism have been completely successful in providing all the elements of healthy development. Moreover, while the Northern world has remained to a great extent tradition bound, Third World countries, having liberated themselves from enslavement to Northern ideologies, are retaining what they see as beneficial and workable in the Northern approach, and adding concepts of their own, derived from their traditional culture, others brand new. Out of the trial and error of these ideological experiments have come some fresh workable ideas, particularly the fashioning of the planning process into a highly flexible institution.

The Third World understands that the real development choice is not reliance on the market or central planning; every country uses the market, and all governments undertake some central planning. The crucial questions are rather "how to plan" and "who plans." Third World governments attach great importance to popular participation in planning, and in recent years they have developed information flows *to* government more sharply pointed toward *social choice* than either the market or established political processes can be. The Third World has thus been forging the planning process into an instrument for unification, problem solving, and conflict resolution which, at

[9] E. M. de Windt, "Business Survival in the Seventies: Is the World Company the Answer?" Speech to Mid-America World Trade Conference, Chicago, Feb. 25, 1971.

the least, can form the basis for making an entire economic organization more efficient; at best, it can lead to the emergence of an integrated economic, social, and political philosophy.

This trend appears to be part of an ideological groundswell in the world of mixed economies towards a variety of "planful" societies. Although the scope and style may vary enormously, from the cooperative aspects of planning in Indonesia to the individualistic approaches suggested for the United States, they still have a common characteristic: the revolutionary concept of establishing new institutions and new channels of communication to make "planning from below" and "diffusion of planning" truly effective. Such communications can at the same time crystallize government policy and lead to consensus rather than coercion. Thus, if everyone concerned has a clear comprehension of the goals and methods of achieving them, the full energies of the development process may be released. A trend towards consensus rather than controls is already visible at the international level.

10

Toward a
new international
economic order

We now return to the question posed in Chapter 1, concerning the "crumbling of the old order." If the old order is crumbling, what is the new order likely to be? Today a trend toward integration of the world economy into a smoother working unit opposes a trend toward self-sufficiency and isolationism. In one respect, the new isolationism is even worse than the scramble for economic independence in the 1930; at that time, nations sought only to prevent capital from going out and goods and people from coming in; but now there is an effort to prevent all these things, plus efforts to prevent capital from coming in and to prevent energy, other resources, and skilled people from going out.

A world of completely isolated and self-sufficient economies could conceivably be a peaceful one, even if totally ignoring the principle of comparative advantage would substantially reduce world income. A moderate degree of self-sufficiency has its points, reducing global instability by dampening transmission of fluctuations from country to country; in times of inflationary boom or recession, harder hit countries would be sustained by relative stability of others. And in these days of energy shortage, a higher degree of self sufficiency, achieved by using local renewable materials wherever possible, could effect some net gains, and could lead to a rich variety of indigenous efforts rather than increasing world uniformity, and to greater independence.

Third World Countries may be able to achieve more independence from the advanced world by trading among themselves through their common market, while the advanced world may eventually reduce its dependence on the Third World for raw materials. However, the attainment of total self-sufficiency is at present an impossibility.

Few countries indeed can hope to be entirely self-sufficient. Advanced countries, particularly the United States and Japan, are increasingly depen-

TABLE 10.1   PRESENT AND PROJECTED IMPORTANCE OF THE UNDERDEVELOPED
WORLD TO THE U.S. ECONOMY

(*Increasing U.S. Dependence on Imports of Strategic Materials*)

	% Imported from All Foreign Sources				% Imported from Underdeveloped Countries
	1950	*1970*	*1985*	*2000*	*1971*
Bauxite	64	85	96	98	95
Chromium	n.a.	100	100	100	25
Copper	31	17	34	56	44
Iron	8	30	55	67	32
Lead	39	31	61	67	32
Manganese	88	95	100	100	57
Nickel	94	90	88	89	71
Potassium	13	42	47	61	n.a.
Sulfur	2	15	28	52	31
Tin	77	98	100	100	94
Tungsten	37	50	87	97	37
Vanadium	24	21	32	58	40
Zinc	38	59	73	84	21

Source: U.S. Department of the Interior, *First Annual Report of the Secretary of the Interior Under the Mining and Minerals Policy Act of 1970* (Overseas Development Council).

dent on the Third World countries for raw materials (see Table 10.1, 10.2), while they in turn are increasingly dependent on the advanced countries (particularly North America and Australia) for food (see Table 10.3, 10.4). Most small countries must trade to survive. Large countries with a wide range of resources such as Brazil and Indonesia nonetheless depend on certain imports. The large socialist countries, Russia and China, which could conceivably be self-sufficient and which have been politically somewhat isolated from the Western world, are still eager to trade, even with the West. Both developing and advanced countries are affected by how and where OPEC invests its profits. In sum, virtually all countries depend on movements of goods and capital.

Since the move towards isolationism is largely to get away from the malfunctioning of the international economic system, any new international economic order must correct its weaknesses, paramount among which are the following:

1. An international monetary system which fosters the export of inflation from one country to another in a highly damaging feedback system.

2. Extreme instability of markets, leading to serious uncertainty with regard to both the balance and the terms of trade.

3. A pattern of trade restrictions which prevents adaptation of the occupational and output structures to true long-run comparative advantage in both advanced and developing countries.

4. A declining share of developing countries in world trade.

Table 10.2 Japanese Raw Material Imports—Major Suppliers

(Share of Total—1972)

	United States	Canada, Australia, New Zealand, South Africa, and Rhodesia	OECD Europe	Developing Countries — Africa exc. South Africa, and Rhodesia	Latin America and Caribbean	Asia[a]	Communist Countries
Aluminum	5	53	1	10	1	10	17
Bauxite/Alumina	1	60	1	–	1	38	12
Chromium ore and concentrates	–	51	–	2	5	29	–
Copper ore and concentrates	2	53	2	–	11	34	–
Copper	10	10	–	57	20	1	2
Iron ore and concentrates	1	48	–	7	21	19	–
Lead ore and concentrates	–	77	–	–	13	10	7
Lead	–	21	10	–	39	23	5
Manganese ore and concentrates	–	54	–	10	3	27	–
Nickel ore and concentrates	–	4	–	–	–	96	–
Nickel	3	36	25	22	1	9	36
Phosphate rock	68	100	–	–	–	–	–
Tin ore and concentrates	–	–	–	–	–	98	4
Tin	–	–	–	–	21	63	–
Tungsten ore and concentrates	–	13	–	–	–	10	–
Zinc ore and concentrates	–	42	–	–	48	10	–
Zinc	–	–	–	1	–	5	93

Source: National Strategy Information Center 111 E 58 St., New York N.Y., 10022. Published in William Schneider, *Food Foreign Policy and Raw Materials Cartels* (New York: Crane Russak & Co., 1976), p. 50.

–Less than 0.5 percent.

[a] Includes Middle East and Oceania.

TABLE 10.3   WORLD AGRICULTURAL PRODUCTION, 1966–73

TOTAL AGRICULTURAL PRODUCTION

(1961–65 = 100)

Year	World[a]	Developed Countries[b]	Developing Countries[c]
1961–65	100	100	100
1966	108	110	105
1967	112	113	110
1968	116	117	114
1969	117	116	119
1970	120	118	123
1971	124	123	126
1972	123	123	124
1973	130	131	129

PER CAPITA AGRICULTURAL PRODUCTION

(1961–65 = 100)

Year	World[a]	Developed Countries[b]	Developing Countries[c]
1961–65	100	100	100
1966	102	106	97
1967	104	108	100
1968	105	111	101
1969	104	109	102
1970	105	110	103
1971	107	113	103
1972	104	112	99
1973	108	117	102

Source: Overseas Development Council.

[a] Excludes Communist Asia.

[b] North America, Europe, USSR, Japan, Republic of South Africa, Australia, and New Zealand.

[c] Latin America, Asia (except Japan and Communist Asia), Africa (except Republic of South Africa).

5. A pattern of capital movements in which developing countries are increasingly bypassed in favor of transfers of capital among advanced countries.

6. A dwindling flow of foreign aid in real per capita terms (i.e., adjusted for price increases and growth of population).

7. Ever more scarce resources, and lack of planning in this regard. (The oil crisis precipitated the worst depression since the twenties; over 100,000 people perished during the food crisis).

8. Disintegration within countries and among the regions of the world as a whole.

In recent years, the most explicit design for a reordered world economy has come from the Third World. Advanced countries have responded with agree-

TABLE 10.4   PROJECTIONS OF FOOD DEMAND VS. FOOD PRODUCTION TO 1985

Area	VOLUME INDICES		VOLUME GROWTH RATES	
	Demand	Production	Demand	Production
	1969–71 = 100		Percent Per Annum	
Developed countries	127	151	1.6	2.8
Market economies	126	143	1.5	2.4
Eastern Europe and USSR	132	168	1.8	3.5
Developing market economies	172	146	3.7	2.6
Africa	177	145	3.9	2.5
Asia and Far East	167	143	3.5	2.4
Latin America	171	152	3.6	2.9
Near East	186	157	4.2	3.1
Asian centrally planned economies	159	146	3.1	2.6
All developing countries	167	146	3.5	2.6
World	145	150	2.5	2.7

Source: Preparatory Committee of the World Food Conference, ECOSOC, *Present Food Situation and Dimensions and Causes of Hunger and Malnutrition in the World*, May 1974.

ments and more proposals evincing a new mood of conciliation, but the pace at which firm agreements and concrete measures have been forthcoming has led some observers to interpret the agreements as mere "stalling" in the face of what is considered "coercion" by the developing countries. In taking a closer look at this attempt to create a new international economic order, we must ask whether the demands are justified, practical and acceptable, whether the responses from the advanced countries are adequate or even called for, and whether it is in the best interest of both advanced and developing countries.

BEGINNINGS OF THE NEW INTERNATIONAL ECONOMIC ORDER

The succession of major international meetings concerned with the need for a New Deal for the less developed countries has produced thousands of pages of documentation. Three initial documents, however, threw down the gauntlet. They outlined the broad demands and proposed lines of action envisioned by the developing countries. The Declaration on the Establishment of a New International Economic Order, a Resolution adopted by the General Assembly of the United Nations on May 9, 1974,[1] stated the case in general terms. It began by protesting continuation of colonial domination, inequitable sharing of technological advance and wealth, lack of proportionate representation in the international decision making process. The Declaration then called for:

sovereignty of all states, including full control over natural resources and economic activity, and for the right of all countries to choose their own economic and social system without reprisals of any kind;

[1] United Nations General Assembly A/RES/3201 (S-VI) 9th May 1974.

full participation on the basis of equality of all countries in solving world economic problems, and broader cooperation among all states;

the assurance of an adequate flow of real resources to developing countries and promotion of their development;

an end to waste of natural resources.

BOX 10.1　PROGRAM OF ACTION ON THE ESTABLISHMENT OF THE
NEW INTERNATIONAL ECONOMIC ORDER

Trade Reforms Required:

I　Improved and stabilized markets for raw materials and foodstuffs produced by developing countries; assurance of sufficient supplies of food to less developed countries by raising output of foodstuffs and the removal of barriers to all kinds of exports from the developing countries; improvements in both the terms and the balance of trade of less developed countries; a halt to increase in freight rates; and the enlarged participation of less developed countries in shipping.

Monetary Reforms and Capital Movements Required:

II　International monetary reforms so as to check world inflation, stabilize the international monetary system, assure adequate liquidity, link Special Drawing Rights (discussed in more detail below) to development assistance, and increase net transfers of real resources to less developed countries, involve less developed countries in decision making.

Encouraging Industralization Required:

III　Measures to increase the Third World's share of world industrial production;

IV　Access to modern technology on improved terms for developing countries;

Economic Rights and Duties Required:

V　Powers to regulate and control activities of transnational corporations;

VI　A Charter of Economic Rights and Duties of States (which was shortly forthcoming).

International Cooperation Required:

VII　Collective self-reliance and promotion of cooperation among the developing countries themselves;

VIII　Assistance in the exercise of permanent sovereignty of States over natural resources;

IX　Strengthening the role of the United Nations system in the field of international economic cooperation;

X　A "special program" to provide short-term relief to countries suffering from sharp increases in prices of imports, for special measures to assist the least developed, landlocked, and island economies, and for debt relief. Assistance of poor countries most injured by events in the world market.

Box 10.2 THIRD WORLD FORUM PROPOSALS FOR INSTITUTIONS AND
OTHER CHANGES TO ESTABLISH THE NEW INTERNATIONAL
ECONOMIC ORDER●

To Improve Their Trade Position:

The establishment of a Commodity Bank to strengthen commodities in a weak bargaining position;

the promotion of producers' associations for suitable commodities for ensuring better supply management and for creating countervailing power against the existing concentration of control at the buying end;

establishment of payment unions within the Third World;

To Improve Capital Flows:

A conference of principal creditors and debtors to reach an agreement on the basic principles of a long-term settlement of past debts of the developing countries by:

establishment of a Third World Development Bank financed by the OPEC and other Third World countries;

a new and more automatic basis for international transfer of resources to the poor nations financed from a development tax on non-renewable resources exported from the Third World to the industrialized countries, royalties from ocean-bed mining and a link between SDRs and aid;

a new alliance of interdependence including the flow of investment toward agriculture production to various Third World countries;

democratization of control over international financial institutions by obtaining at least 50% of the voting power for the Third World;

the termination of all unfavorable contracts, leases, and concessions given to the multinational corporations by the developing countries for the exploitation of their natural resources, and their renegotiation;

setting up of institutions of intellectual self-reliance within the Third World financed by a trust fund of the order of $1 billion.

● Proposed at Inaugural Meeting of the Third World Forum at Karachi January 1975.

A program of action (see Box 10.1) then called for specific measures to open up trade opportunities, to loosen international credit, to assert some economic rights, and to secure strategic world capital flows, rather than requesting straight grant aid (except for emergencies). Specific proposals for new institutions and lines of action were made by the "Group of 77" at the inaugural meeting of the Third World Forum at Karachi in January 1975 (Box 10.2).

TOWARD BETTER TRADE RELATIONS

The first major questions raised by the NIEO concern better trade relations for developing countries. The proposals made concerning international commodity agreements, such as establishment of a worldwide grain reserve system and consumer producer groups for all key materials, have been criticized and suggestions have been made for a more market-oriented system. However, whichever system is chosen, it is obvious that all countries would benefit from more stable prices of energy, raw materials, and foodstuffs.

The question of liberalized trade is much more complex and controversial. The Declaration calls for the removal of all barriers to all kinds of exports from the developing countries. Yet there is little reason to hope that incomes in developing countries could be raised significantly by liberalized trade if the existing pattern of world trade remains unchanged. In the case of primary products there are few barriers to fall. Since tropical agricultural products do not pose serious competition to advanced countries' industries, it has been easier to get reductions on their tariffs, and for some primary products no tariffs exist. The advanced countries have not yet found a cheap and satisfactory substitute for oil, nor for certain other minerals; nor have they been successful in growing coffee or tea. In general, tariff reduction would have relatively little effect on primary exports. In the long run, it is to help developing countries to break into the international market for industrial goods (particularly processed agricultural products) that the repeal of tariffs is most important. Yet, even for manufactured products, liberalized trade would have relatively little immediate impact for two main reasons, which are at the core of the "backwash" theory.

In the first place, many countries would have difficulties attempting to break into even a free international market. Certainly Egyptian and Indian cotton textiles could make more headway in advanced countries' markets. Standardized types of iron and steel products, such as produced in India or Brazil, could also compete favorably in a free world market. Similarly, processing of agricultural products could be promoted. But these are classic cases of comparative advantage based on natural resources. Given the resource base, capital and technology can be attracted from abroad until the domestic capacity is established. But for developing countries seeking to industrialize on the basis of human resources, it is much more difficult to get a start. If they are unable or unwilling to rely on foreign investment for the needed capital and technology, the stake in existing investments in the advanced countries is so high, the basic store of scientific and engineering knowledge so vast, that indigenous industrial firms (despite low wage rates) are hard put to catch up.

In short, many countries are not yet in a position to profit from liberalized trade. Shifting from yesterday's colonial structure to today's comparative advantage requires a good deal of capital, as well as entrepreneurial ability and scientific and technical skills. Here we see the pertinence of items I & II of the NIEO program. "Liberalizing trade" in the old sense of complete *laissez-faire* is not enough; liberalized trade must be supported by other international policies to reverse the "backwash." In this light, the appropriateness of the Lomé Convention format also becomes apparent. The agreement does *not* merely liberalize trade but includes preferential treatment to deal with the first problem, and foreign aid to counteract the second obstacle.

THE LOMÉ CONVENTION

The Lomé Convention, an agreement signed on February 28, 1975 by nine members of the European Economic Community (EEC) and forty-nine countries of Africa, the Carribbean and the Pacific (ACP), mainly former colonies of those same nine European powers responded in substantial degree to the spirit of the New Order, although not without some pressure by the forty-nine on the nine.

In one of its aspects, the Lomé Convention was merely one in a series of agreements by which European members of the Community extended to their ex-colonies, especially those in Africa, various elements of the Common Market. In another of its aspects, however, the Convention was an attempt on the part of the EEC to respond to the demands of the Group of 77, at least for its own Associated States.

To begin with, the Agreement provides for discrimination *in favor* of the developing countries in their trade with the advanced ones, after the pattern of UNCTAD III.[2] Industrial products from the developing countries will be allowed free entry into the markets of the advanced countries, and agricultural products virtually free entry. In return, the advanced countries are accorded merely "most favored nation" treatment in the forty nine developing countries; the latter are not required to lower tariffs against exports of the nine to levels lower than those applied to other nations. There is also a system of commodity stabilization covering a wide range of products, called STABEX. Finally, there is provision for substantial foreign aid from the nine to the forty-nine (up to three billion "Units of Account," or about $3.5 billion).

INTERNATIONAL DIVISION OF LABOR IN INDUSTRIAL PRODUCTS

Clearly, however, for such an agreement to work, and in order to create opportunities for some countries to move towards their true long-run comparative advantage, there must be agreed upon specialization at the world level. Such a division of labor, based on careful study of each country, each sector, each commodity would depend heavily on the cooperation of the advanced countries. The bulk of world trade today takes place among the advanced countries. They are trading among themselves mainly in industrial products and sophisticated services, and to a lesser extent with developing countries. With properly planned specialization, advanced countries could bow out of less technologically advanced industries, as the technological revolution carries them further and further ahead in techniques. On the basis of such specialization, a mutually advantageous pattern of trade and capital flows can be put into effect.

---

[2] *Cf. Proceedings of the United Nations Conference on Trade and Development, Third Session, Vol. 1; Report and Annexes.* United Nations publication Sales No. E-73 II. D.4 (1973). See also Sydney Dell, "An Appraisal of UNCTAD III," *World Development,* vol. 1, no. 5 (1973), pp. 1–13.

COMPLEMENTARY CHANGES IN ADVANCED COUNTRIES

But what about advanced countries which already have serious unemployment and would presumably have more if they decide to lift trade restrictions and help developing countries to industrialize?

Phasing out and Phasing in Techniques. • In the course of removing restrictions on trade with developing countries, some enterprises in advanced countries have been or will be hurt. The United States already has ameliorating legislation under the United States Trade Expansion Act of 1962. The European Economic Community also provides aid to industries and workers injured by tariff reductions. A far more important phase of "internal adjustment" which many advanced countries have yet to make is to higher technology activities involving high education levels, and increased leisure.

Internal Adjustments. • The United States, the United Kingdom, and Canada, for example, have lagged behind Japan in terms of transferring their human resoures to employment in higher technology activities. A well-designed program of reduced restrictions against imports which would compete with the advanced countries' retarded enterprises should actually prove in the long-term interest of the advanced countries. The virtues of the "infant industry" argument should be recognized where the industries are truly infants, or at most vigorous adolescents, and not doddering oldsters in need of constant geriatric treatment like the American and Canadian textile industries. Industries where most of the developing countries could compete—resource based, labor intensive, low wage—are usually not those which are in the advanced countries' interest to promote or even preserve at home. Advanced countries would be well advised to move their labor resources to high productivity industries, rather than tying them to low-wage industries. Sweden's textile industry, for instance, has been required to direct its production to higher grade goods, where the industry can still compete successfully. Meanwhile, in the period from 1950 to 1968, the number of workers in textiles decreased by about 50 percent. This policy's success was facilitated by its acceptance by the Swedish trade union movement, including the union representing workers in these low-wage industries. Policies such as these have allowed Sweden to become the world's second most prosperous society (after Switzerland). Advanced countries would have much healthier economies if obviously inefficient industries disappeared and were replaced either by efficient enterprises in the same fields or by imports. Thus, a global strategy directed towards an optimal allocation of *world* resources would improve both the economic situation of the developing countries and that of advanced countries.

This connection leads to the conclusion that foreign aid, foreign trade, regional disparities, agricultural surpluses, and unemployment and inflation are not individual problems requiring a separate *ad hoc* solution. Inflationary devices such as protection, price supports, and welfare payments on the one hand, and haphazard foreign aid handouts on the other, will solve neither the advanced countries' nor the world's economic problems because they are all part of the same feedback system. As things are, advanced countries, by generating inflation through their inefficient industries, not only undermine their economies but also by high export prices weaken the Third World's terms of trade and delay its adjustment to true comparative advantage. The global economy requires an optimal division of labor to run smoothly. By the same token, aid should no longer be regarded simply as a charitable exercise, but as a device to ensure the best use of resources in developing countries which will lead to a useful feedback within the global economy.

CAPITAL ASSISTANCE: THE NEW LOOK

Despite the shift of emphasis to trade and transfer of technology, the need for an expanded and liberalized program of capital assistance as suggested in the NIEO documents is generally recognized. Today, five main trends in capital assistance are emerging: toward creating "easier money"; toward untying aid; toward giving the Third World a bigger say in world finance; toward directing aid to the poorest countries and to the poorest people within each country, along the lines of the "Basic Needs Approach"; and also a trend towards forgiveness of debts.

LIBERALIZING AID

One of the simplest ways of providing developing countries with aid without threatening their independence and freedom of action is to "untie" it. Untied aid permits each recipient country to shop for equipment, technology, and expertise in the most favorable market available, irrespective of the source of aid. Canada has already partially untied her aid budget, now approaching $1 billion annually. As part of the new foreign aid policy announced during the Bank and Fund meetings, Canada, who like most bilateral donors had previously required procurement financed by Canadian grants and loans to be made within Canada, has agreed to release up to $300 million for procurement by an aid recipient in other developing countries if these are able to win contracts in open bidding against Canadian firms.

REFORM OF INTERNATIONAL MONETARY SYSTEM

Also highly important is the move toward "easy money" for financing trade deficits. Further progress in this direction is linked to reform of the international monetary system. Particular interest attaches to the role of gold in this system. The agreement of September 1975 between the United States and the EEC was a step toward a diminished role of gold in settling international accounts. The developing countries had insisted on removal of gold as the basis of the international monetary system. The agreement reached among the "Group of Ten" advanced countries, and subsequently ratified at the IMF meeting, provides for all references to gold to be removed from the IMF articles of agreement, so that countries will no longer be required to use gold in any transaction with IMF. Secondly, the IMF agreed to sell off one-sixth of its gold reserve, and to use the profits gained thereby to provide financial aid, on concessionary terms, to least developed countries. The industrialized countries that comprise the Group of Ten also agreed not to increase their own aggregate holdings of monetary gold, or allow the IMF to do so. The voting power of the United States and other advanced countries was reduced and that of other countries increased. The OPEC countries will have 10 percent instead of 5 percent of total votes.

BASIC NEEDS APPROACH

Aid flows are also changing direction to bring direct improvement of welfare to the poor. In recent years, the World Bank has helped to support world development projects such as land reform designed to improve productivity, particularly amongst small farmers and the landless, and has conducted a comprehensive revue of possible activities in the field of nutrition. Considering the earlier emphasis of the Bank on having "bankable" projects that could repay loans with interest from their own earnings, mostly in infrastructure or industry, this new approach of the Bank is perhaps the biggest revolution of all. Individual countries are following suit. Canada is now concentrating its aid on the forty neediest countries, and is endeavouring to reach the masses of the poor within those countries. Today more than 70 percent of American aid goes to the really poor countries, and 60 percent of the aid program is devoted to food and nutrition.

But how much aid? As will be discussed later the actual amount needed is very little. In terms of each country, the objective should be to fill the gaps between capital requirements of a country for a takeoff into sustained growth, and domestic capacity for savings and investment. It is no use to provide a country with more capital assistance than it can effectively use. On the other hand, an ideal international economic policy would see to it that all countries were able to invest annually an amount equal to their "absorptive capacities." Capital would be "on tap" in such quantities that its lack would never be a bottleneck in the economic development of any country. Capital flows have never yet reached this optimal level. Moreover, a country's ultimate absorptive capacity can be expanded by technical assistance by experts going directly into the field and by research. In sum, the developing countries can absorb capital far beyond the present levels if it is accompanied by technical assistance supported by research.

TECHNICAL ASSISTANCE: CLOSING THE EFFICIENCY GAP

Ultimate success in advancing credit or granting subsidies, depends on whether or not more goods are produced, and efficiently produced. One of the most strategic and fruitful avenues of foreign aid has been research to adapt

Western scientific knowledge to local needs. These adaptations require financial and personnel resources on a scale which can seldom be met by the developing countries. Items III and IV of the NIEO program concerning transfer of technology, have pertinence here as does Item IX, advocating extension of the role of the United Nations in this field.

As well illustrated in this study, the United Nations specialized agencies (such as WHO, FAO, ILO, UNESCO, UNITAR, UNRISD, etc.) have assembled large cadres of experts engaged in a prodigious range of research and applied knowledge. More experienced countries can design their own programs and call on various types of expertise from these agencies and elsewhere to supplement their own skills. Where enough organizational expertise is not available, various forms of foreign aid machinery can fill the gap.

COMBINING TECHNICAL AND CAPITAL ASSISTANCE

A great deal of international and bilateral aid machinery has already been evolved for supplying combinations of capital and technical assistance for situations where expertise is not available. Although aid agencies sometimes overlap, and some of the aid machinery creaks and groans from time to time, these organizations taken together have the capacity to deal with a wide variety of development projects and problems.

A turn-key project, for example, much favored by bilateral donors where expertise and skills in the recipient country are inadequate, is one in which the donor country may build a factory using its own personnel to supervise the job right through to completion, at which time the "key" is handed over to the recipient country. This arrangement has proven highly successful for a single undertaking,—a cement plant, a sugar refinery. However, when it comes to large integrated development programs involving large-scale multilateral aid, a more complex organization is needed, sometimes international in scope.

A working example of this kind of organization is provided in the Mekong River Project. The countries sharing the Mekong River Valley collaborated to develop the area through a huge hydroelectric and irrigation program. None of the countries had enough capital or expertise to carry such a project through, even if it could have been limited within the boundaries of each country. This joint project is managed by the United Nations Regional Commission (ESCAP). One might expect that the project would have been difficult to realize, involving as it does the cooperation of four countries of varying political complexions (Thailand, Cambodia, Laos, and Vietnam) which share the valley and a complicated mixture of bilateral and multilateral aid. Though restricted by the Vietnam war, and later near paralyzed by the war's aftermath it has been one of the most successful development projects in Asia.

COUNTERACTING CORRUPTION

Foreign aid is never given as a lump sum to governments; it is allocated to worthwhile projects approved by the donors. But graft and corruption do occur at the same level and in the same manner as they do in advanced countries through the allotment of contracts to friends, relatives, and political supporters, in excessive costs for shoddy work, and in excessive profit margins. Here again the turn-key approach has been used to good effect. To limit corruption in the case of a very large aid program the funds usually remain under the control of the donor organization and are dispensed only against work done.

INSTITUTIONAL CHANGE: CAN FOREIGN AID HAVE ANY INFLUENCE OVER SOCIAL REFORM?

Successful economic development sometimes requires effective social reform measures. Foreign aid can sometimes make unpalatable reforms more attractive to recipient governments. For example, a large foreign aid grant can finance land reform as the Americans did in Taiwan. Usually, when unpalatable social or economic measures have to be undertaken as part of a development program, it is harder for vested interests to oppose an international organization than a single bilateral donor. Such a situation sometimes arises in the case of education reform where elitist educational systems are challenged. UNESCO, working with the UN Regional Commissions, and more recently supported by World Bank·finance, has made substantial headway in educational reform. Indeed, those concerned with economic reform in their own countries frequently welcome international control of aid, because it may lead to the accomplishment of projects which might never come to pass if left entirely at the mercy of some of their own politicians.

WHAT IS MISSING?

In terms of creating a smooth working, integrated world economy, the original NIEO documents and the responses make good sense. While the major motivation of the NIEO is the wish to improve the position of the developing countries, yet the documents point to much needed complementary changes in advanced countries' economies, thus preparing the framework for a logical strategy for world development. The strategy falls in line with our own analysis concerning the need for a unified approach.

Moreover, rather than starting from scratch, it is clear that we have a good deal of international machinery already in place to carry out a new international economic order. Some new institutions may be added, but most of the mechanisms for a smooth-working world economy are provided by existing agencies, which have for some time been forecasting, making indicative plans and recommendations for policy, pinpointing future problems and preparing data in much the same way that government departments do for individual countries. A particularly good example is offered by the World Food Conference in Rome in 1974. It provided a timely opportunity to deal with the food crisis, a timing which cannot be dismissed as entirely fortuitous. FAO had long foreseen the possibility of food shortages, having made an Indicative World Plan of Agriculture as far back as 1969; and the agency had a fund of information and solid recommendations at its fingertips when the conference settled down to its agenda.

The new system also allows a good deal of flexibility for individual nations to choose their own "style" of development, and to realize their own blend of dependence, independence, and interdependence.

Given current trends, we need only a fairly short list of additional elements in order to arrive at a unified approach at both national and international levels.

1. The World Bank group is performing many of the functions of a world central bank, but it is hampered by the atomized arena in which it has to work. There is a call for a world monetary system with a global central bank which would regulate the world money supply, (as do central banks in individual countries) to make possible the elimination of unemployment and inflation on a global basis.

Behind the various resolutions regarding the international monetary system is the developing countries' wish to get rid of gold altogether as an instrument for settling international accounts and for determining the rate of growth of the world money supply. They would like to make of the SDRs (or a new international unit with another name) a true international currency, which would be the *major* instrument for international settlements, and which would be linked to an international monetary system which would require each country to make the necessary adjustments to its own economy whenever its balance of payments slipped badly out of line, and permit countries to do so without disastrous inflation or deflation. The IMS would control the total size and rate of growth of monetary reserves. The "paper gold" (SDRs) issued by the International Monetary Fund would become the *principal* asset in the world's monetary reserves.

The broad outlines of such a system are clear enough, and are not far removed from Lord Keynes' original proposals at Bretton Woods. Essentially, the requirements are severing the last cords that tie the international monetary system to gold, establishing the Bank and Fund (or something else) as a true world Bankers' Bank; and introducing a true world currency, such as Keynes' suggested "bancor,"—a better term than "SDRs". The world bank, as a *true* world central bank, would be in a position to make loans in "bancor" to any central bank, to tide the country over temporary balance of payments difficulties. It would also (and this power is perhaps more important) be in a position to assure the expansion of the world money supply at the pace required to avoid both deflation and inflation on a world scale. For the system to work well, of course, some abnegation of sovereignty with respect to control of domestic money supplies would be required of the member states; but without some willingness to transfer elements of sovereignty to world institutions, we are unlikely to avoid a relapse to the conditions of the 1930s or worse. Extensions of the SDR system now under discussion, designed to convert SDRs into a basic reserve asset in the international monetary system, would bring us closer to the flexibility of reserve management which Keynes regarded as so important. But as yet the SDR system does not provide the IMF with the power to create or cancel international currency at will (as central banks create and cancel domestic currencies) a power inherent in the Keynes Plan and one which is probably necessary to assure a completely smooth-working international monetary system.

2. Freedom of migration has not been accorded much emphasis in recent international agreements, perhaps because nearly all countries today, advanced or underdeveloped; have extensive immigration restrictions. While freer immigration could no doubt raise the level and improve the distribution of world income, migration alone cannot provide a solution to the enormous imbalances in population distribution in relation to other resources. With India alone adding 14 million people to her population every year, migration can scarcely be the answer, even if countries could or would receive migrants. In economic terms, and even in social terms, it is probably better to bring the resources to the people, to build a factory in an Indian village, or build an irrigation system, rather than spending the money on transporting villagers elsewhere, where the factory, the irrigation system *and* the villages would still have to be established. Moreover, in environmental terms, it would probably take less of the world's resources to give a person a decent life in India than it would in colder regions. The solution still lies mainly in optimal movements of goods and capital.

3. An element missing from international negotiations is certainty. Today, government representatives meet at international conferences (UNCTAD, GATT, the World Bank Group, Conferences on the Environment, Food Crisis, etc.) at which certain decisions are taken regarding international social and economic policy. The discussion leading to these decisions is based on documentation prepared by the international secretariats. This documentation usually suggests policy conclusions, sometimes makes concrete recommendations. If in accord, each country's own representative signs an international agreement. But international agreements become meaningful *only if ratified by the legislatures of signatory governments and if implemented according to the spirit as well as the letter of the original agreement.*

Signatory governments can take deliberate steps to make agreements ineffective as happened, for example, in the case of UNCTAD II. Some advanced countries signed the agreement according preferential treatment to the manufactured exports of developing countries, and even followed up with legislation and then imposed "voluntary" export restraints on the underdeveloped countries, to make sure that tariff reductions would not damage local industries unable to compete with imports from developing countries. There is some danger that the Lomé Convention could turn into another UNCTAD II. David Wall of the University of Sussex warns that to appreciate the limitations on the agreement it is necessary to read the fine print to discern a number of escape clauses.[3] Similarly, IMF accord on the international monetary system turns out on closer examination to be a declaration of intent and an agenda for action rather than a set of concrete measures. Likewise, the OECD (Orga-

---

[3] David Wall, "The EEC-ACP Lomé Convention: A Model for the New International and Economic Order?" Paper presented to the 1975 Halifax Conference on Canada and the New International Economic Order, St. Mary's University, Halifax, Nova Scotia, Aug. 26, 29, 1975.

nization for Economic Cooperation and Development) had drafted voluntary guidelines for the multinationals,[4] but will they be followed? The existing agreements and guidelines are a start but only a start.

While the success of the NIEO program obviously depends heavily on the commitment of the advanced countries, that does not mean that the advanced countries must accept every proposal made by the developing countries without question. Advanced countries have an enormous fund of expertise to offer in solving economic problems, and advanced as well as developing nations must consider their own "self-interest." However, mutual advantages of a rational international division of labor cannot possibly emerge from a system in which the advanced countries insist on producing everything either at home or abroad, and use their superior power to prevent "unfair competition," labelling as "unfair" any action that could threaten any existing economic activity in an advanced country, no matter how inefficient. What really comes out of our analysis is that the advanced countries can best help themselves and the Third World by committing themselves to getting their own economies in order rather than transferring the effects of their own inefficiencies to the rest of the world. The true "self-interest" of the advanced countries is complementary to, not competitive with, that of developing countries. Apart from agriculture, their true long-run comparative advantage and economic security lies in continually advancing technology, by vigorously promoting research and higher education. This approach will ensure their place in a world economy including increasingly powerful southern neighbours.

PROSPECTS FOR 2010

Let us, however, assume that the missing elements have been added, and that a major concerted effort will be made on a global scale to accelerate development of poor countries while conserving resources and limiting pollution. We will suppose that the world crises will provide the necessary "sharp stimulus" of fear to bestir all countries to deal adequately with global problems. The developing countries will intensify their campaigns for population control, and will make the necessary social and institutional reforms to clear the way for rapid development. The advanced countries will honor commitments for annual transfers of resources to developing countries and will take positive action to expand the export capacity of developing countries, paving the way for necessary structural change in advanced and developing countries alike, within the context of environmental conservation. They would be guided by the projections and forecasts of world indicative planning, provided by the various international agencies.

If the terms of trade of developing countries continue to improve through rising market prices for their primary products, assisted by commodity stabilization schemes (which seems highly likely) and if the OPEC countries con-

[4] OECD, International Investment and Multinational Enterprises, Paris, June 1976.

tinue to provide 2% of their swelling gross national products in aid to poorer countries, achievement of the 0.7% target by the advanced industrial countries would suffice to assure the gradual elimination of poverty in developing countries. In opening the annual Bank Fund meeting in Washington in September 1975, World Bank President Robert McNamara stated that official aid of 0.7% of the GNP of advanced countries would permit growth rates of per capita income of developing countries of 3.5% by 1980. This figure implies a doubling of official aid flows; together with private investment, the total transfers would then reach the 1% target. To put this strategic investment in the world economy into perspective, let us recall that to win World War II, the United States, Canada, and Australia devoted 50% of GNP to the war effort, much of which literally went up in smoke; yet their economies were in better shape at the end of the war than they were in 1939. Compared even to today's military expenditures by advanced countries, the amount required for assuring development is infinitesimal (Compare for example, the United States' 1975 100 billion dollar budget for military purposes with its aid contribution of about 2 billion and the world aid total of 9 billion).

Under these conditions, and with well-construed development plans for the period from now to 1990, growth rates could be 50% higher than they were in the 1960s. With annual growth of per capita income of 3.5%, incomes in 1990 would be double their 1970 level. Thus, in 1990, per capita incomes in Asia and Africa would be approaching $300. If a wholehearted world effort were made, Asian and African countries could from their higher 1990 base enjoy a "Japanese" rate of growth from then on, and double income twice in the following twenty years. Thus in 2010 we would have per capita incomes of around $1,200 in both Asia and Africa. For Latin America, where incomes are already relatively high, we assume a more modest rate of growth after 1990, to reach per capita income of about $1,600 in 2010.

Meanwhile the now advanced "market" economies and the centrally planned countries with incomes above $1,000 in 1970 would have redirected their growth toward a better quality of life, refined services, and leisure, and per capita income of advanced countries as a group would reach $4,000 in 1990 and $5,000 in 2010.

In this scenario, we shift our emphasis from closing income gaps to assuring the poorer countries a level of living comparable to that of advanced countries, which is a very different thing from assuring them the same level of per capita income as measured by standard national accounting procedures, and is a much more attainable goal. The point has already been made that most poor countries lie in the tropics. While the point is also constantly made that economic development has occurred mainly in the temperate climes, it is less often remarked that in the hot countries, highly evolved civilizations have flourished with very little industrialization. Because of a favorable physical environment, a tropical country can do without the large-scale industry needed to clothe and shelter a population in a temperate or cold climate; the great tropical civilizations of the past have been able to feed themselves with a few hours work a week and then devote themselves to the arts and sciences.

Today a family in Canada or New England may need a minimum of $4,000 to stay above the poverty line; most sunny Asian, African, and Latin American countries could attain comparable levels of welfare with substantially less income.

Moreover, while in this scenario per capita GNP remains relatively low in the Third World in comparison to Western standards, GNP estimates do not give a true picture when converted at official exchange rates. For example, according to official exchange rates, the Chinese GNP per capita now stands at about $150. However, the Yuan is grossly undervalued. A recent visitor to China collected retail price information in Shanghai, and calculated that a well-off workers' family would spend about 150 Yuan per month (about $75 at official exhange rates). On his return to the United States, he estimated that it would cost about $400 a month for a family in Ann Arbor Michigan to live *in the same way* (i.e., on a predominately cereal diet with little animal protein, travelling by public transportation, living in a two-room apartment). That of course, is $4,800 per year![5]

THE CHANCES OF SUCCESS

In sum, the world has the potential to solve its economic and social problems and achieve a mature, well functioning economy. In spite of mistakes and waste, a considerable human and physical infrastructure has been built up in the Third World over the last thirty years and a great deal has been learned by painful trial and error about the development process. The most startling single conclusion from this analysis is that success would cost little and be close to our grasp if the world's powerful nations reach an *entente,* and commit themselves to development. As we said in Chapter 1, there is every reason to believe that ingenuity and good management can overcome today's problems *if those responsible make up their minds to do so, take the right decisions, and act on them promptly.*

Without doubt, the most vigorous and imaginative leadership in recent years has come from Third World countries. They have reinterpreted United Nations ideology; they have found new ways to use existing international institutions and have created new ones. Their NIEO offers a global design which implies major policy recommendations for both developing and advanced countries. Their cooperative approach is appropriate to the prevailing global situation. As observed earlier, in a contracting world cooperation is likely to emerge. There seems to be a real possibility that the exigencies of the world's shrinking environment will induce countries to cooperate with each other as they have, in fact begun to do. There is also the possibility that we could slide into disaster.

The 1970s will no doubt go down in history as a threshold era in world economic relations. Not since the discoveries of the 16th century has the scope and nature of the global economy changed so much in so short a period.

[5] Lloyd Reynolds, "China as a Less Developed Economy," pp. 419–27.

However, whereas the discoveries of the great global routes opened up vast new physical and economic horizons, today's less agreeable "discoveries" of environmental limitations and economic inefficencies seem to narrow our horizons. At the same time, they invite accelerated exploration of new frontiers of technological advance, new concepts of international organization, and new approaches to economic analysis and policy. "Often toward the end of an old cultural or artistic period the frenetic search for the new produces things that are worse than the old," Kenneth Boulding mused in 1973. "Cultures move towards a stationary state as the cultural potential that gave rise to a particular pattern is exhausted. In the past we have always escaped this fate by developing a new cultural potential, a new style, a new vision of the world, or a new religion."[6] Today's quests everywhere for new philosophies of development, new ideological interpretations and for a new world order could become just such a global renaissance.

[6] Kenneth Boulding, "The Shadow of the Stationary State" in Olson and Lundsberg, eds., *The No-Growth Society*.

Index